D0209870

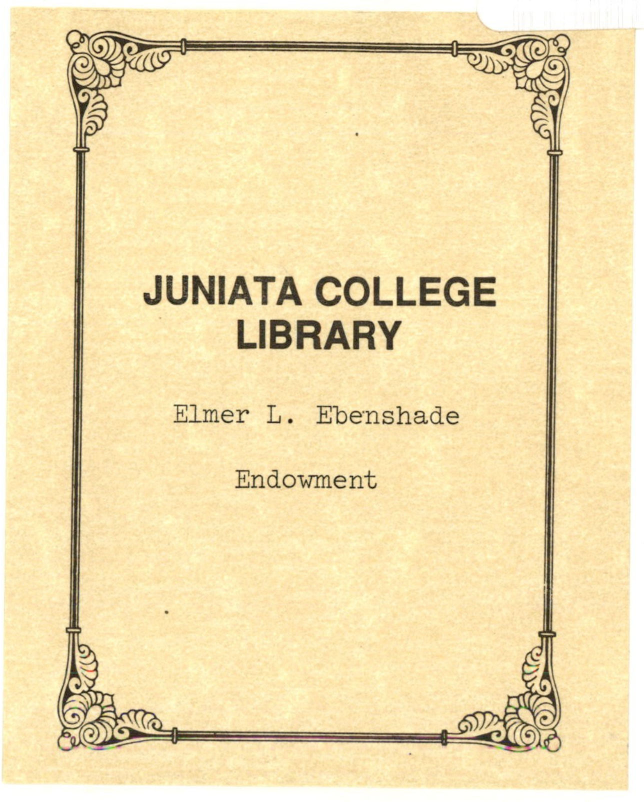
JUNIATA COLLEGE
LIBRARY
Elmer L. Ebenshade
Endowment

Encyclopedia of the Reagan-Bush Years

ENCYCLOPEDIA OF THE REAGAN-BUSH YEARS

Peter B. Levy

Greenwood Press
Westport, Connecticut • London

Library of Congress Cataloging-in-Publication Data

Levy, Peter B.
Encyclopedia of the Reagan-Bush years / Peter B. Levy.
p. cm.
Includes bibliographical references and index.
ISBN 0-313-29018-0 (alk. paper)
1. Presidents—United States—Encyclopedias. 2. United States—Politics and government—1981-1989—Encyclopedias. 3. United States—Politics and government—1989-1993—Encyclopedias. 4. Reagan, Ronald. 5. Bush, George, 1924- . I. Title.
JK511.L48 1996
973.927'03-dc20 95-37336

British Library Cataloguing in Publication Data is available.

Library of Congress Catalog Card Number: 95-37336
ISBN: 0-313-29018-0

First published in 1996

Greenwood Press, 88 Post Road West, Westport, CT 06881
An imprint of Greenwood Publishing Group, Inc.

Printed in the United States of America

The paper used in this book complies with the Permanent Paper Standard issued by the National Information Standards Organization (Z39.48-1984).

10 9 8 7 6 5 4 3 2 1

CONTENTS

INTRODUCTION

"It was the best of times, it was the worst of times." As we approach the end of the twentieth century, Charles Dickens' famous opening line to his novel *A Tale of Two Cities* seems as appropriate for the Reagan-Bush years, 1980–1992, as they were for Victorian England. The period was replete with contradictions and irony and remains an era for which no consensus or agreement has been reached yet by either the public or the scholarly community. For some, Ronald Reagan stands as one of the greatest presidents in American history; for others, he was one of the worst. George Bush left office repudiated, suffering from one of the worst showings by an incumbent ever, yet in the years to come, it may be difficult for students of history to understand why he was defeated or if the election of 1992 represented a repudiation of Bush alone. After all, no major scandals, like Watergate, occurred during Bush's presidency, while President Reagan experienced the **Iran-contra affair.** True, the nation endured a recession during Bush's four years in office, but it was relatively mild in comparison to the recession of Reagan's first term. Moreover, Bush presided over the most successful military expedition since World War II, the **Persian Gulf War.**

The era is even more difficult to understand if one considers Ronald Reagan's promises and ultimate legacy. Reagan promised to enact a "revolution" that would roll back the influence of the federal government, unleash economic growth, balance the budget, and make Americans proud again. He gained fervid support from conservatives who believed he would unleash a social and cultural counterrevolution and from Americans who saw him as a different sort of politician, one of the people bound by principle, not politics. If he had one weak spot, it was his lack of expertise on **foreign policy.** However, by the time he left office, his greatest achievement was in the realm of foreign affairs. Turning away from ideology, Reagan and his secretary of state, **George Pratt Shultz,** held a series of summits with **Mikhail Sergeyevich Gorbachev,** the leader of the **Soviet Union.** These summits produced significant arms reductions and led the way to the end of the cold war. In contrast, on the social and cultural front, no cultural revolution was achieved, and in terms of economics and government spending, his record was mixed. Employment and the economy grew following a severe recession, but so, too, did the federal government and, even more spectacularly, the federal debt.

What makes the era even more fascinating is that many of the things that seemed important at the time and garnered much attention seem trivial today. The media and the public were fascinated and sometimes appalled by **Nancy Davis Reagan**'s extravagant wardrobe and White House affairs. Shortly before the Reagans left office, the First Lady's dependence on a professional astrologer became headline news. In comparison, relatively little attention or clamor was made over the **savings and loan crisis,** the biggest bank failure since the Great Depression. Nor did the public even seem to notice that strong federal government action prevented the crisis from producing a deep depression, as had the banking crisis of the early 1930s. Similarly, it is difficult to comprehend why the media paid so much attention to the relations between Nancy Reagan and Raisa Gorbachev. Rather than try to make sense of these baffling phenomena, this book concentrates on those developments that had more substance and historical significance.

Encyclopedia of the Reagan-Bush Years provides a ready reference source on many of the developments of the Reagan-Bush presidencies mentioned here and much more. From **abortion** to **yuppies,** it presents descriptions ranging from about 100 words to 2,000 words in length on issues, events, laws, and trends of the era. While the book is entitled an encyclopedia, which implies that it is a definitive account of the era, I had to make certain choices. Because of limitations of time and space, I did not try to be exhaustive. Rather, I sought to provide a book of reasonable length that included summaries of the most important events and leads or citations on less important ones. For example, while all the cabinet members are listed under the heading **Cabinet,** the book includes separate entries only on those who had the greatest impact on national affairs. Similarly, the book does not include a separate entry for every piece of legislation. Rather, it presents summaries of the most important laws as well as overviews of broader topics, such as **education** and **civil rights.**

The book's focus is on the Reagan and Bush administrations. While there are some listings on general trends of the era, such as one on **popular culture,** emphasis has been given to individuals and acts associated with Presidents Reagan and Bush. Put a different way, the organizing principle of the book was to include information directly related to Reagan and Bush rather than to the years 1980–1992. The entries seek to present a balanced account; they favor description over judgment while at the same time offering a sense of the controversy that surrounded, and in some cases still surrounds, many of the particulars of the Reagan-Bush years. Almost all the entries include a list of suggested readings. Cross-references to other entries are provided via boldface and also, in some cases, through a related entries section. A number of the entries are accompanied by tables, figures, or photographs. The *Encyclopedia* ends with a timeline and a statistical appendix that displays significant economic trends of the era. An index provides additional references and cross-references.

ACRONYMS

ACLU	American Civil Liberties Union
ADA	Americans for Democratic Action
AFDC	Aid for Families with Dependent Children
AFL-CIO	American Federation of Labor and Congress of Industrial Organizations
AID	Agency for International Development
AIDS	Acquired Immunodeficiency Syndrome
AMA	American Medical Association
AT&T	American Telephone and Telegraph
AWACS	Airborne Early Warning and Control Systems
BCCI	Bank of Credit and Commercial Internationale
CETA	Comprehensive Employment and Training Act
CIA	Central Intelligence Agency
DEA	Drug Enforcement Agency
EDS	Electronic Data Systems
EEOC	Equal Employment Opportunity Commission
FAA	Federal Aviation Administration
FBI	Federal Bureau of Investigation
Fed	Federal Reserve Board
FTC	Federal Trade Commission
GDP	Gross Domestic Product
GM	General Motors

GNP	Gross National Product
GOP	Grand Old Party
HIV	Human Immunodeficiency Virus
IBM	International Business Machines
INF	Intermediate Nuclear Forces
IRS	Internal Revenue Service
MIA	Missing in action
MIT	Massachusetts Institute of Technology
MX	Missile, Experimental
NAACP	National Association for the Advancement of Colored People
NAFTA	North American Free Trade Agreement
NATO	North Atlantic Treaty Organization
NEA	National Endowment for the Arts
NEH	National Endowment for the Humanities
NIS	Naval Investigative Service
NOW	National Organization of Women
NSC	National Security Council
OMB	Office of Management and Budget
OSHA	Occupational Safety and Health Administration
OSS	Office of Strategic Service
PATCO	Professional Air Traffic Controllers Organization
PLO	Palestine Liberation Organization
POW	Prisoner of War
S & L	Savings and Loan
SALT	Strategic Arms Limitations Treaty
SDI	Strategic Defense Initiative
SSDI	Social Security Disability Insurance
START	Strategic Arms Reduction Treaty
UN	United Nations
USSR	Union of Soviet Socialist Republics
VISTA	Volunteers in Service to America

THE ENCYCLOPEDIA

A

ABORTION. One of the reasons Ronald Reagan enjoyed so much support from conservatives was because of his stand on a number of social or cultural issues, including abortion. Despite the fact that he had signed one of the nation's most liberal abortion laws while governor of California, by 1980 Americans viewed him as an outright opponent of a woman's right to choose. During the 1980 presidential campaign, Reagan criticized *Roe* v. *Wade* (the **Supreme Court** decision that had made abortions legal), promised to appoint judges who would overturn the decision, and encouraged antiabortion forces to vote against prochoice candidates.

As president, however, Reagan's record on abortion was more mixed. On the one hand, he fulfilled most of his campaign pledges. He screened his appointments to the courts so as to eliminate prochoice nominees. He convinced Congress to refuse to provide federal funds for abortions. Moreover, he campaigned for, and helped elect, numerous antiabortion candidates. On the other hand, when his first term began he focused his energy and political capital on gaining passage of his economic program and the military buildup rather than on social or cultural issues such as abortion. During his second term in office he continued to speak out against abortion and to call for a constitutional amendment that would make abortions illegal. However, other concerns, especially **foreign policy,** received more of his attention.

In order to solidify his standing with the conservative wing of the Republican Party, George Bush, who initially supported a woman's right to choose, emphasized his opposition to abortion, even terming it "murder," during his 1988 campaign. Like Reagan, Bush sought to nominate justices who promised to overturn *Roe* v. *Wade,* and he advocated a constitutional amendment banning abortions. As president he restricted federal funding for abortion, including limiting medical experiments that used fetal tissue (whether or not the tissue was obtained by abortion). The Bush administration also prohibited or "gagged" prochoice counseling in abortion clinics that received federal funds.

However, the cumulative impact of the Reagan-Bush years on abortion was not revolutionary. While the Supreme Court allowed states to pass laws that limited the procedure, several of the Reagan and Bush Supreme Court nominees, along with holdovers from the pre-Reagan years, refused to overturn *Roe* v. *Wade.* This became clear in *Planned Parenthood* v. *Casey,* a 1992 Supreme Court case involving Pennsylvania legislation aimed at restricting abortions. While the Court allowed the bulk of the state's regulations and restrictions to stand, it also upheld the "essence" of the constitutional right to an abortion. The majority in the case included **Sandra Day O'Connor** and **David Souter,** Reagan and Bush appointees, respectively, suggesting that their attempts to appoint only antiabortion justices had failed.

By 1992, moreover, public polls suggested that abortion no longer was a winning or "wedge" issue for the Republicans. In 1992 some Republican candidates sought to distance themselves from the party's antiabortion stance and, in at least some elections, Democrats won votes by emphasizing their prochoice position. Last, Clinton's victory in 1992 meant that new appointments to the Court would probably support *Roe* v. *Wade,* which in turn would make it more difficult to overturn the decision in the future.

Suggested Readings: David Garrow, *Liberty and Sexuality* (1994); Ronald Reagan, *Abortion and the Conscience of the Nation* (1984); David Sadofsky, *The Question of Privacy in Public Policy* (1993).

Related Entries: Constitutional Amendments (Proposed); Moral Majority; Supreme Court; Women's Rights.

ABRAMS, ELLIOT. (January 24, 1948, New York, N.Y.– .) Assistant Secretary of State for International Organization Affairs, 1981; Assistant Secretary of State for Human Rights and Humanitarian Affairs, 1981–1985; Assistant Secretary of State for Inter-American Affairs, 1985–1989.

Elliot Abrams was one of the Reagan administration's most controversial figures. He helped mold and conduct the administration's policy in Central and South America. This included supporting the contra rebels in **Nicaragua** and the anticommunist government of **El Salvador.** With regard to the latter, Abrams was responsible for certifying to Congress that El Salvador was making progress on human rights. His critics accused him of overlooking numerous abuses and misleading Congress about the diversion of funds to the contras. Abrams and his supporters countered that the Reagan administration's policy had produced a flowering of democracy in Latin America.

Abrams received a B.A. (1969) and law degree from Harvard University (1973) and a master's in international relations from the London School of Economics (1970). He briefly worked as a lawyer in New York City before getting a job in Washington, D.C., first as assistant counsel to the U.S. Senate Permanent Subcommittee on Investigations and then as special counsel for Senators Henry M. Jackson and Daniel P. Moynihan. Since 1989 he has worked as a foreign affairs analyst for the Hudson Institute and as a contributing editor for the *National Review.* He is married to Rachel Mark; they have two sons and one daughter.

Suggested Readings: Elliot Abrams, *Undue Process* (1993); *Current Biography* (1988) p. 9.

ACID RAIN. During the 1980s, debate over the impact of, and proper response to, acid rain figured prominently in discussions over the **environment** and the Reagan administration's environmental policies.

Acid rain is a form of air pollution that forms when oxides of sulphur and nitrogen combine with moisture in the atmosphere to produce sulfuric and nitric acids. These acids get caught in the air currents and fall as rain or settle as dry particles in places far away from the source of their acidity. Acid rain is harmful to forests, crops, and freshwater lakes. It is not a new problem, having originated with the Industrial Revolution, but only recently has the extent of its destructiveness become apparent to the scientific and environmental community. Large areas of eastern Canada and the northeastern part of the United States have been affected.

In the early 1980s the U.S. government issued a report that supported the claims of environmentalists that industrial emissions caused acid rain. However, the Reagan administration resisted calls from the environmental community to strengthen the Clean Air Act. Rather, in part due to its commitment to **deregulation,** it called for further study. As a result, not until 1988 did the U.S. government take any formal action to reduce acid rain, when it signed a United Nations–sponsored protocol that sought to freeze the rate of nitrogen oxide emissions at 1987 levels.

During the 1988 campaign, George Bush pledged to be the "environmental president," suggesting that he would do more to control the effects of acid rain than had President Reagan. While he balked at some of the environmentalists' demands, in 1990 Congress passed, and Bush signed into law, a new clean air act, the **Clean Air Act of 1990.** The new law sought a 50 percent reduction in sulfur dioxide emissions from power plants by the year 2000 and similar reductions in dangerous auto emissions.

Suggested Readings: Bruce A. Forster, *The Acid Rain Debate* (1993); Charles Officer, *Tales of the Earth* (1993); Jacqueline Switzer, *Environmental Politics* (1994).

ACQUIRED IMMUNODEFICIENCY SYNDROME. By the early 1990s, acquired immunodeficiency syndrome (AIDS) was the number-one killer of men age 20 to 40 in the United States. This was remarkable considering that it was not until the early 1980s that medical researchers first diagnosed this syndrome. (Symptoms of AIDS first began to appear in the late 1970s, but the virus that caused it was not isolated until the mid-1980s.) Caused by the human immunodeficiency virus (HIV) type 1, AIDS affects the immune and central nervous systems. Common symptoms of the HIV infection often resemble influenza or mononucleosis, although not all infected individuals experience the same symptoms.

At first there was a great deal of public misunderstanding about AIDS. Since it affected a large number of homosexuals, some called it the "gay cancer." However, scientists asserted from early on that the disease was not limited to the homosexual population and that it is not spread through casual contact. Rather, they noted, the AIDS virus was transmitted through the blood—most commonly via sexual contact, both vaginal and anal—and through the use of infected hypodermic needles, largely by drug addicts. AIDS can also be contracted via blood transfusions, although the public health community has worked hard to guard against this. Revelations that several celebrities, most notably movie actor Rock Hudson and basketball superstar Magic Johnson, had AIDS or had tested positive for the HIV virus raised public awareness about the disease and promoted greater tolerance for its victims. Still, some conservatives continue to insist that AIDS should be viewed as a cultural, not a medical, problem, with some suggesting the virus represents divine punishment for immoral behavior.

The Reagan administration has been harshly criticized for its response to the AIDS epidemic. Even though the U.S. Centers for Disease Control identified AIDS in 1981, federally sponsored research on the disease did not begin for several more years. The president reinforced the public's sense that it was a "gay disease" by refusing to speak about it. He even refused to use the word *AIDS* until the end of his term. When the Reagan administration finally did address the AIDS epidemic, it focused on the need for testing individuals for the disease, including all public officials, so that they could be identified and, presumably, isolated from the public, rather than on treatment or education.

As a result, the United States was much slower than its European partners in sponsoring research on the disease and in educating the public about ways to avoid infection—which include using condoms during sex. Moreover, the disease grew to epidemic proportions before the government took significant action. Evidence of this came in a report by Admiral James Watkins, head of President Reagan's own AIDS panel, which the president had created in 1987. Watkins called the government's response to the disease "slow" and "sluggish" and demanded increased funding for research and education. Surgeon General **C. (Charles) Everett Koop** was just as forthright, criticizing conservatives for their unwillingness to support open sex education as a means toward battling the spread of the disease.

During Bush's tenure in office, federal spending on AIDS research climbed significantly. By the 1990s, it neared $3 billion per year. As of 1994, no cure had been uncovered, although better tests to identify carriers of the virus as well as treatments to prolong the lives of those infected had been developed.

Suggested Readings: Elizabeth Fee and Daniel M. Fox, *AIDS, the Burdens of History* (1988); Chris Jennings, *Understanding and Preventing AIDS* (1988); Randy Shilts, *And the Band Played On* (1987).

ADELMAN, KENNETH LEE. (June 9, 1946, Chicago, Ill.– .) Deputy Permanent Representative, U.S. Mission to the United Nations, 1981–1983; Director, Arms Control and Disarmament Agency, 1983–1988.

Kenneth Adelman served as the director of President Ronald Reagan's Arms Control and Disarmament Agency from 1983 until 1988. This made him responsible for negotiating the **Intermediate-range Nuclear Forces (INF) Treaty** with the Soviet Union and defending the president's **Strategic Defense Initiative (Star Wars)** plan.

Adelman worked his way up the government ladder to the post of chief arms negotiator. He began as an aide in the Department of Commerce in the late 1960s. He worked briefly for Volunteers in Service to America

(VISTA) and the Agency for International Development (AID). At the same time, Adelman went to graduate school, earning an M.A. (1969) and a Ph.D. (1975) in political science from Georgetown University. When **James (Jimmy) Earl Carter** was elected president, Adelman left the government to work as a senior political scientist for the Strategic Studies Center of the Stanford Research Institute in Arlington, Virginia. While there, he specialized on **Africa** and wrote several controversial articles on the region. For the first two years of Reagan's presidency, Adelman worked with a former professor, **Jeane Jordan Kirkpatrick,** as a permanent representative to the United Nations. In 1983 Reagan nominated Adelman to replace Eugene Rostow as director of the Arms Control and Disarmament Agency. Adelman's sharp criticism of Carter's policies, especially the **Strategic Arms Limitation Treaty (SALT) II** and his outspoken criticism of the **Soviet Union,** led to a very stormy confirmation process. Focusing on his lack of experience in arms control, the Senate Foreign Relations Committee barely voted for confirmation (9–8). Adelman remained a controversial figure throughout his tenure as director of the Arms Control agency, in part because of his defense of the Strategic Defense Initiative. Many argued that this project was not feasible and jeopardized arms negotiations with the Soviet Union. The successful negotiation of the INF treaty and the **collapse of communism** in the Soviet Union left Adelman somewhat vindicated. Some credited him with considerable foresight, noting that he simultaneously advocated Star Wars and promoted nuclear weapons agreements.

Adelman is married to Carol Craigle. They have two daughters. Adelman continues to write on defense issues, suggesting ways in which the United States can remain strong in the post–cold war world.

Suggested Readings: Kenneth L. Adelman, *The Great Universal Embrace: Arms Summitry—A Skeptic's Account* (1989); *Current Biography* (1985) p. 2.

AFFIRMATIVE ACTION. Affirmative action has been a controversial issue ever since its origins in the late 1960s. Both Ronald Reagan and George Bush opposed it on the campaign trail and in office. Along with a belief in school prayer and condemnation of **abortion** and crime, it was one of the wedge issues they emphasized in order to win support from traditionally Democratic voters, especially blue-collar workers and southern whites.

Reagan's opposition to affirmative action manifested itself in three main ways. First, his Justice Department presented written and oral arguments that sought to limit affirmative action, if not repeal it in its entirety. For example, in the early 1980s, the administration sought to overturn a lower court decision that had upheld the use of hiring goals in cases involving firefighters and sheet metal workers. Much to the Reagan administration's chagrin, in both cases—*Local 28 of the Sheet Metal Workers* v. *Equal Employment Opportunity Commission* and *Local 93 of the International Association of Fire Fighters* v. *City of Cleveland*—the **Supreme Court** upheld affirmative action plans that sought to hire individuals who had been "actual victims of discrimination." Second, administration members and supporters of President Reagan continuously voiced their criticism of the concept of affirmative action. For one, **William Bradford Reynolds,** the head of the **civil rights** division of the Justice Department during Reagan's presidency, contended that affirmative action represented a betrayal of the color-blind goals of the civil rights movement of the 1960s. The fact that the head of the civil rights division of the Justice Department argued that affirmative action was unconstitutional, in spite of the Supreme Court's rulings that it was not, lent legitimacy to antiaffirmative action sentiment among the public at large.

Third, Reagan sought to appoint judges who opposed affirmative action. The most notable example of this came with his nomination of **Robert Heron Bork.** President Bush followed President Reagan's lead on affirmative action, especially on this front. Bush's nomination of a conservative, Clarence Thomas, to replace Thurgood Marshall, who was a symbol of the revolution in civil rights law in the modern era, sent a clear message to America on where the president stood on this issue. Moreover, since Thomas was a black man who opposed affirmative action, Bush was able to appear less conservative than Reagan while promoting basically the same position.

During Bush's presidency the **courts** further whittled away or restricted the reach of affirmative action. In January 1989, in *Richmond* v. *Croson Co.,* the Supreme Court invalidated a Richmond, Virginia law that set aside 30 percent of public works funds for minority-owned construction companies. Nonetheless, in spite of assaults on it from two presidents, affirmative action programs, as long as they were narrowly constructed, were still deemed constitutional as the Reagan-Bush years came to a close. As with several other social and cultural issues, such as abortion and school prayer, affirmative action resisted conservative attempts to radically alter the status quo.

Suggested Readings: Richard Schaefer, ed., *Racial and Ethnic Groups, 4th ed.* (1990); Steven Shull, *A Kinder, Gentler Racism* (1993); Urban Institute, *Civil Rights and the Reagan Presidency* (1988).

Related Entry: Thomas-Hill Hearings.

AFGHANISTAN. In late December 1979, Soviet forces invaded Afghanistan to prop-up the pro-Soviet government, which had taken power following the Great Saur Revolution of 1978. From the start, the pro-Marxist forces that had taken power during this revolution had faced serious opposition from anti-Marxist, Muslim groups. In response to the invasion, President **James (Jimmy) Earl Carter** announced that the United States would boycott the 1980 summer Olympics in Moscow and placed economic sanctions against the **Soviet Union,** including a grain embargo. These actions, however, largely served only to sharpen the divisions between conservatives and liberals in America and did not compel the Soviet Union to withdraw its forces from Afghanistan.

Even before the invasion, conservatives had been sharply critical of Carter's **foreign policy,** which they considered soft on the Soviet Union. The Soviet action reconfirmed their argument that this was an aggressive, totalitarian nation and bolstered their calls for the United States to build up its defense forces and to take more aggressive actions to counter communist insurgencies around the world.

Once in office, President Reagan pointed to the Soviet invasion of Afghanistan as one of the justifications for a military build up and for conducting covert operations against leftist forces. The Reagan administration granted millions of dollars of aid, largely in the form of weapons and military training, to rebel guerrillas in Afghanistan, known as the *mujahadeen.* The Central Intelligence Agency (CIA) trained Afghan guerrilla warriors and offered other forms of covert aid. With U.S. support and the help of Pakistan, which offered safe haven to them, the *mujahadeen* staged a long and largely successful rebellion against the Soviet-backed government, leading many to term Afghanistan the Soviet's Vietnam in reference to the U.S. war in Southeast Asia.

In June 1986, President Reagan met with Afghan rebel leaders. Shortly afterward, the Soviet Union began to reduce its troop strength in the region. In April 1988, the Soviet-backed, pro-Marxist, Afghanistan government and Pakistan, which had harbored the *mujahadeen,* signed a pact, which was cosigned by the United States and the Soviet Union, aimed at ending the fighting. According to the agreement, the Soviets pledged to withdraw their troops, starting in May 1988. Ultimately, they lived up to this agreement. By February 1989, nearly all Soviet forces in Afghanistan were gone. This development marked a victory for the Reagan administration. However, the victory was somewhat hollowed by the fighting between various Afghan factions that continued after the

Soviet's withdrawal and by the fact that at least some of the *mujahadeen's* weapons, obtained from the United States, ended up in the hands of international terrorists.

Suggested Readings: Arthur Bonner, *Among the Afghans* (1987); Rusteem Galiullin, *The CIA in Asia* (1988); Marvin Weinbaum, *Pakistan and Afghanistan* (1994).

Related Entries: Defense Spending; Foreign Policy; Reagan Doctrine; Terrorism.

AFRICA. U.S. **foreign policy** toward Africa during the Reagan-Bush years marked a general reversal from that pursued by the Carter administration. Following the **Reagan Doctrine,** anticommunism, rather than human rights, became the key concern. This change was most noticeable in terms of U.S. policy toward **South Africa** and Angola. It also influenced the United States relationships with Ethiopia and **Libya,** two pro-Marxist states.

In general, the Carter administration had pursued a human rights–oriented policy in South Africa. This included pressuring the South African government to dismantle apartheid and a refusal to provide direct funding for anti-Marxist forces in Ethiopia and Angola. In contrast, the Reagan administration pursued a policy of "constructive engagement" toward South Africa, whereby it avoided economic sanctions, and sought to provide covert support for anti-Marxist forces in Angola and elsewhere.

The Reagan administration's point man in Africa was **Chester Arthur Crocker.** As assistant secretary of state for African affairs, he focused much of his attention on negotiating a multiparty peace plan, whereby Cuban forces would withdraw from Angola, the United States would quit funding anti-Marxist forces led by Joseph Savimbi, South Africa would withdraw from South-West Africa (Namibia), allowing it to obtain its independence, and white rulers in South Africa would relax their apartheid laws. Crocker pursued these negotiations throughout Reagan's tenure in office.

In 1988, Crocker finally gained an agreement to these terms. This led him and other Reagan officials to claim victory. However, the length of the process led many to argue that the Reagan administration had failed in Africa. In particular, they criticized the administration's failure to whittle away apartheid. Indeed, not until Bush came to office did reforms in South Africa begin in earnest.

During the 1980s, the U.S. government, along with private groups, funneled millions of dollars worth of aid to numerous African nations that were being devastated by widespread famine. The most famous of these efforts emanated from nongovernmental forces. In the summer of 1985, rock musician and music promoter Bob Geldorf helped produce Live Aid, a benefit concert staged simultaneously in London and Philadelphia and broadcast on television around the world. The event raised over $65 million and, just as important, increased awareness about the severity of the famine in Africa. In turn, the U.S. government augmented its effort to get food and medicine to stricken areas.

In December 1992, President Bush sent 1,800 U.S. Marines to Mogadishu, **Somalia,** as part of the United Nations' Operation Rescue Hope. The objective of the military incursion was to provide protection for relief efforts, which had been threatened by civil strife. At least in the short term, the mission succeeded. President Bush received strong support for this action, even from groups that had largely been critical of the Reagan administration's foreign policy initiatives in Africa.

Ironically, civil strife in Somalia had been fueled, in part, by the militarization of the region, which was a byproduct of the cold war and the Reagan administration's policy of providing arms to anticommunist governments. Since Somalia's neighbor, Ethiopia, was run by Marxists and allied with the Soviet Union, the United States had supplied fairly advanced weapons to Somalian forces. As the cold war came to an end, the U.S. strategic interests in the region diminished, but its weapons remained there in the hands of leaders, who often opposed U.S. efforts to distribute relief.

Suggested Readings: Gerald Bender, James S. Coleman and Richard L. Sklar, eds., *African Crisis Areas and U.S. Foreign Policy* (1985); Peter Duignan and Lewis H. Gann, *The United States and Africa* (1987); Peter J. Schraeder, *United States Foreign Policy toward Africa* (1994).

AIDS. See **ACQUIRED IMMUNODEFICIENCY SYNDROME.**

AIRBORNE WARNING AND CONTROL SYSTEM (AWACS). In October 1981 the United States sold five airborne warning and control systems (AWACS) to Saudi Arabia. These aircraft carry advanced, long-range radar and allow for improved human and electronic command of air battles. The sale of these advanced military weapons, along with equipment for F-15 fighters, produced a good deal of controversy. Opponents noted that the Saudis had supported the oil embargo against the United States in 1979 and were enemies of Israel. Despite congressional opposition,

Airborne Warning and Control System (AWAC). Still Media Center, Department of Defense.

Reagan pushed through their sale, which was consistent with the **Reagan Doctrine** of supporting anticommunist nations. The sale of AWACS to Saudi Arabia also was part of the Reagan administration's long-term strategy of developing a moderate block of allies in the region. To an extent, this block manifested itself during President George Bush's presidency with the **Persian Gulf War.** At that time, the AWACS made up part of the military effort to force Iraq out of Kuwait.

The Reagan administration's ability to sell the AWACS over congressional objections was one of the earliest displays of its political power. To gain passage, the administration had to put together a coalition of Republicans and conservative Democrats. This same coalition enacted Reagan's tax and defense policies.

Suggested Readings: *Facts on File* (1981); Kenneth A. Oye, Robert J. Lieber and Donald Rothchild, eds., *Eagle Defiant* (1983); George Venczowski, *American Presidents in the Middle East* (1984); Daniel Yergin, *The Prize* (1991).

Related Entries: Arms Exports; Foreign Policy; Middle East.

AIR TRAFFIC CONTROLLERS (PATCO) STRIKE. On August 5, 1981, two days after United States Air Traffic Controllers, members of the Professional Air Traffic Controllers Organization (PATCO), went on strike, President Ronald Reagan ordered their immediate dismissal. In doing so he cited federal law that outlawed strikes by federal employees. Despite the fact that PATCO was not a member of the American Federation of Labor and Congress of Industrial Organizations (AFL-CIO), the labor federation vociferously objected to the firing of the air traffic controllers, arguing that they were overworked and underpaid and that President Reagan's predecessor had not enforced the law in previous strikes by federal employees. President Reagan, however, refused to budge from his position, contending that while he sympathized with the workers, he could not countenance their breaking of the law. The president added that he had clearly forewarned the union's leaders that he would not tolerate a strike. The president also refused to grant amnesty to the air traffic controllers. Instead, he replaced them with supervisors, military air traffic controllers, and nonstriking employees. While this necessitated the curtailing of a significant number of flights, the president and the Federal Aviation Agency (FAA) insisted that it did not decrease air traffic safety, an assertion that the president's critics challenged.

For many, the PATCO strike came to symbolize labor relations during the Reagan presidency. They argued that by dismissing the strikers, the Reagan administration was intentionally signaling the private sector that it would favor antiunion initiatives. Rather than cooperating with labor, as both government and most large corporations had done since World War II, government and business would now adopt an antagonistic or hostile stance. Labor would be blamed for the country's economic decline; it would be portrayed as a special interest and attacked through new, sophisticated antilabor campaigns.

Sensing that this was the case, on September 19, 1981, the AFL-CIO organized one of the largest demonstrations in the nation's history. Approximately 250,000 labor unionists and sympathizers came to Washington, D.C., to protest the president's antilabor stance in general and his firing of the air traffic controllers in particular. At the "Solidarity Day" demonstration and afterward, AFL-CIO leaders denounced Reagan as a throwback to the antiunion days of the Gilded Age and lobbied their congressional representatives to insure the rights of workers. Public opinion polls, however, suggested that a majority of Americans supported the president's action in the air traffic controllers strike. To make matters worse from labor's perspective, the recession of the early 1980s added to its troubles, as its membership declined both in absolute and relative terms.

Both during the strike and afterward, Reagan contended that he was not opposed to unions. He noted that he was the first union official to have been elected president—Reagan had once headed the Screen Actors Guild. Moreover, Reagan argued that his policies would benefit American workers in the long run, a position he reiterated as the recession ended and the number of jobs increased during the latter half of the 1980s.

Suggested Readings: Michael Pollock, "Why Air Traffic Controllers Are Talking Union Again," *Business Week*, May 27, 1985, p. 124; Ronald Reagan, *An American Life* (1990); Arthur Shostak, *The Air Traffic Controller's Controversy* (1986).

Related Entries: Labor Movement; Recessions.

ALEXANDER, LAMAR. (July 3, 1940, Maryville, Tenn.– .) Secretary of Education, 1991–1993.

Lamar Alexander took over from Lauro Cavazos as President George Bush's secretary of education on March 18, 1991. Alexander earned his B.A. (1962) and law degree (1965) from Vanderbilt University. After graduation, he worked briefly in the private sector, clerked for Judge John Minor Wisdom of the federal Court of Appeals and moonlighted as a piano player. From 1966 through 1970, Alexander worked for **Howard (Henry) Baker, Jr.**, as a campaign and legislative aide. In 1971 he went to work for Dearborn and Ewing, a private law firm in Nashville, Tennessee. In 1974 he won the Republican gubernatorial nomination but lost to Ray Blanton the Democrat in the general election. In 1978 he was more successful, defeating Blanton with 56 percent of the vote. Four years later he was reelected.

As governor of Tennessee, Alexander became best known for his tough stance on crime and attempts to reform **education** in the state. His attempt to link teacher pay to student performance earned him the wrath of the teachers association. Alexander pushed hard to add computers, update textbooks, and lengthen the school year, to be paid for with a special sales tax increase. Building on his actions on the state level, Alexander became a national leader in the crusade to reform education. During Alexander's tenure as governor, the state also attracted a number of new industrial plants, most notably two big car factories, one built by Nissan and the other by General Motors' new subsidiary, Saturn.

As a candidate, George Bush had promised to be the "education president." However, his first secretary of education, Lauro F. Cavazos, had not been as strong an advocate on the subject as Bush would have liked. As a result, in 1991 Cavazos was forced out of the cabinet and Alexander was brought in to take his place. One month after taking office, President Bush and Alexander presented a proposal for educational reform. It called for merit pay for teachers, such as Alexander had implemented in Tennessee; federal funding for the construction of new schools; the establishment of national educational standards; and a complex scheme for promoting competition between schools and a choice of schools by parents. This controversial section of the proposal was not enacted by Congress; parts of the remainder were.

Alexander is married to Leslee Kathryn Buhler. They have four children. In 1995 he announced his candidacy for the presidency.

Suggested Readings: Sam Allis, "George Bush's Point Man," *Time,* September 16, 1991, p. 61; *Current Biography* (1991) p. 11; Dan Goodgame, "Tennessee Waltz," *Time,* March 13, 1995.

ALLEN, RICHARD VINCENT. (January 1, 1936, Collingswood, N.J.– .) National Security Adviser, 1981–1982.

Richard Allen served as President Reagan's national security adviser during his first year in office. In contrast to Zbigniew Brzezinski and Henry Kissinger, Richard Nixon and Jimmy Carter's national security advisers (respectively), Allen was expected to maintain a low profile. However, conflicts with Secretary of State **Alexander Meigs Haig, Jr.,** as well as allegations of misconduct, produced the opposite result and led to his resignation on January 4, 1982. (Allen had directed the White House secretary to place a $1,000 check, paid as an honorarium to Nancy Reagan for an interview she did with a Japanese magazine, *Shufo no Tomo,* into the White House safe. He failed to inform Mrs. Reagan of this action, and he subsequently forgot about the check. When the money was found, rumors spread that Allen had stashed it away for his personal use. By the time investigators demonstrated that these rumors were false, Allen had already resigned.)

Allen earned his B.A. (1957) and M.A. (1958) from the University of Notre Dame and then did postgraduate work at the University of Munich in West Germany. During the 1960s he was employed by various think tanks, including the Center for Strategic and International Studies at Georgetown University (1962–1966) and the Hoover Institution on War, Revolution and Peace at Stanford University (1966–1969). From 1969 through 1972 he worked for President Nixon, first on his National Security Council and then as his deputy assistant. In 1979 and 1980 Allen advised Ronald Reagan on foreign policy and national security issues. He was considered a conservative who favored increased **defense spending** and showing a hard-line toward the **Soviet Union.**

Allen is married to Patricia Ann Mason. They have seven children. He is the author of several books, including *Peace and Peaceful Coexistence* (1966) and *Communism and Democracy: Theory and Action* (1967).

Suggested Readings: *Dictionary of American Diplomatic History* (1989); Thomas Dye, *Who's Running America: The Conservative Years* (1986); *Facts on File* (1981).

Related Entry: Foreign Policy.

AMERICANS WITH DISABILITIES ACT OF 1990. On July 26, 1990, President George Bush signed into law the Americans with Disabilities Act. Proponents of the new law proclaimed that it would do for disabled people what the **civil rights** laws of the 1960s had done for minorities. Opponents warned that it would prove a costly antibusiness measure. The law prohibited discrimination against men and women with disabilities in the areas of employment, transportation, public accommodations, and telephones. Most of its provisions became applicable two years after President Bush signed it into law, although some of them would be phased in over a longer period of time.

The most important section of the act banned employment discrimination. It applied to 500,000 businesses and covered approximately 14 million workers. According to the law, firms of twenty-five or more employees could not discriminate in terms of hiring, advancement, pay, or training because of "physical or mental impairment" as long as the worker was competent to perform the job. (In 1994 the law would be extended to include businesses with a minimum of fifteen workers.)

Another important section of the law dealt with public accommodations. It mandated that new buildings would have to be accessible to the disabled and owners of buildings that were open to the public and housed more than twenty-five workers would have to make a "good faith" effort to make them accessible to the disabled. New buses and trains were to be made accessible to people with wheelchairs. Telephone companies, too, had to establish relay services that would allow all hearing- or voice-impaired individuals to receive and place calls from ordinary phones.

The Equal Employment Opportunity Commission (EEOC) was charged with enforcing the new law. Evan J. Kemp, Jr., the EEOC chairman at the time of the law's enactment, predicted a 20 percent increase in civil rights violations complaints in the first year of the act's life. Subsequent studies, however, suggested that this estimate was very high.

Suggested Readings: *Congressional Quarterly Almanac* 46 (1990); National Council on Disability, *ADA Watch—Year One* (1993); Richard Bryant Treanor, *We Overcame: The Story of Civil Rights for Disabled People* (1993).

ANDERSON, JOHN BAYARD. (February 15, 1922, Rockford, Ill.– .) Independent Presidential Candidate, 1980.

John Anderson, a longtime Republican congressman from Illinois, sought the Republican presidential nomination in 1980. After a strong showing in the early primaries in New England, Ronald Reagan swept to victory in the South and Midwest and Anderson faded from contention. Throughout, Anderson stood as a representative of the moderate wing of the Republican Party (GOP) and earned a reputation for his honesty and integrity. He also attracted considerable attention and enthusiasm, especially from those disillusioned with **James (Jimmy) Earl Carter** and opposed to Reagan.

After Reagan won the GOP nomination, Anderson decided to run as an independent candidate for president. Patrick Lucey, the former governor of Vermont, ran as his running mate. Initially, some polls showed that Anderson would be a major factor in the election. Ultimately, however, he had only a minor impact. He won 6.6 percent of the popular vote and no electoral college votes. In addition, it remains unclear whether he helped or hurt Reagan. Most studies suggest that in 1984 Reagan won the support of the majority of Anderson voters. However, it is unclear whether they would have sided with Reagan in 1980.

Anderson is married to Keke Machakos. They have five children. He has held several academic posts since leaving Congress to run for president in 1980 and has authored numerous books and articles on politics and economics.

Suggested Readings: Mark Bisnow, *Diary of a Dark Horse* (1983); Clifford Brown, Jr., and Robert Walker, eds., *A Campaign of Ideas: The 1980 Anderson/Lucey Platform* (1984).

Related Entry: Election of 1980.

ANDERSON, MARTIN CARL. (August 5, 1936, Lowell, Mass.– .) Economic Adviser to President Ronald Reagan, 1981–1988.

Martin Anderson, an economist, served as a chief adviser to Ronald Reagan throughout his administration. He was a member of the President's Foreign Intelligence Advisory Board (1982–1985), the Economic Policy Advisory Board (1982–1988), and the General Advisory Committee on Arms Control and Disarmament. A conservative intellectual with a B.A. from Dartmouth and a Ph.D. in Engineering and Business from the Massachusetts Institute of Technology (1962), Anderson championed free-market economics and criticized the welfare state. Reagan often turned to Anderson for advice on economic matters during the presidential campaigns of 1976 and 1980. During the 1980s Anderson became identified with those who supported or promoted supply-side economics as opposed to more traditional classical economic views. Prior to serving as an adviser to President Reagan, Anderson worked for President Richard Nixon. He is the author of numerous books and articles, including a largely favorable memoir of the Reagan years. He is married to Annelise Graebner.

Suggested Readings: Martin Anderson, *Revolution: The Reagan Legacy,* updated and expanded ed. (1988); Martin Anderson, *Impostors in the Temple* (1992).

Related Entries: Domestic Policy; Reaganomics.

ARMS CONTROL. One of the cornerstones of the Reagan administration was its determination to build up the U.S. military capability. This included introducing a new generation of nuclear and nonnuclear weapons and deploying arms that had already been developed. Ronald Reagan was a harsh critic of the **Strategic Arms Limitation Treaty (SALT) II** which was negotiated by the **James (Jimmy) Earl Carter** administration but never ratified by the Senate. In addition, through most of his first term in office, he voiced sharp criticism of the **Soviet Union,** even referring to it as an "evil empire." Hence, one of the central paradoxes of the Reagan-Bush years was that they also resulted in the most serious arms control negotiations and agreements in modern American history.

During his first term in office, President Reagan rejected the main thrust of arms control advocates, namely the call for a freeze on the building and deployment of nuclear weapons. This demand was put forth by a large number of European and American antinuclear activists and by Soviet leader Leonid Brezhnev in the spring of 1982. Nonetheless, after suspending arms talks, he initiated a new round of arms talks, headed first by Eugene Rostow and then by **Kenneth Lee Adelman.** At these talks, and in public, the Reagan administration proposed reductions of specific land- and sea-based missiles and by calling for a ceiling on the size of nuclear weapons. Not until after

Mikhail Sergeyevich Gorbachev came to power, however, did these talks lead anywhere. Indeed, Reagan's initial proposals for cuts in specific weapons were rejected by the Soviets outright and were considered disingenuous by many arms control experts given the United States' superiority in air-based nuclear weapons.

In early 1985, nuclear arms negotiations took a new turn. Steady and serious negotiations took place between parties representing both superpowers in Geneva, Switzerland. Talks between Secretary of State **George Pratt Shultz** and Soviet Foreign Minister Eduard Shevardnadze, who replaced Andrey Gromyko, reinforced these efforts. President Reagan and Mikhail Gorbachev held a series of summits which, to a large part, focused on arms control. At one of these, in Iceland, in late 1986, a tentative agreement to reduce nuclear arms fell apart due to the United States' insistence that it would not kill the **Strategic Defense Initiative (Star Wars).** Then, however, at a summit in Moscow, in December 1987, Reagan and Gorbachev signed the historic **Intermediate-range Nuclear Forces (INF) Treaty,** whereby both countries agreed to eliminate intermediate-range nuclear missiles. The U.S. Senate subsequently ratified the treaty, setting the stage for further arms controls agreements between the two superpowers. In 1991, Presidents George Bush and Mikhail Gorbachev signed the **Strategic Arms Reduction Talks (START) Treaty,** which significantly reduced the number of strategic arms held by the United States and the Soviet Union.

The negotiation of arms control agreements are often cited as one of the crowning achievements of the Reagan-Bush years. Supporters of President Reagan credit his strategy of negotiating from strength as the reason why the negotiations proved successful. They add that the president was not simply an ideologue, bound solely by his fierce anticommunism. Rather, he blended his ideological anticommunism with a pragmatic approach to foreign affairs. This allowed him to open earnest discussions with the Soviets when the time was ripe. Supporters of Presidents Reagan and Bush also argue that ultimately, arms control talks worked because the United States engaged in a military buildup that the Soviets could not match. This drove the Soviets to the negotiating table.

Some analysts, however, argue that this interpretation gives too much credit to Presidents Reagan and Bush. They contend that the key development was the ascension of Gorbachev to power. They add that if the United States had been willing to engage in serious arms talks earlier in the decade, they would have been fruitful, in part since the claim that the United States was behind the Soviets in the nuclear arms race had never been true in the first place.

Suggested Readings: David Callahan, *Dangerous Capabilities* (1990); Mathew Evangelista, *Innovations and the Arms Race* (1988); John Lewis Gaddis, "Ronald Reagan's Cold War Victory," *Bulletin of the Atomic Scientists* (1988) Vol. 45, p. 1; Daniel Wirls, *Buildup* (1992).

Related Entries: Defense Spending; Foreign Policy; Nuclear Freeze Movement; Senate, United States; Summits, with Soviet Union.

ARMS EXPORTS. The nearly simultaneous end of the cold war and the **Persian Gulf War** raised concerns about an old issue, worldwide militarization and the exportation of arms by the superpowers. Throughout the cold war the United States and its allies and the Soviet Union provided or sold arms, in many cases conventional arms, to nations around the globe. The cumulative impact of these sales became apparent to many Americans with the Persian Gulf War, as Iraq had constructed one of the largest armies in the world by purchasing arms from both the **Soviet Union** and **North Atlantic Treaty Organization (NATO)** members, including the United States. Even before the end of the cold war, critics of the Reagan administration objected to the sale of arms to nations with poor human rights records. For instance, many Democrats in Congress fought the Reagan administration's sale of **Airborne Warning and Control Systems (AWACS)** to Saudi Arabia and support for the military of **El Salvador.**

In 1987, total arms exports stood at roughly $56 billion dollars, up about 6.5 percent in constant dollars from 1986. The largest exporters were the Soviet Union, with 46.5 percent of all sales, and the United States, with about 26 percent of the total. The NATO nations combined exported more than the entire Warsaw Pact, including the USSR. Middle Eastern nations purchased the most arms. Iraq received $5.6 billion worth of arms in 1987; Israel imported $4.3 billion worth of arms. Saudi Arabia, Egypt, and Japan were only slightly behind these two nations.

Many Americans expected that the end of the cold war would produce an era of security and peace and bring an end to the escalation of arms exports, which increased 50 percent between 1980 and 1988. Much to their surprise, they found that arms exports actually increased. The United States easily surpassed the Soviet Union as the largest arms merchant in the early 1990s. Between 1986 and 1991, U.S. arms exports to the Third World alone rose from $4 billion to $14 billion. In 1992, according to the Congressional Research Service, the Pentagon intended to supply arms and military aid worth $32.7 billion to 154 nations. This included sales to former communist nations, such as Bulgaria and Albania. In the wake of the Persian Gulf War, the United States also increased sales of advanced weapons to Saudi Arabia and Kuwait. In the year following the Persian Gulf War, Middle Eastern nations ordered between $20 and $25 billion worth of arms from the United States.

The reasons for this growth in arms exports were multiple. For one, other advanced nations besides the United States, from Russia to China and France, competed with U.S. defense contractors for orders. This put pressure on the U.S. government to not restrict arms sales—based on the assumption that if American companies did not sell the arms, other companies would. At the same time, the United States faced significant political and economic pressures to continue to produce and sell weapons. American workers in defense industries were hurt by declining arms production, and hence pushed for continued sales. In addition, as Dwight Eisenhower had warned at the end of his presidency, the military industrial complex would make it difficult to deconstruct the arms industry once the original rationale for the arms buildup, namely, the cold war, had ended.

Suggested Readings: "Are U.S. Arms Exports Out of Control?" *Fortune,* February 22, 1993, p. 100; Paul L. Ferrari, Jeffrey Knopf, and Raul L. Madrid, *U.S. Arms Exports* (1988); Michael T. Klare, *American Arms Supermarket* (1984); Mark Thompson, "U.S. Tops the World in Arms Sales, Report Says," Baltimore *Sun,* October 15, 1992, p. 9.

Related Entries: Communism, Collapse of; Defense Spending; Foreign Policy.

ARTS. During the Reagan-Bush years, the arts came under attack from conservatives. One of the **New Right**'s primary targets was the arts community. Conservatives claimed that the arts world was out of touch with the values of most Americans and produced obscene, anti-American, and antifamily works. Moving beyond rhetoric, the Reagan and Bush administrations sought to cut federal funding to the arts, in particular to the National Endowment for the Arts and National Endowment for the Humanities.

Two of the key figures in this effort were **William John Bennett,** head of the National Endowment for the Humanities (NEH) and later secretary of education, and Lynne Cheney, Bennett's successor at the NEH. Both of them took aim at radical, nontraditional arts that they felt the National Endowment of the Arts (NEA) and National Endowment of the Humanities were prone to support.

Debate over the arts was intertwined with criticism of multiculturalism and the **politically correct**, terms often used by conservatives to criticize the liberal drift of scholarship and academic life. Cheney and Bennett argued that the arts establishment sought federal funding for projects that were politically correct but refused to support those that were not. The arts world responded that the government should not be in the business of censoring speech (broadly defined) and that historically, the art world had always been ahead of the masses.

In the late 1980s, the arts debate came to a head with the showing of Robert Mapplethorpe's sexually explicit and homoerotic photographs at the Cochrane Gallery in Washington, D.C. Conservatives demanded that public support for the showing be withdrawn. Numerous artists and the American Civil Liberties Unions (ACLU) condemned this action. The works were removed from the gallery. At about the same time, criminal charges were brought against Mapplethorpe and a Cincinnati museum that had shown his work. In this instance, conservatives lost as a jury found that the works were not obscene.

Despite increasing criticism of the arts, the NEH and NEA were not dismantled during the Reagan-Bush years. Both agencies faced regular struggles for appropriations, especially in the Senate, where North Carolina Senator **Jesse A. Helms** led the crusade against them. One of the reasons why these two agencies remained alive was that they continued to enjoy the support of many moderate Republicans, especially from the Northeast, who resisted cuts to museums and performing arts groups, of which there were many in their states.

Suggested Readings: John Frohnmayer, *Leaving Town Alive: Confessions of an Arts Warrior* (1993); Mark Hertsgaard, *On Bended Knee* (1988); Joseph Zeigher, *Arts in Crisis* (1994).

ASSASSINATION ATTEMPT (RONALD REAGAN). On March 30, 1981, less than three months into his presidency, President Ronald Reagan was shot in the chest outside the Hilton hotel in Washington by **John W. Hinckley, Jr.** Reagan's press secretary, **James S. Brady,** a Secret Service agent, and a Washington, D.C., policeman were also shot by Hinckley. Reagan was rushed to George Washington University Hospital, where he underwent surgery to remove a bullet that had lodged itself only inches from his heart.

While Hinckley nearly killed the president, the incident ironically gave Reagan a boost. His standings in the polls surged and his ability to recover quickly from the gunshot wounds quieted the public's doubts

Assassination Attempt outside Washington, D.C., Hilton Hotel, March 30, 1981. Reagan Library.

about low stamina due to his age. (Reagan was one of the oldest presidents in American history.) The shooting also provided the president with the occasion to display his remarkable sense of humor and calmness during times of duress. Shortly before going into surgery, Reagan quipped to his wife, "I should have ducked." To the doctors he kidded, "I hope you are all Republicans." Nor was the president adverse to taking advantage of the outpouring of sympathy that accompanied the assassination attempt. On April 28, less than a month after leaving the hospital, he made his first public appearance before a joint session of Congress. Smiling and again cracking jokes, he received a tremendous ovation from Republicans and Democrats. Then he proposed deep budget cuts.

On May 13, 1981, Pope **John Paul II (Karol Wojtyla)** was seriously wounded in St. Peter's Square in the Vatican by a would-be assassin. On October 6, 1981, Egyptian President Anwar Sadat was assassinated in Cairo. These events, in combination with the assassination attempt on President Reagan, heightened America's sense of vulnerability and probably reinforced the public's support for an arms buildup and for President Reagan's **foreign policy** in general.

Suggested Readings: Lou Cannon, *President Reagan: The Role of a Lifetime* (1991); *Facts on File* (1981); Nancy Reagan, *My Turn* (1989).

ASTROLOGY. Following the **assassination attempt** on her husband, President Ronald Reagan, Nancy Reagan began to consult regularly with Joan Quigley, a professional astrologer. Entertainer Merv Griffin, a longtime friend of the Reagans, had introduced Quigley to Nancy Reagan prior to the assassination. Quigley advised Reagan about her husband's future. More important, Quigley developed charts that predicted which days would be good ones and which would be bad for the president. Based upon these charts Nancy Reagan helped determine her husband's schedule, ruling out certain days for travel and for other functions. President Reagan, who shared with Nancy a strong streak of superstition, went along with this intervention.

The extent to which Quigley's astrologically based predictions affected the presidency is debatable. Most likely it proved an inconvenience for Reagan's advisers, who had to shuffle schedules to conform with Quigley's advice. **Michael Deaver,** in particular, was placed in the unenviable position of rescheduling flights and appearances, due to Quigley's influence, while at the same time keeping secret the reasons for the changes. (He derisively called her "Madame Zorba.")

After Reagan left the White House, Nancy Reagan's reliance on astrology to determine the operations of the presidency became public record and a matter of considerable controversy. In his memoir, Reagan's chief of staff, **Donald Regan,** criticized the first lady for her intervention. Joan Quigley published a book on her relationship with Nancy Reagan that probably overstated her influence on the White House. Nancy Reagan defended her actions, siding more with Quigley than Regan. Detractors of the president pointed to Nancy Reagan's use of Quigley and President Reagan's compliance with her whims to show that he lacked intellectual vigor. Others, however, found the astrology issue a diversion, a means whereby critics detracted from President Reagan's strong record.

Suggested Readings: Joan Quigley, *"What Does Joan Say?" My Seven Years as White House Astrologer to Nancy and Ronald Reagan* (1990); Nancy Reagan, with William Novak, *My Turn, the Memoirs of Nancy Reagan* (1989); Donald T. Regan, *For the Record, From Wall Street to Washington* (1988).

Related Entry: Assassination Attempt (Ronald Reagan).

ATWATER, (HARVEY) LEE. (February 27, 1951, Atlanta, Ga.–March 29, 1991, Washington, D.C.) Political adviser to Ronald Reagan; Campaign Manager for George Bush, 1988; National Chairman of the Republican Party, 1988–1991.

Until shortly before his premature death in 1991 from a brain tumor, Lee Atwater served as the National Chairman of the Republican Party. Prior to assuming that post he had worked as George Bush's campaign manager and as an adviser to President Reagan.

Atwater was best known for his aggressive or, as his critics termed it, "negative" campaign style. Most particularly, Atwater was associated with the Bush campaign's **Willie Horton commercial,** which painted Democratic candidate **Michael Stanley Dukakis** as soft on crime. Critics alleged that the advertisement was racist and that in general, Atwater used various code words and images to win the support of southern and blue-collar whites. Atwater later apologized for the commercial, but he defended the thrust of his attacks on Dukakis and denied being a racist. Ironically, throughout his adulthood Atwater had struggled to broaden the Republican Party and overcome its minority status by appealing to numerous traditional Democratic constituencies. Thus, while his campaigns emphasized certain wedge issues, like crime, welfare reform, and gun control, Atwater also sought to end the Democratic Party's monopoly on the black vote.

Atwater's first political experience came following his sophomore year in college when he worked as an intern for the longtime conservative senator from South Carolina, J. Strom Thurmond. He quickly moved his way up the Republican ranks, gaining a post as executive director of the College Republicans shortly before his graduation with a B.A. in history from Newberry College. In 1974 he established the political consulting firm called Baker & Associates—but there was no one named Baker at the firm and Atwater had no associates. Among those he advised was President Reagan. Atwater was married to Sally Dunbar. They had two daughters.

Suggested Readings: "Atwater's Legacy," *New Yorker,* October 19, 1992, pp. 40–41; Larry Beinhart, *American Hero* (1993); *Current Biography* (1989) p. 25; *New York Times,* March 30, 1991, p. A:1.

AWACS. See **AIRBORNE WARNING AND CONTROL SYSTEM.**

B

BAKER, HOWARD (HENRY), JR. (November 15, 1925, Cumberland, Tenn.– .) Senate Minority leader, 1977–1981; Senate Majority leader, 1981–1985; Chief of Staff for President Reagan, 1987–1988.

A long-time senator from the state of Tennessee (first elected in 1966), Howard Baker gained national fame in 1973 as the ranking Republican on the Senate select committee to investigate the Watergate scandal. Throughout the 1970s and the early 1980s he was considered a moderate Republican, a centrist in a party that was moving to the right. While this put him at odds with a number of Reagan stalwarts, in February 1987, in the midst of the **Iran-contra affair,** President Reagan asked him to replace **Donald Regan** as his chief of staff. Baker accepted the offer.

In part, Baker had earned Reagan's favor by steering his tax and budget proposals through the Senate as its majority leader in the early 1980s. In 1984, Baker retired from the Senate to spend more time with his wife, who was ill with cancer, and to contemplate a bid for the presidency in 1988. (He had made a brief bid for the Republican nomination in 1980). Baker seemed a wise choice for chief of staff because of his reputation as a consensus builder within Congress. He got along well with Democrats and the press. The extent to which Baker succeeded in limiting the damage of the Iran-contra scandal is debatable. On the one hand, Reagan left office with extremely high popularity ratings. On the other hand, emboldened by Iran-contra, Congress blocked most of the president's domestic initiatives during the last two years of his presidency. One other byproduct of Baker's years as chief of staff was that they closed the door on his candidacy for president. Tied to the Reagan-Bush administration,

James Baker. Reagan Library.

Baker was not in a position to mount an outsider's campaign had he wanted to do so.

Baker was married to Joy Dirksen (deceased) and has two children.

Suggested Readings: J. Lee Annis, *Howard Baker: Conciliator in an Age of Crisis* (1995); Howard Baker, *Howard Baker's Washington* (1982); *Current Biography* (1988) p. 28.

Related Entry: Senate, United States.

BAKER, JAMES (JIM) ADDISON, III. (April 28, 1930, Houston, Tex.– .) Chief of Staff for President Ronald Reagan, 1981–1985; Secretary of the Treasury Department, 1985–1988; Campaign Chairman for George Bush, 1979–1980, 1988; Secretary of State, 1989–1992; Chief of Staff for President Bush, 1992–1993.

The son of a prominent Houston attorney, James Baker was perhaps the most important person during the Reagan-Bush years, aside from Presidents Reagan and Bush. He served as Reagan's chief of staff and secretary of the treasury and as Bush's campaign manager and secretary of state.

Baker first became involved in politics when his longtime friend, Congressman George Bush, decided to run for the Senate in 1970. Bush asked Baker to run his campaign, and though Bush lost to **Lloyd Bentsen,** Baker remained active in Republican politics in the state of Texas and, ultimately, in national politics. Baker managed Gerald Ford's presidential campaign in 1976 and George Bush's run for the Republican presidential nomination in 1980. Despite the fact that Baker had worked for his foes, Ronald Reagan recognized his considerable managerial skills and political astuteness and therefore named him to be his chief of staff shortly after winning the presidential election in November 1980. (Baker had joined the Reagan campaign staff following his nomination.)

Although Reagan's selection of Baker surprised many who had expected him to nominate one of his old friends, such as **Edwin Meese, III,** many considered it one of the wisest Reagan ever made. Alongside with Meese and **Michael Keith Deaver,** Baker made up the so-called big three or troika of the Reagan administration. Together they played a much more important role than the cabinet. Baker helped steer Reagan's policy proposals through Congress and very ably managed White House affairs. Perhaps most important, it was Baker who helped convince Reagan to focus on winning a tax cut and increased **defense spending** early on, rather than spending political capital on more divisive social and cultural issues.

In 1985 Baker switched positions with **Donald Regan**: Baker became secretary of the treasury and Regan took over Baker's position as President Reagan's chief of staff. Many considered this a mistake on the part of the president, as his second term was plagued with scandals and other problems that had not occurred under Baker's watch. While Baker did not distinguish himself as secretary of the treasury, it was Don Regan's job as chief of staff to which most were referring when they called this switch a mistake. As Reagan's second term came to an end, Baker shifted his focus to the election of his old friend, George Bush, to the presidency. Before Reagan's term was up, Baker resigned from the cabinet to devote his full attention to the election. Many credited him with putting together an excellent campaign, one that resulted in a surprisingly easy victory for Bush.

Following Bush's election, Baker was nominated to the post of secretary of state. He was easily confirmed by the Senate. Teaming with President Bush who, many felt, was more at ease with international than domestic affairs, Baker assembled an enviable foreign policy record. Among the most important international developments while Baker was secretary of state were: the **Persian Gulf War,** the **collapse of communism** in Eastern Europe, the negotiation of the **Strategic Arms Reduction Talks (START) Treaty** with the **Soviet Union,** the spread of democracy in **Latin America,** and renewed peace talks in the **Middle East.** While Baker was secretary of state, the cold war ended and, according to Bush, a **new world order** took its place.

As Bush's term came to a close, the president asked Baker to relinquish his post as secretary of state to serve as his chief of staff so that Baker could focus more of his attention on Bush's bid for a second term. (**Lawrence Sidney Eagleburger** became the interim or acting secretary of state, which provided Baker the opportunity to return to his job if Bush won reelection.) Baker's reputation was so great at the time that many felt that only he could salvage Bush's campaign. However, not only was Baker unable to reverse Bush's decline, his switch to political affairs left unresolved a number of international crises—in the Middle East, **Bosnia and Herzegovina,** and **Haiti,** to name just three. Thus, ironically, Baker's ultimate record and legacy ended in a clouded or negative note: a political defeat and evidence that politics (Bush's reelection) counted more than principle (Baker's pursuit of peace in the Middle East).

Suggested Readings: Michael Beschloss and Strobe Talbott, *At the Highest Level* (1993); Lou Cannon, *President Reagan: The Role of a Lifetime* (1991); *Current Biography Yearbook* (1982).

Related Entries: Domestic Policy; Election of 1988; Election of 1992; Foreign Policy.

BALDRIGE, MALCOLM HOWARD. (October 4, 1922, Omaha, Nebr.–July 25, 1987, Walnut Creek, Calif.) Secretary of Commerce, 1981–1987.

Malcolm Baldrige knew both the political and business world. His father, a lawyer, served in the Nebraska state legislature and in Congress for one term (1930–1932). After graduating from Yale University (1944) and serving in the army in the Pacific theater during the tail end of World War II, he went to work at Eastern Malleable Iron in Naugatuck, Conn. Over the next several decades, he moved up the business ladder, becoming the chief executive and chairman of the board of Scovill, Inc., a Connecticut brass-manufacturing firm, and quadrupling its revenues in about ten years' time (to a large degree by expanding its sales abroad).

At the same time, Baldrige became active in Republican Party politics. He served as a delegate to the Republican convention in 1964 and every four years afterwards, through 1980. He headed President Richard Nixon's Connecticut campaign in 1968 and George Bush's unsuccessful campaign in 1980. After Reagan's nomination, he focused on raising funds for the Reagan-Bush ticket. About a month after the election, Reagan nominated him to become the secretary of commerce. He easily won confirmation.

As secretary of commerce, Baldrige advocated free trade and **deregulation.** However, at the same time, as the **trade deficit** grew, he promoted a policy of limiting the imports of Japanese automobiles into the United States. Unlike many of Reagan's other cabinet members, from **James Gaius Watt** to **Edwin Meese III,** Baldrige rarely became a target of heated public criticism. He shared with the president a love for riding. He died, tragically, in a rodeo accident in 1987. He was survived by his wife of thirty-seven years, Margaret Trowbridge Murray, and two daughters.

Suggested Readings: *Current Biography* (1982) p. 625; Clyde Farnsworth, "The Cabinet's Trade Hawk Earns His Spurs," *New York Times Biographical Service,* May 1987, p. 482; *New York Times,* July 26, 1987, p. I26 (obituary).

BANK OF CREDIT AND COMMERCE INTERNATIONAL (BCCI). In July 1991 the assets of the London-based Bank of Credit and Commerce International (BCCI) were seized by regulators around the world as part of an effort to recover $10 billion lost by hundreds of thousands of creditors. The seizure followed probes launched by the Manhattan, New York, District Attorney's Office, headed by Robert M. Morgenthau. These efforts resulted in eleven plea bargains by individuals considered partly responsible for the fraud that was perpetrated on the creditors, as well as the recovery of over $1 billion.

Even before the plea bargains were announced, other probes were already underway. The U.S. Attorney's Office of the Southern District of New York, the **Federal Reserve Board,** and Congress, to name just three, sought to uncover the roots of BCCI's illegal activities and to prosecute the culprits where possible. Over a course of about a year, a series of deals were negotiated between various governmental and private parties in an effort to recover as much money as possible. For example, in January 1994, Abu Dhabi, one of the United Arab Emirates, agreed to provide access to regulators to the files of BCCI in exchange for the dropping of all charges in the United States against Abu Dhabi and Sheik Zayed bin

Sultan Al-Nahayan, the BCCI's biggest creditors. Given the complexity of the case, such an arrangement seemed reasonable to most parties immediately involved in it.

While the BCCI scandal had the potential of hurting the Bush administration, its ultimate impact was not that great. Even though successive Republican administrations had allowed BCCI's fraudulent activities to take place without prosecution and had been friendly to several of the key players in the scandal (due to broader **foreign policy** concerns), the Democrats shared part of the blame. This was due, in part, to the fact that one of the key figures indicted by federal investigators was Clark Clifford, a major figure in the Democratic Party since the days of President Harry Truman. If anything, the BCCI scandal hurt both political parties. Like the **Iran-contra affair** and the **savings and loan crisis,** it furthered the public's distrust of politics as usual and of the federal government.

Suggested Readings: Robert Emmet Long, ed., *Banking Scandals: The S & L's and BCCI* (1993); Jonathan Ready, *The Outlaw Bank* (1993); Peter Truell, *BCCI: The Inside Story of the World's Most Corrupt Empire* (1992).

BARR, WILLIAM P. (May 23, 1950, New York, N.Y.– .) U.S. Attorney General, 1991–1992.

On November 26, 1991, William P. Barr succeeded **Richard L. Thornburgh** as President George Bush's U.S. attorney general. Thornburgh had left to run in a special election for the U.S. Senate, which he unexpectedly lost. Barr was easily confirmed, with Congress seeing him as a welcome relief from a string of highly political appointees to the post.

Barr earned his B.A. (1971) and M.A. (1973) in Chinese studies from Columbia University, hoping to one day become the director of the Central Intelligence Agency (CIA). Unlike many of his college cohorts, Barr did not protest against the Vietnam War. On the contrary, he helped organize a counter demonstration during the infamous Columbia University takeover in 1968. After earning his M.A., he went to work for the CIA, working under George Bush, the CIA's director, from 1976 to 1977. At same time he attended law school, earning his law degree from George Washington University in 1978. Rather than staying with the CIA, Barr accepted a clerkship with Judge Malcolm Wiley of the U.S. Court of Appeals and then went to work for Shaw, Pittman, Potts and Trowbridge, a private Washington, D.C., law firm. In 1980 he worked on President-elect Ronald Reagan's transition team and then joined the White House staff as a member of the Domestic Policy Council. In 1983 he returned to his former law firm. In 1988 he worked for the Bush campaign and subse-

Bombed out U.S. Marine barracks, Beirut, Lebanon. Still Media Center, Department of Defense.

quently accepted a post as assistant attorney general for the Office of Legal Counsel. A year later he became deputy attorney general, and a year after that he ascended to the top post at the Justice Department. As an insider, he enjoyed the support of many of his coworkers. His focus as attorney general was on crime. This included a reorganization of the Federal Bureau of Investigation in order to devote more of its manpower to domestic crime and less to counterintelligence.

Barr is married to Christine Moynihan. They have three daughters.

Suggested Readings: *Current Biography* (1992) p. 53; David Johnston, "Attorney General Choice with Low Key Style," *New York Times Biographical Service,* October 1991, p. 1097.

BEIRUT, LEBANON (BOMBING OF U.S. MARINE BARRACKS). Shortly after dawn on October 23, 1983, a truck laden with approximately 12,000 pounds of TNT crashed through barricades at the headquarters of U.S. Marines at Beirut airport in Lebanon. Upon impact, the truck exploded, collapsing a four-story building on top of 300 American marines, soldiers, and sailors, many of whom were still asleep. It took weeks to identify all the victims. All told, 241 died from this terrorist attack.

President Ronald Reagan had first sent marines to Beirut in September

1992, in an effort to restore peace to the capital of Lebanon, which had been torn apart by civil strife. For over a year they remained there as part of a multinational peacekeeping force of five thousand. During the summer of 1993, as the civil war in Lebanon heated up, they often came under attack. On August 29, 1983, two marines were killed and fourteen were wounded. Eight days later, two more marines died and three more were injured when they were caught in cross-fire between Christian and Muslim forces.

In response, President Reagan increased the size of the U.S. contingent, both in Beirut and offshore aboard U.S. naval vessels. Since the troops had been there longer than sixty days, he was compelled to invoke the 1973 War Powers Act, which commands the president to obtain congressional authorization to keep troops in combat for more than sixty days. Both houses of Congress granted Reagan the power to do so. The House voted 253–156 in favor of the resolution; the Senate approved it by a margin of 54–46.

Then came the bombing of the Marine barracks. In response to widespread criticism of the U.S. presence in Beirut, President Reagan insisted that the United States would not be driven out. To leave following the bombing, Reagan argued, would reward the terrorists. Criticism was somewhat muted by the invasion of **Grenada,** which turned America's attention away from its losses and toward its successes. Moreover, shortly after the bombing, Defense Secretary **Caspar Willard Weinberger** informed the nation that the United States had evidence implicating a Syrian-backed, pro-Iranian, Shiite Muslim group. In early December, twenty-eight U.S. jets bombed Syrian positions east of Beirut. During the attack, two planes were lost.

These events, however, never totally quieted Reagan's critics nor convinced America that the marines should remain in Beirut. On February 7, 1984, President Reagan announced that U.S. Marines would be "redeployed" offshore. By the end of February, all had left Beirut. Even before this action, Syrian-backed Muslim forces had taken control of most of the capital of Lebanon. A report written by a five-member commission blamed the military chain of command for the terrorist attack. President Reagan responded by announcing that "if there is blame, it rests here in this office and with this president."

The bombing of the marine barracks in Lebanon was clearly the biggest **foreign policy** setback of President Reagan's first term in office. Even his admirers were forced to admit that the goal of the mission had not been well defined and, moreover, that the removal of the marines suggested that Lebanon had never been a vital interest to the United States in the first place. Nonetheless, public opinion polls suggested that President Reagan did not suffer much from the affair. His ability to maintain his popularity in spite of the high casualties led many to describe him as the "teflon president." (In other words, as with a teflon frying pan, nothing seemed to stick to him.)

Suggested Readings: George W. Ball, *Error and Betrayal in Lebanon* (1984); Eric M. Hammel, *The Root: The Marines in Beirut, August 1982–February 1984* (1993); David Martin and John Walcott, *Best Laid Plans* (1988).

Related Entries: Foreign Policy; Middle East; "Teflon Presidency"; Terrorism.

BENNETT, WILLIAM JOHN. (July 31, 1943, Brooklyn, N.Y.– .) Chairman, National Endowment for the Humanities, 1981–1985; Secretary of Education, 1985–1987; Director, Office of National Drug Control Policy (Drug Czar), 1989–1990.

A graduate of Williams College (B.A., 1965) and University of Texas (Ph.D. in philosophy, 1970), Bennett rose to national prominence in the 1980s as one of the Ronald Reagan and George Bush administrations' most articulate spokespersons. In contrast to his predecessors at the National Endowment for the Humanities (NEH) and the Department of Education, Bennett raised the ire of educators, artists, and the liberal intelligentsia by supporting President Reagan's proposed cuts in funding for student aid and conservative educational reforms, and through his sharp critique of the arts establishment.

A one-time director of the National Humanities Center in Chapel Hill, North Carolina (1976–1980), Bennett focused much of his scholarship on cultural and moral issues. As director of the NEH, he turned the agency in a more conservative direction, cutting its budget and eliminating programs that had historically funded liberal projects. He also supported grants to **New Right** groups, such as one for $30,000 that went to Accuracy in Media to produce a conservative alternative to the widely watched documentary on Vietnam produced for the Public Broadcasting System by Stanley Karnow. While he was director of the NEH, it issued a report, *To Reclaim a Legacy: A Report on the Humanities in Higher Education,* which lamented the decline of the humanities, as traditionally defined, in **education.** Using the report as a springboard, Bennett launched an attack on various "politically correct" developments, from multiculturalism to **affirmative action.**

Bennett became known for his advocacy of issues that went well be-

William Bennett and Nancy Reagan. Reagan Library.

yond the NEH. He supported a constitutional amendment that would allow school prayer and a school voucher program that would provide tax credits to those who sent their children to private schools. In 1989 he became the Drug Czar, commanding the Bush administration's massive **war on drugs.** Under his leadership, the federal government vastly increased the funds spent on drug control and law enforcement. Critics claimed that the federal government should be spending more on drug education and rehabilitation and less on criminal prosecution.

Bennett left the Bush administration in 1990. Afterward, he published several very widely read books, most notably, *The Book of Virtues* (1993) and *The Index of Leading Cultural Indicators* (1994), both of which purported to show that the nation was in cultural decline and that this decline could be traced to the social programs and values of liberal America. He gained so much attention from these books and from his public appearances and newspaper and magazine articles that some thought he would make a strong presidential candidate in 1996. In 1995, however, he declared that he would not run.

Suggested Readings: William J. Bennett, *Completing the Reagan Revolution* (1986); William J. Bennett, *The Book of Virtues* (1993); William J. Bennett, *The Index of Leading Cultural Indicators* (1994); *Current Biography Yearbook* (1985); *New York Review of Books,* March 1, 1990, pp. 29–33.

Related Entries: Arts; Constitutional Amendments (Proposed); Moral Majority; Politically Correct.

BENTSEN, LLOYD. (February 11, 1921, Mission, Tex.– .) U.S. Congressman, 1955–1970; U.S. Senator, 1971–1993; Democratic Vice Presidential candidate, 1988; Secretary of Treasury, 1993–1995.

Lloyd Bentsen crossed paths with Ronald Reagan and George Bush numerous times in his career. In 1970 Bentsen defeated George Bush in their race to represent the state of Texas in the U.S. Senate. From 1980 to 1992, as chairman of the Senate Finance committee, Bentsen presided over many of the hearings regarding President Reagan's and, then, President Bush's tax and budget proposals. In 1988 he ran as **Michael Stanley Dukakis**'s running mate against George Bush and **Danforth (Dan) James Quayle.** Moreover, in 1993, he became President **William (Bill) Jefferson Clinton**'s secretary of the treasury.

Considered a moderate-to-conservative Democrat who favored quiet negotiations rather than combative politics, Bentsen generally got along well with both Presidents Reagan and Bush. During the 1988 campaign his stature increased, to the point where some Dukakis supporters lamented that Bentsen was not the presidential nominee. Although rumored to be interested in the presidency, he did not run for the White House in 1992.

Suggested Readings: Richard Cohen, "Second Fiddles," *National Journal,* October 29, 1988, p. 2725; Jack Germond, "Inside Politics," *National Journal,* October 29, 1988, p. 2744.

BERLIN WALL, FALL OF. On November 9, 1989, twenty-eight years after it was first erected, the Berlin Wall came tumbling down. First built in 1961 to prevent residents of East Berlin (part of communist East Germany) from escaping into noncommunist West Germany via West Berlin, the wall became the most important symbol of the divisions between the communist and noncommunist worlds during the cold war, and of the separation of Germany itself. Its fall symbolized the end of the cold war and harkened the reunification of Germany. (Technically, the wall did

Fall of the Berlin Wall. Still Media Center, Department of Defense.

not fall right away. Rather, the East German government announced that, starting at midnight on November 9, 1989, its borders to the noncommunist west would be opened up. This included the border between East and West Berlin, which had been cut off for years by the wall.)

Initially, the wall was built of barbed-wire fencing alone. Then, East Germany constructed a twenty-eight-mile-long and ten-foot-high concrete wall, combined with barbed-wire fencing, minefields, and guard towers, to keep people from escaping into West Berlin. On occasion, individuals attempted to scale the wall or to tunnel under it, but almost always, these attempts failed.

The opening up of the border between East and West Berlin was an occasion of rejoicing in Germany and other parts of the world. Thousands celebrated the event in Berlin, climbing the wall, carting away pieces of it and, most important, simply traveling from one section of the city to the other. Over a three-day period, an estimated 2 million East and West Berliners crossed into the West and East, respectively. The subway between the two halves of the city was reconnected and large chunks of the wall were carted away. Summing up the significance of the moment, *Time* magazine reported: "It was one of those rare times when the tectonic plates of history shift beneath men's feet, and nothing after is quite the same." Based upon the fall of the Berlin Wall, in combination with the collapse of communist regimes throughout Eastern Europe in the fall of 1989, President Bush remarked: "If the Soviets are going to let the communists fall in East Germany, they've got to be really serious—more serious than I realized."

This said, many feared that East Berlin would be depopulated by the tearing down of the wall. Others worried that refugees from East Germany would swamp West Germany. By and large, however, neither of these developments took place. East Germans, in general, returned to their homes, and the reunification of Germany took place with remarkable speed and minimal violence.

Suggested Readings: "After the Wall," *Time,* November 13, 1989, p. 44; "Crossing the Divide," *Nation,* December 4, 1989, p. 665; Doris Elper, *The Berlin Wall: How and Why It Rose and Why It Fell* (1992); Lisa Mirabella, *The Berlin Wall* (1992).

Related Entry: Communism, Collapse of.

BHOPAL, INDIA. In one of the worst industrial accidents in history, more than 2,500 people were killed and an additional number (estimated at between 50,000 and 200,000) were injured when toxic, methyl isocyanide gas escaped from a pesticide plant and spread into a residential section of Bhopal, India, in the early morning of December 3, 1984. The plant was owned by an Indian subsidiary of Union Carbide of Danbury, Connecticut. Investigations revealed that the catastrophe resulted from substandard operating and safety procedures. In 1989, India's Supreme Court ordered Union Carbide to pay $470 million in compensation to the victims of the accident. The accident heightened concern about the **environment** in the United States and added to the pressure to adopt new environmental legislation.

Suggested Readings: Joshua Karliner, "Bhopal: Ten Years Later," *The Nation,* December 10, 1994, p. 726; Larry Everest, *Behind the Poison Cloud* (1986); Paul Shrivastava, *Bhopal: Anatomy of a Disaster* (1987).

BITBURG CEMETERY. On May 5, 1985, following an economic summit in Bonn, West Germany, President Reagan made an extremely controversial visit to a German military cemetery in Bitburg, West Germany. This visit, which was done at the request of German Chancellor Helmut Kohl, overshadowed President Reagan's entire visit to Europe and the economic summit. Coming on the fortieth anniversary of the end of World

President Reagan and West German Chancellor Helmut Kohl at Bitburg Cemetary, May 5, 1985. Reagan Library.

War II, the visit was supposed to display the healing of old wounds between the United States and Germany and their contemporary friendship. However, the discovery, made prior to the visit itself, that forty-nine German SS soldiers—from the notorious elite Nazi unit—lay buried at the cemetery clouded the entire affair.

Prior to the visit, Reagan defended his decision to go to Bitburg. He argued that the German soldiers buried there were "victims just as surely as the victims in the concentration camps." Jewish and veteran groups responded with outrage to this claim, with Elie Wiesel, the noted Holocaust survivor and author, pleading with the president during a public White House ceremony not to go through with the visit. Nancy Reagan and other top Reagan advisers similarly urged him not to go. However, Reagan insisted that he had made a promise to Chancellor Helmut Kohl on which he could not renege without jeopardizing relations with Germany.

The actual Bitburg visit lasted only eight minutes, and the president sought to compensate for the visit by stopping at the Bergen-Belsen concentration camp site the same day. Still, the episode remained a blemish on the Reagan administration. Jewish and other groups were not placated by his visit to the concentration camp, in part because it revealed the degree to which Germany downplayed the Holocaust. Unlike many trips abroad, this one did not lead to a boost in the president's popularity. Perhaps most important, the decision to go to Bitburg created a rift between Nancy Reagan and **Donald Regan,** the president's new chief of staff, whom she blamed for the controversy. Long afterward, she insisted that the Bitburg incident would not have taken place had **James (Jim) Addison Baker III,** still held the post.

Suggested Readings: *Facts on File* (1985); Ilya Leukoff, *Bitburg and Beyond* (1987); Nancy Reagan, *My Turn: The Memoirs of Nancy Reagan* (1989).

Related Entry: Summits, Economic.

BLOCK, JOHN RUSLING. (February 15, 1935, Galesburg, Ill.– .) Secretary of Agriculture, 1981–1986.

John R. Block served as President Ronald Reagan's secretary of agriculture from 1981 to 1986. Block's views and those of the president dovetailed. Both believed in less government and greater reliance on the free market. However, during his tenure, the Reagan administration attained only minimal cutbacks in farm subsidies and the Department of Agriculture remained one of the largest government bureaucracies in the nation. Political pressure from Republicans and Democrats from farm states, along with consumer fears that deregulation would produce price rises, helped convince both Reagan and Block to go slow in the realm of agriculture.

Born in 1935 on his family's farm in Galesburg, Illinois, Block graduated from the United States Military Academy in 1957. After three years of service, he returned to rural Illinois to work with his father in the hog, corn, and soybean raising business. Over a period of twenty years, their farm grew from 300 to 3,000 acres and hog production went from 100 to 6,000 a year. Named the Outstanding Young Farmer of the Year by the American Jaycees in 1969, Block became an advocate for farmers throughout the region. From 1977 until 1981, he served as the Illinois secretary of agriculture under Republican Governor James R. Thompson, Jr.

Shortly after becoming the secretary of agriculture, the Reagan administration announced the end of the grain embargo against the **Soviet Union** which had been initiated by President Carter following the Soviet invasion of **Afghanistan.** Block explained that this action symbolized the administration's commitment to expanding the sales of U.S. agricultural products abroad as a way to keep up prices without artificial price supports. This implied that the Reagan administration would seek drastic cuts in federal subsidies to American **farmers.** However, difficult times for farmers, resulting partly from high interest rates and the recession of the early 1980s, made it virtually impossible for Block to push through major cuts in governmental aid.

Block resigned in 1986 in the face of criticism from farmers and consumer groups. Afterward, he became the president of the National-American Wholesale Owners Association. He was succeeded as secretary of agriculture by Richard Lyng. Block is married to Susan Rathjo. They have three children.

Suggested Readings: *Current Biography* (1982) p. 37; *New York Times,* January 15, 1986, p. 1.

Related Entry: Recessions.

BOB JONES UNIVERSITY. On May 24, 1983, the **Supreme Court,** in the cases of *Bob Jones University* v. *United States* and *Goldsboro Christian Schools, Inc.* v. *United States,* ruled 8–1 that private schools that followed racially discriminatory policies could be denied tax-exempt status. The decision marked a setback for the Reagan administration, which had joined Bob Jones University in arguing that Congress had not granted the Internal Revenue Service (IRS) the power to deny tax-exempt status to schools that discriminated. The case was additionally important because it reflected on the Reagan administration's **civil rights** policies. As far as most civil rights groups saw it, the Reagan administration's decision to support Bob Jones University, a school run by religious fundamentalists and founded by **New Right** leader **Jerry Falwell,** in combination with its opposition to **affirmative action** and busing, showed that the president sought to reverse the drift on civil rights of the past twenty-five years.

After the Supreme Court ruled against the administration, Reagan and many of his supporters claimed that their support of Bob Jones University did not imply that they sanctioned segregation. Reagan claimed that the case had not been presented to him as one involving racial discrimination but rather as one involving the overreach of the federal government or, more precisely, harassment by the IRS. Neither Attorney General **William French Smith,** nor his top adviser, **Edwin Meese III,** had advised Reagan that the three previous administrations (two Republican and one Democratic) had authorized the IRS to deny schools tax-exempt status if they had racially discriminatory policies. Moreover, Reagan's supporters argued that the president was genuinely surprised when he discovered that Bob Jones University did discriminate—the university admitted a small number of minorities but banned interracial dating and marriage, citing the Bible as justification for these racial restrictions.

However, Reagan's ignorance in this case reflected the degree to which advocates of civil rights were denied his ear while its opponents had access to him. The administration's decision to support the university grew out of a plank put in the 1980 Republican platform by the New Right in which the party pledged to halt the IRS's "regulatory vendetta" against independent schools. Shortly after Reagan's election, Mississippi congressman Trent Lott wrote the president requesting that the government change its policies and side with Christian schools. In the margins of the letter, Reagan wrote that he concurred. Subsequently, the Justice Department filed an amicus curae brief in support of Bob Jones University. **William Bradford Reynolds,** Reagan's director of the civil rights division of the Justice Department, did nothing to deter the president from doing this. Notably, during this period and after, there was no one within the administration to point out the obvious racial implications of the case, whereas even presidents Dwight Eisenhower and Richard Nixon had had black aides who would have been in a position to notify them of the civil rights implications of such a matter.

Suggested Readings: *Facts on File* (1983); Richard Nathan, "Reflections on Pragmatic Jurisprudence: A Case Study of *Bob Jones University* v. *United States,*" *American Business Law Journal* (1984); Steven Shull, *A Kinder, Gentler Racism?* (1993).

BOESKY, IVAN FREDERICK. (March 6, 1937, Detroit, Mich.– .) Financier.

Ivan Boesky was born and raised in one of Detroit's tougher neighborhoods. Street-smart and driven, he earned his law degree from Detroit College and then worked as a tax accountant. In the mid-1960s he began devoting his full energies to the securities industry in New York City. By the early 1980s, Boesky presided over Ivan F. Boesky & Company (renamed CX Partners Limited Partnership), a financial empire that specialized in arbitrage. He also headed Cambrian & General Securities, based in London. His ability to spot or predict takeover stock deals earlier than the market made him extremely rich and one of Wall Street's most famous traders. Boesky bragged about his own abilities and powers in his semiautobiographical work, *Merger Mania—Arbitrage: Wall Street's Best Kept Money-Making Secret,* published in 1985.

In 1986, however, Boesky's empire and life began to crumble. He was indicted and subsequently convicted on insider-trading charges. News stories revealed that Boesky had obtained information from traders in a manner likened more to that of an underworld figure or petty thief than that of the highly sophisticated and suave Wall Street banker. In a plea bargain agreement with the federal government, Boesky agreed to pay $100 million in fines to the Securities and Exchange Commission and to inform on others who had committed securities fraud. In exchange he received a light sentence of two years in federal prison and was barred for life from trading in American securities.

Many see Boesky's rise and fall as symbolic of the course of the 1980s. He came to represent the successes and excesses of the decade. President Ronald Reagan's economic policies encouraged financial speculation and resulted in the creation of new, vast fortunes, with Boesky being only one of the better-known new multimillionaires. He helped give rise to the movement of **corporate takeovers** that swept through Wall Street. Toward the end of the decade, however, the stock market crashed, the savings and loan industry collapsed, and the takeover movement and economy slowed. Several of the best-known businessmen of the era, including Boesky and **Michael Milken,** who had made unheard-of fortunes, ended up in jail or on the verge of bankruptcy.

Suggested Readings: Gwen Kinkhead, "Ivan Boesky: Crook of the Year," *Fortune,* January 5, 1987, p. 48; Jonathan B. Stewart, *Den of Thieves* (1991).

Related Entries: Economy, U.S.; Savings and Loan Crisis; Stock Market Crash of 1987.

BOLAND AMENDMENT. The Boland Amendment, named after Congressman Edward P. Boland, a Democrat from Massachusetts and the chairman of the House Intelligence Committee, restricted the ways in which the federal government could use funds to help the Nicaraguan contras. It banned federal funding for the contras except for humanitarian purposes. The Boland Amendment first appeared in the classified section of the authorization bill for the Central Intelligence Agency (CIA) (PL 97–269) for fiscal year 1983. Congress passed it in September 1982. Later that same year, the House voted 411–0 in favor of applying the Boland Amendment's restrictions to a continuing appropriations resolution (PL 97–377) for fiscal year 1983. The amendment stated: "None of the funds provided in this act may be used by the Central Intelligence Agency or the Department of Defense to furnish military equipment, military training or advice, or the support for military activities, to any group or individual not part of a country's armed forces, for the purpose of overthrowing the government of **Nicaragua** or provoking a military exchange between Nicaragua and Honduras." In fiscal years 1984 and 1985, Congress provided nonmilitary aid to the contras. It continued to insist that the Boland Amendment was still in place.

By then, the Reagan administration had come to see the Boland Amendment as nuisance and a barrier to its **foreign policy** in Central America. This led to a search for alternative ways to fund the contras. This process led to the decision to divert funds obtained from secret arms-for-hostages deals with the Iranians to the anticommunist rebels. When reports of this diversion of funds appeared, many alleged that the Reagan administration had violated the Boland amendment. Attorneys for the president, however, contended that technically, the administration had not broken the law since it had not used congressionally appropriated funds. In addition, Reagan's aides suggested that they would challenge the constitutionality of the Boland Amendment if charges were filed. This said, **William Joseph Casey,** director of the CIA, and other administrative officials were accused of lying to Congress during questions regarding the contras, and several administrators were eventually charged and convicted of committing perjury and obstruction of justice. Ironically, Boland initially offered his amendment, in part, to deter attempts by some Democrats in the House of Representatives to cut off all aid to the contras. Nonetheless, by trying to get around the amendment, the administration virtually assured that Congress would cut off all military aid, which it did.

Suggested Readings: "Congress Set to Place Early Limits on Covert Aid to the Contras," *Congressional Quarterly Almanac* (1985) p. 76; Roy Gutman, *Banana Diplomacy* (1987); Peter Kornblum, *Nicaragua* (1988).

Related Entries: Iran-Contra Affair; Iranian Hostages.

B-1 BOMBER. The B-1, an advanced strategic bomber, was first deployed in 1974. From early on, however, it encountered criticism that it cost too much, performed poorly, and would become obsolete within a short period of time. As a result, in 1976 President **James (Jimmy) Earl Carter** canceled plans to build more. When Ronald Reagan became president, he pledged to renew the B-1 program. He lobbied for funding to build

B-1 bomber. Still Media Center, Department of Defense.

more of them, while simultaneously building modified B-52s, which had been used since the 1950s, and developing a new generation of bombers, known as the B-2 or Stealth bomber. Reagan's advocacy of the B-1 bomber encountered considerable opposition in Congress. Nonetheless, Reagan and Secretary of Defense **Caspar Willard Weinberger** refused to back down. They insisted that the military needed the bombers and that the nation could afford to fund all three projects. Reagan won the battle, gaining support from conservative Democrats and almost all Republicans for renewed appropriations of the B-1. As a result, by 1986, there were about one hundred of the bombers in service.

Suggested Readings: Noble Frankland, ed., *The Encyclopedia of Twentieth Century Warfare* (1989); Caspar Weinberger, *Fighting for Peace* (1990).

Related Entries: Defense Spending; MX (Missile, Experimental) Missile.

BORK, ROBERT HERON. (March 1, 1927, Pittsburgh, Pa.– .) U.S. Supreme Court Nominee, 1987.

On July 1, 1987, Ronald Reagan nominated Judge Bork to a seat on the United States **Supreme Court** to replace Lewis F. Powell, Jr. His nomination resulted in one of the most tumultuous confirmation hearings in American history, as liberal Democrats mounted a vigorous campaign to deny Bork a seat on the nation's top court. Bork was one of the best-known conservative jurists in America. He opposed **abortion** and gay rights and favored the death penalty. More broadly, he was a well-known proponent of judicial restraint and favored interpreting the Constitution in a narrow manner, often termed "original intent." His writings

President Reagan and Supreme Court nominee Robert Bork. Reagan Library.

and legal decisions, as a member of the U.S. Court of Appeals, made him one of the best-known critics of the Earl Warren Court and of the liberal drift of the judiciary through much of the twentieth century. This included an initial criticism of early **civil rights** decisions—though he supported *Brown v. Board of Education,* the landmark civil rights case—and a particularly harsh critique of the reasoning of the court in *Roe v. Wade,* the case that protected a women's right to have an abortion. Bork's nomination was further clouded by his role in the Watergate scandal. As solicitor general at the time, he was responsible for dismissing special prosecutor, Archibald Cox during the so-called "Saturday Night Massacre." Nixon had ordered Cox to be fired due to the latter's insistence on pursuing Nixon's involvement in the scandal. Whereas other justice department officials had resigned rather than carry out Nixon's order to fire Cox, Bork had chosen to save his own career and executed Nixon's command.

Following weeks of contentious hearings, the Senate Committee on the Judiciary voted against recommending his nomination, largely because it disagreed with Bork's conservative ideology and due to fierce political opposition from a broad coalition of liberals. Nonetheless, the president refused to withdraw Bork's name, thus forcing further debate and a vote from the floor of the Senate. On October 23, the Senate voted 58–42 against confirmation, as six moderate Republicans broke party ranks and voted with fifty-two Democrats against Bork (two Democrats voted for Bork). Ironically, although liberals celebrated Bork's defeat, shortly afterward Reagan nominated and won confirmation for another conservative, **Anthony McLeod Kennedy.**

Bork received his B.A. (1948) and J.D. (1953) from the University of Chicago. For nearly a decade he worked at Kirkland, Ellis, Hodson, Chaffetz & Masters, a private Chicago law firm. From 1962 to 1981 he taught law at Yale University. After a brief stint back at his old firm (1981–1982), President Reagan nominated him to the U.S. Court of Appeals for the D.C. Circuit. After winning confirmation from the Senate, he held this post until Reagan nominated him to the Supreme Court in 1987. In 1988, after being rejected by the Senate, Bork resigned from the Court of Appeals. He went to work for the American Enterprise Institute, a conservative think tank, where he wrote *The Tempting of America* (1990), a sharp attack on liberals and the drift of the Court in the twentieth century.

Bork is married to Mary Ellen Pohl. They have two children through his prior marriage to Claire Davidson (deceased, 1980).

Suggested Readings: Robert Bork, *The Tempting of America: America and the Political Seduction of the Law* (1990); Ethan Bronner, *Battle for Justice* (1989); Mark Gitenstein, *Matters of Principle* (1992); *New York Times,* July 2, 1987, p. 1; *New York Times,* October 24, 1987, p. 1.

Related Entries: Courts; Senate, United States.

BOSNIA AND HERZEGOVINA. In March 1992, Bosnia and Herzegovina declared independence from the former Republic of Yugoslavia. Bordered on the north and west by Croatia and on the east and south by Serbia and Montenegro, Bosnia and Herzegovina form a multiethnic republic, part Muslim, part Croatian, and part Serbian, which contained about one-quarter of the land of the former Yugoslavia and one of its most famous cities, Sarajevo. On the eve of independence, Bosnia and Herzegovina had about 4.1 million residents. Muslims comprised over 40 percent of the population; Serbs represented the second largest group, with about 31 percent of the total population; approximately 17 percent of the population was Croatian. When the winter Olympics were held in Sarajevo in 1984, the world celebrated the city's ethnic diversity and the ability of different people to live together in harmony. Beginning in 1991, however, Bosnia and Herzegovina in general, and Sarajevo in particular, became synonymous with strife, violence, and ethnic genocide.

When Croatia and Slovenia declared their independence from Yugoslavia in 1991, following the end of Communist rule in Yugoslavia, many smaller republics declared their allegiance to the Serbian-dominated Yugoslavia. Bosnia, which was controlled by non-Serbs, was not one of them. It refused to align itself with the Yugoslavian government. The European Community and the United Nations recognized Bosnia and Herzegovina's independence. This action did not stop Serbs within Yugoslavia or Bosnia from arguing that the new nation was illegitimate. Aided by Yugoslavian national troops, Serbs within Bosnia and Herzegovina gained control of the majority of the republic and laid siege to its capital, Sarajevo. Efforts to peacefully resolve the dispute between the Serbs, who favored alliance, and the Muslims and Croats, who did not, failed.

Most Americans had a great deal of difficulty understanding the conflict in the former Yugoslavia. They were repulsed by media reports of unprecedented wartime atrocities, most notably the systematic rape of 20,000 Muslim women by Serbian soldiers. However, they had few clues as how to end the fighting. In line with his generally cautious **foreign policy**, President George Bush accepted the European decision to recognize Bosnia and Herzegovina and supported the European Community and United Nations peace efforts. During the campaign, Bill Clinton criticized Bush's tempered response to the situation there. (Ironically, Clinton would find that it was easier to criticize Bush than to develop a workable alternative for the region.) Not until the final weeks of his presidency did Bush take a tougher stance, supporting the United Nations decision to establish a flight ban over Bosnia. By then, approximately 150,000 had already died.

Suggested Readings: Andrew Bell-Fialkoff, "A Brief History of Ethnic Cleansing," *Foreign Affairs* (Summer 1993) p. 110; John Newhouse, "No Exit, No Entrance," *New Yorker* (1993) p. 44.

Press Secretary James Brady, November 19, 1982. Reagan Library.

Related Entries: Clinton, William (Bill) Jefferson; Communism, Collapse of.

BRADY, JAMES S. (August 29, 1940, Centralia, Ill.– .) Ronald Reagan's White House Press Secretary, 1981–1989.

On March 30, 1981, James Brady was shot and nearly killed by **John W. Hinckley, Jr.** during Hinckley's attempt to assassinate President Ronald Reagan. While both President Reagan and Brady survived the shooting, a bullet wound above Brady's eye left him near death. For several months, thousands of Americans rooted for him to hang onto life. Not until Thanksgiving was he well enough to return home, and he battled with serious complications from the bullet wound for years afterward.

Although Brady returned to work for the president in November 1982, his life was never quite the same. His job for President Reagan was largely symbolic, as **Larry Speakes** and **Marlin (Max) Fitzwater** took over the day-to-day duties of the Press Secretary's Office. Moreover, with the assassination attempt, Brady's name became synonymous with the drive to pass federal **gun control** legislation. By the end of the 1980s, Brady's wife, Sarah, the daughter of a Federal Bureau of Investigation agent from a conservative Virginia community, had become the leading crusader for handgun restrictions. Ironically, it was not her husband's near murder but rather the discovery of a loaded handgun by her five-year-old son, Scott, that transformed Sarah Brady into a gun control advocate.

Throughout most of Reagan's presidency, James Brady did not join his wife's crusade, which conflicted with his boss's position. However, shortly before Reagan's term ended, James joined his wife in the effort to convince Congress to pass the so-called Brady Bill. On March 28, 1991, virtually the tenth anniversary of the assassination attempt, at George Washington University, President Reagan endorsed the Brady Bill with his old aide at his side. Later that summer the Senate passed the Brady Bill. Even though President Bush vetoed the bill in 1992, a year later, Congress passed it again. This time, the new president, **William (Bill) Jefferson Clinton,** signed it into law at a moving ceremony personally witnessed by Jim and Sarah Brady.

Suggested Readings: *Current Biography* (1991) p. 77; Mollie Dickenson, *Thumbs Up: The Life and Courageous Comeback of White House Press Secretary Jim Brady* (1987); *Historic Documents* (1993) p. 203; *New York Times Magazine,* December 9, 1990, pp. 42–45.

Related Entries: Assassination Attempt (Ronald Reagan); Gun Control.

BRADY, NICHOLAS. (April 11, 1930, New York, N.Y.– .) Secretary of the Treasury, 1988–1993.

When **James (Jim) Addison Baker III** resigned as President Ronald Reagan's secretary of the treasury in the summer of 1988 to focus his attention on George Bush's presidential campaign, Nicholas Brady, a moderate Republican and a close friend of Bush, took Baker's place. After Bush's election, Brady stayed on as secretary of the treasury.

Brady's father, James C. Brady, was a financier. His grandfather, James Cox Brady, was one of the founders of Maxwell Motor Company, which merged with the Chrysler Corporation before Nicholas Brady's birth. His great grandfather, a close associate of Thomas Alva Edison, had accumulated a fortune of approximately $100 million. Brady grew up on the family estate in Far Hills, N.J. He earned a B.A. from Yale (1952) where, like George Bush, he played sports. Afterward, he earned his M.B.A. from Harvard (1954). Upon graduation he went to work for Dillon, Reed & Company, one of the country's oldest and most famous investment banking firms. He quickly rose through the ranks, becoming the firm's president and chief executive officer in 1971.

At about the same time, Brady became active in politics. In 1980, he cochaired George Bush's presidential campaign. Two years later, New Jersey Governor Thomas Kean nominated Brady to serve out the remaining eight months of Senator Harrison Williams's term, as the latter had resigned following a conviction stemming from the Abscam affair. (Abscam stands for Abdul "scam," which was an elaborate federal undercover operation aimed at countering corruption in government. Seven members of Congress were convicted on charges stemming from the operation.) Knowing that he would not run for the Senate, Brady put forth some unorthodox views from the Senate floor. For instance, he called for cutting social security and warned that Reagan's economic forecasts were far too rosy. After leaving the Senate, Brady worked for various government commissions. Most important, he chaired the Task Force on Market Mechanisms, which President Reagan had created following the October 1987 stock market crash, to investigate its causes and suggest possible reforms. Even though the commission called for greater regulation of the stock market, which most Republicans opposed, his nomination to take Baker's post at the Department of Treasury was well received.

During the Bush administration, Brady advocated a pragmatic approach to the economy. He supported the President's decision to renege on his no tax pledge, favored the bailout of the savings and loans (S & Ls), and promoted a capital gains tax cut—which he did not get. As the recession worsened and the 1992 election neared, Brady was often a target of criticism, particularly from conservative Republicans. On February 25, 1992, Florida's Republican Senator, Connie Mack, called for his resignation. Along with twenty-six other Republicans, Mack charged that Brady was not "one of them." Nonetheless, Bush stuck by his old friend, only suggesting that during a second term the nation could expect some cabinet changes and implying that the treasury would be one of them.

Brady is married to Katherine Douglas. They have four children.

Suggested Readings: *Current Biography* (1988) p. 86; Susan Dentzer, "The Pick-and-Shovel Work of Nick Brady," *U.S. News and World Report,* March 20, 1989, p. 23; Louis Rickman, "Who Is Nick Brady?" *Fortune,* May 22, 1989, p. 59.

Related Entries: "No New Taxes"; Savings and Loan Crisis; Stock Market Crash of 1987.

BROCCOLI. "My mother made me eat it," President Bush declared about the vegetable broccoli, "and I'm President of the United States, and I'm not going to eat any more broccoli.'' This statement by the president, which accompanied stories that President Bush hated broccoli and refused to eat it at the White House, caused a major flap in 1990, which never completely died. In response to initial stories regarding the president's tastes, California broccoli growers sent seven tons of their vegetable to Washington, D.C. (All but two cartons went to a food bank. The remaining two cartons were sent to the White House.) When it was revealed that the president had a thyroid problem, numerous Americans wrote the president to say that he should have eaten his broccoli. The release of scientific studies in the early 1990s that showed that broccoli, along with other foods, could have a positive impact on health added to the punch of this jibe.

Suggested Readings: *Time,* April 2, 1990, p. 68; *Time,* June 10, 1991, p. 82; *Time,* January 6, 1992, p. 53.

BUCHANAN, PATRICK J. (November 2, 1938, Washington, D.C.– .) Assistant to the President and Director of Communications, 1985–1987; conservative columnist; candidate for 1992 Republican presidential nomination.

Patrick J. Buchanan, a conservative newspaper columnist, cohost of ''Crossfire,'' a debate-style television show, and a former aide to Presidents Richard Nixon and Ronald Reagan, gained national fame in 1992 when he challenged George Bush for the Republican presidential nomination. While Buchanan had little chance of winning, he rallied the right wing of the Republican Party against the president. He promised, if elected, to pursue an ''America First'' strategy, an explicit critique of Bush's focus on foreign policy. At the Republican Party (GOP) national convention, Buchanan delivered an all-out attack on the Democrats, rattling off a sharp criticism of liberalism and contrasting it to the Republican Party's defense of traditional values. Afterward, he endorsed Bush. In March 1995 he announced his candidacy for the presidency.

After attending Georgetown University (B.A., 1961) and earning his master's degree in journalism from Columbia University (1962), Buchanan went to work for the St. Louis *Globe-Democrat,* where he quickly distinguished himself via several editorials that blasted liberals. Almost at the same time he aligned himself with Richard Nixon, who Buchanan expected would run for president in 1968. When Nixon became president, Buchanan got a job working for him as a speechwriter. His most famous speeches were those that he wrote for Vice President Spiro Ag-

Pat Buchanan. Reagan Library.

new, which lambasted the media and liberals. During the 1970s he befriended several prominent conservatives, including Richard Viguerie, founder of the American Conservative Union. Following Nixon's resignation, Buchanan became an early supporter of Ronald Reagan.

From 1985 to 1987 Buchanan worked as President Reagan's director of communications. He adopted a much more adversarial approach to the press than had his predecessors, **David Richmond Gergen** and **Richard Darman.** He endorsed speeches that unequivocally endorsed the all-white government of **South Africa** at the very time that the anti-apartheid movement was gaining steam. He staunchly supported the Nicaraguan contras in spite of the **Iran-contra affair.** Ironically, he disapproved of the arms exchange, preferring open support for the anticommunist rebels over covert aid. Reminiscent of the age of McCarthyism, Buchanan questioned the patriotism of those who opposed the contras, stating that the communists would "be in San Diego" soon if they were not stopped in Nicaragua. However, unlike McCarthy, Buchanan proved unable to intimidate Congress, which not only went ahead and held investigations into the Iran-contra affair but also cut support for the contras.

Buchanan is considered by many to be too extreme to be elected to high office. He often says things that even other conservatives find embarrassing. At the same time, his pugnacious style appeals to those who are tired of traditional politicians who answer almost every question in double-speak. Ironically, while he claims to speak for the little guy, Buchanan's work as a columnist and authorship of a conservative newsletter, *PJB,* has made him a multimillionaire. He lives lavishly in a mansion in McLean, Virginia. Buchanan is married to Shelley Scarney.

Suggested Readings: Pat Buchanan, *The New Majority* (1973) p. 85; Pat Buchanan, *Right from the Start* (1988); *Current Biography* (1985) p. 49; Ann Reilly Dowd, "President Buchanan?" *Fortune,* February 10, 1992, p. 30; Norman Podhoretz, "Buchanan and the Conservative Crack-Up," *Commentary,* May 1992.

Related Entries: Election of 1992; New Right; Nicaragua.

BUDGET DEFICIT. During the 1980 presidential campaign, Ronald Reagan promised to balance the federal budget. To prove his seriousness on this issue, as president he continuously called for a constitutional amendment that mandated a balanced budget. As vice president and president, George Bush did likewise. However, one of the most significant phenomena of the Reagan-Bush years was the rapid increase in the federal budget deficit and the resulting accumulation of federal debt, as seen in Table 1. In fiscal year 1981 (President **James (Jimmy) Earl Carter**'s last budget year), the federal budget deficit was $79 billion. By 1993, Bush's last fiscal budget year, the deficit stood at $254.7 billion and the federal debt had skyrocketed to over $4 trillion. At no time during the Reagan-Bush years was the deficit ever below $100 billion, and most of the time it was much higher.

The rapid rise in the deficit and federal debt can be blamed on many different groups. Republicans liked to point out that the Democratic Party controlled the House of Representatives, the branch responsible for originating all appropriations bills, throughout this period. They added that the Democrats by and large opposed a Republican-favored balanced budget amendment and the idea of granting the president a line-item veto, which would have allowed him or her to cut unnecessary expenditures. However, in the final analysis the blame must lie at least as much with Presidents Reagan and Bush as with Congress. They claimed that they

Table 1
The Federal Deficit and Debt

Fiscal Year	Deficit (in bils. of $s)	Gross Federal Debt (in bils. of $s)	Debt as % of GDP
1980	−78.3	908.5	34.4
1981	−79.0	994.3	33.5
1982	−128.0	1,136.8	36.4
1983	−207.8	1,371.2	41.3
1984	−185.4	1,564.1	42.3
1985	−212.3	1,817.0	45.8
1986	−221.2	2,120.1	50.3
1987	−149.8	2,345.6	52.7
1988	−155.2	2,600.8	54.1
1989	−152.5	2,867.5	55.4
1990	−221.4	3,206.2	58.5
1991	−269.5	3,598.3	63.4
1992	−290.4	4,001.9	67.4
1993	−254.7	4,351.2	69.1

could raise military spending, cut taxes, and cut the budget deficit at the same time. (Bush initially called this "**voodoo economics**" but backed away from this critique after Reagan nominated him to be his running mate.)

Nonetheless, "**Reaganomics,**" the theory that underlay the claim that both taxes and the deficit could be cut, lay on some flimsy assumptions. Most important, it presumed that the tax cuts would generate enough growth to offset revenues lost by decreasing tax rates and increasing **defense spending.** However, this presumption rested on an extremely rosy economic forecast of the economy. When **recessions** hit the United States in 1981 and 1982, rather than adjusting taxes, cutting defense spending, or informing the public that the budget deficit would increase precipitously, the Reagan administration insisted that no modifications in its economic package were necessary. As the deficit grew, Reagan blamed Congress and continued to call for a balanced budget amendment, but he refused to decrease defense spending or significantly increase taxes. Indeed, during the 1984 presidential campaign, when the Democratic candidate **Walter Frederick Mondale** declared that he would raise taxes

Table 2
Selected Budget Forecasts (billions of $s)

Fiscal Actual Year Deficit	Proposed Budget, by President	Budget Adopted by Congress	Predicted Deficit	Actual Deficit
1982	695.3	695.5	45	128
1983	757.6	769.8	91.5	207.8
1986	973.7	967.6	180	221.2
1988	1,002	1,000	107.8	155.2

since it was the only way to cut the budget, President Reagan attacked him as a tax-and-spend liberal who had no interest in balancing the budget.

Reagan's director of the Office of Management and Budget, **David Alan Stockman,** observed early on during the Reagan presidency that the numbers did not "add up." Stockman had hoped that Reagan could win larger cuts in domestic spending than he did. When Congress refused to cut entitlement programs and Reagan himself pledged not to cut social security Stockman admitted in a widely-read interview published in the *Atlantic Monthly* (December 1981) that the deficit would grow. For making this claim, many conservatives called on Stockman to resign. Reagan stood by his budget director, but he did not alter his economic policy.

Every year President Reagan submitted to Congress budgets larger than the previous year. Every one contained sizable budget deficits. In almost every case, the administration vastly underestimated the deficits to come in future budget years. For example, in 1981 Reagan sent to Congress a $695.3 billion budget for fiscal year 1982. At the time, he predicted that this would generate a $45 billion deficit. Congress approved a $695.5 billion budget for the year, almost exactly the amount requested by the president. However, the real deficit ended up being $128 billion, nearly three times as large as Reagan had predicted (see Table 2).

To make matters worse, by the time George Bush became president it was becoming harder and harder to balance the budget. The **savings and loan crisis,** which was arguably precipitated by the **deregulation** policies promoted by conservatives, added to the sums of money that the federal government had to spend. The recession of the early 1990s made things even worse (and it was arguably a byproduct of the large deficits). Furthermore, an increasing part of the federal budget was being spent on entitlement programs, which neither party seemed willing to touch, and on servicing the federal debt. In 1980, less than 10 percent of federal budget outlays went for federal interest payments. By 1992 the figure had risen to nearly 15 percent and was continuing to rise rapidly. The cost of entitlement programs, especially medicare, grew faster than those for other programs.

As a result, by the end of the Reagan-Bush years, the deficit was a much bigger political issue than it had been when Reagan had first come into office. It underlay America's dissatisfaction with the federal government. Ironically, some analysts have contended that the real blame lay with the American people, who have punished politicians who sought to address the deficit by either raising taxes or cutting popular and widespread government programs.

Suggested Readings: Alberto Alesina and Geoffrey Carliner, eds., *Politics and Economics in the Eighties* (1992); Peter Bernstein, *The Debt and the Deficit* (1989); David Stockman, *The Triumph of Politics: How the Reagan Revolution Failed* (1986).

Related Entries: Constitutional Amendments (Proposed); Economy, U.S.

BURFORD, ANNE MCGILL (GORSUCH). (March 6, 1937, Casper, Wyo.– .) Administrator, Environmental Protection Agency, 1981–1983.

On March 19, 1983, Anne Burford (formerly Gorsuch) resigned from her post as head of the Environmental Protection Agency (EPA). She did so following six months of controversy and allegations regarding mismanagement of the agency's funds for cleaning up hazardous waste sites.

The storm over the EPA's use of funds began in October 1982 when Representative John Dingell, Democrat from Michigan and chairman of the House Commerce and Energy Investigations Subcommittee, issued a subpoena requesting information regarding the EPA's toxic waste cleanup fund. Based on President Ronald Reagan's instructions, Burford refused to comply with the subpoena for nearly four months, claiming executive privilege. In response, the House of Representatives, which argued that executive privilege did not protect her from answering the subpoena, cited her for contempt. This earned her the dubious honor of being the highest executive branch official so charged in history.

Shortly after she was cited for contempt, new allegations of improper activities surfaced. These implicated **Rita Marie Lavelle,** head of the EPA's toxic waste cleanup program. On February 7, 1983, President Reagan dismissed Lavelle and several of her top aides. A couple of weeks later, the White House changed its mind regarding the subpoena and agreed to turn over agency documents to Congress, except for those marked "enforcement sensitive." Dingell and the chairs of other congressional committees investigating the charges proclaimed that the administration's actions did not go far enough. On March 5, 1983, President Reagan declared that Burford enjoyed his "full confidence" and could maintain her post "as long as she wants to." However, faced with growing opposition from both Democrats and Republicans in Congress, Burford resigned four days later.

Burford received her B.A. (1961) and law degree (1964) from the University of Colorado. She was a Fulbright scholar in Taipur, India (1964–1965), and then worked alternately in academia and the public and private sectors. She is married to David Burford and has three children.

Suggested Readings: *Current Biography* (1982) p. 123; *New York Times,* March 10, 1983, pp. A1, B12.

Related Entries: Environment; House of Representatives, United States; Watt, James Gains.

BURGER, WARREN EARL. (September 17, 1907, St. Paul, Minn.– .) Chief Justice, United States Supreme Court, 1969–1986.

Nominated to the Supreme Court by Richard Nixon in 1969, Warren Burger retired in 1986 after fifteen years as its chief justice. During his seventeen years of leadership, the **Supreme Court** became a bit more conservative than it had been under the direction of Earl Warren, yet not conservative enough to please many of the Warren Court's critics, including Ronald Reagan. Reagan nominated **William Hubbs Rehnquist,** a sitting Supreme Court judge with a conservative reputation, to replace Burger as Chief Justice, and **Antonin Scalia,** another conservative, to fill the vacancy left by Burger's retirement. By doing so, Reagan hoped to turn the Court in a dramatically new direction.

Burger attended the University of Minnesota from 1925 to 1927 and received his law degree from St. Paul Law College, a night school, in 1931. After working in the private sector for two decades, he joined the Justice Department as assistant attorney general for civil rights in 1953. Three years later, President Dwight Eisenhower nominated him—and he was confirmed—to the U.S. Court of Appeals, a post he held until 1969. In 1969, Eisenhower's former vice president, Richard Nixon, nominated Burger to become the new chief justice of the Supreme Court.

At the time, Nixon hoped that Burger would move the Court in a more conservative direction, reversing the drift of the Warren Court. However, Burger did not preside over a counterrevolution in the law. As suggested by a book title referring to his tenure on the Court, *The Burger Court: The Counterrevolution That Wasn't* (ed. Vincent Blasi, 1983), no revolution took place during his fifteen years as Chief Justice. The most notable cases decided by the Court under Burger's leadership were *Roe v. Wade* (1971), which decriminalized **abortion,** and *University of California Regents* v. *Bakke* (1978), which upheld **affirmative action** yet banned quotas. His most important opinions dealt with the separation of powers. He wrote the majority opinion in *United States* v. *Nixon* (1974), in which he rejected Nixon's claim to keep the Watergate Tapes based on executive privilege. During Ronald Reagan's presidency, he wrote the majority opinions in *Immigration and Naturalization Service* v. *Chadha* (1983) and in *Rowsher* v. *Synar* (1986), which invalidated the legislative veto and struck down much of the Gramm-Rudman bill, respectively. He sided with the majority of the Court in its opposition to the Reagan administration in the case of *Bob Jones University* v. *United States* (1983).

Upon his retirement from the Court, Burger devoted much of his time to commemorating the two hundredth anniversary of the U.S. Constitution. This activity reflected one of Burger's long-standing interests, that of making the Court accessible to the general public.

Suggested Readings: Vincent Blasi, ed., *The Burger Court: The Counterrevolution That Wasn't* (1983); *New York Times,* June 18, 1986, pp. 1, 31; Bernard Schwartz, *The Ascent of Pragmatism: The Burger Court in Action* (1990); Herman Schwartz, ed., *The Burger Years* (1987).

Related Entries: Bob Jones University; Courts; Gramm-Rudman-Hollings Act (Balanced Budget and Emergency Deficit Control Act of 1985).

BUSH, BARBARA PIERCE. (June 8, 1925, Rye, N.Y.– .) First Lady, 1989–1993.

For nearly her entire adult life, Barbara Pierce Bush devoted herself to her husband's career, first in the Texas oil business and then in politics. For her devotion, integrity, and humility, she earned widespread admiration, with some suggesting that she was the most popular First Lady in recent history.

Barbara Bush grew up in Rye, New York, an affluent suburb of New York City. The daughter of an executive with McCall Publishing, she was descended from a long line of political leaders. Her maternal grandfather had served on the Ohio Supreme Court and her great-great-great-uncle was President Franklin Pierce. She attended public elementary school and then enrolled in a series of private educational institutions, including Ashley Hall boarding school in Charleston, South Carolina, where she received her high school diploma, and Smith College. Shortly before enrolling at Smith, she met **George Herbert Walker Bush** at a dance at the Round Hill Country Club in Greenwich, Connecticut. At the time, he was a senior at Phillips Academy. After graduating from high school, in 1942 George enlisted in the navy, where he became a fighter pilot. While on duty he corresponded regularly with Barbara, who was still attending Smith College. In 1943 Barbara dropped out of college. Around the same time, George's plane was shot down over the Pacific. Shortly afterward, the two were married in Rye, New York. Years later Barbara remarked that she married the "first man I ever kissed."

While George was still attending Yale, Barbara gave birth to their first child, George Walker Bush, in 1946. In 1948 the family relocated to Texas, as George began his career in the oil industry. Several more children were born during this stage of their lives: John (Jeb), Pauline Robin (who died in her first year, of leukemia), Neil, Marvin, and Dorothy. While George built a prosperous business, Barbara devoted herself to rearing her children and to charitable affairs and volunteer work. In 1966 George was elected to Congress, and for the most of the next twenty-five years of their lives, the Bushes resided in Washington, D.C.

During George Bush's campaigns and his presidency, Barbara served as his political adviser and confidant. She was fiercely loyal to her husband. Although she had a grandmotherly appearance, especially when contrasted to the stylish **Nancy Davis Reagan** and the more aggressive Hillary Clinton, she could be a dynamic speaker and was an active first lady. While residing in the White House, she focused much of her attention on the battle against illiteracy. She was often pictured nurturing young children, including her numerous grandchildren.

During the 1992 campaign, the Republican Party juxtaposed Barbara Bush's image, as a symbol of traditional values, to that of Bill Clinton's wife, Hillary, who was cast as a fierce feminist who opposed traditional values. In an unusual appearance, Barbara presented a major address in which she emphasized the virtues of the traditional mother as opposed to the career woman. Many contended, however, that this frontal assault on Hillary Clinton, by Barbara and others at the Republican convention, backfired. It not only dissuaded voters, it tarnished Barbara's virtually impeccable image.

Suggested Readings: Barbara Bush, *Barbara Bush: A Memoir* (1994); *Current Biography* (1989) p. 84; Diane Sansevere-Dreher, *Barbara Bush* (1991); Pamela Kilian, *Barbara Bush: A Biography* (1992).

The Reagans and the Bushes at the 1984 Republican Convention. Reagan Library.

BUSH, GEORGE HERBERT WALKER. (June 12, 1924, Milton, Mass.– .) Vice President of the United States, 1980–1988; Forty-first President of the United States, 1989–1993.

On January 20, 1993, George Bush departed the White House to witness the swearing in of his political rival **William (Bill) Jefferson Clinton** to the presidency. Shortly afterward, he and his wife, Barbara, departed Washington, D.C. for their new home in Dallas, Texas. It was one of the low points in what was otherwise a remarkable career.

Although born in Massachusetts, George Herbert Walker Bush spent most of his youth in Greenwich, Connecticut. His father, Prescott Bush, was a Wall Street Banker and a U.S. senator. As the son of a prominent financier and politician, George Bush enjoyed a comfortable life. He attended the finest private schools and was affected little by the Great Depression. When World War II broke out, George Bush enlisted in the navy. He served as a aircraft carrier fighter pilot, for which he received the Distinguished Flying Cross. Shortly after he returned from the war, where he had been shot down over the Pacific, he married Barbara Pierce, whom he had met at a dance while a senior in preparatory school at

Phillips Academy. When the war ended, George enrolled at Yale University, where he played baseball and earned his degree in economics.

In 1948, after graduating, Bush made one of the more important decisions in his life. Rather than joining his father's Wall Street firm, he journeyed with Barbara to Texas to start his own business in the oil industry. During the late 1940s and 1950s, both his family and business grew rapidly. Barbara and he had six children (one died in childhood), and he became a millionaire. Later in his career Bush would often cast himself as a self-made man. While his success in the oil industry was of his own making, critics noted that he had begun with important political and business connections and enjoyed the luxury of knowing that if his business failed he could always return home and work with his father.

In 1964 Bush ran unsuccessfully for the U.S. Senate. Two years later, however, he won a seat in the U.S. House of Representatives, representing a Houston district long held by Democrats. In 1968 he was reelected to Congress. In 1970, he ran again for U.S. Senate and lost, this time to **Lloyd Bentsen.** This defeat, however, did not end his public career. Rather, he accepted President Richard Nixon's nomination to become the U.S. ambassador to the United Nations, a post he held for two years (1971–1972). Afterwards he held a series of other high political posts, including chairman of the Republican Party (1973–1974), chief liaison officer in Beijing, China (1974–1975), and director of the Central Intelligence Agency (1976–1977).

During Jimmy Carter's presidency, Bush set his eyes on winning the Republican presidential nomination and ultimately, the presidency itself. His journey to the White House was dealt a setback by Ronald Reagan. After winning an upset victory in the Iowa caucus, Bush suffered a series of defeats to the former California governor. At times the campaign became heated, but after Reagan won the presidential nomination, he extended an olive leaf to Bush, nominating him to become his running mate. At the time, Bush was seen as a moderate Republican with Washington experience who nicely balanced the Republican Party (GOP) ticket, which was headed by a conservative outsider. The two went on to easily defeat **James (Jimmy) Earl Carter** and **Walter Frederick Mondale.**

For eight years Bush dutifully served as President Reagan's vice president. Twice, Bush temporarily assumed the reins of the presidency, first following the assassination attempt on the president and later during Reagan's surgery for colon cancer. Bush was a relatively active vice president.

During Reagan's presidency, Bush moved toward the political right. For instance, whereas prior to 1980, he had criticized supply-side economics and supported women's right to choose, during the 1980s he became an advocate of Reagan's economic policies and an opponent of **abortion.** In 1988, he defeated several Republican opponents to win his party's nomination. In his race against **Michael Stanley Dukakis,** Bush emphasized the accomplishments of the Reagan-Bush years and promised to continue the Reagan Revolution. Moreover, Bush pledged not to raise taxes. Following an aggressive, somewhat dirty, campaign, he enjoyed a stunning victory over Michael Dukakis, winning even more votes than Ronald Reagan had in 1980.

Bush's presidency was one of the strangest in recent history. His popularity rose as the economy grew and as communism collapsed in Eastern Europe in 1989 and 1990. Then, with conclusion of the **Persian Gulf War,** the biggest and most decisive military victory since World War II, his approval rating soared to record heights. However, even before Operation Desert Storm, the offensive campaign against Iraq, the seeds for Bush's demise, had begun to sprout. The **savings and loan crisis** turned already large deficits into enormous ones. In reaction, Bush broke his campaign pledge and acceded to the congressional demand to raise taxes. While this stabilized the **budget deficit,** it left many conservatives outraged. At the same time, the economic expansion of the Reagan years, which had already begun to run out of steam, ended. Bush's early denials that the economy was in a recession combined with his tepid reaction to the economic downturn, which he ultimately acknowledged, led many to believe that he was out of touch with the needs and concerns of most Americans. Earlier in his career, people had expressed doubts about Bush's leadership capabilities, and as the 1992 election neared, such concerns reappeared.

Ultimately, Bush proved unable to reignite the fervor that had swept Reagan into office and himself in 1988. With many Reagan supporters casting their ballot for **H. Ross Perot,** Bush won less than 38 percent of the popular vote. It was one of the worst Republican showings in years. Despite the loss, Bush left office proud of his record, pointing especially to his **foreign policy** achievements.

Suggested Readings: Colin Campbell and Bert A. Rockman, eds., *The Bush Presidency* (1991); Michael Duffy, *Marching in Place: The Status Quo Presidency of George Bush* (1992); Tony Hedra, *Born to Run Things: The Unauthorized Biography of George Bush* (1992); Dilys M. Hill and Phil Williams, eds., *The Bush Presidency* (1994); William Pemberton, *George Bush* (1993).

Related Entries: Communism, Collapse of; Economy, U.S.; Election of 1980; Election of 1984; Election of 1988; Election of 1992; "No New Taxes"; Reaganomics; Recessions.

C

CABINET.

President Reagan's Cabinet (January 20, 1981–January 20, 1989)

Secretary of State	**Alexander Meigs Haig, Jr.**
	George Pratt Shultz (assumed post Jul. 16, 1982)
Secretary of Treasury	**Donald Regan**
	James (Jim) Addison Baker III (assumed post Feb. 25, 1985)
	Nicholas Brady (assumed post Aug. 18, 1988)
Secretary of Defense	**Caspar Willard Weinberger**
	Frank Charles Carlucci 3rd (assumed post Nov. 21, 1987)
Attorney General	**William French Smith**
	Edwin Meese III (assumed post Feb. 25, 1985)
	Richard L. Thornburgh (assumed post Aug. 12, 1988)
Secretary of Interior	**James Gaius Watt**
	William Patrick Clark (assumed post Nov. 21, 1983)
	Donald Paul Hodel (assumed post Feb. 7, 1985)

President Reagan, Vice President Bush, and cabinet, February 4, 1981. Reagan Library.

Secretary of Agriculture	**John Rusling Block**
	Richard E. Lyng (assumed post Mar. 7, 1986)
Secretary of Commerce	**Malcolm Howard Baldrige**
	Calvin W. Verity, Jr. (assumed post Oct. 19, 1987)
Secretary of Labor	**Raymond James Donovan**
	William (Bill) E. Brock, 3rd (assumed post Apr. 29, 1985)
	Ann D. McLaughlin (assumed post Dec. 17, 1987)
Secretary of Health and Human Services	**Richard Schultz Schweiker**
	Margaret Mary Heckler (assumed post Mar. 9, 1983)

	Otis R. Bowen (assumed post Dec. 13, 1985)
Secretary of Housing and Urban Development	**Samuel Riley Pierce, Jr.**
Secretary of Transportation	Drew L. Lewis
	Elizabeth Hanford Dole (assumed post Feb. 7, 1983)
	James H. Burnley, 4th (assumed post Dec. 3, 1987)
Secretary of Energy	James B. Edwards
	Donald Paul Hodel (assumed post Dec. 8, 1982)
	John S. Herrington (assumed post Feb. 7, 1985)
Secretary of Education	Terrel H. Bell
	William John Bennett (assumed post Feb. 7, 1985)
	Lauro F. Cavazos, Jr. (assumed post Sept. 20, 1988)

President Bush's Cabinet (January 20, 1989–January 20, 1993)

Secretary of State	**James (Jim) Addison Baker III**
Secretary of Treasury	**Nicholas Brady**
Secretary of Defense	**Richard Bruce Cheney**
Attorney General	**Richard L. Thornburgh**
	William P. Barr (assumed post Nov. 20, 1991)
Secretary of Interior	Manuel Lujan, Jr.
Secretary of Agriculture	Clayton K. Yeutter
	Edward Madigan (assumed post Mar. 7, 1991)
Secretary of Commerce	Robert A. Mosbacher
Secretary of Labor	**Elizabeth Hanford Dole**
	Lynn Martin (assumed post Feb. 2, 1991)

Secretary of Health and Human Services	**Louis Wade Sullivan**
Secretary of Housing and Urban Development	**Jack French Kemp**
Secretary of Transportation	**Samuel Knox Skinner**
	Andrew H. Card (assumed post Jan. 22, 1992)
Secretary of Energy	James D. Watkins
Secretary of Education	Lauro F. Cavazos, Jr.
	Lamar Alexander (assumed post Mar. 14, 1991)
Secretary of Veterans' Affairs	Edward J. Derwinski

CABLE TELEVISION REGULATION. On October 3, 1992, President Bush vetoed legislation to increase federal regulation of the cable television industry, arguing that even though the bill had good intentions, it would not reduce the price of cable television and contradicted one of the fundamental principles of the Reagan-Bush years, a faith that competition and the free market, not the government, operated in the best interest of the American public. Two days later both the Senate and House of Representatives overrode Bush's veto. While the two branches of the federal government had clashed many times, the vote represented a major setback for President Bush and the first time one of his vetoes had been overridden.

Rising cable television rates and the lobbying efforts of noncable television broadcasters underlay the demand for regulation of the industry. The major noncable television broadcasters favored regulation because it allowed them to charge cable operators for the rebroadcast of their programs. Since 1965 the Federal Communications Commission had required broadcasters to provide cable operators with their shows free of charge. Consumer groups sought the legislation on the grounds that cable television rates had risen drastically due to the monopoly positions these broadcasters enjoyed. Despite the fact that President Bush emphasized the broadcasters' interest in the legislation and sought to cast the veto override vote as a test of Republican loyalty, and despite Senate Minority leader **Robert Joseph Dole**'s efforts to sustain the president's veto, eighteen Republican senators joined fifty Democratic senators in support of the legislation. The House overrode Bush's veto by an even larger margin, 308–114.

Suggested Reading: "Hill Enacts Cable TV Law over Veto," *Congressional Quarterly Almanac* (1992), p. 171.

CAMPAIGN FINANCE REFORM. In the spring of 1992 Congress passed legislation aimed at curbing spending by congressional candidates. On May 9, 1992, President George Bush vetoed the bill, arguing that it did not accomplish the goal of reducing the influence of special interests nor the advantages of incumbency. Four days later, the U.S. Senate, voting largely along party lines, fell nine votes short of overriding his veto.

In the early and mid-1970s, at first partly in reaction to increased campaign expenditures and then because of the Watergate scandal, Congress established public financing for presidential candidates. This system limited the amount of funds that candidates for all federal positions could receive from individuals. Subsequent court decisions forced Congress to modify the act, leaving large loopholes in the plan, including a lack of limits on the amount that could be spent by candidates for the House of Representatives. For over fifteen years, attempts to reform campaign financing went nowhere in Congress. Democrats, who were in the majority, differed sharply with Republicans over what type of reform to enact. The former favored spending limits and public financing, while the latter feared that this would only reinforce the Democrat's advantages. The **"Keating Five"** scandal, along with the ever-increasing costs of campaigns, however, prodded Congress to pass a campaign finance reform measure in 1992. Bush vetoed the bill because it did not reduce the advantage of incumbency—the same reason Republicans had opposed such reform throughout the 1980s. During the 1992 campaign, **William (Bill) Jefferson Clinton** pointed to campaign finance reform as symbolic of the **gridlock** that plagued Washington. He promised to enact it if elected, but once in office he proved unable to prod Congress to pass a new reform measure. (Threats of Republican filibusters kept the Senate from enacting campaign finance reform.)

Suggested Readings: "Bush Rejects Campaign Finance Legislation," *Congressional Quarterly Almanac* (1992), p. 63; Meredith Whiting, *Campaign Finance Reform* (1990).

Related Entries: Election of 1992; House of Representatives, United States; Senate, United States.

CARIBBEAN BASIN INITIATIVE. In February 1982, President Ronald Reagan announced his Caribbean Basin Initiative, an economic recovery plan for the Caribbean and Central America. Under the program, Reagan pledged to provide $350 million in direct aid to the region and agreed to remove trade barriers to products that the United States imported. In addition, the plan called for establishing tax incentives to encourage private investment by U.S. corporations in the area.

The initiative grew out of the Reagan administration's broader goal of checking Cuban influence in the region and, even more broadly, from Reagan's anticommunism. The plan dovetailed with the invasion of **Grenada,** aid to the Nicaraguan rebels, termed contras, and military and economic support for anticommunist forces in **El Salvador.** Critics of the initiative complained that it was really a ploy to increase aid to El Salvador, whose government was accused of vast human rights violations, in the guise of a broader effort to help the region in general.

Congress originally opposed the initiative. In 1982 it limited the amount of funds that El Salvador could receive to $75 million. In 1983, however, Congress moderated its position. To bolster his case, Reagan established the National Bipartisan Commission on Central America, headed by former Secretary of State Henry Kissinger. Not surprisingly, this group issued a report that lent support for the Reagan initiative. It concluded that Soviet- and Cuban-backed Marxists posed a serious threat to the region and recommended enacting a five-year, $8 billion aid program. The success of the invasion of Grenada helped undercut congressional opposition; so, too, did the victory of Jose Napoleon Duarte, a moderate, in El Salvador's presidential elections. Ironically, the president's impatience with this process led to the administration's decision to fund the Nicaraguan contras from outside sources. In turn this led to the **Iran-contra affair** which ultimately undercut one of the original major thrusts of the Caribbean initiative.

Suggested Readings: Cynthia J. Arnson, *Crossroads* (1994); Walter LaFeber, *Inevitable Revolutions* (1993); Gaddis Smith, *The Last Years of the Monroe Doctrine* (1994).

Related Entry: Nicaragua.

CARLUCCI, FRANK CHARLES, 3RD. (October 18, 1930, Scranton, Pa.– .) Deputy Secretary of Defense, 1981–1983; National Security Adviser, 1986–1987; Secretary of Defense, 1987–1988.

In 1987, following the resignation of Admiral **John Marlan Poindexter** as President Ronald Reagan's national security adviser, stemming from Poindexter's involvement in the **Iran-contra affair,** Frank Carlucci became President Reagan's sixth national security adviser. Shortly afterwards, his long-time mentor, **Caspar Willard Weinberger,** resigned as secretary of defense and Carlucci assumed that post. Carlucci's years of service in the defense department and as national security adviser made him one of the most influential voices in military and **foreign policy** during Reagan's presidency.

Frank Carlucci went to Princeton University (A.B., 1952) and then enlisted in the U.S. Navy. Afterward Carlucci earned his M.B.A. from Harvard in one year. In 1956 he joined the State Department, rapidly moving up its ranks. In 1970 he left the State Department to take over for his old friend, Donald Rumsfeld, as director of the Office of Economic Opportunity. A year later Carlucci became the associate director of the Office of Management and Budget, working under Caspar Willard Weinberger. Subsequently Carlucci worked as Weinberger's undersecretary at the Department of Health, Education and Welfare. In 1974 he was appointed the ambassador to Portugal. Four years later he became the number two man at the Central Intelligence Agency (CIA). Following Reagan's election, he was nominated to serve as Weinberger's deputy. Given his previous work for the Office of Economic Opportunity and Department of Health, Education and Welfare, some conservatives balked at his nomination. Nonetheless, he easily won confirmation.

Weinberger and Carlucci enjoyed a very close working relationship throughout the 1980s. Together they helped oversee the tremendous U.S. military buildup. Carlucci's nomination to succeed John Poindexter as national security adviser was generally well-received, as was his subsequent nomination to head the Defense Department. During his tenure in the latter post, **defense spending** continued to increase and relations with the **Soviet Union** continued to improve.

Carlucci is married to Marcia Myers. He has two children by his first marriage to Jean Anthony.

Suggested Readings: *Current Biography* (1981) p. 49; *Dictionary of American Diplomatic History* (1992); Elaine Sciolino, "Carlucci: A Tough Pragmatist," *New York Times Biographical Service,* November 1987, p. 1152.

CARTER, JAMES (JIMMY) EARL. (October 1, 1924, Plains, Ga.– .) Thirty-ninth President of the United States, 1977–1981.

Jimmy Carter swept into national prominence in early 1976, defeating a number of better-known figures to win the Democratic presidential nomination and then beating the Republican incumbent, Gerald Ford, in the general election. Four years later, however, Carter was defeated by Ronald Reagan. Following Reagan's election, Carter returned to his home state of Georgia, where he had spent the majority of his life.

Raised in Plains, Georgia (population 550), the son of Earl and Lillian Gordy Carter, Jimmy spent much of his youth on his family's peanut plantation until he left to attend the U.S. Naval Academy at Annapolis in 1943. He stayed in the navy for a decade, rising to the rank of commander. In 1953, on his father's death, Carter returned to Plains to run his family's business. Active in the local Baptist Church and a lone opponent of the local White Citizens Council, which had formed to oppose desegregation, Carter first ran for public office in 1962. His opponent for a position in the state senate flagrantly stuffed the ballot box. This led to the Democratic Party's decision to overturn the primary results and made Carter the Democratic nominee. It also helped create Carter's image as a clean politician. Carter went on to win a seat in the Georgia State Senate, which he held until 1967. In 1970 Carter was elected governor of Georgia and then, in 1976, he won the presidency.

Since his 1980 defeat, Carter has remained very active, proving himself one of the most active ex-presidents in American history. He became particularly involved in Habitat for Humanity, a nonprofit organization dedicated to helping the poor and homeless. Carter also commented frequently on foreign affairs (and served as a peacemaker during **William (Bill) Jefferson Clinton**'s first years in office). Carter is married to Rosalyn Smith. They have four children.

Suggested Readings: Jimmy Carter, *Keeping Faith: Memoirs of a President* (1982); Jimmy Carter, *Turning Point: A Candidate, a State and a Nation Come of Age* (1992).

Related Entries: Debates, Presidential; Election of 1980; Iranian Hostages.

CASEY, WILLIAM JOSEPH. (March 13, 1913, Elmherst, N.Y.–May 6, 1987, Glen Cove, N.Y.) Director, Central Intelligence Agency (CIA), 1981–1987.

William Casey died not far from his birthplace in 1987 in the midst of controversy revolving around his involvement in the **Iran-contra affair.** Less than twenty-four hours prior to his death, General Richard V. Secord testified, during the first day of congressional hearings on the Iran-contra affair, that Casey had played an active role in the effort to arm the contra rebels. Subsequent testimony and Bob Woodward's bestseller, *Veil* (1987), further implicated Casey.

CIA Director William Casey meets with President Reagan. Reagan Library.

The son of a sanitation worker, William Casey gained wealth and fame through hard work, intelligence, and what some claimed was the lack of an ethical or moral center. After graduating from Fordham University and St. John's law school, Casey obtained employment in Washington, D.C., with the Research Institute of America. During World War II he worked for the Office of Strategic Services (OSS), the predecessor of the CIA, directing spies from the OSS office in London. After the war he became a well-known tax lawyer and a partner with Republican Party leader Leonard Hall in the New York law firm, Hall, Casey, Dickler, and Howley. During the Richard Nixon and Gerald Ford administrations, he held several positions, as chairman of the Securities Exchange Commission, undersecretary of state for economic affairs, and chairman of the Export-Import Bank. After Ford's loss, he became affiliated with Roger's and Wells, a large New York law firm.

In 1980 Casey served as Ronald Reagan's campaign manager, focusing much of his attention on raising large sums of money for the former governor of California. On Reagan's election, Casey was nominated and agency was suffering from poor morale, due largely to congressional findings on the intelligence community's unethical behavior. Casey helped rebuild morale in the CIA, in part by turning it into an active arm of the Reagan **foreign policy** apparatus. Under his direction, the CIA increased its covert support for anticommunist insurgencies around the world, from Angola to **Nicaragua.** In addition, Casey lobbied Congress for increased **defense spending,** citing CIA studies that revealed the advantages the Soviets enjoyed in numerous military systems. Whether Casey played *the* key role in conceiving the plan to divert funds obtained from the arms deals with Iran to the contras will probably never be known. Ironically, his probable involvement in the affair, in combination with several **espionage** scandals involving CIA agents, left the intelligence community in at least as much disarray on his death as it had suffered from when he became director.

Casey was survived by his wife of forty-six years, Sophia Kurz Casey, and by one daughter.

Suggested Readings: *Current Biography* (1987) p. 628; *New York Times,* May 7, 1987; Joseph E. Persico, *Casey* (1990).

***CHALLENGER* DISASTER.** On January 28, 1986, the U.S. space program suffered the worst disaster in its history when the space shuttle *Challenger* exploded shortly after liftoff, killing all seven of its crew members: Commander Francis R. "Dick" Scobee; Pilot Michael J. Smith; Mission Specialists Judith A. Resnik, Ellison S. Onizuka, and Ronald E. McNair; Payload Specialist Gregory Jarvis; and (Sharon) Christa McAuliffe, a civilian schoolteacher. The launch and midair explosion were witnessed by onlookers at the Kennedy Space Center and by a worldwide television audience, which included many schoolchildren, who were paying special attention to this flight because of Christa McAuliffe's participation.

President Reagan appointed a thirteen-member panel termed the Rogers Commission—after its chairman, former Secretary of State, William P. Rogers—to investigate the disaster. The commission included Neil Armstrong, the first astronaut to land on the moon, and Nobel Prize–winning physicist Richard P. Feynman. On June 6, 1986, the commission issued its findings that a chain of events, beginning with a malfunction of the O-ring seal between sections of the external fuel tank, led to the explosion. Cold weather, the commission added, caused the O-ring's rubber seal to fail. The commission criticized the National Aeronautics and Space Administration (NASA) and Morton Thiokol, the producer of the seal, for laxity regarding the testing and safety of equipment.

The explosion grounded the space program for the longest time period in its history. Thirty-two months passed before another space shuttle was launched while NASA undertook a $2.4 billion effort to redesign the craft. Among the changes made were the inclusion of an escape system for the astronauts—which would not have aided the *Challenger* crew even if it had existed at the time—and redesign of the O-ring seal. The disaster also led to the reinstitution of an expendable launch vehicle program. (This move was already under consideration before the *Challenger* incident.)

Clearly, one of the most devastating aspects of the disaster was its impact on the youth, who were paying special attention because of Christa McAuliffe's participation. Some psychologists warned that the incident could leave permanent emotional scars on some who witnessed it. Nevertheless, President Reagan and the public remained committed to the manned space program and further space exploration.

Suggested Readings: Richard Lewis, *Challenger: The Final Voyage* (1988); Malcolm McConnell, *Challenger: A Major Malfunction* (1987); Joseph J. Trento, *Prescription for Disaster* (1987).

CHENEY, RICHARD BRUCE. (January 30, 1941, Lincoln, Nebr.– .) Secretary of Defense, 1989–1992.

Richard Cheney easily won confirmation as secretary of defense after the Senate rejected President George Bush's first choice for the post, former Texas Senator John Tower. As secretary of defense, Cheney presided over the **Persian Gulf War,** the **Panama invasion,** and the downsizing of the U.S. military. In each instance, he gained a reputation as a pragmatic and likable administrator. Some even suggested that he would make a strong presidential candidate in 1996.

The son of a soil-conservation agent with the U.S. Department of Agriculture, Cheney grew up in Wyoming, where he excelled as an athlete and student. After dropping out of Yale, he worked for two years laying power lines in the Rocky mountain states. In 1965 he received his B.A. from the University of Wyoming. Two years later, he earned his M.A. in political science from the same institution. Cheney then moved to Madison, Wisconsin, where he enrolled in a Ph.D. program while working on the staff of Governor Warren Knowles at the same time. Although Madison was known for its political radicalism, Cheney tended toward conservatism. Rather than completing his degree, he accepted a fellowship to work for Congressman William Steiger. Then he went to work for Donald Rumsfeld, a leading Republican in the Richard Nixon administration. As Rumsfeld moved up the political ladder, serving as Nixon's counselor and then President Gerald Ford's chief of staff, so, too, did Cheney. On November 5, 1975, when Rumsfeld became Ford's secretary of defense, Cheney took over as Ford's chief of staff. Following Ford's defeat in 1976, Cheney turned his energy to winning a seat in Congress. He returned to Wyoming for two years, and in 1978 he won the first of six elections. During the Reagan years he won a reputation as a conservative, pragmatic, and popular member of the House of Representatives, ascending to one of the top Republican Party (GOP) posts. He supported almost all of President Reagan's programs. As the vice chairman of the House committee that investigated the **Iran-contra affair,** Cheney declared that there was no evidence of any direct involvement by the president in the incident or in any cover-up.

During the **Persian Gulf War,** Cheney staunchly defended the president's decision to invade Kuwait rather than rely further on economic sanctions. As the cold war came to an end, Cheney called for gradual and deliberate defense cuts, so as not to risk American preparedness. One feature report on Cheney called him the "most important Secretary of Defense since Robert S. McNamara." Unlike McNamara or Ronald Reagan's secretary of defense, **Caspar Willard Weinberger,** Cheney enjoyed generally high popularity ratings. Perhaps the most controversial incident of his tenure came when he predicted that Soviet president **Mikhail Sergeyevich Gorbachev**'s reforms would fail which would lead to the ascension of an anti-Western leader or communist hawk in the USSR. This prediction created a temporary public rift with President Bush, but in the long run it did little to damage their close working relationship or Cheney's reputation.

Cheney is married to Lynne Anne Vincent (Cheney), the former chairman of the National Endowment of the Humanities. Together with the Doles, they constitute one of the most famous political couples in the nation. They have two daughters.

Suggested Readings: Richard B. Cheney, *Kings of the Hill* (1983); *Current Biography* (1989) p. 162; *New York Times Magazine,* January 27, 1991, pp. 16–17.

Related Entries: Dole, Elizabeth Hanford; Dole, Robert Joseph; House of Representatives, United States; Soviet Union.

CHERNOBYL, UKRAINE. On April 26, 1986, the nuclear power plant at Chernobyl in the **Soviet Union** experienced the worst nuclear accident in the history of the atomic power industry. The accident began when technicians at the plant violated several safety procedures while running tests on one of Chernobyl's four nuclear reactors. A chain of events, beginning with a decision to shut down the emergency water-cooling system and culminating with several explosions, produced a large fireball that blew the steel and concrete lid off the reactor. This explosion, in combination with a concurrent fire in the core of the plant, led to the release of massive amounts of radioactive material into the atmosphere.

The Soviet Union did not initially announce the disaster to the public. However, on April 27, after the fire had been brought under control, 30,000 residents of nearby Pripyat were evacuated. The following day, monitors in Sweden reported abnormally high levels of radioactivity in the air and demanded an explanation. This forced the Soviets to admit that there had been an accident, producing an international outcry and alarm throughout the region.

Over thirty people were killed by the accident and at least two hundred more suffered from severe radiation sickness. The explosion and fire dumped over eight tons of radioactive material into the atmosphere, more than that created by the atomic bombs that the United States dropped at the end of World War II on Hiroshima and Nagasaki, Japan, combined. The wind spread traces of the poisonous material as far west as Italy and France. Parts of the Soviet Republics of Ukraine and Byelorussia experienced serious environmental damage from the fallout.

The Chernobyl disaster posed a serious setback to the Soviets' nuclear power program and increased resistance to building more nuclear energy plants in Europe and the United States. Perhaps just as important, Chernobyl came to symbolize to many the corruption and inefficiency of the Soviet system. It damaged the Communist Party's prestige and further depleted the USSR's treasury. It also bolstered **Mikhail Sergeyevich Gorbachev**'s push for reform, which in turn helped lead to the **collapse of communism** in Eastern Europe, including Russia.

Suggested Readings: Grigori Medvedev, *The Truth about Chernobyl* (1991); Grigori Medvedev, *No Breathing Room: The Aftermath of Chernobyl* (1993); Piers Paul Reed, *Ablaze: The Story of the Heroes and Victims of Chernobyl* (1993).

CHINA. While the Ronald Reagan administration took a hard-line policy toward communism worldwide, relations between the People's Republic of China and the United States, which had been normalized by President **James (Jimmy) Earl Carter,** generally continued to improve during the Reagan and George Bush years. Even after Chinese Communist rulers cracked down on the democratic insurgency in their nation at Tiananmen Square, President Bush resisted calls for reversing the trend toward détente begun by President Richard Nixon in the early 1970s.

Evidence of the Reagan administration's less-antagonistic posture toward China, as compared to the **Soviet Union** and Cuba, came in 1984. In January 1984, China's prime minister, Zhao Ziyang, became the first Communist leader of China to visit the United States. From April 26 to May 1, 1984, President Reagan reciprocated, touring the People's Republic of China and meeting with Chinese leaders, including Deng Xiaoping, Premier Zhao Ziyang, and Communist Party General Secretary Hu Yaobang. During the trip, the United States and China agreed to allow for new cultural exchanges and greater economic cooperation. Afterward, the Chinese press described the visit as a "significant step forward," and President Reagan declared that a "new level of understanding" had been reached. (The only real flap of the trip took place when the Chinese censored a Reagan interview in which the American president praised American freedoms and criticized the **Soviet Union.**)

While the United States and China were unsuccessful in their attempt to negotiate a nuclear weapons agreement in 1984, a year later, leaders from both countries signed one. Cultural and scientific exchange reached new heights in the years that followed, and economic trade and cooperation between the two countries boomed. As a result, despite broad support in America for the prodemocracy movement in China and the public outcry that followed the ruthless crackdown on insurgents in late spring 1989, the Bush administration did its best not to avoid a breakdown in relations with the People's Republic of China. In late 1989, President Bush sent a team of American officials led by National Security Adviser **Brent Scowcroft** to China to maintain amicable relations. In 1992, Bush vetoed an act by Congress that would have placed restrictions on Chinese most-favored nation status. (Congress sustained his veto.)

Critics of these actions claimed that they allowed China to become one of the greatest abusers, if not the greatest, of human rights in the world. However, Bush's supporters countered that the best leverage that the United States had with China was to maintain open relations so as to foster the trend within the country toward free markets and a less planned economy. When **William (Bill) Jefferson Clinton** became president, he largely continued Bush and Reagan's policies, despite the fact that he had criticized them on the campaign trail. One favorable byproduct of this policy (at least from Bush's perspective), in addition to the economic one, was that the Chinese generally cooperated with or supported the United States in its international endeavors. Most notably, China backed the U.S. action against Iraq during the **Persian Gulf War.** (It did so by refusing to veto UN resolutions.)

Suggested Readings: John Gittings, *China Changes Face* (1990); Harry Harding, *A Fragile Relationship* (1992); Michael Schaller, *The United States and China in the Twentieth Century* (1989).

Related Entry: Tiananmen Square Incident.

CIVIL RIGHTS. Many observers considered the Reagan-Bush years to have been dark ones in terms of civil rights. Both Presidents Ronald Reagan and George Bush courted white southern voters; spoke out against **affirmative action,** claiming it represented reverse racism; and hindered the passage of new civil rights legislation.

Even before the 1980 campaign, Ronald Reagan had established himself as an opponent of busing, affirmative action, and other civil rights measures. As president he took a number of actions that seemed to confirm his animosity to the main drift of civil rights policy since the early 1960s. Early in his presidency, he opposed establishing the birthday of Martin Luther King, Jr., as a national holiday. He nominated **William Bradford Reynolds,** an outspoken critic of affirmative action, to head the civil rights division of the Justice Department. In turn, with Reagan's blessing, Reynolds sided with **Bob Jones University** in a case involving the college's racially discriminatory policies. When the 1965 Voting Rights Act came up for renewal, President Reagan initially called for killing it. After Congress renewed the law in spite of Reagan's protests, the Justice Department failed to side with blacks in their suits aimed at obtaining more representation. Instead, it aggressively prosecuted southern black officials accused of corruption. Furthermore, Reagan replaced liberal members of the U.S. Civil Rights Commission with conservatives while at the same time seeking to reduce the powers of the commission itself. Even more important, President Reagan appointed conservatives, who had records in opposition to affirmative action and other civil rights measures, to the courts. This policy climaxed with President Reagan's unsuccessful attempt to nominate **Robert Heron Bork** to the Supreme Court.

As part of his pledge to promote a "kinder and gentler America," George Bush backed away somewhat from President Reagan's attacks on civil rights. In part, Bush was motivated by signs that the nation wanted new action on the civil rights front. On November 21, 1991, President Bush signed the Civil Rights Act of 1991. This law made it easier for employees to sue employers on charges of racial and sexual discrimination and put the burden of proof on employers. The legislation grew out of a 1989 Supreme Court decision which had placed the burden of proof on employees while at the same time allowing Congress to pass new legislation that specifically made employers responsible. Initially Bush opposed the legislation, claiming it imposed quotas on hiring. However, following lengthy negotiations with Congress and minor modifications in the law by Senate leaders, he decided to sign it. Bush's appointments to the Justice Department and various commissions were also more moderate than Reagan's.

However, two incidents during Bush's term in office stood out above all others and put him at odds with civil rights advocates. First, his nomination of Clarence Thomas to the Supreme Court generated tremendous controversy. Second, the Central Los Angeles riot of 1992, which seemed to catch President Bush totally unprepared, suggested that neither the Reagan and nor Bush administrations had done much to improve conditions in the predominantly black inner cities and reinforced the division between civil rights groups and the Republican Party.

Throughout, both Reagan and Bush defended their civil rights records, arguing that their policies, which were not liberal, best promised to improve the lot of blacks in the United States and to ameliorate tensions between whites and blacks. However, based on their votes, black Americans did not accept this argument. While the number of well-known black conservatives increased, blacks as a group remained more committed to the Democratic Party than any other group in America. While President Reagan made inroads among other traditional Democratic voting blocks, he did not win a large number of black votes. In the 1992 election, **William (Bill) Jefferson Clinton** won in part due to President Bush's inability to gain black support.

Ironically, on the local level blacks gained more political power during the Reagan-Bush years than at any other time in American history. For example, America's largest cities elected black mayors. In 1989 David Dinkins became mayor of New York City. This followed the reelection of Thomas Bradley as mayor of Los Angeles and the even more spectacular election of Harold Washington as mayor of Chicago. During the same time period, the number of black members of Congress and state and local officials climbed dramatically, including the election of Douglas Wilder to the post of governor of Virginia in 1989. One might even argue that blacks owed their political success to the Reagan and Bush administrations, which they used as foils to attract support.

However, the Reagan-Bush years were also marked by one serious racial incident after another, from a shootout that culminated in a deadly fire at the Philadelphia headquarters of the radical black group MOVE to the killing of a black man by white teenagers in the Howard Beach neighborhood of New York City. Public opinion polls showed that tensions between blacks and whites were on the rise and that increasing numbers of blacks distrusted the government and felt they were the victims of persistent discrimination. Not surprisingly, this helped give rise to a number of opportunistic black leaders who sought to play up racial incidents even when the particulars of the incident (or alleged incident) did not support charges of racism. The best example of this involved Tawana Brawley, a black teenager from New York State. In early 1988 she proclaimed that she had been abducted and raped by a group of white men, including law enforcement officials—a charge that Reverend Al Sharpton and other New York black leaders supported. Only later in the year did Brawley admit that she had made up the story. By then Sharpton and others had moved on to more verifiable racial incidents.

Suggested Readings: Gerald D. Jaynes and Robin M. Williams, eds., *A Common Destiny* (1989); Steven A. Shull, *A Kinder, Gentler Racism?* (1993); Urban Institute, *Civil Rights and the Reagan Administration* (1988).

Related Entries: Los Angeles Riot; Thomas-Hill Hearings.

CLARK, WILLIAM PATRICK. (October 23, 1931, Oxnard, Calif.– .) Deputy Secretary of State, 1981; National Security Adviser, 1982; Secretary of the Interior, 1983–1985.

William Clark grew up in California. As a youth he worked on a ranch, spent a year at a seminary in Austria with thoughts of becoming a priest, and then enrolled at Loyola Law School. Without obtaining a degree, he passed the bar exam and became a practicing attorney. Clark was an early supporter of Ronald Reagan and remained one of his closest advisers through much of his political career. Despite the fact that Clark was a lifelong Democrat, Reagan named him to become his chief of staff upon assuming the governorship of California in January 1967. Along with **Edwin Meese III** and **Michael Keith Deaver,** Clark acted as one of Reagan's inside advisers, even after leaving this post. In 1969 Reagan appointed Clark to the California Superior Court, and three years later, he named him to the California Supreme Court.

When Reagan won the presidency, Clark was considered for a number of positions. He assumed the post of deputy secretary of state, serving under **Alexander Meigs Haig, Jr.,** who was not a Reagan insider. Despite his lack of background in foreign affairs, which became apparent during his confirmation hearings, he won approval from the full Senate. A very hard worker, Clark won general praise for his work at the State Department. In January 1982 Clark replaced **Richard Vincent Allen** as national security adviser. Along with **Caspar Willard Weinberger,** he often clashed with Alexander Haig.

Many predicted that Haig's resignation and the appointment of **George Pratt Shultz** as secretary of state would strengthen Clark's role within the administration. However, President Reagan's October 15, 1982, announcement that Clark would give up his position as national security adviser to replace **James Gaius Watt** as secretary of the interior proved these predictions wrong. Some hypothesized that Clark was moved to Interior because of some rift with Shultz. However, a more likely explanation for Clark's change in jobs was that Reagan wanted his longtime friend and adviser to settle the situation at the Interior Department which, while run by Watt, had received an inordinate amount of attention. During confirmation hearings, some critics complained about Clark's lack of expertise. However, by 1985, when he resigned to return to private life, it was generally accepted that he had, in fact, stabilized the situation at the department, even though his policies may have differed little from his predecessor.

Clark is married to Joan Brauner. They have five children.

Suggested Readings: *Current Biography* (1982) p. 68; Deanne Kloepfer, *The Watt/Clark Record* (1984); *New York Times,* October 15, 1983, p. 1; *New York Times,* January 2, 1985, p. 1.

CLEAN AIR ACT OF 1990. In October 1990 Congress passed the Clean Air Act of 1990. Technically the act consisted of tens of amendments that strengthened the Clean Air Act of 1970 (renewed in 1977). The new law tightened emission standards for automobiles, power plants, and other industrial polluters. It represented the first time in thirteen years that federal air pollution laws had been strengthened. Its passage came after nearly ten years of bitter debate between environmentalists and conservatives. The latter contended that the new regulations threatened American businesses and jobs while the former argued that only stricter regulations would end the problems associated with **acid rain.**

As a candidate for president, George Bush had given the Clean Air Act a shot in the arm by promising to be the "environmental president." In June 1989 he followed up on his campaign pledge by proposing a new clean air package. For over a year, however, the bill went nowhere as the administration and key Democrats in Congress haggled over many of the particulars. Bush threatened to veto the Clean Air Act if it contained overly stringent regulations. Democrats balked at some of Bush's proposals. Ultimately, the final measure that Congress passed contained the basics of Bush's proposal. Most notably, it phased in new emission standards for the automobile industry over a period of years and contained a market-based system of incentives to get utility companies to decrease pollutants. On signing the bill, Bush stated: "This legislation isn't just the centerpiece of our environmental agenda. It is simply the most significant air pollution legislation in our nation's history."

While many environmentalists felt that this statement was an exaggeration, they had to admit that it was the best environmental law to come out of a Republican administration in years.

Suggested Readings: *Congressional Quarterly Almanac* (1990); John-Mark Stensvagg, *Clean Air Act: Law and Practice* (1991).

Related Entry: Environment.

CLINTON, WILLIAM (BILL) JEFFERSON. (Hope, Ark., August 19, 1946– .) Governor of Arkansas, 1979–1981, 1983–1992; Forty-second President of the United States, 1992– .

In 1980, when **Ronald Wilson Reagan** defeated **James (Jimmy) Earl Carter,** Bill Clinton, who was only thirty-four years old at the time, seemed an unlikely candidate to end the Republican reign in the White House. (With the exception of Jimmy Carter's presidency, Republicans controlled the White House from 1968 through 1992.) Although he had become the youngest governor in the nation in 1978, his loss to Frank White in the 1980 Arkansas gubernatorial race made the odds against him becoming president extremely long. However, during the Reagan-Bush years Clinton emerged as one of the young stars of the Democratic Party, and in 1992 he captured the Democratic nomination and the presidency on his first try, something neither Reagan nor Bush themselves had achieved.

Clinton was born shortly after the end of World War II. His father died in a car accident three months before his birth. His mother, the former Virginia Cassidy (a hairdresser), married Roger Clinton (a car dealer—and alcoholic), when Bill was four. When he was fifteen, Bill legally changed his last name to Clinton.

From a young age Clinton displayed an interest in politics. In 1963 he took a trip to Washington, D.C., where he met and shook the hand of

President John Kennedy. Several years later he enrolled at Georgetown University, where he earned his B.A. After winning a Rhodes scholarship and studying at Oxford, England, he entered Yale Law School, receiving his law degree in 1973. Four years later, after returning to Arkansas to practice law, he married Hillary Rodham, another Yale Law graduate. A year later, their only child, Chelsea, was born. Even before marrying, Clinton had run unsuccessfully for Congress, barely losing to four-term Republican incumbent John Paul Hammerschmidt. In 1976 he directed Jimmy Carter's presidential campaign in the state and was elected state attorney general. Two years later, he became the youngest governor in the nation.

During his first term as governor, Clinton raised taxes, using the new revenues to expand the highways and to fund several progressive programs. Frank White convinced voters to turn Clinton out of office in 1980 in part by focusing on Clinton's tax hike. In 1982, running on a more moderate platform which called for education reform, Clinton made a comeback. He regained the governorship and was easily reelected in several subsequent bids. By 1992 Clinton had earned a national reputation. He served as the head the National Governor's Association and helped found the Democratic Leadership Council, a group of Democrats that sought to moderate their party's position with the hope of winning back the White House. Unlike many other Democratic stalwarts, such as New York Governor Mario Cuomo, Clinton supported the death penalty. In 1988, as a sign of his growing status in the party, Clinton nominated **Michael Stanley Dukakis** at the Democratic Party convention.

Clinton announced his candidacy for president in 1991 and quickly established himself as one of the front-runners. Positioning himself as a moderate, Clinton staved off challenges by former Massachusetts Senator Paul Tsongas and former California governor Jerry Brown to win the Democratic nomination. During the campaign, Clinton focused on the stagnation of the economy under Bush's helm and promised health and **welfare** reform and tax relief for the middle class. His nomination of **Albert Gore, Jr.,** a Senator from Tennessee, enhanced his appeal in the South, a region that historically had supported Democrats but had voted solidly Republican during the 1980s. Although he won only 43 percent of the popular vote, **H. Ross Perot**'s presence in the race allowed him to easily win the electoral college, making him one of the youngest presidents in U.S. history.

Suggested Readings: David Gallen, *Bill Clinton as They Know Him* (1994); Connor O'Cleary, *America: A Place Called Hope?* (1993).

The collapse of communism as symbolized by the fall of the Berlin Wall. Still Media Center, Department of Defense.

Related Entries: Economy, U.S.; Election of 1992.

COLD WAR. See **COMMUNISM, COLLAPSE OF; FOREIGN POLICY; REAGAN DOCTRINE; SOVIET UNION.**

COMMUNISM, COLLAPSE OF. With blistering speed, communism collapsed in Eastern Europe between 1989 and 1992. Less than a decade earlier, the **Soviet Union**'s Communist Party seemed to reign with an iron grip in the Union of Soviet Socialist Republics (USSR) and over other Eastern Bloc nations. In the early 1980s, Solidarity, the prodemocracy movement in Poland, had been crushed by Soviet-backed Polish forces. Warsaw Pact nations had joined with the Soviet boycott of the 1984 Olympics in Los Angeles, in retaliation against the U.S. boycott of the 1980 Olympic Games in Moscow. The arms race between the United States and the Soviet Union had escalated, and repression of dissidents in countries ranging from East Germany and Bulgaria to the Soviet Republics continued as a matter of course. However, beginning in the fall of 1989 and culminating in December 1991, the Communist Party lost power in one Eastern Bloc nation after another, culminating with the end of Communist rule in the Soviet Union.

Evidence of communism's demise appeared in a flurry in the fall and early winter of 1989–1990. Poland's Solidarity Party, which had won control of the Polish parliament in June, took power. On October 7, 1989, Hungary changed the name of its ruling party from the Hungarian Socialist Workers' Party to the Hungarian Socialist Party. Earlier in the year, Hungary and Austria had opened their border. Then, on October 13, 1989, while commemorating the 1956 uprising against the Soviet Union, Hungary proclaimed itself a free republic. A little more than two weeks later, on November 9, East Germany opened all its borders, including the border between East and West Berlin. This set off a mass celebration of individuals at the Berlin Wall, one of the symbols of the cold war and the division between the communist and noncommunist worlds. Thousands streamed from East to West Berlin, while others tore down the wall. On December 29, 1989, Vaclav Havel, a writer and human rights advocate, was elected president of Czechoslovakia. The day before, Alexander Dubcek, the leader of the liberation movement in Czechoslovakia in 1968 (which the Soviet Union had crushed), had been named chairman of the Czech parliament. By the end of the winter of 1989–1990, talks for reunifying Germany were underway and Communist rulers in Bulgaria, Lithuania, Romania, and Yugoslavia had either resigned or been removed from power.

Meanwhile, in the Soviet Union, the Communist Party encountered challenges to its power from nationalists (often anticommunists) in various Soviet republics. The Balkan states of Estonia, Latvia, and Lithuania were among the first to assert their right of self-rule. They were quickly joined by protesters in Armenia, Georgia, Byelorussia, the Ukraine, and many of the trans-Caucasian republics, such as Azerbaijan. At the same time, **Mikhail Sergeyevich Gorbachev** promoted reforms (under the rubric of *perestroika*) within the Communist Party itself, chipping away at its power. As early as April 1989, Gorbachev successfully orchestrated the restructuring of the Soviet Communist Party's Central Committee. About a year later, the Soviet parliament expanded President Gorbachev's powers and repealed constitutional provisions which guaranteed the Communist Party's monopoly on political power.

However, the pace of reform was not rapid enough for Russian maverick **Boris Nikolayevich Yeltsin.** On July 12, 1990, less than two months after the parliament of the republic of Russia elected him president, he resigned from the Communist Party and lent his support for declarations of sovereignty by the Ukraine, Byelorussia, Georgia, and other Soviet republics. In the first part of 1991, the pace of change sped up even more. The citizens of Latvia and Estonia voted for independence; hundreds of thousands of demonstrators marched through Moscow demanding Gorbachev's resignation, in defiance of a ban against such protests, and the Warsaw Pact disbanded.

Then, in August 1991, the Soviet Union experienced a "bloodless" revolution. The revolution began on August 19 when, after having initially announced that Gorbachev was missing, a group of Soviet State Security (KGB), military, and Communist Party leaders reported that he been replaced. In response to this development, Boris Yeltsin called for nationwide resistance. Thousands of Russian citizens surrounded the Kremlin. Faced with protestors in Moscow, rebellion in many of the Soviet republics, and a military that, by and large, supported Yeltsin, the coup leaders released Gorbachev and turned themselves over to the authorities. In the wake of this bizarre event, in rapid succession, Gorbachev resigned, the Soviet parliament suspended the Communist Party, and the Soviet parliament then voted itself out of existence.

The Ronald Reagan and George Bush administrations' role in this dramatic turn of events is a matter of much debate. Some argue that President Reagan deserves credit for communism's collapse, noting that his hard-line stance, including the arms buildup, pushed the near-bankrupt Soviet Union over the brink. Others, however, contend that communism's demise came about much more due to internal developments within the Soviet Union (largely beyond the control of the United States), including the Soviet invasion of Afghanistan, rather than external pressures. They also emphasize the significance of Gorbachev's rise to power and the independent rebellions in the Eastern Bloc. In so far as the Reagan and Bush administrations' actions caused the collapse of communism, credit must go to a long list of Republicans and Democrats as well, starting with Harry Truman, who developed and maintained a long-term, bipartisan policy of containing communism. Still others, on the left, contend that all along the power of the Soviet Union had been exaggerated by advocates of containment. The speed with which the Communist Party and the Soviet economy collapsed in the late 1980s and early 1990s, they declared, displayed how exaggerated conservative estimates of Soviet power had been all along. Put another way, communism had never been the bogeyman it was portrayed to be, and a long-term policy of cooperation would have produced virtually the same results with much lower costs to both nations and much less danger to the world as a whole.

Regardless of which interpretation is the most accurate, the collapse of communism caught almost everyone by surprise. Critics charged President Bush with reacting too slowly to the change in Eastern Europe, demanding that he recognize the sovereignty of various Soviet republics and align the United States behind Yeltsin at a faster pace than he did. However, even his critics had to acknowledge that none of them had predicted the course of events in Eastern Europe and that no fully developed contingency plan for dealing with these events existed.

Suggested Readings: John Lewis Gaddis, *The United States and the End of the Cold War* (1992); Michael Hogan, ed., *The End of the Cold War* (1992); Richard Lewbow and Janice Gross Stein, *We All Lost the Cold War* (1993); Nicholas Rizopoulous, *Sea-Changes* (1990).

Related Entries: Berlin Wall, Fall of; Defense Spending; Foreign Policy; New World Order.

CONSERVATIVE COALITION. Ronald Reagan's ascendancy represented the coming of age of a new conservative coalition. (It might be accurate to refer to this as the Reagan Coalition.) Not only did Reagan rewin the votes of those who had elected Richard Nixon in 1968 and 1972, he elevated the conservative wing of the Republican Party in the process.

From early on in his political career, Reagan had been a darling of both traditional conservatives and those who considered themselves part of the **New Right.** Like traditional conservatives, the New Right was anti–big government and fervidly anticommunist. Unlike many traditional conservatives, the New Right contained a religious or fundamentalist edge and adopted new political methods, such as the expert use of direct-mail fund-raising. Among the New Right's leaders were Richard Viguerie, founder of the American Conservative Union, and William F. Buckley, Jr., editor of the *National Review.* Several conservative think tanks and political action committees added to the intellectual and organizational backbone of the New Right, most notably the Heritage Foundation, the Hoover Institute, the **Moral Majority,** and Paul Weyrich's Committee for the Survival of a Free Congress.

The Reagan or conservative coalition also drew support and advice from neoconservatives, former liberal intellectuals who broke with the Democratic Party because of its weak foreign policy—in their eyes—and overreliance on the state in economic and social matters. The conservative coalition gained support from Reagan Democrats as well. This group consisted of blue-collar voters who had traditionally voted for the Democratic Party. While they continued to vote for Democrats for Congress and local offices, they supported Reagan in the general elections. Reagan won the vote of this group, in part, by emphasizing certain wedge issues, ranging from **affirmative action, welfare,** and **abortion,** which in most cases white ethnic voters opposed, to the death penalty, which they generally favored.

While some described the rise of the conservative coalition as a revolution in American politics equal to shifts that took place with the Civil War and the rise of the New Deal, many historians and political analysts are not so sure that Reagan's elections signified as much. Democrats strengthened their grip on the House of Representatives in 1982 and retook the U.S. Senate in 1986. Even though George Bush was able to soundly defeat **Michael Stanley Dukakis** in 1988, he did so in part by suggesting that he would be less conservative than Reagan, a "kinder and gentler" president. Furthermore, even after winning in a landslide in 1984, Reagan was unable to win passage of many of his initiatives. On the contrary, in 1987 and 1988 the Democratically controlled Congress even managed to pass several liberal reforms over Reagan's veto.

William (Bill) Jefferson Clinton's victory in 1992, accompanied by a Democratic sweep of Congress, raised further doubts about the significance of conservative victories in the early 1980s. This said, the Republicans' resounding midterm elections in 1994 suggested that it was possible that the conservative coalition had laid deep roots when it came into power in 1980 and would be a dominating factor in political life for years to come.

Suggested Readings: Sidney Blumenthal, *The Rise of the Counter-Establishment: From Conservative Ideology to Political Power* (1986); Thomas Ferguson and Joel Rogers, *Rights Turn: The Decline of the Democrats and the Future of American Politics* (1986); Gillian Peele, *Revival and Reaction: The Right in Contemporary America* (1984); Peter Steinfels, *The Neoconservatives: The Men Who Are Changing America* (1980).

Related Entries: House of Representatives, United States; Senate, United States.

CONSTITUTIONAL AMENDMENTS (PROPOSED). During the Ronald Reagan–George Bush years, Republican Party leaders called for the passage of a number of amendments to the United States Constitution. Several of the proposed amendments dealt with social or cultural issues. By altering the Constitution, conservatives hoped to undo what they saw as the inaccurate decisions of the Supreme Court and reverse dangerous trends by the national government. The constitutional amendments that received the most attention called for allowing prayer in schools, mandating a balanced federal budget, outlawing **abortion,** and making the action of burning an American flag a crime. None of the amendments were enacted. Indeed, none of them ever went before the states for ratification, despite the backing that they received from Presidents Ronald Reagan and George Bush.

During his campaign for the presidency, Reagan had decried the moral decline of America and pledged his support for a constitutional amendment that would permit prayer in the public schools. During the early 1960s, the U.S. **Supreme Court** had deemed mandatory prayer in public schools a violation of the constitutional guarantee of separation of church and state. In March 1984, a constitutional amendment that would allow for prayer in the public schools reached the floor of the U.S. Senate but fell eleven votes short of the two-thirds majority necessary for passage. The prayer amendment did not again come up for a vote during the Reagan-Bush years.

In 1990 Democrats and Republicans battled over whether to pass a constitutional amendment that would make burning the flag of the United States a crime. Flag burning had become an issue in 1989 when the Supreme Court had ruled that flag burning was a form of protest protected by the guarantee of free speech. Democrats blocked Republican efforts to pass a constitutional amendment, offering in its place a simple law that made desecrating the flag a federal crime. In part since the constitutionality of this law was suspect, during the 1992 campaign President Bush and the Republican Party vowed to enact a flag-burning amendment. Bush's loss to **William (Bill) Jefferson Clinton** put at least a temporary end to this issue.

The proposal to mandate a balanced budget was put forth by Reagan as a way to prove his sincerity on reducing the federal deficit. However, it never gained the necessary two-thirds vote from both houses of Congress. Opponents claimed it was unenforceable and would endanger the nation in times of economic crisis and produce drastic cuts in Social Security and other parts of the economic safety net built up since the 1930s. Lacking the votes to pass a balanced budget amendment, Congress passed the so-called **Gramm-Rudman-Hollings Act (Balanced Budget and Emergency Deficit Control Act of 1985).** The Supreme Court ruled that important parts of this law, which established a binding timetable for cutting the deficit, were unconstitutional. Hence, the balanced budget amendment remained an important issue on through the 1992 election.

Presidents Reagan and Bush pushed for a constitutional amendment to make abortion illegal. As with the other amendments, this one never made it through Congress. Democrats argued that the majority of people did not favor making abortions illegal, a view supported by many public opinion polls. By the campaign of 1992, there was evidence that the Republican Party was losing votes by pursuing this constitutional change.

While Democrats blocked Republican efforts to enact constitutional amendments in these areas, the Reagan-Bush years also witnessed the final closing of the door on the Equal Rights Amendment, which had been passed by Congress in the 1970s but failed to win ratification in enough states to become part of the Constitution. As a candidate President Reagan criticized the proposed Equal Rights Amendment. By the time Bush became president, the issue was moot.

Suggested Readings: John Biskupic, "Congress Snaps to Attention over New Flag Proposal," *Congressional Quarterly Weekly Report,* June 16, 1990, p. 1877; George Chressanthis, "Ideology, Constituent Interests and Senatorial Voting: The Case of Abortion," *Social Science Quarterly* September 1991, 72: 588; George Hager, "Balanced Budget Redux," *Congressional Quarterly Weekly Report,* June 27, 1992, p. 1864.

Related Entries: Budget Deficit; Election of 1992; Madison Amendment (Twenty-seventh Amendment to the U.S. Constitution); New Right; Senate, United States.

CORPORATE TAKEOVERS. The Reagan-Bush years witnessed a wave of spectacular corporate takeovers and mergers (see Figure 1). In August 1981, Du Pont announced the acquisition of Conoco, the ninth largest oil company in the United States. At the time, this purchase, at a price of $7.6 billion, represented the biggest takeover in U.S. corporate history. By the end of the decade, this deal would be paled by much more spectacular ones. These included the acquisition of some of the oldest and most renowned companies in America. In 1985, for instance, General Electric bought RCA for $6 billion. Four years later, in the biggest corporate takeover of the era, Kohlberg, Kravis, Roberts and Co. bought RJR Nabisco, Incorporated, itself the product of a merger between RJR Reynolds and Nabisco company, for $25 billion (see Table 3).

Several factors fueled this wave of mergers and acquisitions. The Reagan administration pursued an antitrust policy that encouraged, or at least did not discourage, business consolidation. The Council of Economic Advisors, in their 1985 annual report to Congress, rebutted arguments made by critics of the merger mania, arguing that even hostile

Figure 1
Corporate Mergers

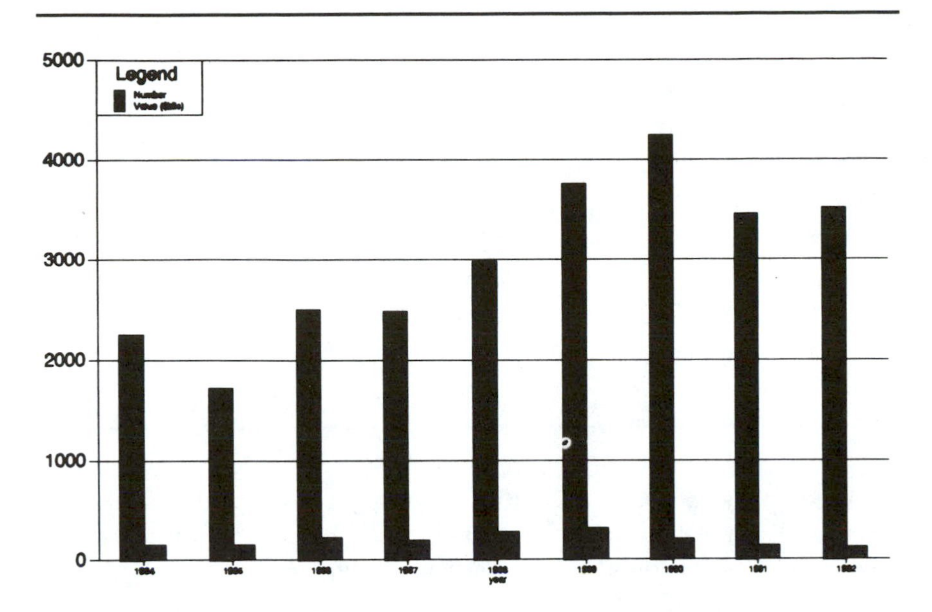

takeovers were good for the economy. The **Tax Reform Act of 1986,** which disallowed individuals to deduct interest on consumer debt but continued to allow for the deduction of interest on business debt (the mechanism by which most of the takeovers were financed), further promoted the takeover wave. Arguably, even the 1981 tax cut played a role, since it lowered the tax rates on the wealthy and the mergers and acquisitions of the 1980s created a new class of super-rich individuals.

Two other key factors that helped give rise to the takeovers of the 1980s were a growing recognition that many stocks were undervalued—meaning that the value of a company's assets was much higher than the value of outstanding stock—and the development of new tools to finance acquisitions. This included the selling of "junk bonds" (corporate bonds that paid a high interest rate but whose rating was low—meaning a greater risk of failure than with most corporate bonds).

In addition, many of those involved in the takeovers had a self-interest in promoting them. Corporate raiders from Carl Icahn to **Ivan Frederick Boesky,** investment bankers such as **Michael Milken,** and attorneys and management consultants, who helped put together the finances and details of the buyouts, benefited greatly from this wave of consolidation. They received hefty fees—in the millions of dollars—for their services.

Table 3
Ten Largest Takeover Deals Involving U.S. Companies

Bidder	Target	Value ($ bils.)	Year
Kohlberg, Kravis Roberts & Co.	RJR Nabisco	25.1	1988
Standard Oil Co. of CA	Gulf Corp.	13.2	1984
Philip Morris Co.	Kraft, Inc.	13.1	1988
AT&T	McCraw Cellular	12.6	1993
Bristol-Meyers Co.	Squibb Corp.	12.0	1989
Time Inc.	Warner Commun.	11.7	1989
British Petroleum	Standard Oil	7.9	1987
SmithKline Beckman	Beecham Group	7.9	1989
E.I. Dupont	Conoco	7.6	1981

Likewise, many corporate executives who might have fought acquisition by outside companies so as to maintain their position of power did not do so because they found it financially rewarding to cooperate with outside corporate raiders. In exchange for their cooperation they often received "golden parachutes," (lucrative severance packages). For example, F. Ross Johnson and E. A. Horrigan, the chief executive officer (CEO) and vice chairman of RJR Nabisco, received golden parachutes totaling upwards of $100 million when the takeover of their corporation was completed.

By the end of the Reagan-Bush years, the corporate takeovers and the raiders who promoted and profited from them seemed to represent, for many, the primary mood or theme of that period. Novels and movies, such as Tom Wolfe's *Bonfire of the Vanities* (1988), which explored the world of the takeover artist, became big hits. Similarly, numerous works of nonfiction that examined the takeover world sold millions of copies.

During the 1992 campaign, as the recession put a stop to the takeovers and dampened the spirit of economic boosterism that went with it, **William (Bill) Jefferson Clinton** and other Democrats railed at the greed and waste of the Reagan-Bush years. Critics claimed that the takeovers were responsible for the growing division between rich and poor in the United States, the stagnation of the economy, and the mounting pile of debt that threatened to undermine the American standard of living. However, whether the mergers and acquisitions actually played this role—and whether they would have taken place even with the Democrats in the

White House—remains debatable. Given the profound changes that were taking place in the economy, and especially the globalization of trade and finance, some sort of consolidation was probably inevitable. Suffice it to say, the Reagan and Bush administrations, via both specific policies and their general philosophies or attitudes, fostered the development.

Suggested Readings: Walter Adams and James Brock, *Dangerous Pursuits: Mergers and Acquisitions in the Age of Wall Street* (1989); Alan J. Auerbach, ed., *Corporate Takeovers: Causes and Consequences* (1988); Connie Bruck, *The Predators' Ball* (1988).

Related Entries: Economy, U.S.; Recessions.

COURTS. One of the main thrusts of the "Reagan Revolution" was its attempt to reverse the liberal drift of the federal courts. Both Presidents Ronald Reagan and George Bush aimed at remaking the courts into a bulwark of conservatism. Among the areas of the law which they sought to affect were **civil rights,** civil liberties, **abortion,** and criminal procedure. They did so through their appointments to the bench, via the politicization of the Solicitor General's office and positions of the Justice Department. While most scholars agree that the courts did not undergo a revolution, they add that the verdict is still somewhat problematic since it is impossible to determine what impact the Reagan and Bush appointments will have, especially in the lower federal courts, in coming years.

From early on in his administration, President Reagan took aim at reversing the course of civil rights law. Via proposed legislation, as a party litigant and *amicus curiae* (friend of the court) and through the arguments of the Solicitor General's office, Reagan sought to end **affirmative action** and limit the scope of the Voting Rights and Civil Rights Acts. While the courts narrowed the scope of affirmative action during the Reagan-Bush years, they continued to maintain that narrowly constructed affirmative action programs were constitutional as long as they addressed specific past discrimination. The administrations took similar stances and had similar experiences in the realm of civil liberties. Despite its efforts, the courts, in general, continued to uphold First Amendment guarantees of separation of church and state and maintained a relatively broad construction of the right to freedom of speech, as in the decision to protect flag burning as a form of free speech guaranteed by the Constitution.

The administration had a bit more success in the realm of criminal procedure. President Reagan's first solicitor general, Rex E. Lee, helped convince the **Supreme Court** to expand the number of exceptions it would allow to the exclusionary rule, which placed limits on the admissability of illegally obtained evidence. For instance, in *Nix* v. *Williams* (1984) and *United States* v. *Leon,* the Supreme Court sided with the Reagan administration, ruling that evidence collected despite police misconduct and defective search warrants was admissible.

Clearly, the Reagan and Bush administrations had the greatest impact on the courts via their power to nominate justices. During his eight years in office, Reagan appointed 290 district and 78 appeals court judges, comprising slightly less than a majority of all of the federal judges. By the time **William (Bill) Jefferson Clinton** took office, a majority of the Supreme Court (five of nine) and a majority of all federal district and appellate court judges were Reagan and Bush appointees.

While the appointment of judges has always been affected by the politics, Presidents Reagan and Bush developed a much more rigorous test of the ideological views of their appointees than had most of their predecessors. They only appointed individuals who had conservative records. In 1984, President Reagan established the Office of Legal Policy which advised the attorney general on the selection of judges. Subsequently, the president appointed a special Committee on Federal Judicial Selection. In 1985, when **Edwin Meese III** took over as attorney general, he tightened the review process even further, transferring responsibilities for appointments to one of his personal advisers. During the Reagan years, every judicial nominee was personally interviewed by staff members of the Justice Department, leading to the charge that candidates had to pass a litmus test that had little to do with their judicial experience or qualifications. Unlike previous Republican presidents, including Dwight Eisenhower, Richard Nixon, and Gerald Ford, Reagan did not seek the evaluation of candidates by the American Bar Association until after he had made their nomination. While the Reagan administration tended to follow the time-honored practice of senatorial courtesy, whereby the president granted senators from the states for which there was a vacancy a choice over the nominee, this was not always the case.

One example of the politicization of the courts came with the 1986 nomination of Daniel A. Manion to the Court of Appeals of the Seventh Circuit. Manion, an Indiana attorney, was the son of Charles Manion, one of the founders of the far-right John Birch Society. He was not a particularly distinguished attorney, and the American Bar Association gave him its lowest positive rating. Manion garnered the wrath of many liberals, in part because of his argument that the Bill of Rights did not apply to state laws. The Senate Judiciary committee split, nine to nine, on his confirmation, and he barely won confirmation by the entire Senate.

One final impact that Reagan and Bush had on the courts was that they promoted a climate that cast doubt on the legal views of the federal bench since at least World War II. By doing so they further legitimized disrespect for the federal government and may have encouraged violation of certain laws, under the pretext that the laws were unconstitutional. Without a doubt, they did so not only for reasons of principle. Polls showed that their attacks on the courts helped them win political support among groups traditionally aligned with the Democratic Party, especially white ethnic groups and southerners, who found the courts' rulings on civil and criminal rights in conflict with their own views.

Suggested Readings: Charles Fried, *Order and Law: Arguing the Reagan Revolution* (1991); Richard L. Pacelle, *The Transformation of the Supreme Court's Agenda* (1991); Herman Schwartz, *Packing the Courts* (1988).

Related Entries: Burger, Warren Earl; Civil Rights; Rehnquist, William Hubbs; Reynolds, William Bradford.

CRIME BILL. Calls to "get tough" on crime predominated the Ronald Reagan–George Bush years, as crime and arrest rates rose (Figure 2). Both Presidents Reagan and Bush demanded stiffer penalties for breaking the law, and both houses of Congress passed bills aimed at reducing crime in America. However, none of the bills made it through both houses, and even if they had, they probably would have been vetoed by either President Reagan or President Bush. They failed largely because of differences over the death penalty, the rights of the accused, and **gun control.**

The inability of Congress and the president to arrive at a compromise on crime became particularly apparent during President Bush's final years in office. Early in 1991 he demanded that Congress enact an anticrime measure within its first one hundred days in session rather than putting such legislation off until shortly before adjourning, as had been the practice through most of the 1980s. Bush supported a bill that sought to apply the federal death penalty to forty crimes, limit appeals by death-row inmates, and make it easier for prosecutors to introduce tainted evidence in criminal trials. Democrats countered with their own bill, which added to Bush's requirements a ban on assault weapons, funding for state and local law enforcement agencies, and a "racial-justice" safeguard for death penalty candidates, which would require the courts to consider the fact

Figure 2
Crime (Rates per 100,000)

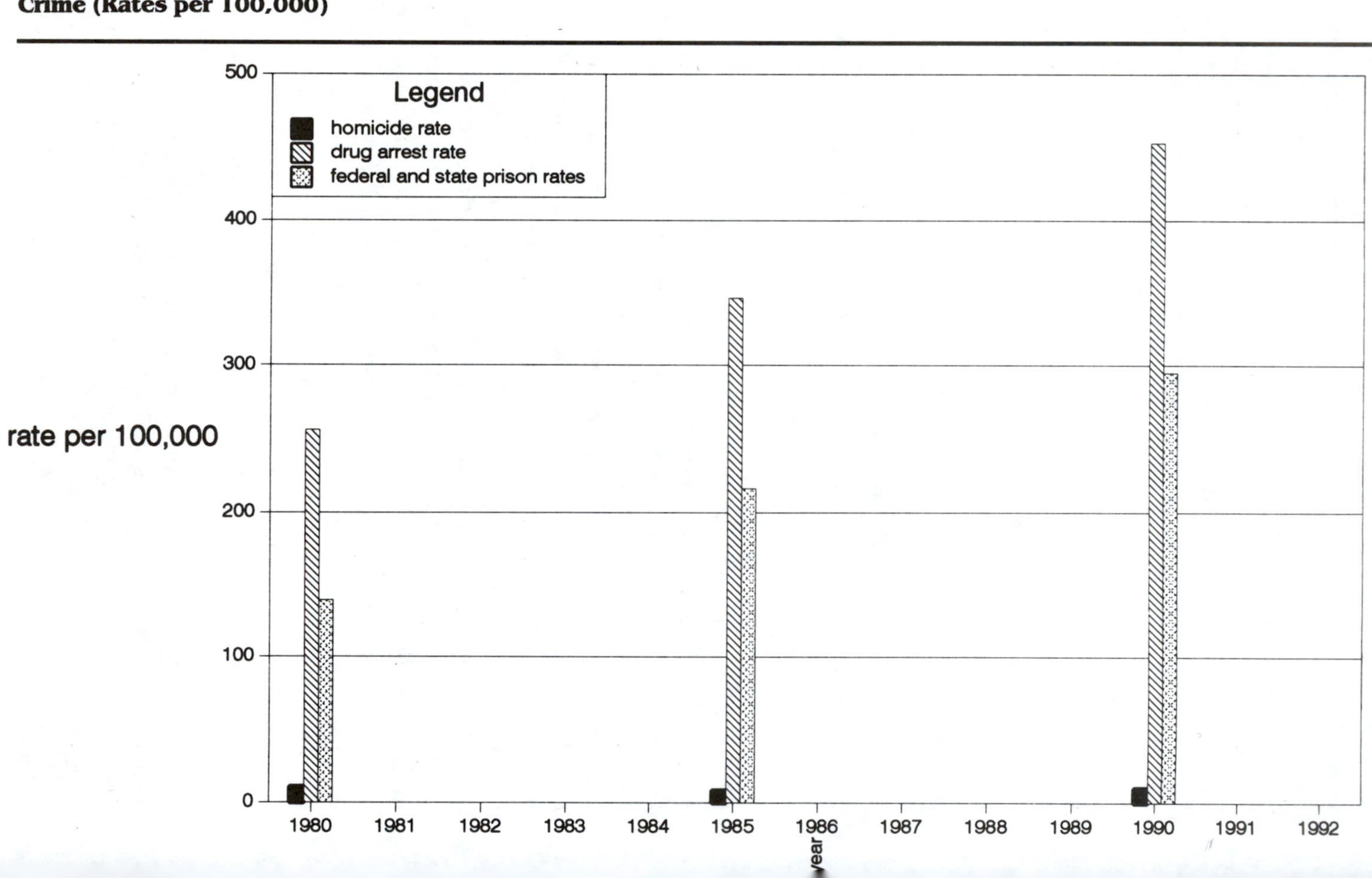

that a disproportionate number of nonwhites received the death penalty. In 1991 the House of Representatives passed the Democrats' measure, but the Senate, largely due to Bush's opposition to the assault gun ban, failed to pass the bill. (Democrats in the Senate, who favored the bill, lost a key cloture vote, 49–38, which would have allowed them to kill a threatened Republican filibuster.)

In 1992, despite claims by both the president and Democratic and Republican leaders in Congress that they favored an anticrime bill, none was enacted. Continued differences over gun control and the death penalty blocked its passage. Separate attempts to pass restrictions on handgun ownership, known as the Brady Bill, failed to make their way through the Senate. To many, the failure of Congress and the president to arrive at a compromise represented the poor state of affairs in Washington. In spite of claims from both parties that they favored anticrime legislation, the two sides remained in **gridlock.**

Suggested Readings: "Crimebuster Bush," *Economist,* May 20, 1989, p. 27; "No Compromise Forged on Crime Bill," *Congressional Quarterly Almanac* (1992) p. 311.

Related Entries: Brady, James S.; Crime; House of Representatives, United States; Senate, United States; War on Drugs.

CROCKER, CHESTER ARTHUR. (New York, N.Y., October 29, 1941– .) Assistant Secretary of State for African Affairs, 1981–1989.

Chester Crocker was the chief architect of the policy of "constructive engagement," which the Ronald Reagan administration used to guide its actions in **Africa.** According to this policy, the United States sought to improve relations with the all-white minority government of **South Africa** so as to induce it to introduce reforms. This policy conflicted with the one called for by the antiapartheid movement in the United States, which demanded stiff sanctions by the U.S. government and divestment by private corporations.

Chester Crocker, a distant relative of former president Chester Arthur, grew up in New York City and attended Ohio State University (B.A., 1963). He received his M.A. (1965) and Ph.D. (1969) from the Johns Hopkins School of Advanced International Studies, writing for *Africa Report* at the same time. He briefly worked as a lecturer at American University in Washington, D.C., and then joined the Richard Nixon administration as the African affairs expert on the National Security Council. In 1972 Crocker returned to academia, directing Georgetown University's foreign service program and teaching courses on African politics and international relations. While at Georgetown's Center for Strategic and International Studies, he helped coauthor a book that argued that the Soviets sought to create turmoil in Africa, as evidenced by their sponsorship of Cuban troops in Angola. During the 1980 presidential campaign, Crocker advised Reagan on African issues. An article published in *Foreign Policy,* which criticized the Carter administration's policy in Africa, "South Africa: Strategy for Change" (Winter, 1980–1981, 59:323), further attracted the attention of Reagan's top advisers and helped land him a post as assistant secretary of state under his former mentor, **Alexander Meigs Haig, Jr.** Ironically, North Carolina Senator **Jesse A. Helms** held up Crocker's nomination for nine months because of his doubts about the latter's conservative credentials.

According to his "constructive engagement" doctrine, the United States would aim at convincing South African and Cuban forces to withdraw from Namibia and Angola and to promote the former's independence. In the late 1980s, Crocker finally realized this objective, as Cuban military troops left Angola and South Africa recognized the independence of Namibia. In *High Noon in Southern Africa* (1992), Crocker described this turn of events as vindication of his policy. However, many others argued that constructive engagement had proved a failure and emphasized that apartheid had remained unscathed for too long. Even Reagan, they observed, had placed limited sanctions on South Africa because of the resistance of the all-white government to reform. Moreover, Crocker's refusal to support sanctions often put him at odds with Democrats in Congress. They added that "constructive engagement" was hypocritical or inconsistent with the rest of the Reagan administration's policies. If a hard-line policy was used toward communist nations based on the principal that peace or reform would be gained through strength, the administration should have applied the same logic to South Africa.

Crocker is married to Saone Baron, a native of Zimbabwe (formerly Rhodesia). They have three children.

Suggested Readings: Christopher Coker, *The United States and South Africa* (1986); Chester A. Crocker, *High Noon in Southern Africa* (1992); Peter J. Schroeder, *United States Foreign Policy toward Africa* (1994).

Related Entry: James (Jimmy) Earl Carter.

CROWE, WILLIAM JAMES, JR. (LaGrange, Ky., January 2, 1925– .) Chairman, Joint Chiefs of Staff, 1985–1989.

Admiral William Crowe served as chairman of the Joint Chiefs of Staff during President Ronald Reagan's second term in office. His appointment represented the culmination of a long career of military and government service. It also signified a first in modern military history, as Crowe was the first chairman of the Joint Chiefs of Staff not to have served in World War II.

Crowe spent most of his youth in Oklahoma. After spending a year at the University of Oklahoma, in 1943 he enrolled at the United States Naval Academy. He graduated in 1946, the same class as **James (Jimmy) Earl Carter.** Following a tour of duty on the U.S.S. *Carmick,* Crowe became a specialist in submarines, serving as the assistant to the naval aide to the president from 1954 to 1955. Then he took a leave of absence to study at Stanford, receiving his M.A. in 1956. Rather than joining Admiral Hyman Rickover's prestigious nuclear submarine group, he enrolled in Princeton University, earning his Ph.D. in politics in 1965. While completing his doctoral work Crowe returned to active duty, commanding the U.S.S. *Trout.* By the early 1970s he had moved up to the rank of rear admiral and was involved in strategic planning for East Asia and the Pacific. In the mid-1970s he served as commander of the Middle East Task Force and then was named commander in chief of the North Atlantic Treaty Organization (NATO). In 1983 Crowe was appointed commander in chief of the Pacific and Indian Ocean forces, having gained a reputation for political dexterity and strategic insight. He earned the favor of Defense Secretary **Caspar Willard Weinberger,** who recommended Crowe to replace General **John W. Vessey, Jr.,** as Reagan's head of the Joint Chiefs of Staff (JCS) in 1985.

While chairman of the JCS, Crowe's main goal was to rid the military of interservice rivalry, which produced wasteful spending and, in Crowe's mind, inefficient operations. He acted as the president's top military adviser, although he did not play a key role in early arms negotiations with the **Soviet Union.** In 1987 he served as the president's top military adviser at the Washington, D.C., summit with **Mikhail Sergeyevich Gorbachev,** which culminated with the signing of the **Intermediate-range Nuclear Forces (INF) Treaty.** Investigators found that he was not involved with the **Iran-contra affair.** He oversaw operations in the Persian gulf growing out of the **Iran-Iraq war,** which included the decision to protect shipping in the area.

Crowe is married to Shirley Mary Grennell (Crowe). They have three children.

Suggested Readings: William Crowe, *The Line of Fire* (1993); *Current Biography* (1988) p. 133.

Related Entries: Soviet Union; Summits, with Soviet Union.

CULVAHOUSE, ARTHUR BOGGESS, JR. (July 4, 1948, Athens, Ga.– .) Counsel to the President, 1987–1989.

Arthur Culvahouse, a graduate from the University of Tennessee (1970) and New York University Law School (1973), was Ronald Reagan's legal counsel during the last two years of his second term. This meant that he served as his lawyer in the midst of the **Iran-contra affair.** Culvahouse first came to Washington following graduation from law school. He went to work for Tennessee Senator **Howard (Henry) Baker, Jr.,** who, at the time, was the ranking Republican on the Senate committee investigating the Watergate scandal. From 1973 through 1986 he worked for O'Melveny & Myers and then Vinson, Elkins, and Washington. As counsel to the president, Culvahouse was responsible for providing legal advice regarding the Iran-contra scandal and negotiating with the Tower Commission and congressional investigators over what information the president would be willing to share. He advised in favor of cooperating with the investigations while at the same time limiting the reach of the investigators. For instance, he rejected a congressional request for a wide variety of National Security Council documents, arguing that he would not support a "fishing trip" by Congress.

Culvahouse is married to Mari Lou Vatter. They have four children.

Suggested Readings: *New York Times,* March 26, 1987, II:8; *New York Times,* April 14, 1987, I:15.

D

DARMAN, RICHARD. (May 10, 1943, Charlotte, N.C.– .) Adviser to President Ronald Reagan, 1981–1985; Deputy Secretary, Department of Treasury, 1985–1987; Director of Office of Management and Budget, 1989–1993.

Richard Darman, the son of a New England textile magnate, has spent most of his adult life in Washington, D.C., in various executive branch jobs. After earning a B.A. (1964) and an M.B.A. (1967) from Harvard University, he went to work for the Department of Health, Education and Welfare (HEW). He soon became part of Elliot Richardson's inner circle—Richardson was the secretary of HEW at the time. As Richardson moved from one cabinet post to another, including Defense, Justice, and Commerce, Darman moved with him. However, his association with Richardson, a moderate Republican, made him suspect to many conservatives, a suspicion Darman labored to overcome for years. Nonetheless, when **James (Jim) Addison Baker III,** whom Darman knew from their years together at the Commerce Department, became President Reagan's chief of staff, Darman gained a post working under him as an adviser for the new president. Along with **David Alan Stockman,** he developed budget positions and political strategies. He helped craft deals on social security and tax reform and edited Reagan's speeches. When Baker became secretary of the treasury, Darman moved with him, serving as his deputy.

During 1988 Darman's stature rose further. He played an active role in George Bush's campaign, providing economic advice and playing **Michael Stanley Dukakis** during mock debates. Following Bush's election, Darman was named the new head of the Office of Management and Budget. Given the rising **budget deficit** and the president's pledge to not raise taxes, this was not an enviable post. His advocacy of a tax hike and budget cuts earned him few friends. As the recession worsened and the 1992 election approached, many conservative Republicans called for his resignation. While Bush stuck by Darman, the president also suggested that if he was reelected, after the election changes would be made, presumably among his economic advisers.

Darman is married to Kathleen Emmet (Darman). They have two sons and live in Virginia.

Suggested Readings: "Bush Indicates Cabinet Shake-Up," *Baltimore Sun*, August 19, 1992, p. 1A; Fred Barnes, "White House Wonk," *New Republic*, January 2, 1989, p. 19; *Current Biography* (1989) p. 125.

Related Entry: Recessions.

D-DAY CELEBRATION. See **NORMANDY, FRANCE, D-DAY CELEBRATION**

DEAVER, MICHAEL KEITH. (April 11, 1938, Bakersfield, Calif.– .) Deputy Chief of Staff, 1981–1985.

Michael Deaver, a long-time associate and friend of Ronald and **Nancy Davis Reagan,** served as deputy chief of staff for the president from his inauguration until 1985. Along with **Edwin Meese III** and **James (Jim) Addison Baker III,** Deaver made up part of the so-called Reagan troika or inner cabinet. His relationship with the Reagans went back to the mid-1960s when he worked as Governor Reagan's cabinet secretary and assistant. Deaver was often considered a voice for political pragmatism within the White House and was especially close to the president's wife, Nancy. He played an important role during Reagan's 1980 presidential campaign, as a political strategist and fund-raiser.

Two years after leaving office he was indicted for violating federal ethics laws that limit lobbying by former top government officials. Shortly thereafter, he was convicted of lying about his lobbying activities to Congress. The conviction proved especially painful to the Reagans due to their long-standing friendship. Ironically, if Reagan had appointed Deaver as his chief of staff in 1985, when James Baker became secretary of the treasury and Meese became attorney general (as was the president's original intent), then Deaver might not have left the White House to set up a powerful lobbying firm which ultimately led to his indictment and conviction. Reagan did not do so because Baker and Regan arranged their swap of

The "troika": James Baker, Edwin Meese, and Michael Deaver. Reagan Library.

positions and presented it as a package deal to the president, who accepted their proposal.

Deaver was raised in California, received his B.A. in Public Administration from San Jose State University (1960), and became active in Republican politics after his graduation. He is married to Carolyn Judy (Deaver). They have two children.

Suggested Readings: Michael Deaver, *Behind the Scenes* (1987); *New York Times,* December 17, 1987 p. I:1.

DEBATES, PRESIDENTIAL. During the Ronald Reagan–George Bush years, debates between the presidential and vice presidential candidates became a regular part of the campaigns. In 1980, 1984, 1988, and 1992, the Democratic and Republican nominees squared off against one another before nationally televised audiences. The vice presidential running

President Reagan and Walter Mondale (Democratic nominee) during a presidential debate. Reagan Library.

mates debated each other during every campaign except 1980. While none of the debates proved to be the deciding factor in the election, nearly every one was important and drew large television audiences. Debates also became common during the primary campaigns and, unlike those between the two final candidates, had a clear impact on the final outcome.

In 1980 President **James (Jimmy) Earl Carter** and **Ronald Wilson Reagan** held a debate on October 28, just one week before the election, in Cleveland, Ohio. The debate followed months of haggling between advisers over whether to include independent candidate **John Bayard Anderson.** Carter objected to his inclusion; Reagan did not and thus debated him without Carter on September 21 in Baltimore. Sponsored by the League of Women Voters, the debate between Carter and Reagan saw a panel of journalists ask a series of questions and follow-up questions to the candidates. The debate also allowed for rebuttals and a closing statement. During the debate the candidates differed sharply over several issues. President Carter attempted to question Reagan's ability to lead the nation and to paint him as an extremist. Most observers felt that these attacks failed, as Reagan appeared friendly and even-tempered when responding to Carter's attacks. While it is doubtful that Carter could have won the 1980 election, Reagan's strong showing in the debate, according to pollsters, helped account for the extent of his margin of victory.

Four years later President Reagan twice debated the Democratic nominee **Walter Frederick Mondale.** On October 7 the two met in Louisville, Kentucky, to discuss domestic issues. Two weeks later they squared off on **foreign policy** matters in Kansas City, Missouri. Mondale went into the first debate far behind in the polls, but he scored what some saw as a near-knockout punch. Reagan appeared tired and disorganized, allowing Mondale to raise questions about the president's age in the minds of the voters. (He was seventy-three years old.) In addition, by focusing on the size of the **budget deficit** and the power that Christian fundamentalists had gained with Reagan in office, Mondale was able to raise doubts as to the direction in which Reagan would bring the nation during his second term. During the second debate, however, Reagan appeared much more relaxed and in control. The two clashed over Reagan's proposed **Strategic Defense Initiative (Star Wars)** proposal and U.S. policy in **Nicaragua.** While Reagan's concluding statement was not as polished as many of the other major public addresses of his life, he did well enough to stave off doubts about his ability to continue to lead the nation and went on to win the election in a landslide.

In 1988 George Bush and **Michael Stanley Dukakis** met in two 90-minute debates, the first at Wake Forest University in Winston-Salem, North Carolina, on September 25 and the second at the University of California at Los Angeles on October 13. Reversing the momentum that Bush had built since his nomination, Dukakis was viewed as the winner of the first debate. He appeared "cool and confident," according to one analyst, and capable of upsetting the vice president. At the same time, Bush, who repeatedly sought to paint Dukakis as a liberal and to link him with various controversial liberal positions, such as support of the American Civil Liberties Union (ACLU), put the Democratic candidate in a defensive position. During the second debate Dukakis was much less effective. Perhaps even more important than the debates themselves was the spin that advisers sought to put on them. Both camps argued that their candidates had won. Bush's eventual victory either confirmed that Dukakis had not won the debates or that he had not scored the knockout he needed to win the election.

The 1992 debates between President Bush, **William (Bill) Jefferson Clinton** and **H. Ross Perot** were perhaps the most entertaining of the era. The presidential candidates met three times; the vice presidential candidates held one debate. Perot, who had dropped out of the race and then reentered it, probably benefited the most from the ability to reach millions of Americans—without cost. However, at the same time, Perot's running-mate, Admiral James Stockdale, performed terribly, leading some Americans to wonder about the seriousness of Perot's campaign. Clinton displayed a command of the issues and a presidential demeanor during the debates. While Bush demonstrated his experience on foreign affairs, at times he appeared tired and resigned to his ultimate defeat. A variation in the format added to the public's interest in these debates. The first debate followed the traditional format, with each candidate answering questions from a panel of journalists. In the second meeting a single moderator, Carole Simpson of ABC News led the discussion, but the audience asked most of the questions. In their third meeting, on October 19 in East Lansing, Michigan, the candidates answered questions from the moderator and then from three journalists.

While none of the debates proved decisive and most likely will never be compared to the Abraham Lincoln–Stephen Douglas or John Kennedy–Richard Nixon debates, they did influence the elections. At the least, by performing capably, the candidates who led in the polls going into the debates did not lose their leads. Just as important, the debates became an expected part of the political landscape, and it is likely that voters would punish a candidate who refused to participate in them.

Suggested Readings: Peter Goldman and Tony Fuller, *The Quest for the Presidency* (1984); Kathleen Hall Jamieson and David Birdsell, *Presidential Debates and the Challenge of Creating an Informed Electorate* (1988).

Related Entries: Election of 1980; Election of 1984; Election of 1988; Election of 1992; Great Communicator, The.

DEBT CRISIS, FOREIGN. While the **U.S. economy** rebounded in the mid-1980s, the foreign debt crisis worried investors, threatened the banking world, and troubled many economists. By 1989 developing nations owed creditors over $1.2 trillion. Latin American countries were particularly plagued by high debts. Mexico alone owed more than $100 billion.

American banks that had invested heavily in many developing countries feared they would default on loan payments. Mexico and Brazil, in fact, both threatened to do so. American manufacturers also worried that foreign debts would hurt them by slowing the growth of the developing nations, thus limiting their exports. In turn, this would further exacerbate the **trade deficit.**

The foreign debt crisis resulted from several factors. Falling commodity prices (particularly oil), made worse by the fact that many developing nations had borrowed heavily when prices had been high during the 1970s, placed many developing nations in a difficult situation. The recession in the United States, which limited its imports from many debtor nations, contributed to the crisis as well, as did the tight money policy pursued by the **Federal Reserve Board,** because it attracted money into U.S. financial markets while driving up the cost of loans to developing nations.

The debt crisis first appeared in Mexico in 1982 and quickly spread (or became apparent) to other Latin American nations. To avert an international financial collapse, banks scrambled to renegotiate loan agreements. While the Reagan administration resisted calls to provide a U.S. bailout, it helped the International Monetary Fund and World Bank extend new loans to the debtor nations. These new loans, however, were contingent on the foreign governments accepting severe austerity programs, which served to increase anti-American sentiment abroad, as many foreigners argued that the United States was dictating internal or domestic policies. The foreign debt crisis began to ease in the early 1990s, but some critics contended that the fundamental problems that had produced it in the first place had not been resolved.

Suggested Reading: Barry Eichengreen and Peter Lindert, eds., *The International Debt Crisis in Historical Perspective* (1989).

Related Entry: Recessions.

DEFENSE SPENDING. One of the cornerstones of President Ronald Reagan's 1980 campaign, and one of the main legacies of his presidency, was increased defense spending aimed at rebuilding the military and a credible nuclear threat. During Reagan's first four year term, defense spending nearly doubled, rising from $134 billion in 1980 to $252 billion in 1985. By 1989, with George Bush in the White House, defense spending stood at $304 billion. Even with the fall of the Berlin Wall and the end of the cold war, military outlays remained at very high levels. The mili-

Table 4
Defense Expenditures (Billions of Dollars)

Date	Total	Personnel	Weapons	Research and Development
1980	134	41	29	13
1984	227	64	62	23
1988	290	76	77	35
1992	298	79	74	36

tary buildup did not focus on one branch of the military or a particular weapons program. Rather, it was widespread and comprehensive. All the services enjoyed increased appropriations; numerous new weapon programs were developed or deployed. Spending increased for training and military salaries as well as for hardware and research and development (see Table 4).

While Reagan highlighted the need to increase defense spending during the 1980 campaign, he did not unveil the particulars of his plan until after he had gained passage of the bulk of his economic program. On October 2, 1981, he announced the government's program to renew development, production, and deployment of the **B-1 bomber** and **MX (missile, experimental) missile,** both of which had been halted or slowed by President **James (Jimmy) Earl Carter.** He also announced his intention to go ahead with the production of neutron bombs and other nuclear weapons programs. The following year, despite growing opposition to his military buildup from the **nuclear freeze movement,** President Reagan pressed forward with his national defense agenda.

In May 1982 the Defense Department issued a report on its plans for the rest of the decade, entitled *Fiscal Year 1984–88: Defense Guidance.* It spelled out more fully than had previous documents the administration's long-range plans for military weapons research, development, procurement, and deployment, as well as improvements in the capabilities of conventional forces. Drawing on this report, in 1983, after describing the **Soviet Union** as an "evil empire," President Reagan launched another broad military initiative. He called for the United States to develop a high-technology space-based defense against nuclear missiles. He termed this project the Strategic Defense Initiative; critics called it Star Wars. This plan for an entirely new weapons system assured that defense expenditures would continue to increase regardless of the results of nuclear arms negotiations with the Soviets.

The military buildup did not include a significant increase in the number of military personnel. In 1980 there were about 2 million men and women on active duty. A decade later this number remained virtually unchanged. Nor did the military buildup involve a revival of the draft. Young American men still had to register with the Selective Service, but the military continued to be made up of volunteers.

Presidents Ronald Reagan and George Bush insisted that increased defense spending was necessary for several reasons. First, they argued that the United States had grown soft and had allowed the Soviet Union to develop a military advantage during the 1970s. This, they contended, had to be countered. Second, they claimed that a strong defense was the surest way to assure peace and stability, not only with the Soviets but worldwide. Last, some defense and foreign policy strategists claimed that a massive military buildup by the United States had the potential of producing a crisis in the Soviet Union. In turn, this process could lead to the **collapse of communism.**

The actual fall of communism in the Soviet Union in the early 1990s seemed to prove the validity of this theory. The Soviet Union was unable to keep up with the U.S. military buildup, and its attempt to do so contributed to the Communist Party's demise. However, some experts argued that communism was already on the verge of collapse before Reagan initiated a new round of the arms race and that talks of an arms gap had always been vastly exaggerated. Even more important, critics contended that the military buildup of the 1980s had produced massive federal budget deficits, which put the nation at a competitive disadvantage compared to the other leading industrial nations of the world. Paradoxically, the end of the cold war compelled President Bush and his secretary of defense, **Richard Bruce Cheney,** to begin the process of demilitarization. Bases were either closed or plans for their closing had to be made. New weapon systems were scaled back and orders for existing systems were reevaluated. This produced a decrease in defense spending, as measured in real dollars. Perhaps just as important, demilitarization contributed to the recession and probably hurt Bush politically. Defense cuts often hit those regions of the nation that had benefited the most from the military buildup during the 1980s. Southern California, which had seen its economy boom during the middle 1980s, began to bust. While the cuts were inevitable and much smaller in scale than those that followed the end of World War II, they still caused personal pain and political fallout.

Suggested Readings: H. Haflendorn and J. Schissler, eds., *The Reagan Administration: A Reconstruction of American Strength* (1988); Caspar Weinberger,

Table 5
Changes in Employment (Distribution of Workers)

Year	Goods-Producing Workers (percent of workforce)	Service Workers (percent of workforce)
1960	43.5	56.5
1970	36.5	63.5
1980	30.8	69.2
1990	24.8	75.2

Fighting for Peace (1990); Phil Williams, "The Reagan Administration and Defense Policy," in *The Reagan Presidency,* ed. by Dilys Hill, Raymond A. Moore and Phil Williams. (1990).

Related Entries: Berlin Wall, Fall of; Budget Deficit; Recessions; Strategic Defense Initiative (Star Wars).

DEFICIT. See **BUDGET DEFICIT; TRADE DEFICIT.**

DEINDUSTRIALIZATION. The deindustrialization of the United States, which began during the 1970s, continued apace during the 1980s. While President Ronald Reagan pointed to the fifteen million new jobs created during his presidency, few were in manufacturing. Many traditional industries, such as steel, textile, and shoes, virtually disappeared from the American scene. Others, most notably electronics and automobiles, continued to shed workers (see Table 5). Moreover, statistics on the total number of manufacturing jobs, which grew slightly, hid the more pertinent fact that wages were on the decline. Real hourly earnings fell from $7.78 in 1980 to $7.42 in 1992. Blue-collar workers without a college education were particularly hard hit. Those who were unionized found that their unions were less powerful than in the past. Employers demanded concessions and threatened to farm out jobs to nonunion firms or relocate to low-wage areas, either in the South or abroad, if they did not accept them. Nonunionized manufacturing workers faced even more dire straits.

Deindustrialization resulted from many causes. Critics of Presidents Ronald Reagan and George Bush argued that their policies fostered the decline of the manufacturing sector and did little to protect American workers from the loss of jobs. Reagan's tax cuts spurred corporate restructuring, to the advantage of the corporate elite but not wage workers.

The president's decision to fire striking air traffic controllers, members of the Professional Air Traffic Controllers Organization (PATCO), encouraged corporations to take a much tougher stance with labor. The tight money policy pursued by the **Federal Reserve Board** with the backing of President Reagan aided investors but hurt job growth.

Reagan was not hurt politically by the process of deindustrialization. Many Americans were not directly affected by it, and some benefited. In addition, many accepted his argument that big government and high taxes were the problem and that **Reaganomics** was the answer to America's economic decline. George Bush, in contrast, found it much more difficult to deflect the political anger that grew out of more than a decade of stagnating wages and economic insecurity. Unlike Reagan, he proved unable to convince Americans that the nation was on the right track. Furthermore, for political reasons he could not blame the previous administration for the nation's economic troubles. Ironically, by the time the recession of the early 1990s hit, many American industries were much stronger than they had been in years. The automobile companies, in particular, had developed much better-made cars and, when the economy recovered, they posted record profits. As a result, their workers enjoyed their first real gains in real earnings in years.

Suggested Readings: Michael A. Bernstein and David Adler, eds., *Understanding American Economic Decline* (1993); Barry Bluestone and Bennett Harrison, *The Deindustrializing of America* (1982); Hudson Institute, *Workforce 2000* (1987).

Related Entries: Air Traffic Controllers (PATCO) Strike; Economy, U.S.; Recessions.

DEREGULATION. Ronald Reagan made deregulation one of the centerpieces of his presidency. Many conservative think tanks, including the American Enterprise Institute and the Heritage Foundation, contended that overregulation of private industries by the federal government had crippled American businesses. This argument meshed with Reagan's broader criticism of big government. However, by the time George Bush entered the White House, the clamor for deregulation had quieted. Indeed, the **savings and loan crisis** produced calls for reregulation of one of the industries that had been deregulated.

Even before Ronald Reagan became president, the federal government had already begun to deregulate a number of key industries. Under President **James (Jimmy) Earl Carter,** the Civil Aeronautics Board initiated the deregulation of the airline industry. Subsequently, deregulation took place in the trucking and banking industries. Moving beyond merely supporting these efforts, the Reagan administration cut funding for several existing regulatory agencies—most notably, for the Environmental Protection Agency and the Occupational Health and Safety Administration. In addition, Reagan appointed administrators and cabinet members who opposed the strict enforcement of existing regulation.

Perhaps the most significant example of deregulation during the 1980s involved the telephone industry. In 1982, American Telephone & Telegraph (AT&T) was broken apart into several regional telephone carriers or "baby bells." Several new long-distance telephone companies, most notably Microwave Communications Incorporated (MCI), were allowed to compete more fairly with AT&T. By the time **William (Bill) Jefferson Clinton** had become president, the telecommunications industry was in the midst of a major revolution, with regional carriers merging with cable television networks and cellular phone consortiums in an effort to build diversified telecommunications empires.

While the verdict on the long-term impact of deregulation is still out, most economists feel that it produced greater competition and consumer choice and led to decreased prices and increased innovation. However, the deregulation of several industries also resulted in declining consumer confidence and worsened morale among employees in the deregulated industries. It may also ultimately produce greater market concentration.

Suggested Readings: Elizabeth Bailey, David Graham, and Daniel Kaplan, *Deregulating the Airlines* (1985); John Richard Felton and Dale G. Anderson, *Regulation and Deregulation of the Motor Carrier Industry* (1989); Thomas McCraw, *Prophets of Regulation* (1984).

Related Entries: Corporate Takeovers; New Federalism.

DESERT SHIELD, OPERATION. See **PERSIAN GULF WAR.**

DOLE, ELIZABETH HANFORD. (July 26, 1936, Salisbury, N.C.– .) Secretary of Transportation, 1983–1987; Secretary of Labor, 1989–1990; Director, American Red Cross, 1990– .

Elizabeth Hanford Dole was one of the most prominent women in Washington, D.C., during the Ronald Reagan–George Bush years. She and her husband, Senator **Robert Joseph Dole,** made up perhaps the most powerful political team of the era.

Born, raised, and educated in North Carolina, Elizabeth Dole graduated from Duke University with honors in 1958. After studying at Oxford University, she earned her master's in education and her law degree (1965) from Harvard University. A Democrat at the time, she worked for the Committee on Consumer Interest under President Lyndon Johnson. In the late 1960s she switched her party affiliation, first to independent and then to the Republican Party. In the early 1970s she held the position of deputy director of the White House Office of Consumer Affairs. In 1973, Richard Nixon appointed her to the Federal Trade Commission (FTC), a job she held until 1976. She resigned to work on the Gerald Ford–Robert Dole presidential–vice presidential campaign. (A year earlier, she had married Dole, the Republican senator from Kansas.) After their loss, she returned to the FTC. She departed again in 1979, this time to work, first, for her husband's brief presidential bid and, then, for the Reagan-Bush ticket.

First as secretary of transportation and then as secretary of labor, Elizabeth Dole earned a reputation as a moderate Republican who got along well with members of both parties. Unlike many of Reagan's other appointees, she rarely raised or encountered controversy. Organized labor largely supported her nomination for secretary of labor and, to certain extent, lamented her departure. In 1990 she resigned as secretary of labor to become the director of the Red Cross, leading some to wonder if she and the president had disagreed over his response to the weakening economy.

While her husband is renowned for his sarcastic wit and rather rough demeanor and look, she is personally liked by nearly all in Washington. At times her name has been mentioned as a possible vice presidential nominee, but nothing has yet come of such rumors.

Suggested Readings: Elizabeth and Robert Dole, *The Doles* (1988); Carolyn Mulford, *Elizabeth Dole: Public Servant* (1992).

DOLE, ROBERT JOSEPH. (July 23, 1923, Russell, Kans.– .) U.S. Senator, 1968– ; Candidate for Republican presidential nomination, 1980, 1988, and 1996.

First elected to the Kansas state legislature in 1950, Robert Dole has been one of the most prominent Republicans since the 1970s. After serving in the Kansas State Legislature, he worked as the prosecuting attorney for Russell County, Kansas, his birthplace. Eight years later, in 1960, he ran for, and won, a seat in the House of Representatives. He held this seat for four terms. In 1968 he ran for the Senate. Maintaining his perfect record, he won again. During the 1960s and 1970s, Dole largely had a conservative voting record. He opposed many of Presidents John Kennedy and Lyndon Johnson's policies, although he was not a dogmatic conservative and supported aid to agriculture and the handicapped. His strong support for Richard Nixon gained him the post of chairman of the Republican National Committee, a post he resigned during the Watergate scandal. In 1976 Dole ran as Gerald Ford's vice presidential running mate, returning to the Senate after the two narrowly lost to **James (Jimmy) Earl Carter** and **Walter Frederick Mondale.**

In 1980 Dole briefly campaigned for the Republican presidential nomination. After losing to Ronald Reagan and George Bush in the early primaries, he refocused his efforts on rewinning his seat in the U.S. Senate, which he did with ease. He was one of the top Republicans in the Senate when it enacted most of President Reagan's domestic and defense measures, from 1980 to 1984. In 1984 he became the majority leader of the Senate. He helped push through the **Tax Reform Act of 1986,** but otherwise he was unable to help Reagan enact several of his other proposals—largely due to opposition in the Democratically controlled House of Representatives. In 1987 he was forced to relinquish this position, as the Democrats retook control of the Senate.

In 1988 he ran again for the Republican presidential nomination. This time he was defeated by George Bush. While some expected Bush to nominate him as his running-mate, after Bush chose **Danforth (Dan) James Quayle,** Dole returned to the Senate as the minority leader, a post he held throughout Bush's presidential term. He helped deliver Republican support for several of Bush's policies, such as the **Clean Air Act of 1990,** but he had a much more difficult time rallying his party around controversial subjects, such as increased taxes. All in all, he maintained a reputation as a Washington insider with a moderate to conservative voting record. Whether or not this reputation would help him gain the Republican presidential nomination in 1996 remained to be seen.

Dole was raised in Russell, Kansas. When World War II broke out, he left college to join the military. During the fighting in Italy, he was severely wounded. After the war he returned to college, earning his A.B. and law degrees from the University of Topeka (J.D., 1952).

Throughout his career he has often been criticized for his rather acerbic personality. In 1975 he married Elizabeth Hanford who at the time was a member of the Federal Trade Commission. In the 1980s and early 1990s she served in both Presidents Reagan's and Bush's cabinets, making the

Doles one of the most prominent and powerful political families in America.

Suggested Readings: Stanley Holton, *Bob Dole: American Political Phoenix* (1988); Jake Thompson, *Bob Dole: The Republican Man for All Seasons* (1994).

Related Entries: Dole, Elizabeth Hanford; House of Representatives, United States; Senate, United States.

DOMESTIC POLICY. As a candidate for president, Ronald Reagan promised to usher in a revolution in domestic affairs. When he ran in 1988, George Bush asked America to allow him to continue the Reagan revolution. At the core of this revolution lay a dislike of big government, a faith in the free market, and a commitment to promote a conservative social and cultural agenda. However, twelve years later, on the domestic front the revolution remained incomplete. Taxes had been reduced dramatically for the wealthy, but not for the average citizen. Government spending and the federal **budget deficit** had increased precipitously. Moreover, rhetorical criticisms of recent social and cultural trends did little to reverse them.

Reagan's greatest successes on the domestic front came during the first two years of his presidency. He cut the top tax rate and reduced spending for a number of domestic programs. However, he proved unable to reduce federal spending or the deficit. At the same time, Reagan's advisers convinced him to put off action on social and cultural issues, such as **abortion** and school prayer. As a candidate in 1984, Reagan restated his commitment to cutting federal spending, balancing the budget, and restoring traditional values. However, the only major domestic achievement of his second term was further tax reform. Spending and the federal debt continued to grow, and Congress blocked efforts to pass a balanced budget or school prayer amendment.

Another aspect of Reagan's domestic policy was his support for **deregulation.** He consolidated the deregulation of industries initiated by President **James (Jimmy) Earl Carter** and cut federal oversight in other areas. However, even here Reagan failed to achieve a revolution.

Faced with anxiety over the **savings and loan crisis,** a reawakened concern about the **environment,** and a humongous national debt, George Bush promised to be a "kinder and gentler" president. The result of this pledge was a somewhat contradictory and befuddled domestic policy. He signed into law a revised clean air act, the **Clean Air Act of**

1990, and new **civil rights** legislation. He also oversaw the federal bail out of the savings and loan industry and supported a tax hike to address the enormous federal deficit. All of this suggested a break from Reagan's domestic policies. However, at the same time, Bush nominated conservative judges to the federal **courts,** with the goal of reversing several liberal social and cultural trends.

Suggested Readings: Larry Berman, ed., *Looking Back on the Reagan Presidency* (1990); William Berman, *America's Right Turn* (1994); Lou Cannon, *President Reagan: The Role of a Lifetime* (1991); Dilys Hill, Raymond A. Moore and Phil Williams, eds., *The Reagan Presidency: An Incomplete Revolution?* (1990).

Related Entries: Constitutional Amendments (Proposed); Economic Recovery Act of 1981; Reaganomics; Tax Reform Act of 1986.

DONOVAN, RAYMOND JAMES. (August 31, 1930, Bayonne, N. J.– .) Secretary of Labor, 1981–1985.

Raymond Donovan came from a working-class background. He grew up in Bayonne, New Jersey, the son of an oil company clerk, the seventh of twelve children. He was of Irish decent, and his family was devoutly Roman Catholic. Like several of Reagan's other top associates, he flirted with becoming a priest. However, by the time he became secretary of labor, Donovan had worked his way up the social ladder. He was a top executive with Schiavone Construction Company, one of the largest firms of its type in the Northeast. With Schiavone he specialized in labor relations and finance and earned a reputation among construction trade leaders as a tough but fair man. In the late 1970s he became attracted to Ronald Reagan, although he was a Democrat, raising hundreds of thousands of dollars for his 1980 presidential bid.

While Donovan's nomination was met warmly by representatives of the business community, organized labor responded more coolly. Indeed, his confirmation was put on hold while the Federal Bureau of Investigation (FBI) investigated allegations of improper conduct by the Schiavone Corporation, including accusations of underworld connections. Shortly after the FBI reported that it could not corroborate the charges, Donovan's nomination was confirmed by the Senate.

As secretary of labor, Donovan carried out a number of what many perceived as antilabor measures, from a diminishment of the powers of the Occupational Safety and Health Administration (OSHA) to a delay in a hike in the minimum wage. Donovan also supported Reagan's decision to end the Comprehensive Education and Training Act (CETA), a federal jobs program, and to fire striking air traffic controllers, who were members of the Professional Air Traffic Controllers Organization (PATCO).

Throughout his tenure, Donovan was bogged down by allegations of corruption. In December 1981, a special prosecutor was appointed to investigate Donovan's past. Several times the special prosecutor declared that there was insufficient evidence to charge Donovan with any federal crime, yet charges of various types kept appearing. In September 1984, a Bronx, New York, grand jury indicted Donovan on fraud charges, making him the first sitting cabinet member in American history to be indicted. The following March, Donovan resigned. Two years later, in September 1986, a trial finally began. On May 25, 1987, Donovan was acquitted of all charges. Afterwards, President Reagan declared: "I have always known Ray Donovan as a man of integrity, and I am happy to see this verdict."

Donovan is married to Catherine Sblendorio (Donovan). They have three children.

Suggested Readings: *Current Biography* (1982) p. 103; *New York Times,* May 26, 1987, p. 1.

Related Entry: Air Traffic Controllers (PATCO) Strike.

DRUGS. See **WAR ON DRUGS.**

DUBERSTEIN, KENNETH. (April 21, 1944, Brooklyn, N.Y.– .) Presidential Adviser, 1982–1983, 1988–1989.

During the early years of the Ronald Reagan presidency, Ken Duberstein worked in the White House promoting the policies of the new president. Initially hired as the deputy assistant for legislative affairs, he served as the chief White House congressional liaison in 1982 and 1983. He played a seminal role in getting various Reagan proposals passed by Congress. Then he left the White House to work in private firm as a lobbyist and public relations expert. In 1987, he returned to the White House as deputy chief of staff, working under **Howard (Henry) Baker, Jr.,** who had taken the helm from **Donald Regan** in the midst of the **Iran-contra affair.** Duberstein was considered to be close with **Nancy Davis Reagan** and perceived as a political pragmatist. Following the Republican convention in summer 1988, Duberstein focused much of his attention on developing and delivering White House support for Vice President George Bush's campaign for the presidency. For example, while Baker was chief of staff, three cabinet posts became vacant. Duberstein helped influence Reagan to name individuals to these posts who he felt would help Bush attract voters, such as **Richard L. Thornburgh,** a former governor of Pennsylvania.

Duberstein's involvement in national politics went back to his college days when his political science teacher at Franklin and Marshall (F&M) College, Sidney Wise, landed him a job as an intern with Senator Jacob Javits of New York. After graduating from F&M, he worked for the General Service Administration and the Department of Labor. At the same time he earned his master's degree in government from American University. He is married to the former Sydney Greenberg and they have three children.

Suggested Readings: *New York Times,* June 15, 1988, p. 24; *New York Times,* August 29, 1988, p. 13.

DUKAKIS, MICHAEL STANLEY. (November 3, 1933, Brookline, Mass.– .) Governor of Massachusetts, 1975–1979, 1983–1991; Democratic candidate for president, 1988.

Michael Dukakis, the son of Greek immigrants, was the Democratic nominee for the presidency in 1988. A two-term governor from Massachusetts, he was initially the dark horse in the race. He emerged as the front-runner after the preprimary favorite, **Gary W. Hart,** was derailed by a scandal regarding his sexual fidelity. Dukakis defeated an assortment of candidates for the nomination, most notably **Jesse Louis Jackson.** However, the road to the nomination was not an easy one and both Dukakis and the Democratic Party were bruised by it. At the time of his nomination, most national polls showed him ahead of Vice President George Bush. However, Dukakis's lead soon evaporated. Bush attacked Dukakis's record as governor, painting him as a left-wing liberal. Dukakis proved especially vulnerable to Bush's diatribes against his record on crime. While Bush's pledge not to raise taxes provided his campaign with a sharp focus, Dukakis's message remained muddled. He promised to run an efficient government, but what exactly this meant remained unclear. In November he lost to Bush by a fairly wide margin.

Suggested Reading: Charles Kenney, *Dukakis: An American Odyssey* (1988).

Related Entries: Debates, Presidential; Election of 1988; Horton, Willie (commercial).

DUKE, DAVID ERNEST. (July 1, 1950, Tulsa, Okla.– .) White Supremacist.

David Duke, a former Ku Klux Klan leader and member of the American Nazi Party, became a national political figure and a symbol of the racial backlash of the Ronald Reagan and George Bush years during the latter part of the 1980s and early 1990s. Duke grabbed the national limelight in 1990 when he won 44 percent of the vote in the Louisiana Senate race. During his campaign, Duke claimed that he was no longer a white supremacist and that he should be judged by what he proposed, as a candidate, rather than for his youthful past, when he was the youngest Grand Wizard of the KKK and marched around in Nazi uniforms. However, Duke's proposals echoed with many racist implications, including drastic **welfare** reform, stringent crime measures, and opposition to **affirmative action,** leading many to wonder if he had changed at all. Moreover, Duke's presidency of the National Association for the Advancement of White People (1980–1990) further undercut his claim that he was no longer a racist. Even though Reagan and Bush favored welfare reform and opposed affirmative action, both they and the national Republican Party disassociated themselves from Duke. Nonetheless, some of their critics contended that their **civil rights** policies and proclamations legitimized individuals like Duke.

Initially the press helped make Duke into a national figure by paying much attention to him. As the possibility that he might actually win a top office grew, however, the press became one of his primary foes. Journalists probed Duke's record, revealing his ties to various white supremacist groups, and they analyzed his proposals, demonstrating that his views had not changed as much as he contended they had. Such critical stories, along with the emergence of **Patrick J. Buchanan** and **H. Ross Perot** in 1992, helped deflate Duke's popularity. The latter two were seen as more legitimate antiestablishment political figures than Duke, as neither had his racist past.

Duke was a member of the Louisiana State Legislature from 1989 to 1992. He was married to the former Chloe Hardin. They divorced in 1984. They have two children.

Suggested Readings: Tyler Bridges, *The Rise of David Duke* (1994); Julia Reed, "His Brilliant Career," *New York Review of Books,* April 9, 1992, p. 20; Michael Zafarain, *David Duke, Evolution of a Klansman* (1990).

E

EAGLEBURGER, LAWRENCE SIDNEY. (August 1, 1930, Milwaukee, Wis.–). Undersecretary of State for Political Affairs, 1982–1989; Deputy Secretary of State, 1989–1992; Acting Secretary of State, 1992–1993.

In August 1992, when James (Jim) Addison Baker III stepped down as secretary of state to focus on President George Bush's bid for reelection, Lawrence Eagleburger assumed his place. This move marked the culmination of over three decades of work in the arena of foreign affairs.

The son of a physician and an elementary school teacher, Eagleburger received his B.A. (1952) and M.A. (1957) in political science at the University of Wisconsin. Rather than pursue a Ph.D., Eagleburger took the foreign service exam and, upon passing, joined the State Department. From 1957 through 1965 he rotated through various posts. In the mid-1960s he was promoted to special assistant to Dean Acheson, the former assistant secretary of state. Subsequently he worked on the staff of Walt W. Rostow, the head of the National Security Council. During the early 1970s Eagleburger became closely allied with Henry Kissinger, serving as his executive assistant and undersecretary. When **James (Jimmy) Earl Carter** became president in 1977, he appointed Eagleburger as ambassador to Yugoslavia.

Even though his close ties with Henry Kissinger and association with the Carter administration put him at odds with hard-line conservatives, Ronald Reagan's secretary of state, **Alexander Meigs Haig, Jr.**, named Eagleburger assistant secretary of state for European affairs in 1981. From there he moved up to the third highest spot in the State Department, undersecretary for political affairs, a position that many considered the highest a career diplomat could achieve.

In 1984 Eagleburger resigned from the government, largely due to physical and emotional exhaustion. For four years he worked with his old mentor, Henry Kissinger, in the private sector. Although he earned close to a million dollars a year, Eagleburger still remained interested in public service. Hence, in 1989 he readily accepted the number two job in the State Department, deputy secretary of state, when James (Jim) Addison Baker III offered it to him. Aside from brief opposition mounted by Senator **Jesse A. Helms,** Eagleburger easily won confirmation to this post. While serving as Baker's deputy, Eagleburger conducted numerous key tasks. During the **Persian Gulf War** he rushed off to Israel following Iraqi Scud missile attacks. There he helped convince the Israelis not to retaliate so as to keep the war from widening. With Bush's defeat, Eagleburger retired from public service.

Eagleburger has a reputation for candor, humor, and a lack of pretention. Although reared in a very conservative family, throughout his career Eagleburger worked well with state department leaders of various political stripes. He is married to Marlene Ann Heinemann and has three children.

Suggested Readings: *Current Biography Yearbook* (1992); *Time,* September 27, 1992, pp. 56–58.

Related Entry: Foreign Policy.

ECONOMIC RECOVERY ACT OF 1981. On August 13, 1981, President Ronald Reagan signed the Economic Recovery Act, also known as the Kemp-Roth tax cut, into law. The bill, which called for a 25 percent reduction in personal income tax rates over three years, was one of the cornerstones of the president's economic or **domestic policy.** Based on the theory of supply-side economics, the president and his supporters argued that the tax cut would stimulate economic growth and spur savings while at the same time reducing the **budget deficit.** The House of Representatives approved the measure by a vote of 238–195 on July 29, 1981. The Senate passed the bill, 89–11, shortly afterward.

Specifically, the Kemp-Roth tax cut—named after **Jack French Kemp,** a Republican congressman from upstate New York, and William Roth, a Republican senator from Delaware—was to be implemented over three years. It cut all income tax rates by 5 percent on October 1, 1981; an additional 10 percent on July 1, 1982; and 10 percent more on July 1, 1983. The cuts would appear in the lower withholding rates. The law also reduced the top income tax rate from 70 percent to 50 percent,

Table 6
Shift in Effective Federal Tax Rates by Population Income Decile

Decile	1977	1984	1988	Change in Rate, 1977–1988
First	8.0%	10.5%	9.6%	+1.6
Second	8.7	8.5	8.3	−.4
Third	12.0	13.2	13.3	+1.3
Fourth	16.2	16.3	16.8	+.6
Fifth	19.1	18.5	19.2	+.1
Sixth	21.0	20.1	20.9	−.1
Seventh	23.0	21.5	22.3	−.7
Eighth	23.6	23.0	23.6	−1.5
Ninth	24.5	23.8	24.7	+.2
Tenth	26.7	23.6	25.0	−1.7
Top 5%	27.5	23.3	24.9	−2.6
Top 1%	30.9	23.1	24.9	−6.0

indexed tax rates to offset the impact of **inflation,** and increased the tax exemption on estates and gifts. To win broad support for the measure, the Republicans offered a number of tax incentives to special interest groups, including shorter depreciation periods for capital equipment, tax breaks for oil producers, and an expansion of individual retirement accounts (IRAs).

While the president had to scale back his plans—he originally called for a 30 percent cut over three years—the passage of the Kemp-Roth bill with bipartisan support represented a major political victory. Whether the tax cut achieved its objective, however, remains a hotly debated subject. Coinciding with the recession of 1981–1982, the tax cut did not lead to deficit reductions. Moreover, while the economy grew in the mid-1980s, so, too, did the federal deficit. Thus, while Reagan's supporters contended that supply-side economics worked, his critics countered that deficit spending, driven by increased defense spending, was the primary engine of economic growth. In addition, while Reagan cast tax cuts as a broad-based measure, studies showed that the wealthy got most of the benefits (Table 6). Reagan's supporters countered that even though the wealthy enjoyed the greatest reductions in their tax rates, they ended up paying out more total dollars in taxes.

Suggested Readings: *Congressional Quarterly Almanac* (1981); Kevin Phillips, *The Politics of Rich and Poor* (1989); Paul Craig Roberts, *The Supply Side Revolution* (1984).

Related Entries: Domestic Policy; Economy, U.S.; Reaganomics; Recessions; Tax Reform.

ECONOMY, U.S. The performance of the economy during the Ronald Reagan–George Bush years can be divided into three distinct phases. Shortly after Reagan took office, the nation experienced a severe recession. The recession began in the fall of 1981 and lasted until early 1983. This was followed by over five years of expansion, one of the longest sustained periods of growth in modern American history. Not long after George Bush became president, the economy began to stagnate and finally fell into a second recession.

Overall, the gross national product (GNP), unadjusted for inflation, nearly doubled from 1980 through 1992, and per capita income grew at almost the same rate. Unemployment, however, remained relatively high compared to other periods of sustained growth, never dipping below 5.3 percent in any given year. In contrast, during the 1960s, unemployment rarely got above 5 percent. Similarly, the gross national product and per capita income, when adjusted for inflation, did not grow as fast during the 1980s as during other economic expansions. Unlike in the twenty-five years following World War II, the additional national income was not evenly distributed throughout the population. The richest Americans benefited the most and careful studies of the average American family showed that their real earnings, after taxes, barely grew over the twelve year period of 1981–1992. Only through working harder—in particular, through increased participation by women in the labor force—did many families make any economic gains at all.

Four important economic developments during the Reagan-Bush years were (1) the taming of **inflation,** (2) a dramatic rise in the **budget deficit** and overall federal debt, (3) the **deindustrialization** of the economy as the manufacturing sector shrank relative to the service sector, and (4) the persistence of a high **trade deficits,** especially with Japan. The combined result of these four developments meant that while the American people had escaped the double-digit inflation that Reagan had inherited from President **James (Jimmy) Earl Carter,** and while many partook in the expansion of the mid-1980s, they still faced an economy beset by serious problems as the Reagan-Bush years came to a close. In 1979, President Carter had declared that the United States was no longer sure that the "days of our children would be better than our own." Ironically, during the 1992 campaign, conservative and independent candidates, such as **Patrick J. Buchanan** and **H. Ross Perot** were making virtually the same claim. Many youths feared that they would not live a better life than their parents. Put another way, the economic boom of the 1980s notwithstanding, the Reagan-Bush years did not put an end to deep concerns about the future.

This said, conservative supporters of President Reagan contended that George Bush, and not Reagan, deserved the blame for the economy's malaise. They insisted that **Reaganomics** worked but that Bush's break from its basic principles of cutting taxes and spending had produced the recession of the early 1990s and gotten the nation off the track that President Reagan had left it on when he left office. Conservatives also blamed the Democrats for the nation's economic malaise, arguing that all along they had controlled Congress and prevented both President Reagan and President Bush from fully implementing their economic programs.

Most economists, however, disagree with this analysis. While they criticize Democrats for their unwillingness to cut federal spending, they find Reaganomics seriously flawed. Indeed, some of the harshest criticism of President Reagan came from one of his former aides, **David Alan Stockman,** who contended that the president sacrificed real economic reform for political reasons. Rather than cut popular entitlement programs (especially social security) Reagan chose instead to insist that the budget could be balanced without either trimming **defense spending** or scaling back tax cuts. Reagan, Stockman added, was more comfortable criticizing the Democrats, playing symbolic politics—for instance, by proposing a constitutional amendment to balance the budget—than he was in taking the political risk of demanding a freeze on social security payments. This ensured that budget deficits would continue to spiral upward and that Bush would inherit a fragile economy.

Suggested Readings: Alberto Alesina and Gregory Carliner, eds., *Politics and Economics in the Eighties* (1991); Robert L. Bartley, *Seven Fat Years* (1992); Benjamin M. Freeman, *Day of Reckoning* (1988); David Stockman, *The Triumph of Politics* (1986).

Related Entries: Constitutional Amendments (Proposed); Recessions.

EDUCATION. Debates over the state of education did not appear for the first time during the Ronald Reagan–George Bush years, but heightened public concern over education and support for alternative means for im-

Figure 3
Education (Federal Outlays)

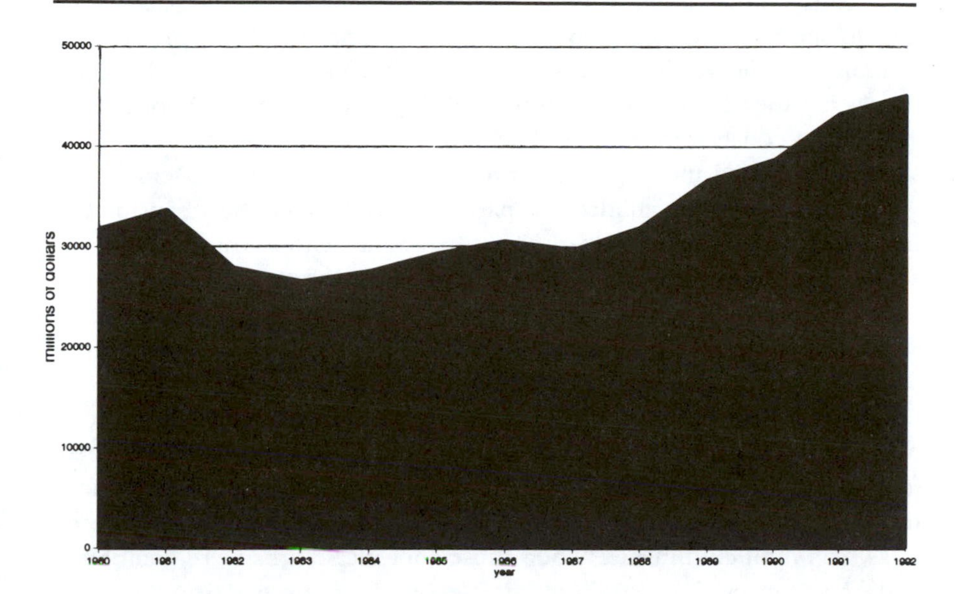

proving it did. Both Presidents Reagan and Bush lent their support for various initiatives aimed at improving primary, secondary, and higher education (see Figure 3). Among the most significant of these were ones that called for school vouchers, reestablishing conservative values in schools, and decreasing federal funding for education. Due in part to Democratic opposition to most of these specific proposals, however, little came from the initiatives.

In 1983 the Department of Education issued *A Nation at Risk,* a study commissioned by Secretary of Education Terrel Bell. Ironically, the department originally undertook the study to provide it with ammunition to fend off proposed spending cuts. The study brought together many of the complaints and concerns about education that had been raised for a number of years. As the title suggested, mediocre education, as evidenced by declining test scores and high dropout rates, put the United States in a precarious position. American students, the report argued, were ill-suited to compete with students around the globe, who were better trained in math and science. Moreover, many schools were utterly failing to deliver in the basics to their constituents.

Even before *A Nation at Risk* appeared, conservatives had called for a number of reforms, most notably the provision of school vouchers. According to this plan, families would receive vouchers or tax credits from the government to allow them to send their children to private schools. This, conservatives argued, would provide a means for working-class families to send their children to private schools and would prompt public schools to improve themselves. Critics of the vouchers argued that they would kill the already underfunded and overtaxed public schools. They added that conservatives favored school vouchers for political reasons—the issue allowed the Republicans to appeal to traditionally Democratic voters who sent their children to parochial schools—rather than for educational ones. Conservatives countered that school vouchers represented a market-based approach to improving education consistent with other aspects of the Reagan administration's **domestic policy.** Regardless of who was right, Democrats blocked Republican attempts to enact a federal school voucher plan.

Reagan's second secretary of education, **William John Bennett,** spent much of his time railing at the decline of values in America and the need for school vouchers and stiffer discipline. He attacked the liberal educational establishment, claiming it was polluting education through its emphasis on multiculturalism. When these rhetorical barbs were combined with the Reagan administration's attacks on **affirmative action** and calls for spending cuts for nearly all education programs, they produced an extremely antagonistic relationship between educators and the White House. To make matters worse, Bennett advocated abolishing the Department of Education, over which he presided. Reagan supported this goal but, as with school vouchers, proved unable to convince the Democratic majority in Congress to do so.

During the 1988 campaign, George Bush pledged to be the "education president." Like Reagan, he backed school vouchers and emphasized the need to return to the basics and to restore traditional values to the classroom. This included a call for a constitutional amendment that would allow prayer in school. However, Bush favored a more active role by the federal government in the effort to reform education than had Reagan. In 1989 he attended an education summit with the nation's governors which aimed at raising awareness over the need to reform education. It called for establishing national standards for schoolchildren, a proposal the president supported and the National Endowment for the Humanities funded. When Secretary of Education Lauro Cavazos, a Reagan appointee, proved unable to rally support behind the goals of the conference, Bush replaced him with **Lamar Alexander** who, as governor of Tennessee, had gained national fame by enacting major changes in education in his state.

In terms of higher education, Bush took a somewhat different tack than Reagan. Whereas federal spending for education decreased during Reagan's presidency, it was increased during Bush's term. Funding for **Head Start,** college loans, and research all went up.

At the end of the Reagan-Bush years, many people still felt that education still lay in a perilous state. **William (Bill) Jefferson Clinton** pointed to his own record as an educational reformer while governor of Arkansas in order to win votes. However, little consensus existed on which direction the federal government should take. The Republicans tended to call for the federal government to get out of the business of education, to turn control back over to the states and the private sector. The Democrats, in contrast, argued that education was one place where the federal government had a clear role as a catalyst for improvement and reform.

Suggested Readings: Terrel H. Bell, *The Thirtieth Man: A Reagan Memoir* (1988); Lynne Cheney, *Tyrannical Machines* (1990); James J. Horgan and Joseph A. Cernik, eds., *The Reagan Years: Perspectives and Assessments* (1988).

Related Entries: Constitutional Amendments (Proposed); Election of 1988.

ELECTION OF 1980. With the defeat of President Gerald Ford by **James (Jimmy) Earl Carter** in 1976, Ronald Reagan began his campaign for the 1980 Republican presidential nomination and the White House itself. Four years later, overcoming the doubts of oddsmakers, who proclaimed in 1976 that he was too conservative to win in the general election, he easily defeated Jimmy Carter.

Reagan's planning for the campaign began almost immediately after Ford's loss. He quickly developed a network of loyal partisans, drawn from his supporters in 1976, and established a political action committee to raise funds for a possible future run for office. By the time he announced his candidacy in 1979, he already had a sound organizational and financial base and a lead over his main Republican opponents.

However, in the Iowa caucus, the first test of the voters' sentiments, he nearly suffered a devastating defeat. His campaign director, **John Patrick Sears,** assumed that Reagan was the front-runner and advised him to pursue a strategy that kept him above the fray and moved him closer to the political center. This included declining to debate other major Republican candidates. This seemed to backfire when **George Herbert Walker Bush,** a former congressman, ambassador, and director of the Central Intelligence Agency, won. This led many pundits to suspect that

Table 7
Election Results of 1980

Candidate and Party	Popular Vote (Total and Percentage)		Electoral College Votes
Ronald Reagan (Rep.)	43,904,153	50.7%	489
Jimmy Carter (Dem.)	35,483,883	41.0	49
John B. Anderson (Ind.)	5,720,060	6.6	
Ed Clark (Libertarian)	921,299	1.1	
Other	465,826	.7	

Reagan would become just one more preprimary front-runner who would fail to secure the nomination.

However, Reagan revived his campaign in New Hampshire. He fired Sears—technically, Sears did not resign until after the New Hampshire vote—turning back to his long-time California aides **Edwin Meese III, Michael Keith Deaver, William Joseph Casey,** and **Lyn Nofziger.** He agreed to debate his Republican opponents and emphasized his traditional conservative views. This strategy worked, and he won the New Hampshire primary. Indeed, he went on to win every primary but four. At the same time, he easily won the vast majority of delegates selected by party caucuses.

Only George Bush did not withdraw from the field. Arguing that Reagan was too conservative to be elected and warning that the former California governor threatened to turn the clock back to the 19th century, Bush stayed in the race up until the convention. Bush also described Reagan's supply-side economics as unworkable, once decrying them as **"voodoo economics."** However, Bush was unable to counter Reagan's popularity and organizational strength. Reagan easily won nomination on the first ballot. Afterwards, he healed rifts within the Republican Party by nominating Bush as his running mate.

During the general election campaign, Reagan sought to focus the voters' attention on President Carter's "failed" economic policies, represented most clearly by double-digit **inflation** and lingering unemployment. Carter tried to counter by painting Reagan as "trigger happy" and inexperienced in foreign affairs. However, Carter himself could not escape the claims that he was an incapable leader, an image reinforced by the Iran hostage crisis, which dragged on day after day through the campaign. While Carter closed Reagan's lead in the polls from a high of 15 percent to less than 10 percent, leading some to see the election as too close to call, he was never able to secure the vote of those who felt that Reagan was too conservative for their tastes. A number of moderate voters turned instead to Independent candidate **John Bayard Anderson,** a Republican congressman from Illinois (see Table 7).

Not only did Reagan defeat Carter, the 1980 election marked a significant defeat for the Democratic Party in Congress. While the Democrats retained control of the House of Representatives, the Republicans won control of the U.S. Senate for the first time since 1955. In addition, a number of well-known liberals, including Senator Frank Church of Idaho, were defeated. This made it easier for Reagan to claim that he enjoyed a broad mandate, despite the fact that he had won only 50.7 percent of the popular vote.

Suggested Readings: Lou Cannon, *Reagan* (1982); Thomas Ferguson and Joel Rogers, eds., *The Hidden Election* (1981); Jack W. Germond and Jules Witcover, *Blue Smoke and Mirrors: How Reagan Won and Why Carter Lost the Election of 1980* (1981).

Related Entries: Conservative Coalition; Debates, Presidential; Iranian Hostages.

ELECTION OF 1984. While President Ronald Reagan's approval rating declined during the 1981–1982 recession, leading some to predict that he would be only a one-term president, as the economy rebounded in 1983 and 1984, so, too, did his popularity. His renomination as the Republican Party's presidential candidate never was in doubt, except by those who suggested that he might not seek reelection.

On the Democratic Party side, former Vice President **Walter Frederick Mondale** was the early front-runner. He won early endorsements from the American Federation of Labor and Congress of Industrial Organizations (AFL-CIO) and the National Organization of Women (NOW), two key Democratic constituencies. Building on these endorsements and a strong organizational base, he overcame an early upset loss to Colorado Senator **Gary W. Hart,** in New Hampshire, to build an insurmountable lead going into the Democratic convention. Still, on the eve of his nomination, polls showed him trailing President Reagan by a wide margin. Hence, Mondale took the dramatic and historic step of nominating **Geraldine Anne Ferraro** as his running mate. She was the first women to ever receive such a nomination, and Mondale hoped this would galvanize the electorate behind him.

Table 8
Election Results of 1984

Candidate and Party	Popular Vote (Total and Percentage)		Electoral College Votes
Ronald Reagan (Rep.)	54,455,074	58.80%	525
Walter Mondale (Dem.)	37,577,137	40.60	13
David Bergland (Lib.)	228,314	.25	
Lyndon LaRouche (Ind.)	78,807	.08	
Other	241,261	.26	

However, Mondale was never able to significantly narrow the gap between himself and the president. Reagan ran an extremely well-orchestrated campaign. Generally upbeat in its message, the Reagan campaign team tagged Mondale with the malaise of the "Carter-Mondale" years. Mondale sought to turn the public against Reagan by emphasizing the skyrocketing **budget deficit.** However, his pledge to raise taxes to cut the deficit won him few, if any, converts. Neither were they won by his claim that Reagan would do the same thing. Mondale's only glimmer of hope came following their first debate, in which Reagan performed badly. He looked old and unprepared, rekindling concerns about his age and intellectual capacity. However, Reagan overcame these doubts during their second debate.

On Election Day, Reagan won in a landslide, losing only the state of Minnesota (barely) and the District of Columbia (Table 8). Ferraro's impact was negligible. Concerns about her husband's possible ties to organized crime and her own worthiness to be president may even have lost Mondale votes.

Despite the wide margin of victory, Reagan's coattails proved much shorter than in 1980. The Democratic Party retained control of the House of Representatives, and the Republican majority in the Senate remained slim. Hence, while the election represented a personal victory for Reagan, it did not clearly translate into a mandate for further conservative initiatives during his second term.

Suggested Readings: Jack W. Germond and Jules Witcover, *Wake Me Up When It's Over: Presidential Politics of 1984* (1985); Steve Gillon, *The Democrat's Dilemma: Walter Mondale and the Liberal Legacy* (1992); Jane Mayer and Doyle McManus, *Landslide: The Unmaking of the President, 1984–88* (1988).

Related Entries: Debates, Presidential; Economy, U.S.; House of Representatives, United States; Recessions; Senate, United States.

ELECTION OF 1988. The Democratic Party considered 1988 a year of opportunity. It had achieved impressive midterm election gains in 1986, winning back control of the Senate and increasing its majority in the House of Representatives. The **Iran-contra affair, stock market crash of 1987,** and growing criticism of conservatism suggested that the citizenry was ready to put a Democrat back in the White House. Perhaps even more important, Democrats were buoyed by the fact that they would not have to face Reagan again and, most likely, would face George Bush, whose personal popularity never equaled that of his boss. However, the 1988 election largely ended up as a repeat of those of 1980 and 1984, leaving many Democrats wondering if they would ever regain the White House.

While Bush secured the Republican nomination with relative ease, beating back an early challenge from Senator **Robert Joseph Dole,** the Democratic Party waged a fractious battle for the nomination. Early front-runner **Gary W. Hart** was derailed by a sex scandal. Afterward, dark horse **Michael Stanley Dukakis,** the governor of Massachusetts; **Jesse Louis Jackson,** a protégé of Martin Luther King, Jr.; and others slugged it out in state after state. Dukakis managed to win enough primaries and caucuses to secure the nomination by the time of the convention, but in contrast to the Republican Party, the Democrats were divided and still feeling the sting of the primary battles as they turned their attention to the general election.

Bush initiated his aggressive fall campaign with a rousing acceptance speech at the Republican convention, which some termed the speech of his life. He hammered at Dukakis's liberalism, defended **family values** and the Reagan-Bush record of prosperity, and revived patriotism. In the most famous line of his campaign, Bush vowed not to raise taxes—"Read my lips," he declared. "No new taxes." Stealing a page from Machiavelli's *The Prince,* Bush promised a kinder and gentler America while at the same time viciously attacking Dukakis's record on crime. This latter tactic included the use of the infamous Willie Horton commercial, which played to the latent racism of many Reagan Democrats. In contrast, until shortly before the election, Dukakis ran a defensive campaign.

As a result, Bush won a convincing victory, receiving a greater percentage of the popular votes than had Reagan in 1980 (Table 9). By winning, he became the first vice president to secede a two-term president

Table 9
Election Results of 1988

Candidate and Party	Popular Vote (Total and Percentage)		Electoral College Votes
George Bush (Rep.)	48,886,097	53.4%	426
Michael Dukakis (Dem.)	41,809,074	45.6	111
Ron Paul (Lib.)	432,179	.5	
Other	467,459	.5	

since Martin Van Buren, Andrew Jackson's vice president, had done so in 1836. Nonetheless, the Republican Party did not benefit from Bush's success. The Democrats actually picked up one seat in the Senate and two in the House of Representatives, which portended badly for Bush.

Suggested Readings: Michael Barone, *Our Country* (1989); Sidney Blumenthal, *The Last Campaign of the Cold War* (1990); Jack Germond and Jules Witcover, *Whose Broad Stripes and Bright Stars* (1989).

Related Entries: Debates, Presidential; Horton, Willie (Commercial); House of Representatives, United States; Senate, United States.

ELECTION OF 1992. The 1992 presidential campaign was one of the strangest in modern history. Following the **Persian Gulf War,** George Bush's public approval ratings reached new highs, leading most political pundits to predict that he would easily win reelection in 1992. Bush's chances seemed so good that many Democrats who were expected to run for president, from New York Governor Mario Cuomo to New Jersey Senator Bill Bradley, chose not to seek the presidency. By the summer of 1992, as the recession lingered and public anger grew over political **gridlock** in Washington, D.C., Bush's star fell and that of his contenders rose.

By the summer of 1992, **William (Bill) Jefferson Clinton,** the youngest governor in Arkansas history, had sewn up the Democratic nomination. Steering a middle course, Clinton outmaneuvered his rivals in the primaries, most notably former Massachusetts Senator Paul Tsongas and former California Governor Jerry Brown—who ran one of the most quixotic campaigns ever. Just as important, Clinton secured the Democratic Party's nomination without antagonizing many of its traditional constituencies so that, unlike in the past, the Democrats revealed a united front at their convention.

In contrast, the Republican Party took on characteristics generally associated with the Democrats. Bush had to beat back a biting primary challenge from the pugnacious **Patrick J. Buchanan.** To gain the support of the right wing of the party, he endorsed extremely conservative platform pledges on **abortion** and other social issues. Moreover, unlike Reagan's carefully orchestrated and upbeat campaigns of the 1980s, Bush's campaign was shrill and disorganized.

However, it was not simply Democratic unity and Republican infighting that made 1992 so unusual. Rather, it was **H. Ross Perot**'s in, out, and back in again independent campaign that made the race for the presidency so different. A billionaire from Texas with a homespun look and populist message, Perot attracted voters from both parties who were disillusioned with politics as usual. He also energized Americans who usually did not take an active interest in politics. His popularity soared in the spring and summer of 1992. However, then he shocked even many of his closest supporters by withdrawing from the race following Clinton's nomination in July. Unpredictable and irascible to the end, Perot rejoined it in early October, mounting a furious campaign filled with lengthy "infomercials" paid for with his own funds. Perot gained further exposure during a series of presidential debates with both Bush and Clinton. Performing admirably, he regained much of the support he had held earlier in the summer.

In the end, however, Perot's third-party candidacy, like others before, failed. While he garnered nearly 20 percent of the popular vote, he did not win a single vote in the electoral college. Clinton, who maintained his focus and drive until the final day, easily gained a majority of the electoral college vote, even though he won only 43 percent of the popular vote. Bush won just 38 percent of the popular vote, one of the worst showings by an incumbent or a Republican presidential candidate ever (Table 10). At the same time the Democrats maintained control of both houses of Congress, leading many to argue that the public had turned against the policies of the Reagan-Bush years. Clinton's relatively small proportion of the popular vote and Perot's popularity, however, suggested that the verdict on the Reagan-Bush years was still not in.

Suggested Readings: Jack W. Germond and Jules Witcover, *Mad as Hell: Revolt at the Ballot Box, 1992* (1993); Mary Matalin and James Carville, *All's Fair*

Table 10
Election Results of 1992

Candidate and Party	Popular Vote (Total and Percentage)		Electoral College Votes
Bill Clinton (Dem.)	44,909,326	43.0%	370
George Bush (Rep.)	39,103,882	37.4	168
Ross Perot (Ind.)	19,741,657	18.9	
Other	670,149	.7	

in Love and War and Running for President (1994); Gerald M. Pomper, ed., *The Election of 1992* (1993).

Related Entries: Debates, Presidential; Recessions.

EL SALVADOR. President Ronald Reagan's policy toward El Salvador flowed out of his broader concern with the spread of communism in Central America. It was connected to the Reagan administration's efforts to overthrow the Sandinistas in **Nicaragua.** His policies toward El Salvador were highly controversial and the extent to which the administration achieved its objective in the region remains a matter of heated scholarly debate.

In February 1981 the State Department issued a white paper claiming that there was "definitive evidence" that Marxist Cuban and Nicaraguan forces had supplied leftist Salvadoran rebels with military arms. The State Department added that Cuban advisers had helped create a united guerrilla force in El Salvador, which in turn had launched an offensive against the U.S.-backed government in the country. It called this action a "textbook case of indirect armed aggression by Communist powers." In response to these developments, the Reagan administration suspended a $75 million economic aid program for Nicaragua and called for sending more military advisers and an additional $25 million in military aid to El Salvador. Many people, however, questioned the veracity of the white paper. This prompted the Reagan administration to declare that it favored a political, not a military, solution for the region and, perhaps more important, forced the president to delay plans to arm El Salvador's military forces to the extent he had originally proposed.

On February 24, 1982, in a nationally televised address, President Reagan once again focused the nation's attention on the region. He called for a massive **Caribbean Basin Initiative,** whereby the United States would foster economic growth in Central America and the Caribbean while simultaneously supporting anticommunist forces in the region. To bolster this plan, he appointed a special commission headed by former Secretary of State Henry Kissinger to study the situation. The commission subsequently issued a report that largely reiterated the goals enunciated by President Reagan on February 24.

Meanwhile, events in El Salvador undercut the administration's goal of fostering either a middle course or a political solution. Right-wing forces led by Roberto d'Aubuisson won the elections (partly because the leftists boycotted the ballot boxes). Once in power, the right initiated a wave of terror and kidnapping. The simultaneous failure of the El Salvadoran government to prosecute individuals suspected of killing Americans prompted the U.S. ambassador to call the legal system "rotten" and led to calls in the United States to suspend military aid to the country.

Nonetheless, the Reagan administration refused to cut off the d'Aubuisson government. On April 27, 1983, before a joint session of Congress, the president called for passage of an earlier request for $298 million in aid for the region. On May 25, Lieutenant Commander Albert A. Schaufelberger III, a U.S. military adviser in El Salvador, was shot and killed, allegedly by rebel forces. Two days later, the Reagan administration replaced Ambassador Robert White, a critic of the right-wing government, with Deane Hinton. On June 14, 1983, one hundred U.S. Special Forces arrived in Honduras to train Salvadoran forces. Meanwhile, Congress approved $55 million in military aid to El Salvador, representing half the president's original request. Congress made this funding contingent on the administration certifying that El Salvador was making progress on human rights. Biannually the administration did so, sending **Elliot Abrams** or another top official to report that, in fact, progress was being made. Quite often human rights groups challenged these reports, but Congress continued to provide the funds.

In May 1984, Jose Napoleon Duarte defeated Roberto d'Aubuisson in national elections in El Salvador. As a moderate, Duarte enjoyed the support of the Reagan administration. His election made it easier for Congress to provide funding in spite of growing concerns over the veracity of Abrams's reports. Indeed, two days after Duarte's election, the House of Representatives approved a large military and economic aid package for El Salvador (over $500 million).

In 1987, with fighting still dominating the region, Costa Rican President Oscar Arias Sánchez signed a pact with the presidents of Guatemala, Honduras, Nicaragua, and El Salvador calling for a cease-fire between all forces and an end to intervention by outside forces, including the United States. President Reagan termed the plan "fatally flawed," largely because it favored the Sandinistas over the contras in Nicaragua. However, Arias Sánchez won international support for his efforts. House Speaker **James (Jim) Claude Wright** applauded the plan as well. Peace, however, was delayed. Not until January 1, 1992, was a United Nations–sponsored agreement signed and implemented.

Unlike Reagan, George Bush took a more pragmatic and less visible approach to El Salvador and the region in general. For instance, whereas Reagan once called El Salvador the "last domino," Bush rarely spoke publicly about the area. The end of the cold war made the communist presence less threatening. Moreover, Bush was more accustomed to using the quiet channels of diplomacy than Reagan.

Suggested Readings: Kenneth M. Coleman and George Herring, eds., *Understanding the Central American Crisis* (1991); Walter LaFeber, *Inevitable Revolutions* (1993); Sue Montgomery, *Revolution in El Salvador* (1990).

Related Entries: Communism, Collapse of; House of Representatives, United States; Latin America; Senate, United States.

ENDERS, THOMAS OSTROM. (November 28, 1931, Hartford, Conn.– .) Assistant Secretary of State, Inter-American Affairs, 1981–1983; U.S. Ambassador to Spain, 1983–1986.

Central America was one of the primary foci of the Reagan administration's foreign policy during the early 1980s. Secretary of State **Alexander Meigs Haig, Jr.,** promoted a hard-line approach, providing aid to the anticommunist government of **El Salvador** and placing sanctions on the Marxist Sandinista government of **Nicaragua.** At the center of this policy was Thomas Enders, a lifelong diplomat. Enders, however, did not always share the administration's hard-line views. He criticized the human rights records of right-wing military officials in El Salvador and took a more temperate view of the Sandinistas than Secretary of State Haig or President Reagan. As a result, in 1983 he was replaced as assistant secretary of state for inter-American affairs. He was, however, appointed to be ambassador to Spain, a position he held through 1986.

Enders received his B.A. from Yale in 1953 and then attended the University of Paris and Harvard (M.A., 1957). He held several high-level positions within the State Department in the late 1960s and 1970s, including assistant secretary of state for economic and business affairs

(1974–1976), U.S. ambassador to Canada (1976–1979), and U.S. ambassador to the European Communities (1979–1981).

He is married to Gaetana Marchegiano. They have four children.

Suggested Reading: *Dictionary of American Diplomatic History* (1989) p. 175.

ENVIRONMENT. The Reagan and Bush administrations' records on the environment were mixed. President Reagan ran for office pledging to cut back on the government regulation of business, including environmental restrictions enacted by Congress during the 1970s. **James Gaius Watt,** Reagan's first secretary of the interior, quickly implemented this policy. With the president's approval, Watt opened up the Pacific coast to oil companies for exploration and drilling, loosened restrictions on the use of wilderness areas to the benefit of mine and timber companies, and voiced the administration's opposition to further environmental regulations. In 1983, when public outcry against Watt mounted, he resigned. Reagan replaced him with **William Patrick Clark,** one of his oldest political associates. Even though Clark sparked less controversy, the administration's environmental policies remained generally unchanged. The same can be said for the tenure of **Donald Paul Hodel,** who took Clark's place in 1985.

During Reagan's second term, Congress pressured the president to become a bit more active on the environmental front. In 1986, House and Senate conferees worked out differences between bills to extend the Superfund hazardous-waste cleanup program, a special project aimed at making safe several especially polluted sites. After legislators convinced him that they would override his veto, President Reagan reluctantly signed the bill into law on October 17, 1986. In the same year, however, Reagan pocket-vetoed an $18 billion reauthorization of the Clean Water Act, claiming it was too expensive. In response, in early 1987 the new Congress repassed virtually the same bill and dramatically overrode his veto. (The final vote on the Water Quality Control Act was 401–26 in the House of Representatives and 86–14 in the Senate.)

Part of George Bush's 1988 campaign pledge to create a "kinder and gentler" America included promises to strike a more even balance between the environment and business than had Reagan. While Bush was president, Congress passed the **Clean Air Act of 1990** and he signed it into law. Even if the bill included many compromises, it represented one of the most far-reaching environmental measures ever enacted and required reduced emissions from automobiles, power plants, and other industries. Nonetheless, by the end of President Bush's term, he, too, was caught in a fierce battle with environmentalists, who argued that his administration was not enforcing various conservation laws. On the campaign trail, Bush often responded by arguing that overzealous environmentalists threatened economic recovery and the livelihood of numerous western communities. One specific controversy revolved around the spotted owl in the northwestern woods of the United States. Bush's critics claimed that the owl was on the endangered species list, and thus had to be protected, according to government regulations, from encroachments by the forestry industry. President Bush challenged these claims and sought to portray the environmentalists as radicals who cared more about owls than they did about people. Bush also clashed with environmentalists when they pressured him to sign agreements to combat global warming and other worldwide environmental problems. Bush attended the "Earth Summit," a massive meeting of 160 world leaders held in Rio de Janerio in June 1992, but he refused to commit the United States to binding agreements aimed at reducing emissions of carbon dioxide and other gasses.

Suggested Readings: Robert Shanley, *Presidential Influence and Environmental Policy* (1992); Brant C. Short, *Ronald Reagan and the Public Lands* (1989).

Related Entries: Acid Rain; Burford, Anne McGill (Gorsuch); Lavelle, Rita Marie.

ESPIONAGE. In the mid-1980s, several major spy or espionage rings were uncovered involving the trading of classified secrets by U.S. military or intelligence agents. One of the most notorious of these rings involved Jerry A. Whitworth, a former Navy communication specialist. On August 28, 1986, he was sentenced to 365 years in prison and fined $410,000 for providing secrets to the **Soviet Union** over a period of many years. Whitworth's conviction grew out of testimony that the spy ring's leader, John Walker, provided as part of a plea bargain arranged with federal prosecutors. In exchange for a confession, Walker received a sentence of life in prison. The sentence for his son, Michael, who was also implicated in the case, was reduced to twenty-five years. During Whitworth's trial, the director of naval intelligence stated that the information that had been provided to the Soviets was extremely significant and could give the USSR an advantage in case of war.

The arrest and conviction of Whitworth and Walker followed several other incidents involving intelligence operators that threw doubt on the internal security measures of the Central Intelligence Agency (CIA) and various other defense intelligence–gathering departments. In February 1986, Larry Wu-Tai Chin, a one-time analyst for the CIA, committed suicide after being convicted of spying for China for a quarter of a century. In September 1985, CIA veteran Edward Howard sought asylum in the Soviet Union after he learned that the Federal Bureau of Investigation (FBI) suspected him of spying for the Soviets. He was the first CIA agent to defect to the Soviet Union in the agency's history. Suspicion regarding Howard surfaced after Vitaly Yurchenko, a Soviet State Security Agency (KGB) agent, defected to the United States. (Yurchenko subsequently returned to the Soviet Union, leading some to wonder if he had planted false information.) Yurchenko also provided information that led to the conviction of Ronald Pelton, an employee with the National Security Agency.

Both the Defense Department and Central Intelligence Agency claimed that they had taken the necessary steps to prevent such breakdowns in internal security in the future. Navy officials stated that the cost of developing new cryptographic and communications material, which the Walker spy ring had rendered inoperable, was about $100 million. Clearly, the $410,000 fine that Whitworth had to pay on his conviction did not even make a dent in the cost of the new equipment. In addition, shortly after Whitworth's conviction, FBI Director **William H. Webster** became director of the CIA. Many people hoped he could help the agency regain its esteem and improve internal security.

Suggested Readings: John Barron, *Breaking the Ring* (1987); Howard Blum, *I Pledge Allegiance: The True Story of the Walkers* (1987); Pete Early, *Family of Spies* (1987).

EUROPEAN UNION. On November 1, 1993, the European Union (EU) was established when the Maastricht Treaty, which had been signed by twelve European nations—Belgium, Denmark, France, Germany, Great Britain, Greece, Ireland, Italy, Luxembourg, the Netherlands, Portugal, and Spain—went into effect. The EU superseded the European Community, which had originally been comprised of three organizations, the European Coal and Steel Community, the European Atomic Energy Community, and most important, the European Economic Community, best known as the Common Market. The founding of the EU represented the culmination of years of consolidation in Europe and was first envisioned by French and other thinkers prior to World War II. The economic power of the European Community helped prompt the United States to push for the **North American Free Trade Agreement (NAFTA)** and to negotiate economic agreements with other large economic blocks. (Common market countries worked toward eliminating all tariffs and other economic restrictions and toward a common currency.) In general, the United States supported the formation of the European Union.

Suggested Readings: Desmond Dinan, *Ever Closer Union?* (1994); Alex Roney, *The European Community Fact Book,* 3rd ed. (1993).

EXXON *VALDEZ*. In the early morning hours of March 24, 1989, the oil tanker Exxon *Valdez* struck Bligh Reef in Prince William Sound, Alaska, causing the largest oil spill ever in North American waters. The spill covered at least 900 square miles of shoreline in one of the world's largest wildlife areas.

The *Valdez,* which was enroute from Alaska to Long Beach, was captained by Joseph J. Hazelwood. Under his command, the ship had left the port of Valdez, Alaska at 9 P.M. on March 23. Shortly before midnight, Hazelwood requested and received permission to move the ship from the outbound to the inbound shipping lane because of reports that the former contained ice from the Columbia Glacier. About ten minutes later, Captain Hazelwood turned control of the ship over to the third mate, Gregory Cousins, and helmsman, Robert Kagen, neither of whom was licensed to pilot the ship through Prince William Sound. Before leaving the bridge, though, he ordered Cousins and Kagen to make a right turn back into the outbound lane when the ship reached a navigational point near Busby Island, which is three miles north of Bligh Reef. According to the ship's log, at 11:55 P.M., Hazelwood phoned Cousins to remind him to begin to turn, but Cousins did not carry through with this command for another seven minutes. At 12:04 A.M. on the 24th, the *Valdez* ran aground. Hazelwood quickly returned to the bridge to stabilize the ship, so as not to capsize and spill more oil. By then, however, eight of the *Valdez*'s thirteen tanks had already been damaged.

To make matters worse, the initial response to the accident was insufficient. The Alyeska Pipeline Service Company, which was responsible for oil spills in the area, took fourteen hours to arrive. The Exxon Corporation, which took full responsibility for the accident and ultimately spent over $2 billion on the cleanup effort, was slow to respond. As a result, the spill spread further and made the ultimate cleanup effort more difficult. On April 7, two weeks after the accident, President George Bush declared that "Exxon's efforts, standing alone, are not enough." Hence, he sent military troops to assist in the cleanup of the area.

Following the accident, Hazelwood, Cousins, and Kagen were relieved from their duties by the Exxon Corporation. Questions regarding Hazelwood's sobriety soon emerged, in part due to the fact that he had been arrested twice in the previous five years on drunk driving charges. However, charges against Hazelwood for reckless endangerment and operating a vessel while intoxicated were subsequently dropped. The Exxon Corporation, on the other hand, was fined over $1 billion for its actions, much of which was paid to local fishermen, whose livelihood suffered greatly due to the spill. The spill also led to the enactment of new legislation which mandated double hulls for all newly built large oil tankers. Procedures for cleanup efforts were tightened in the area as well.

Suggested Readings: Sharon Begley, "Smothering the Waters," *Newsweek,* April 10, 1989, p. 54; Andrea Dortman, "Alaska's Billion-Dollar Quandry," *Time,* September 28, 1992, p. 60; John Keeble, *Out of the Channel* (1991); Michael D. Lemonick, "The Two Alaska's," *Time,* April 17, 1989, p. 56.

Related Entry: Environment.

F

FALKLAND ISLANDS WAR. On April 2, 1982, Argentine troops invaded and seized control of the Falkland Islands, a longtime British colony in the South Atlantic Ocean off the coast of Argentina. Argentines hailed the invasion as the end to 150 years of British colonial rule and celebrated the return of what they termed part of their nation's territory. British Prime Minister Margaret Thatcher, however, denounced the attack, ordered British naval forces to the area, and froze all Argentine assets in Britain. She defended these actions by noting that the residents of the Falkland Islands, almost all of whom came from British ancestry, preferred to remain part of Great Britain.

The invasion initially put the Ronald Reagan administration in a quandary. The president was very close to Prime Minister Thatcher, and he did not want to offend an important ally. However, the administration also did not want to weaken its ties to the Argentine military government of President Leopoldo Galtieri. As a result, Secretary of State **Alexander Meigs Haig, Jr.,** flew back and forth between the capitals of both nations, seeking to arrive at some sort of diplomatic solution. However, neither side expressed satisfaction with the United States' balanced approach, and Britain insisted that it would protect its citizens with force if necessary.

On April 30, after it had become clear that his diplomatic efforts would lead nowhere, Haig announced that the United States would support Great Britain. The Reagan administration accused Argentina of illegal aggressive actions, suspended arms exports to that nation, and signaled that it would not interfere with British military maneuvers. When war broke out between Great Britain and Argentina, the United States did not intervene. It did not object to the torpedoing of an Argentine cruiser, the *General Belgrano* (which killed 320), nor to the retaking of the island, which began on May 21 and ended with the surrender of Argentine forces on June 14.

In order to help repair its relations with Argentina, in November 1982 the United States supported a resolution submitted to the United Nations that called for Britain to negotiate an end to the dispute over the Falkland Islands. Britain, which opposed this resolution, largely shrugged it off, and President Reagan and Prime Minister Thatcher maintained their very close ties in spite of it.

Suggested Readings: Paul Eddy, *War in the Falklands* (1982); Max Hastings, *The Battle for the Falklands* (1983); R. Reginald, *Tempest in the Teapot: The Falkland Islands War* (1983).

Related Entries: Latin America; Thatcher (Roberts), Margaret Hilda.

FALWELL, JERRY. (August 11, 1933, Lynchburg, Va.– .) Founder and head, Moral Majority.

In 1979, Jerry Falwell founded the **Moral Majority,** one of the best-known and most powerful conservative political organizations in the country. Under his leadership, the Moral Majority prodded the Republican Party to oppose **abortion** and the Equal Rights Amendment and to pursue other conservative goals.

Falwell's father, a successful small businessman, died of alcoholism when Jerry was just fifteen years old. As a student, Falwell excelled both in the classroom and on the athletic field. He skipped second grade and earned a 98.6 percent grade point average at Brookville High School. However, Falwell also had a reputation for rowdiness and was barred from presenting the school's valedictorian address because of his participation in a scheme to use counterfeit lunch tickets. In 1950, Falwell enrolled in Lynchburg College, expecting to major in mechanical engineering. He earned the B. F. Goodrich citation for his performance in math during his freshman year. In his sophomore year he became a born-again Christian and transferred to the Baptist Bible College in Springfield, Missouri.

Falwell's commitment to a religious life was influenced by the preaching of Charles E. Fuller, a trailblazer in radio evangelism, to whose program he regularly listened as a youth. His final conversion was prompted by a service that he heard Reverend Paul Donnelson deliver at the Park Avenue Baptist Church on January 20, 1952. As Falwell put it, "[I] surrendered my life to God.'' Falwell became active in the youth department of the church, taught Sunday school, and graduated with a Th.G. from Baptist Bible in 1956.

The same year he established the Thomas Road Baptist church, a small, independent congregation, in Lynchburg. A half-year later he presented his first religious service over the television, the ''Old Time Gospel Hour.'' Falwell's congregation and television viewership grew rapidly. Falwell also opened Lynchburg (now Liberty) Baptist College. During this part of his career, Falwell opposed intermingling religion with politics. His 1965 sermon, ''Ministers and Marches,'' which was aimed at the **civil rights** movement, emphasized that ministers were ''nowhere commissioned to reform the externals.'' However, in the late 1970s, Falwell dramatically changed his views in this regard and began to stridently discuss a variety of controversial political issues, from homosexuality and abortion to pornography and women's liberation. The basis of his political views lay in his fundamentalist interpretation of the Bible. Even before he founded the Moral Majority, in 1979, he cooperated with Anita Bryant in a campaign to defeat the Equal Rights Amendment (ERA) and gay rights ordinances.

Falwell's influence waned in the latter part of the 1980s, particularly after a scandal hit the Praise the Lord (PTL), a religious organization headed by Jim Bakker, with which Falwell was associated.

Falwell was married in 1958 to Macel Pate. They have three children.

Suggested Readings: Jerry Falwell, *Listen America* (1980); Frances Fitzgerald, ''Reporter at Large,'' *New Yorker* 57 (May 18, 1981): 53; M. Murphy, ''Next Billy Graham?'' *Esquire* 90 (October 10, 1978): 25; Jerry Strober and Ruth Tomczak, *Jerry Falwell: Aflame for God* (1979).

FAMILY VALUES. During the Ronald Reagan–George Bush years, and especially during the 1992 campaign, Republicans sought to gain support by presenting their party as a proponent of family values while at the same time painting the Democratic Party as antifamily. Among the issues that Republicans included under the rubric of family values were **abortion** and gay rights, which they opposed, and school prayer, which they favored. To a large degree, the term *family values* came to stand for a broad critique of years of domestic policies supported by the Democratic Party, from the welfare programs of the Great Society, which Republicans argued undermined the family by encouraging women to have children out of wedlock, to decisions by the Earl Warren and **Warren Earl Burger** Courts, which diminished the reach of the church.

Among the best known speeches on family values was one delivered in the wake of the **Los Angeles riot** by Vice President **Danforth (Dan) James Quayle.** It was known as the "Murphy Brown" speech because in it, Quayle criticized an episode on the popular television series in which the lead character, Murphy Brown, a single woman, decides to have a child. Quayle used this episode to highlight the conservative argument that the nation had experienced a revolution in cultural values, which was supported by the mass media and intellectual elite, groups that, Quayle contended, made such a decision acceptable. By doing so, Quayle and others argued, the elite legitimized both immoral and counterproductive behavior.

Many liberals counterattacked Quayle's "Murphy Brown" speech, arguing that he misrepresented the issue of the show—Murphy Brown made the decision after painful thought about its pros and cons—and, more important, they argued that he sought to divert attention away from the real problems that beset America, which were economic. He blamed the victims of the Los Angeles riot for their problems through his focus on family values, rather than admitting the shortcomings of the economic policies of the Reagan and Bush years, particularly in terms of addressing the problems of the underclass. Others saw the speech as symbolic of the hypocrisy of the Republican Party's use of the term, *family values.* While they preached family values, critics pointed out, many well-known Republican leaders often practiced the opposite. President Reagan's problems with his children were infamous. Quayle harangued others about the need to get back to the basics, yet as a youth he had not taken school very seriously.

Even some conservatives felt that the Republican Party went too far during the 1992 convention. Rather than winning votes, the party's focus on issues of family values backfired. It alienated swing voters who, while they sought to prod individuals to act responsibly, disliked being dictated to by the extreme right. This said, by 1992 it was clear that conservatives had managed to redirect the debate over American culture. Whereas in the 1960s and through much of the 1970s, the momentum rested with those who favored the creation of a counterculture or some variant of traditional culture, by the early 1990s, talk of the counterculture was relegated to the realm of nostalgia and supporters of abortion, greater rights for women, and the like, had been placed on the defensive.

Suggested Readings: David Blankenhorn, Steve Bayne, and Jean Elshtorn, *Rebuilding the Nest: A New Commitment to the American Family* (1990); Kurt

President Reagan bids farewell on his last day in office, January 20, 1989. Reagan Library.

Finsterbusch and George McKenna, eds., *Taking Sides: Views on Controversial Social Issues* (1992); Ellen Goodman, *Value Judgments* (1993).

Related Entries: Election of 1992; Falwell, Jerry; Moral Majority; New Right; Politically Correct; Supreme Court.

FAREWELL ADDRESS (RONALD REAGAN). On January 11, 1989, President Ronald Reagan delivered his last televised address from the

Oval Office of the White House. At the time, public opinion polls showed that he enjoyed the highest popularity rating of any president since pollsters started taking the pulse of Americans in the 1930s. In his farewell address, Reagan focused on what he termed his "two great triumphs," the nation's "economic recovery" and its "recovery of morale." Much of his speech reiterated his basic or core philosophy, expounding on the beliefs that he had been describing for over two decades: the need to free people from the burdens of government taxation and regulation and the importance of gaining peace through a strong defense.

As with other farewell addresses, Reagan added a word of caution. While he reveled in the "resurgence of national pride" or "new patriotism," Reagan warned "it won't last unless it's grounded in thoughtfulness and knowledge." He emphasized the importance of teaching the youth of America their history, particularly the story of "what's important," such as why the Pilgrims came to the country. "We've got to do a better job of getting across that America is freedom—freedom of speech, freedom of religion, freedom of enterprise. And freedom is special and rare." Characteristic of his presidency and his speeches in general, Reagan concluded on an upbeat note, referring to the famous Puritan leader John Winthrop's statement that America represented a "shining city upon a hill." "I've spoken of the shining city all my political life," Reagan declared, "but I don't know if I ever quite communicated what I saw when I said it. . . . In my mind," he continued, "it was a tall proud city built on rocks stronger than oceans, wind-swept, God-blessed, and teeming with people of all kinds living in harmony and peace, a city with free ports that hummed with commerce and creativity, and if there had to be city walls, the walls had doors and the doors were open to anyone with the will and the heart to get there. That's how I saw it, and see it still." Reagan threw in some self-congratulatory remarks in his final lines: "We made a difference. We made the city stronger. We made the city freer, and we left her in good hands. All in all, not bad, not bad at all."

The speech was vintage Reagan; it displayed why many had called him **the Great Communicator.** It was upbeat, had a personal touch, was peppered with illustrative anecdotes, and was relatively simple in its theme. Even its warning paled in comparison to the much more somber words of advice offered by other presidents in their farewell addresses, such as Dwight Eisenhower's statements regarding the potential dangers of the military-industrial complex or George Washington's counsel against factionalism. Eleven days later, following another brief personal farewell address to his aides, Ronald Reagan left office. He was the first president to be elected and to serve out two terms since Dwight Eisenhower.

Suggested Readings: *Historic Documents* (1989) p. 15; Kathleen Hall Jamieson, *Packaging the Presidency* (1992); Kurt Ritter, *Ronald Reagan: The Great Communicator* (1992).

FARMERS. Particularly during the mid-1980s, the plight of the American farmers became headline news in the United States. In 1985 the American Agriculture Movement and other farm groups staged a mass march on Washington, D.C., demanding aid to help them pay off their debts, higher food prices, and subsidies. In the same year, Country Western singer Willie Nelson and others organized Farm Aid, a benefit concert held in Champaign, Illinois. It raised over $10 million to help American farmers.

What these events suggested about the political sentiments of American farmers is difficult to determine. During the Washington protest, many criticized the Ronald Reagan administration's policies, which aimed at decreasing the role of the federal government in farming and increasing the power of the market. However, in 1980, 1984, and 1988, Reagan and George Bush won solid victories in farm states and scored well in rural areas of other regions of the United States. This suggested that even if farmers found problems with the Reagan administration's agricultural policies, they liked Reagan personally and supported the Republican Party's broader political agenda.

Until the twentieth century, farmers constituted the bulk of the American population. By 1980, however, those who earned a living by farming had fallen to less than 5 percent of the population. Whereas there were over 6.5 million farms in 1930, by 1982 there were only about 2 million. Long-term trends as well as macroeconomic forces hurt many farmers in the 1980s, particularly family farmers. Farmers needed to spend more on expensive machinery and technology. They faced increased foreign and domestic competition. The tight money policy pursued by the federal government in the early 1980s added to their debt load. In 1985, farm debt stood at about $210 billion, up 27 percent since 1980. At the same time, many farmers suffered from a declining value of their assets, as land prices in the Midwest declined. This made it even harder to obtain loans.

Despite their declining numbers, farmers remained very important in the United States. Agriculture constituted a significant part of the economy. The farmers enjoyed political power disproportionate to their numbers, due to the fact that the Senate provides equal representation to rural states, as it does to urban ones. In addition, the farmers enjoyed a particular cultural allure. Perhaps because of their political and cultural power, the Reagan administration did not end price subsidies and other farm programs during the 1980s. Put another way, in spite of his conservative free-market agenda, Reagan did not push hard for removing all government intervention in the farm economy. Nor did President Bush make a strong effort. Not surprisingly, the Department of Agriculture remained one of the largest segments of the federal government.

At the same time, American farmers continued to prove very adaptive, growing new crops, introducing new methods for processing food, and finding new markets abroad as well as at home. Needless to say, on the whole the American people remained very well fed, enjoying a varied and relatively cheap supply of food.

Suggested Readings: Philip Cagan, ed., *The Impact of the Reagan Program* (1986); William Galston, *A Tough Row to Hoe: The 1985 Farm Bill and Beyond* (1985).

Related Entries: Block, John Rusling; Domestic Policy; Economy, U.S.; Election of 1980; Election of 1984; Election of 1988.

FEDERAL BUDGET DEFICIT. See **BUDGET DEFICIT.**

FEDERAL RESERVE BOARD. During the Ronald Reagan–George Bush years, the Federal Reserve Board (popularly known as the Fed) was headed by two monetary conservatives, **Paul Volcker,** who was nominated by **James (Jimmy) Earl Carter** and renominated by President Reagan, and **Alan Greenspan.** Volcker pursued a tight monetary policy, aimed at breaking the back of **inflation.** Greenspan largely followed Volcker's lead until after the recession of the early 1990s had begun.

When President Reagan began his term, inflation stood upward of 10 percent and was considered by many to be the most significant threat to the **U.S. economy.** Not only did high inflation signify higher prices, it discouraged savings and investment, thus threatening long-term economic growth. The Federal Reserve Board, under the lead of Paul Volcker, had already begun to combat this inflation by tightening the money supply. It did so, in part, by rapidly raising the federal discount rate, the interest rate at which it loaned money to commercial banks. Seeing inflation as a threat to his economic program, President Reagan encouraged the Federal Reserve Board to maintain its tight money policy, and the board complied. Hence, whereas the discount rate stood at 6.83

Table 11
Interest Rates (Selected Years)

Year	3-month Rate, Treasury Bills	AAA Corp. Bonds	New Home Mortgages	Fed Discount
1977	5.26	8.02	9.02	5.46
1980	11.50	11.94	12.66	11.77
1981	14.03	14.17	14.70	13.42
1982	10.69	13.79	15.14	11.02
1984	9.58	12.71	12.38	8.80
1986	5.98	9.02	10.17	6.33
1988	6.69	9.71	9.19	6.20
1990	7.51	9.32	10.05	6.98
1992	3.45	8.14	8.24	3.25

percent in 1977, it peaked at 11.02 percent in 1982 and stood higher than the 1977 rate for all but four of the Reagan-Bush years.

Since the interest rates of various securities, from Treasury bills to corporate bonds, tend to parallel the discount rate, this meant that the returns (not adjusted for inflation) on these investments reached all-time highs during the early 1980s (Table 11). However, at the same time, since lenders had to borrow at a higher price, mortgage, credit card, and other commercial loan rates skyrocketed. For individuals who had money to invest but few expenditures or debts, this could be a blessing. For others, however, it was not. Regardless of the impact on different groups, the Federal Reserve Board felt that a tight monetary policy was the necessary prescription for killing high inflation. Most economists agree that the medicine worked, as inflation dropped dramatically.

Suggested Readings: William Greider, *Secrets of the Temple: How the Federal Reserve Board Runs the Country* (1987); Richard Sylla, *A History of Interest Rates*, 3rd ed. (1991); Paul Volcker and Toyoo Gyohten, *Changing Fortunes: The World's Money and the Threat to American Leadership* (1991).

Related Entry: Recessions.

FELDSTEIN, MARTIN (STUART). (November 25, 1939, New York, N.Y.–) Chairman of the Council of Economic Advisers, 1982–1984.

In August 1982, President Ronald Reagan nominated Martin Feldstein, a prominent conservative economist from Harvard University, to head the

Council of Economic Advisers. When Reagan was elected he had asked Feldstein to accept this post, but Feldstein had turned down Reagan's offer. In 1982, however, with the economic situation deteriorating, Reagan's first chair of the Council of Economic Advisers, **Murray Lew Weidenbaum,** resigned. Reagan again asked Feldstein to serve as his chief economic adviser. This time Feldstein accepted the offer and the Senate confirmed his nomination.

Feldstein grew up in Manhattan and Long Island, New York. He earned his B.A. in economics from Harvard in 1961, attended Oxford University on a Fulbright scholarship, and then stayed on to complete his graduate studies in economics, earning an M.A. (1965) and Ph.D. (1967). After completing his doctorate, he accepted a post as an assistant professor of economics at Harvard, rising to the rank of full professor within two years. At the time, Feldstein was a Keynesian, a member of the liberal school of economics that favored government intervention in the economy to ensure steady growth. In the late 1960s he began to change his views, however, breaking with the Keynesian school on a number of major points.

In the mid-1970s Feldstein sparked controversy by criticizing social security, one of the cornerstones of liberal economic policies for over thirty years. He blamed Keynesian theories for high **inflation** and slow growth and favored tight monetary policies, tax reforms, and reduced government regulation as the cure to the nation's economic troubles. These ideas, of course, dovetailed with those of President Reagan. However, Feldstein was not a doctrinaire conservative. He supported national catastrophic health insurance and expressed doubts about **Reaganomics,** particularly the ability to cut taxes, increase **defense spending,** and balance the federal budget at the same time.

In 1977 Feldstein became the president of the National Bureau of Economic Research, an economic think tank that sought to affect public policy. Along with **David Alan Stockman,** Feldstein opposed speeding up tax cuts or establishing public works programs since he saw both as threatening to increase the **budget deficit.** He further sided with Stockman by resisting the rosy economic forecasts put forth by more doctrinaire supply-siders. At times, Feldstein's economic forecasts contrasted sharply with those of Secretary of Treasury **Donald Regan.** However, when the economy began to recover in 1983, and even more so in 1984, divisions between the two diminished. In 1984 Feldstein returned to academia, later becoming the governor of the American Stock Exchange (1991–1994).

Feldstein is married to Kathleen Foley Feldstein. They have two children.

Suggested Readings: *Current Biography* (1983) p. 133; Ann Reilly, "Feldstein Talks Back," *Fortune,* August 6, 1984, p. 100; Lawrence Seidman, "A Third Way for Feldstein," *Challenge,* September–October 1983, p. 44.

FERRARO, GERALDINE ANNE. (August 26, 1935, New York, N.Y.– .) Democratic vice presidential nominee, 1984.

In 1984 the Democratic presidential candidate, **Walter Frederick Mondale,** nominated Geraldine Ferraro, a three-term congresswoman from Queens, New York, to be his running mate. This made her the first woman to be nominated by a major political party for the vice presidency in the history of the United States. Her nomination quickly became one of the focal points of the campaign, due both to its uniqueness and to the attention paid to the possible criminal activities of her husband, John Zaccaro.

Ferraro is the daughter of Dominick and Antonetta (Corrieri) Ferraro. Her father, a first-generation immigrant, owned a successful deli and dime store, which afforded her a pampered existence as a child. However, her father's death in 1943 dramatically changed her life, as her family was forced to move to a number of much more humble abodes in the Bronx and Queens, New York. With the help of a scholarship, she enrolled at Marymount College in New York City, graduating in 1956 with a B.A. in English. For four years she taught in the New York City public schools by day while going to law school at night. In 1960 she graduated from Fordham Law School and married John Zaccaro. For the next fourteen years she raised three children while working part-time as a lawyer, primarily for her husband's real estate business. She also became an active member of the local Democratic club. In 1974 she was hired as an assistant district attorney (DA) in Queens, handling child abuse, domestic violence, rape, and other cases. In 1978 she resigned from the DA's office to run for a seat in Congress that had been vacated by James J. Delaney. She was successful in her first attempt.

As a member of the House of Representatives, Ferraro earned the backing of House Speaker **Thomas (Tip) Philip O'Neill, Jr.,** gained the reputation as a team player, represented the views of her constituents on matters of economic concern, and became known as a strong advocate of **women's rights,** from equal pay to **abortion.** Her stance on abortion put her at odds with many Catholics in her home district. Nevertheless, she easily won reelection in 1980 and 1982. In 1984 she was appointed chairwoman of the Democratic platform committee, a position that gained her national prominence and ultimately led to Mondale's decision to nominate her as his running mate.

Ferraro's impact on the final vote remains unclear. Perhaps more women and Italian-Americans voted for Mondale because she was on the ticket, but questions regarding her qualifications and her husband's business dealings may have lost Mondale votes. Without a doubt, the highlight of her campaign came during a debate with Vice President George Bush, in which she made a very impressive showing. While the Democratic Party ticket suffered a devastating defeat, most political pundits agreed that Ferraro's nomination further opened the way for women to run for political office.

Suggested Readings: *Current Biography* (1984) p. 118; Geraldine Ferraro, *My Story* (1985); Geraldine Ferraro, *Changing History* (1993).

Related Entries: Election of 1984; House of Representatives, United States.

FITZWATER, MARLIN (MAX). (November 24, 1942, Salines, Kans.– .) Press Secretary to President Ronald Reagan, 1987–1989; Counsel and Press Secretary to President George Bush, 1989–1993.

In 1987 Marlin Fitzwater took over for **Larry Speakes** as President Ronald Reagan's principal press secretary. When George Bush became president, Fitzwater maintained this post. He was generally respected by the press for his professionalism, although critics claimed that he did a poor job of communicating Bush's message during the 1992 campaign.

Fitzwater was born in a small farming community. He attended Kansas State University, while working as an editor for the Lindburg *News Record,* a small-town weekly, and as a free-lance reporter for the larger Topeka *Capital-Journal.* After graduating in 1965, he turned down a post with the *Wall Street Journal* to work instead as an assistant in the public affairs department of the Appalachian Regional Commission, part of President Lyndon Johnson's War on Poverty. After serving for two years in the United States Air Force, Fitzwater returned to Washington, D.C., where he worked for various government agencies, including the Department of Transportation and the Environmental Protection Agency.

In 1981 Fitzwater landed his first political post, becoming the deputy spokesman for the Treasury department. There he worked under **Donald Regan.** In 1983, Fitzwater took a cut in pay to work in the White House as deputy press secretary for domestic affairs. In spring 1985 Fitzwater became Vice President George Bush's press secretary. He quickly established a close relationship with Bush, which lasted through the presidency. When Reagan's press secretary, Larry Speakes, left Washington in 1987, Fitzwater took his place. Coming in the midst of the **Iran-contra affair,** it was not an enviable time to do so. Ironically, Fitzwater was backed for the job by his former boss, Donald Regan, who was subsequently fired as the President's chief of staff. By taking Speakes's job, Fitzwater gave up a chance to play a leading role in Bush's 1988 campaign. Nonetheless, he was the obvious choice for press secretary when Bush assumed the presidency.

Fitzwater is divorced. He has two children.

Suggested Readings: Paul Chin, "Marlin Fitzwater," *Broadcasting,* January 30, 1989, p. 95; *Current Biography* (1988) p. 163.

FOLEY, THOMAS STEPHEN. (March 6, 1929, Spokane, Wash.– .) Speaker, U.S. House of Representatives, 1989–1995; Member, U.S. House of Representatives, 1964–1995.

In June 1989, upon the resignation of **James (Jim) Claude Wright** of Texas amidst allegations that Wright had abused his office as speaker of the House, Thomas Foley ascended to the top spot in the House of Representatives. Foley became speaker at a difficult time. Public confidence in Congress had dropped following a series of scandals. Growing disapproval with the federal government and Bush's victory over **Michael Stanley Dukakis** added to the Democrats' declining morale. In contrast to the feisty Wright, Foley sought to rebuild the Democratic Party's strength by adapting a conciliatory approach. This dovetailed with his reputation as a soft-spoken, honest, and collegial representative.

While relations between Foley and Bush were at times cantankerous, he helped win support from Democrats and the president for several reforms, most notably the Civil Rights Act of 1990 and a stricter version of the original Clean Air Act. Even though he opposed escalating the **Persian Gulf War,** he ultimately supported American intervention once the fighting began. Foley also played a leading role in putting together the budget package and tax hike of 1990, which Bush signed. This said, as the 1992 election approached, **gridlock** seemed to predominate in Washington, D.C. Democrats in the House enacted bills, Bush vetoed them, and Congress proved unable to override them in almost all cases. This added to the public's disillusionment with the federal government. Even after **William (Bill) Jefferson Clinton** became president, Foley had a tough time rallying Democrats in the House behind several of their party president's key programs. To make matters worse, Foley gained the animus of voters back home for his opposition to a Washington State term limit law.

Foley represented the Fifth Congressional District of the state of Washington for twenty-five years. In the late 1970s and early 1980s, he beat back several stiff challenges from Republicans who sought to paint him as an arch-liberal who was out of touch with his constituents. In the mid-1980s he widened his margin of victory back home and moved up the political ladder in Washington, D.C. In the November 1994 election he was defeated by his Republican challenger, making him one of few standing speakers to fail to be reelected in U.S. history.

Foley is married to the former Heather Strachan, who has worked as his administrative assistant and adviser since their marriage in 1968.

Suggested Readings: *Current Biography* (1989) p. 177; Thomas Egan, "The No. 1 Congressman," *New York Times Biographical Service,* October 1994, p. 1684; Mike Mills, "Thomas Foley," *Congressional Quarterly Weekly Report,* June 10, 1989, p. 1379.

Related Entries: Civil Rights; Clean Air Act of 1990; House of Representatives, United States.

FOREIGN AID. From the time of the Truman Doctrine until the end of the 1980s, the United States provided military and economic aid to numerous nations around the world. Aid went to democratic allies, such as Israel, and to anticommunist dictatorships, such as the **Philippines.** Following the end of the war in Vietnam, a large number of Democrats opposed providing foreign aid to undemocratic regimes—such as **El Salvador.** Some conservative Republicans, most notably Senator **Jesse A. Helms,** had no problems sending aid to anticommunist dictatorships but argued against providing funds to "leftist-led" governments. In general, however, most foreign aid packages continued to make their way through Congress with relatively few changes.

In 1991 the measure to provide appropriations for foreign aid for fiscal year 1992 was temporarily blocked by a dispute over whether or not to provide Israel with loan guarantees. Israel sought the guarantees so that it could more easily absorb new emigrés from Russia, in part by building new settlements on the occupied western bank. Some in Congress and within the Bush administration saw this action as a threat to the peace process in the **Middle East** and, hence, held up the loan guarantees, which in turn, delayed the general foreign aid package.

At the same time, broader opposition to foreign aid was on the rise.

The recession weakened the public's support for spending American tax dollars to help foreign countries. The end of the cold war ended one of the prime reasons, if not the central cause, for providing aid in the first place. Paradoxically, proposals for foreign aid for parties that had not received funding in the past, most notably the **Soviet Union,** were simultaneously on the increase.

Probably the best-known opponent of foreign aid was **Patrick J. Buchanan,** a former aide to Presidents Richard Nixon and Ronald Reagan and a candidate for the Republican presidency in 1992. He campaigned on an "America First" platform that echoed the cries of isolationists of the pre–World War II era. Among his favorite targets was the United Nations (UN), whose peacekeeping forces had been deployed all over the globe. Buchanan and others noted that while these forces relied on American tax dollars, they were free from U.S. control. He also contended that UN forces were involved in regions of questionable importance to the United States.

While his criticism stung, it did not stop Bush from promoting a foreign aid appropriation measure. Bush favored keeping the United States involved in the world arena, and he combated efforts to cut foreign aid. In 1992 he requested $26 billion for foreign aid. Feeling the political pressure from isolationists, Congress heatedly debated his proposal. In the end it trimmed only $1 billion from his request. However, whether Congress would continue to support foreign aid in the future remained uncertain.

Suggested Readings: *Congressional Quarterly Almanac* (1992) p. 609; Michael J. Hogan, ed., *The End of the Cold War: Its Meanings and Implications* (1992).

Related Entries: Communism, Collapse of; Foreign Policy; Recessions.

FOREIGN POLICY. Ronald Reagan and George Bush's records on foreign policy represent the greatest paradox of their administrations. Critics noted that as a two-term governor of California without any national experience, Reagan lacked foreign policy expertise. Many moderates within the Republican Party feared that Reagan could never win a general election because of his lack of experience and extreme views on international affairs. The two biggest setbacks during Reagan's years in office were in the realm of foreign policy—the killing of marines by a terrorist car-bomb in Beirut, Lebanon, and the **Iran-contra affair.** In contrast, George Bush came to office with a plethora of foreign policy experience.

He had served as director of the Central Intelligence Agency, ambassador to the United Nations, and vice president before taking command. As president, his moments of greatest glory revolved around U.S. foreign policy triumphs, most notably the defeat of Iraq during the **Persian Gulf War.** Yet, in the final analysis, Reagan's greatest achievement came in the realm of foreign policy—namely, the signing of nuclear arms agreements with the **Soviet Union**—while Bush proved unable to deliver the so-called **new world order** that he promised in the wake of communism's collapse.

Especially early in his administration, Reagan tended to see the world in black-and-white terms. He portrayed the Soviet Union as an evil empire and pursued a policy, dubbed the **Reagan Doctrine,** bent on opposing communism worldwide, regardless of the virtues, or lack thereof, of any particular anticommunist ally. He viewed nearly all world problems through the lens of the cold war, blaming insurgencies in Central America and **Africa** on Soviet provocateurs rather than problems indigenous to these regions. The Reagan administration offered a fairly simple response to the global Soviet threat—increased militarization and arming of anti-communist rebels and regimes. Nearly every weapons system, from the controversial **MX (missile, experimental) missile** and **B-1 bomber** programs to the cruise missile and Trident II submarine, were justified on the grounds that they demonstrated the strength and will of the United States. Along the same lines, the Reagan administration supported selling sophisticated weaponry to nations whose fealty to the United States was suspect yet promised to contribute to the broader anticommunist campaign. Such was clearly the case with the decision to sell **Airborne Warning and Control Systems (AWACS)** to Saudi Arabia and arms to Pakistan. Furthermore, the style of the Reagan presidency promoted a revival of uncritical nationalism. He called for Americans to overcome the Vietnam syndrome, defined as a fear that all forms of intervention would result in another quagmire from which the United States could not disentagle itself, and to revitalize their sense of mission and exceptionalism.

While these views resulted in the largest military buildup during peacetime in U.S. history and support for several ineffective global adventures, most notably the Iran-contra affair, they ultimately did not inhibit the Reagan administration from adopting pragmatic measures that produced significant foreign policy achievements. Particularly after Secretary of State **George Pratt Shultz** established himself as a key player within the Reagan administration, the United States moved in a more moderate or centrist direction. This became apparent with the rise of **Mikhail Ser-**

geyevich Gorbachev to power within the Soviet Union. Shultz helped convince the president to meet with the new Soviet leader. (Reagan had not met with any of Gorbachev's predecessors.)

Whether Reagan's hard-line policy or Gorbachev's rise to power was the key to the successful negotiation of arms agreements and the ultimate end of the cold war will prove a subject of debate for years. Reagan's strongest supporters emphasize that his strident anticommunist policies produced this end, while others argue that internal developments within the Soviet Union mattered much more and that Reagan's policy may even have delayed the end of the cold war. Regardless of who is correct on this debate, by the time Reagan handed over the reins of power to Bush, he appeared to be a much more pragmatic and experienced and tempered leader than when he had come to office. Indeed, even the Iran-contra scandal and lingering unresolved conflicts in the **Middle East**—a region in which the Reagan administration enjoyed few triumphs—took away little from his major achievement of improving relations with the Soviet Union.

George Bush inherited the achievements and weaknesses of the Reagan administration's foreign policy. Overall, the Bush administration adopted a cautious policy toward the Soviet Union and the Eastern Bloc. It supported further arms agreements and encouraged the decline of communism in East Germany, Poland, Czechoslovakia, and ultimately, the Soviet Union itself. Whereas Reagan's foreign policy had at least originally been driven by ideology and aimed at achieving dramatic global changes, Bush openly pursued a more conservative, pragmatic, and nonideological course. In contrast to the Reagan administration, which had backed controversial anticommunist policies in Central America, the Bush administration lent support for the Arias peace plan, which aimed to end the armed conflict between leftists and right-wing regimes and rebels.

The one exception to this rule came in the Middle East. At first the Bush administration pursued a centrist course there. Some even argue that the State Department encouraged Iraqi leader Saddam Hussein to invade Kuwait by not sending him a stronger message as he amassed troops along the border and fired rhetorical salvos at the world community. Once Iraqi troops crossed into Kuwait, Bush adopted a hard-line stance. He quickly sent troops to the region to defend against a possible invasion of Saudi Arabia and notified Hussein that his troops must leave Kuwait. While Secretary of State **James (Jim) Addison Baker III** rounded up international support for the U.S. lead in the region, Bush directed the military to ready a plan for turning back the Iraqi invasion. In the face of potential congressional opposition to a military solution, Bush stood firm. On January 16, 1991, with congressional support, he ordered the aerial bombardment of Iraq. About five weeks later, ground troops drove Iraqi troops out of Kuwait, suffering remarkably few casualties. The Persian Gulf War even gave a boost to the Middle East peace process, as Baker shuttled between one Arab country after another in an effort to secure an elusive accord.

However, the military triumph in the Persian Gulf combined with the collapse of communism in Eastern Europe provided only a temporary political boost. More important, Bush and his administration's foreign policy produced few long-term foreign policy achievements. Americans expressed dissatisfaction with the fact that Saddam Hussein remained in power and even greater disapproval of the Bush administration's focus on foreign affairs, given the declining economy and growing problems at home. In spite of his fury of activity, Baker was unable to secure a peace accord between Israel and the Arabs. New conflicts erupted all over the globe, from **Bosnia and Herzegovina** (the former Yugoslavia) to **Haiti,** toward which Bush seemed to lack a coherent and clear policy. Liberals, for example, wondered why the president refused to intervene in Haiti given his decisive actions in the Persian Gulf.

Of course, much of America's ambivalence toward Bush's record was due more to changing historical circumstances than to the particulars of his foreign policy. For years Americans had expected that the end of the cold war would produce a "peace dividend," ushering in an era of economic prosperity and an end to American intervention abroad. When neither of these phenomena took place Bush received part of the blame.

At root of much of America's foreign policy malaise lay several problems that, even if they had not been created by the cold war, certainly had been promoted by it. As became apparent with Saddam Hussein's invasion of Kuwait, many nations maintained tremendous arsenals of weapons, which they had accumulated to a large degree because of the cold war rivalry between the Soviet Union and the United States. This reality promised to unleash an endless string of small-scale armed conflicts, from the shores of **Somalia** to the mountains of Bosnia and Herzegovina, all of which threatened to involve the United States. At the same time, the cold war had drained resources and distorted economic priorities. Japan and Germany, in particular, did not have to worry about downsizing their military establishments, while the businesses in the United States were burdened by high debts, accumulated in part by the huge defense buildup of the Reagan years.

In sum, in terms of foreign policy, the Reagan-Bush years did not result in a peaceful and prosperous new world order. This said, the end of the cold war meant that the average American citizen was more secure and that the nation had the opportunity to redirect its attention to developing new, peaceful technologies rather than new means of destruction.

Suggested Readings: Coral Bell, *The Reagan Paradox: American Foreign Policy in the 1980s* (1989); John Lewis Gaddis, *The United States and the End of the Cold War* (1992); Kenneth Oye, Robert J. Lieber and Donald Rothchild, eds., *Eagle Resurgent? The Reagan Era in American Foreign Policy* (1987).

Related Entries: Beirut, Lebanon (Bombing of U.S. Marine Barracks); Communism, Collapse of; Defense Spending; Economy, U.S.; El Salvador; Foreign Aid; Nicaragua.

FULLER, CRAIG L. (February 16, 1951, Pasadena, Calif.– .) Chief of Staff for Vice President George Bush, 1985–1989.

Craig Fuller served as Vice President George Bush's chief of staff from 1985 to 1989 and was one of his closest companions and most important advisers during the 1988 presidential campaign. When President Bush did not offer Fuller the post of chief of staff, appointing **John Henry Sununu** instead, Fuller returned to the private sector, as an executive with the Philip Morris Company.

Fuller grew up in California, earned a B.S. (1973) in political science from the University of California at Los Angeles and a master's degree in urban affairs (1974) from Occidental College. Active in politics, he went to work for President Ronald Reagan, as an assistant for cabinet affairs, in 1981. In 1985 he moved up to chief of staff for the vice president. While many political pundits commended his work, they also argued that Bush needed a stronger, more visible chief of staff, such as Sununu. Ironically, Sununu quickly became a target of much criticism and was one of the first Bush appointees to resign.

Suggested Readings: *New York Times,* February 17, 1985, p. 4; *New York Times,* November 18, 1988, p. 1.

G

GATES, ROBERT M. (September 25, 1943, Wichita, Kans.– .) Director of Central Intelligence Agency, 1991–1992.

In November 1991, Robert Gates became the youngest director of the Central Intelligence Agency (CIA) in its history. His appointment came at a time of turmoil and flux for the agency.

Gates grew up in Wichita, Kansas. He was a very good student and an Eagle Scout. He received his B.A. from the College of William and Mary and an M.A. in history from the University of Indiana. He then joined the Central Intelligence Agency, rising, step by step, through its ranks. At the same time he completed his Ph.D. in history at Georgetown University (1974). After graduating, Gates went to work for the National Security Council. He returned to the CIA in 1980.

When **William Joseph Casey** took over as the intelligence agency's director in 1981, he named Gates as his executive assistant. Gates simultaneously maintained his duties as national intelligence officer for the **Soviet Union.** In January 1982, Gates became deputy director for intelligence, making him responsible for the entire analytical division of the CIA. Throughout the early and mid-1980s, Gates remained a "hawk" on the Soviet Union, even claiming as late as 1987 that **Mikhail Sergeyevich Gorbachev**'s reforms were a ruse aimed at camouflaging the Soviet's traditional expansionist goals. A year later, Gates continued to caution against developing too close a relationship with Gorbachev. In June 1987, two months after Gates became deputy director of the CIA, William Casey underwent an operation for a brain tumor, making Gates the agency's acting director. The following January, on Casey's resignation, President Ronald Reagan nominated him to become the permanent director. His nomination, however, produced very stormy confirmation hearings. Several senators refused to accept Gates's declaration that he knew little about the **Iran-contra affair.** This criticism forced Reagan to withdraw Gates name for consideration for the top post. In spite of the rebuff, Gates remained deputy director of the CIA until December 1988, when he became the deputy national security adviser, under **Brent Scowcroft.**

Throughout the early years of the George Bush administration, Gates remained skeptical about the chances for real reform in the Soviet Union. In December 1991, President Bush nominated him to succeed **William H. Webster** as director of the CIA. Once again, Gates faced tough confirmation proceedings. Some midlevel CIA intelligence officers even testified that Gates had hampered the collection and dissemination of intelligence information, which contradicted Gates's hawkish views of the Soviet Union. Nonetheless, this time, Gates won confirmation.

Ironically, while director, Gates announced a major reorganization of the CIA. Accepting that communism had collapsed in the Soviet Union, he directed the agency to spend more time and resources on other issues, from the proliferation of nuclear weapons to the international drug trade. Gates also oversaw the downsizing of the CIA.

Gates and his wife, Rebecca, have two children.

Suggested Readings: *Current Biography* (1992) p. 219; Mark Perry, *Eclipse: The Last Days of the C.I.A.* (1992); *Time,* May 27, 1991, p. 46.

Related Entries: Communism, Collapse of; Foreign Policy.

GEPHARDT, RICHARD ANDREW. (January 31, 1941, St. Louis, Mo.– .) Congressman, 1979– ; Candidate for Democratic nomination for President, 1988.

Richard Gephardt was one of the early front runners for the Democratic nomination for the presidency in 1988. He sought organized labor's support and cast himself as a representative of middle America. However, following a successful showing in the Iowa caucus, Gephardt was outdueled in New England and the South by **Michael Stanley Dukakis** and **Jesse Louis Jackson,** putting an end to his campaign.

Gephardt received his B.S. in drama and speech from Northwestern University (1962) and a law degree from the University of Michigan (1965). Upon graduation, he returned to his hometown of St. Louis, Mo., and almost immediately turned his attention to politics. He became a leader in the local Democratic Party while at the same time working for Thompson & Mitchell, one of St. Louis's largest law firms. He also served as an officer with the National Guard. The retirement of Leonor Sullivan, Missouri's twenty-four-year veteran representative in Congress, in 1976, provided him with an opportunity that he seized. After winning the Democratic nomination, he soundly defeated his Republican opponent, Joseph L. Badaracco. He has represented the third congressional district of Missouri ever since.

Within the House of Representatives, Gephardt quickly moved up the political ladder, winning important committee appointments and Democratic Party positions. By 1984 he was chairman of the Democratic caucus, the fourth highest position; several years later he moved up to majority whip and then majority leader, making him the second-ranked Democrat in Congress. Politically, Gephardt has been difficult to pigeonhole. While he attained high rankings from the Americans for Democratic Action (ADA), a liberal organization, he also helped to establish the Democratic Leadership Council, which aimed at moving the party in a more centrist direction.

Gephardt is married to the former Jane Byrnes. They have three children.

Suggested Readings: Peter Bragdon, "Profile: Richard Gephardt," *Congressional Quarterly Weekly Report,* June 10, 1989, p. 1379; *Current Biography* (1987) p. 200; Mickey Kaus, "The Many Faces of Dick Gephardt," *Newsweek,* March 7, 1988, p. 46.

GERGEN, DAVID RICHMOND. (May 9, 1942, Durham, N.C.– .) Presidential adviser.

David Gergen surprised many Americans on May 30, 1993, when he accepted a post as communications director for President **William (Bill) Jefferson Clinton.** The move was surprising because Gergen had held a similar post for President Ronald Reagan and was considered by many to be one of the masterminds of the Republicans' success.

During the 1970s Gergen worked as a writer and as a director of communications, for Presidents Richard Nixon and Gerald Ford, respectively. He distinguished himself by playing a key role in the 1972 Republican nominating convention. He promoted the notion that conventions should be aimed at framing the party nominee's candidacy. Traditionally, they had lacked such coordination. Nixon followed this script; so, too, did Reagan in 1980 and 1984.

As President Reagan's communication adviser, Gergen's "100 days" memo, which alluded to Franklin D. Roosevelt's first 100 days in office, served as the game plan for selling Reagan's **domestic policy** to the public. As with Nixon's campaign, Gergen sought to coordinate everything from public appearances to speeches and announcements to the press.

Gergen received a B.A. from Yale (1963) and a law degree from Harvard (1967). He spent nearly four years in the navy before joining the Nixon administration as an assistant speechwriter in 1971. In 1983 he left the White House, going to work for *U.S. News & World Report* and serving as a commentator on national television. He is married to Anne Gergen. They have two children.

Suggested Readings: *New York Times,* May 30, 1993, p. 1; Maureen Orth, "Sultan of Spin," *Vanity Fair,* August, 1993, p. 100.

Related Entry: Great Communicator, The.

GINGRICH, NEWTON (NEWT) LEROY. (June 17, 1943, Harrisburg, Pa.– .) Member, House of Representatives, 1979– ; House Minority Whip, 1989–1993; Speaker of the House, 1993– .

Ever since he first entered Congress, in 1979, Newt Gingrich has distinguished himself through his brashness and unwillingness to play by the rules. As a member of the minority party in the House, from 1979 to 1994 Gingrich concentrated on winning Republican control of the body for the first time since the mid-1950s. Defying custom, he attacked senior members of the House. This included charging House Speaker **James (Jim) Claude Wright** with unethical conduct, which led to Wright's resignation.

Throughout his tenure, Gingrich has maintained a staunch conservative record. Along with other younger Republicans, Gingrich forced votes on controversial subjects, and he publicly attacked his fellow members in front of live television cameras. (In 1980, when the cable television channel C-Span began broadcasting House proceedings, Gingrich was one of the first to seek publicity via the broadcasts.) These actions earned Gingrich a mixed reputation, even within his own party. Some Republicans viewed him as arrogant and a loose cannon. In 1989 he had to overcome the opposition of Republican Minority leader Robert Michels to win post of minority whip. Many Democrats considered Gingrich more of a nuisance than a real threat.

However, following **William (Bill) Jefferson Clinton**'s election in 1992, Gingrich loomed a much larger player in Washington. He led the opposition to the Democratic president's policies and commandeered one of the most sweeping changes in history, the Republicans' midterm election success in 1994. Their stunning victory turned Democrats out of control of both houses of Congress and resulted in Gingrich's election as speaker of the House.

As the adopted son of a career army officer, Gingrich grew up all around the world. He earned a B.A. from Emory University (1965) and an M.A. (1968) and Ph.D (1971) from Tulane University. Although he later became one of the nation's most prominent conservatives, Gingrich accepted student deferments rather than face the draft. For six years he taught at West Georgia College. In 1974 he unsuccessfully ran for Congress, barely losing to the incumbent, Democrat John J. Flynn, Jr. (by 2,800 votes). Two years later he lost again to Flynn, but the third time was a charm for Gingrich and he defeated Virginia Sharp. (Flynn had retired.)

Gingrich has been married twice. He has two daughters.

Suggested Readings: *Current Biography* (1989) p. 256; *New Republic,* November 7, 1994, p. 32; Katherine Seelye, "Gingrich's Life," *New York Times Biographical Service,* November 1994, p. 1800.

GINSBURG, DOUGLAS HOWARD. (May 25, 1946, Chicago, Ill.– .) Supreme Court Nominee, 1987.

Following the U.S. Senate's rejection of the nomination of Judge **Robert Heron Bork** to the **Supreme Court,** President Ronald Reagan nominated Douglas H. Ginsburg to fill the post left vacant by the resignation of Justice Lewis Powell. Reagan's nomination of Ginsburg showed that the president did not intend to back away from his goal of shifting the Court in a more conservative direction. Like Bork, Ginsburg had a conservative reputation. However, the Senate showed that it too had no intention of allowing a conservative to win confirmation without opposition. Indeed, Reagan, himself, had been advised that it would be easier to win confirmation for one of the other possible candidates, Judge **Anthony McLeod Kennedy.** However, Reagan initially refused to nominate the more politically acceptable Kennedy in Bork's place.

Senate opponents to Ginsburg focused on several things. Some noted that he lacked experience—Ginsburg had been on the Appeals Court for less than a year. Others criticized his conservative philosophy. Ironically, Ginsburg's undoing came when he acknowledged that he had experimented with drugs while in law school, both as a student and professor. This lost him support among traditional conservatives and led him to withdraw his name from consideration less than a week after being nominated.

Ginsburg received a B.A. from Cornell University and a law degree from Harvard University. After serving as a clerk to Supreme Court Justice Thurgood Marshall, Ginsburg accepted a post at Harvard Law School, where he taught for ten years. He then accepted a series of posts within the Reagan administration, including head of the Antitrust Division of the Justice Department. In 1986 Reagan nominated him to the U.S. Court of Appeals, to which he won confirmation despite a lukewarm endorsement from the American Bar Association. Had he been confirmed, he would have been the youngest Supreme Court justice in over fifty years.

Suggested Readings: Brian Duffy, "Up in Smoke," *U.S. News & World Report,* November 10, 1987, p. 24; *New York Times,* October 30, 1987, pp. 1, 23; Stuart Taylor, "Youthful Conservative Judge," *New York Times Biographical Service,* October 1987, p. 1128.

GOETZ, BERNHARD (BERNIE) HUGO. (November 7, 1947, Queens, N.Y.– .) Criminal defendant; folk hero.

On December 22, 1984, Bernhard (Bernie) Goetz, a thirty-seven-year-old small businessman from New York City, shot four black teenagers who he alleged had been trying to mug him on the No. 2 IRT subway train in Manhattan. After the shooting, Goetz escaped down the underground tunnel. Nine days later he turned himself in to authorities in New Hampshire to face attempted murder and illegal weapons possession charges.

Nearly from the moment of the shooting, Goetz became a folk hero to many Americans, who viewed him as a symbol of the honest citizen terrorized by a growing criminal element. For instance, George Clark, head of the New York State Republican Committee, offered $5,000 to Goetz to help him defend himself against criminal charges, arguing that Goetz's response had been proper. Others portrayed him as a defender of civilization.

Still others, however, saw Goetz and his defenders as representative of the darker side of American society. Noting that all his alleged muggers were black, they argued that Goetz's appeal was fundamentally racist. They also emphasized that those who applauded the action encouraged further acts of vigilantism. Taking place in New York City, the Goetz incident and the lengthy trial that followed received an inordinate amount of media coverage.

A graduate from New York University, Goetz was the owner and sole employee of his own technical equipment business. Divorced, with no children, he lived alone in a one-bedroom apartment on 14th Street in

Manhattan. He headed a tenants' activist group that sought to clean up his neighborhood, but otherwise was a fairly anonymous individual. Two years before the shooting, Goetz had been mugged while waiting at a subway station. While one of the three muggers was arrested and subsequently convicted, the incident clearly traumatized him and convinced him to begin to carry a pistol. Goetz's critics argued that afterward, he went looking for trouble. They noted that he was not mugged on the subway in December 1984. Rather, they contended, he was looking for an excuse to shoot individuals who resembled those who had previously mugged him. Goetz's defenders emphasized that several of the alleged muggers had long criminal records and that Goetz rightfully felt threatened by them.

The Goetz case was significant because it represented many of the central themes of the Ronald Reagan–George Bush years, from rising crime to increasing tensions between blacks and whites. Views of Goetz largely split along political lines, with conservatives rallying to his cause and liberals criticizing him. More than three years after the incident, Goetz was acquitted on all but one of the weapons charges, a verdict that seemed to satisfy no one. Conservatives still considered him a hero, while liberals argued that he deserved a stiffer sentence.

Suggested Readings: *Facts on File* (1984); George Fletcher, *A Crime of Self Defense* (1988); *New York Times Biographical Service* (1988) 211:32.

Related Entry: Gun Control.

GORBACHEV, MIKHAIL SERGEYEVICH. (March 2, 1931, Privolnoye, Russia– .) Former President, the Soviet Union.

Along with Ronald Reagan, the most important world leader of the 1980s and early 1990s was Mikhail Gorbachev. His reform policies, along with his efforts to open up Eastern Europe and improve relations with the United States, helped produce historical **arms control** agreements between the United States and the **Soviet Union,** hastened the end of the cold war and the **collapse of communism** in Eastern Europe, and ultimately led to the fall of the Communist Party in the Soviet Union. Ironically, Gorbachev himself was overwhelmed by the forces he had helped unleash and lost power in 1991.

Gorbachev, who joined the Communist Party at the age of twenty-one, rose quickly through its ranks. Trained as a lawyer at Moscow State University, he became a leader in the regional party hierarchy in the Stavropol region of Russia before moving to Moscow as a protegee of

President Reagan and Soviet leader Mikhail Gorbachev at summit meeting in Geneva, Switzerland, November 18, 1985. Reagan Library.

Yuri Andropov in 1978. In 1980, Gorbachev became a full member of the Politburo. Two years later, when Yuri Andropov replaced Leonid Brezhnev as the Soviet leader, Gorbachev moved up to second in command. In 1984, when Andropov died, Gorbachev remained second in command during Konstantin U. Chernenko's brief rule. Then, on Chernenko's death in 1985, Gorbachev took over as general secretary of the Communist Party. Three years later, he augmented his power, becoming president of the Soviet Union.

While relations between the United States and the Soviet Union soured during Andropov and Chernenko's reigns, things changed rapidly when Gorbachev assumed power. Faced with a collapsing economy, a military defeat in **Afghanistan,** and a massive arms buildup by the United States, Gorbachev pushed for *perestroika*—the Russian term for *restructuring*—and *glasnost*—the Russian word for *openness*—with the West. He held a series of summits with Presidents Reagan and Bush and with other Western leaders and signed several arms agreements, including the **Intermediate-range Nuclear Forces (INF) Treaty** in 1987. When reformers in Eastern Bloc countries challenged their Communist Party rulers, unlike many of his predecessors, he did not send in Soviet troops or tanks to suppress their uprisings. In 1990, in recognition for his actions, he was awarded the Nobel Peace Prize.

By 1991, however, Gorbachev faced challenges from foes from the left and right. The left, at times represented by **Boris Nikolayevich Yeltsin,** felt that reform was preceding too slowly within the Soviet Union, while the right, often made up of hawks within the Communist Party, felt it was moving too fast. In August, members of the right-wing opposition staged a coup, which quickly failed, when reformers, led by Boris Yeltsin (supported by important members of the military), rallied to Gorbachev's defense. The coup leaders released Gorbachev, but afterward, Yeltsin, not Gorbachev, assumed power. Gorbachev resigned as general secretary of the Communist Party, and shortly afterward, the party itself disintegrated.

Gorbachev has continued to promote peace and to travel abroad. He is married to Raisa Maximova.

Suggested Readings: Thomas G. Butson, *Gorbachev* (1985); Dusko Doder, *Gorbachev* (1990); Neil Felshman, *Gorbachev, Yeltsin and the Last Days of the Soviet Empire* (1992).

Related Entries: Arms Control; Summits, with Soviet Union.

GORE, ALBERT, JR. (March 31, 1948, Washington, D.C.– .) U.S. Senator, 1984–1993; Vice President of the United States, 1993– .

Albert Gore, Jr., was born into politics. His father, Albert Gore, Sr., was a prominent congressman and senator from Tennessee. Gore followed, and ultimately transcended, his father's footsteps. Spending much of his youth in Washington, D.C., Gore attended and graduated from Harvard University in 1969. Even though he opposed the Vietnam War, he served in the U.S. Army for two years, from 1969 to 1971. Upon his return from Southeast Asia, he worked as a journalist for the *Tennessean,* a leading Nashville newspaper. At the same time he studied philosophy and earned his law degree from Vanderbilt University. Following graduation, in 1976 he ran for, and was elected to, the U.S. House of Representatives, a post he held for four terms. In 1984 he was elected to the U.S. Senate. He was reelected in 1990.

While in Congress, Gore earned a reputation as a moderate Democrat with a particular interest in **arms control** and the **environment.** In 1988 he ran unsuccessfully for the Democratic presidential nomination. Many predicted that he would run again in 1992, but he chose not to. When **William (Bill) Jefferson Clinton** asked him to be his running mate, Gore accepted. Gore and Clinton were the first all-southern Democratic ticket in memory, and one of the youngest in history. While he was initially criticized for his stiff style, Gore loosened up a bit during the campaign, especially while on a cross-country bus tour with Clinton and during a biting debate with Vice President **Danforth (Dan) James Quayle.**

Gore is married to Mary Elizabeth "Tipper" Gore. They have four children. He is the author of several books on the environment, including *Earth in the Balance: Ecology and the Human Spirit* (1992).

Suggested Readings: John Baden, ed., *Environmental Gore* (1994); *Current Biography* (1987) p. 211; Albert Gore, *Earth in the Balance: Ecology and the Human Spirit* (1992).

Related Entry: Election of 1992.

GRACE COMMISSION. In June 1982, President Ronald Reagan established the Grace Commission to investigate ways for the federal government to save money. Headed by J. Peter Grace, chief executive of W. R. Grace and Co. and made up of 161 business leaders, the privately financed commission issued its 650-page final report on January 16, 1984. It recommended 2,478 managerial and structural reforms, which, it claimed, would save the government $428 billion over a three-year period. Among the reforms the commission called for were providing the president with a line-item veto, which would allow him to cut funding for specific programs without vetoing the entire budget; means-testing social welfare benefits, including civil service and military pensions; repealing the Davis-Bacon Act, which required the federal government to pay prevailing wages rather than the lowest bid in its contracts; and privatizing numerous federal agencies.

A little over a month after the Grace Commission issued its report, the Congressional Budget Office (CBO) and General Accounting Office (GAO) issued their own reports, which cast doubt on the Grace Commission's findings. Whereas the Grace Commission claimed that its reforms would save the government over $400 billion, the CBO and GAO figured that the reforms would save less than $100 billion. Others noted that many of the reforms proposed by the Grace Commission had been suggested in the past but had proven politically untenable.

Most of the major changes recommended by the Grace Commission were never passed, although it remained a starting point for conservative critiques of the Democratic Party throughout Reagan's and George Bush's tenures in office. They used its findings to argue that there was tremendous waste in the government and to bolster their call for a line-item veto and other measures.

Suggested Readings: *Facts on File* (1984); *Historical Documents* (1984) p. 169.

Related Entries: Budget Deficit; New Federalism.

GRAMM-RUDMAN-HOLLINGS ACT (BALANCED BUDGET AND EMERGENCY DEFICIT CONTROL ACT OF 1985). In response to an ever-growing federal **budget deficit,** which was forecast at $200 billion for fiscal year 1986, two Republican freshman senators, Phil Gramm of Texas and Warren Rudman of New Hampshire, along with veteran Democrat, Ernest Hollings of South Carolina, proposed the Balanced Budget Bill of 1985, shortly after Ronald Reagan's second term began. Better known as the Gramm-Rudman Act, the bill promised to balance the federal budget by October 1990. It promised to do so by mandating automatic budget cuts in case Congress proved unable to meet certain targets on its own. The bill's sponsors attached it to another Senate measure, which raised the ceiling on the amount of debt the federal government could incur—a measure made necessary by the budget deficits of the first half of the 1980s.

The Reagan administration applauded the bill while, at the same time, expressing concern over some of the programs that the automatic cuts might affect, most importantly, **defense spending.** Reagan wanted defense spending to continue to grow. The balanced budget bill threatened to reduce all federal spending except for some exempted programs, most notably social security. On December 12, 1985, President Reagan signed the bill into law, stating that he hoped it would compel Congress to reduce spending on its own so that automatic cuts, which might hurt the defense department, would not have to be made.

Hours after Gramm-Rudman became law, Representative Mike Synar of Oklahoma filed suit in a federal court challenging its constitutionality. Synar and others argued that Gramm-Rudman illegally stripped the legislative branch of some of its basic powers. Opponents also expressed concern that the measure could damage the nation's health, safety, and defense. On July 7, 1986, the Supreme Court voted 7–2 to strike down some of the most important provisions of the law. In the majority opinion, written by Chief Justice **Warren Earl Burger**, the Court argued that the law violated basic constitutional principles and disregarded the separation of powers established in the Constitution by granting to members of the executive branch the ability to cut the budget when such authority rested solely with Congress.

Despite the legal setback, members of Congress sought to live up to the spirit of Gramm-Rudman by enacting budgets aimed at meeting the targets of the bill. However, this effort ultimately failed for several reasons, including the fact that the **savings and loan crisis** added considerably to federal expenditures, as did cost-of-living expenses for certain entitlement programs exempted by Gramm-Rudman in the first place. In order to keep the budget deficit under control, Congress enacted, and President George Bush signed into law, a tax increase in 1990. Phil Gramm, one the sponsors of the original bill, was one of the most vociferous opponents of this tax hike.

Suggested Readings: *Congressional Quarterly Almanac* (1985); *Historical Documents* (1985) p. 803.

Related Entry: "No New Taxes."

GREAT COMMUNICATOR, THE. One of President Ronald Reagan's greatest strengths was his ability to communicate with the American public, a skill that earned him the accolade, "great communicator." Tens of books and articles have been written aimed at understanding Reagan's talent in this realm. They tend to agree that Reagan's training in radio, movies, and television helped him communicate. They also recognize that Reagan's personality, which was generally upbeat, and his penchant for humor complemented his training. In addition, Reagan surrounded himself with a team of talented advisers who knew how to accentuate his strengths. For instance, chief of staff **James (Jim) Addison Baker III** scheduled few press conferences, the type of public appearance in which the president was the weakest, due to his poor command of details. Rather, the Reagan team made the most of public ceremonies, such as the anniversary of the invasion of Normandy. They used these occasions for major speeches, carefully crafted by **Peggy Noonan** or other professionals, which the president delivered with poise and confidence rarely matched by other politicians.

President Reagan's ability to communicate stood out both in formal and informal situations. He uttered some of his most memorable words shortly after **John W. Hinckley, Jr.,** shot him in 1981. While in the emergency room with a bullet still in his chest, Reagan kidded to his wife, "Honey, I forgot to duck." Then, just before the doctors operated, he added, "I hope you're all Republicans." In times of great tragedy, such as the spacecraft ***Challenger* disaster,** Reagan had the ability to deliver moving speeches that portrayed a deep-felt sorrow. By doing so, Reagan disarmed those who, based upon his demand for spending cuts in social programs, sought to portray him as an uncaring president.

Reagan's ability to communicate stood out during his presidential campaigns. His 1984 campaign commercials were masterly crafted to invoke a feeling of patriotism. Similarly, the 1984 Republican convention looked like a Broadway production, in part because his campaign team paid attention to every detail. Reagan's campaign speeches aimed at making the greatest impact possible in the brief coverage they would receive on the nightly news. Even though television had been around for a generation, Reagan was probably the first president to understand the multifaceted way it could be used to his advantage, from live coverage of public ceremonies and television addresses to sound bites and photo opportunities on the nightly news.

Perhaps the greatest testimony to Reagan's communication skills came from his political opponents. **Thomas (Tip) Philip O'Neill, Jr.,** the Speaker of the House during most of Reagan's tenure, admitted that he enjoyed socializing with the president and trading stories. Other politicians paid him the greatest complement by trying to mimic his style, peppering their speeches with anecdotes. Doubtless hoping that some of Reagan's magic might rub off on him, when his standings in the polls began to decline, President **William (Bill) Jefferson Clinton** even hired Reagan's former communication director, **David Richmond Gergen.** Unfortunately for George Bush, analysts were constantly comparing his speeches to Reagan's, which made Bush look like a worse communicator than if he had been compared to other recent leaders, such as **James (Jimmy) Earl Carter,** Richard Nixon, and Gerald Ford.

Suggested Readings: Paul D. Erickson, *Reagan Speaks: The Making of an American Myth* (1985); David Houck, *Ronald Reagan: Actor, Ideologue, Politician* (1993); Kathleen Jamieson, *Packaging the Presidency* (1992); Kurt Ritter, *Ronald Reagan: The Great Communicator* (1992).

Related Entries: Election of 1984; Farewell Address (Ronald Reagan); "Morning in America"; Normandy, France, D-Day Celebration.

GREENSPAN, ALAN. (March 6, 1926, New York, N.Y.– .) Chairman, Federal Reserve Board, 1987– .

Although he has never been elected to office, Alan Greenspan has played a prominent role in government since the early 1970s. He served as chairman of the Council of Economic Advisers (from 1974 to 1977), was a member of numerous economic and domestic policy boards under Reagan, including a stint as chairman of the National Commission on social security reform, and has been chairman of the **Federal Reserve Board** since 1987.

Greenspan grew up in the Washington Heights section of Manhattan and initially studied music at the Julliard School in New York before earning a B.S. (1948) and M.A. (1950) in economics from New York University (NYU). He started a doctorate program at Columbia University, where he befriended Arthur Burns, who served as chairman of the Federal Reserve Board from 1970 to 1978, but before completing his degree—which he later earned from NYU—he opened an economic consulting firm. In the early 1950s, Greenspan came to personally know Ayn Rand, the conservative philosopher. She helped convince him to become involved in public affairs.

During much of his tenure as chairman of the Economic Advisers, under Richard Nixon and Gerald Ford, and as chairman of the Federal Reserve Board, Greenspan has focused on keeping **inflation** in check. In the mid-1970s, Greenspan asserted that "everyone was hurt by inflation." Confirmed to the post of chairman of the Federal Reserve Board on August 3, 1987, Greenspan faced a very serious crisis in mid-October when the stock market took its biggest single-day fall. Greenspan, himself, had already predicted a possible decline, and some argued that he helped precipitate it by increasing the federal discount rate to combat inflation. However, his calm handling of the crisis drew praise from the *Wall Street Journal* and other business voices.

On various occasions during the Bush administration, Greenspan voiced his concern over the size of the federal **budget deficit,** suggesting that Congress needed to cut entitlement programs to get it under control and to encourage savings. As the recession lingered on during the early 1990s, Greenspan and the Federal Reserve Board gradually decreased the federal discount rate, which produced a decline in interest rates. This helped the economy recover, although Greenspan's critics argued that he reacted too slowly to the recession and should have lowered interest rates more quickly.

Suggested Readings: *Current Biography* (1989) p. 214; David M. Jones, *The Politics of Money: The Fed under Alan Greenspan* (1991).

Related Entries: Economy, U.S.; Recessions; Stock Market Crash of 1987; Volcker, Paul.

GRENADA, INVASION OF. Two days after suffering the worst setback of his first four years in office, the bombing of U.S. marine barracks in Beirut, Lebanon, President Ronald Reagan ordered the invasion of Grenada, a tiny Caribbean island of fewer than 100,000 people. Reagan justified the invasion by pointing to the need to protect approximately 1,000 Americans who lived on the island, most of whom were students at St. George's School of Medicine. Reagan claimed that recent political developments placed them in grave danger. The invasion also dovetailed with the administration's determination to combat left-wing governments in the Western Hemisphere. American forces encountered little resistance and took full control of the island in a few days time.

Since 1979, Grenada, a former British colony, had been ruled by Maurice Bishop, a self-proclaimed Marxist. Bishop accepted the aid of the Cuban government, including a contingent that was in the process of building a modern airport. Bishop claimed that the modern runway strip at the airport was necessary to accommodate jet planes which, he hoped, would bring tourism to the island. President Reagan countered (during his remarks explaining the invasion), that the runway was intended for Soviet and Cuban military use.

About two weeks before the invasion, a militant faction of Marxists, led by General Hudson Austin, overthrew and then murdered Bishop. Austin then imposed martial law. The Reagan administration argued that this situation put American lives in danger. It noted that the militant New Jewel movement, of which Austin was part, had no intention of using the airport for tourists. Rather, Reagan suggested that the movement would provide Cuban and Soviet military sources with a base of operations dangerously close to American borders.

Critics of the invasion wondered about its timing. They felt its primary

Aerial photograph of airport runway displayed by President Reagan during the invasion of Grenada. Still Media Center, Department of Defense.

goal was to divert attention away from the disaster in Beirut. They also challenged Reagan's claim that the invasion was ordered to protect the lives of American medical students, suggesting it had much more to do with his broader objective of restoring American patriotism, noting that Grenada was an easy and convenient target. The military effort could hardly fail there. Regardless of his purpose, the invasion produced a groundswell of support for the president and a revived sense of patriotism at home. During the 1984 election, film footage of grateful medical students was shown to the American public, and Reagan pointed to the successful operation as evidence of the efficacy of his military buildup. As Reagan's supporters argued, the invasion demonstrated that America had overcome the "Vietnam syndrome," defined as an unwillingness to involve American forces abroad because of a fear that the conflict would become another quagmire like Vietnam. Fortunately for Reagan, few Americans ever learned that the invasion was full of snafus. While news cameras beamed pictures of happy medical students returning to America, a media blackout kept them from showing that American troops had been unable to communicate with each other due to incompatible radios. Soldiers were forced to use travel brochures because the massive arms buildup had not included accurate maps of the tiny island. While casualties were low on both sides, U.S. forces mistakenly bombed a mental health institution, injuring over two dozen Grenadans. Moreover, while many Grenadans initially welcomed American soldiers as saviors who would bring free elections and tourism, not much changed in Grenada after the invasion. While more American tourists ventured to Grenada than before, making use of the new airport, the daily lives of most Grenadans improved little.

Suggested Readings: Roy Gutman, *Banana Diplomacy* (1988); Gordon K. Lewis, *Grenada* (1987).

Related Entries: Beirut, Lebanon (Bombing of U.S. Marine Barracks); Caribbean Basin Initiative; Election of 1984; Latin America.

GRIDLOCK. In contrast to the early years of the Ronald Reagan administration, which were marked by action, the latter years of the Reagan administration and, even more so, those of the George Bush administration were marked by political gridlock. In 1981 and 1982, President Reagan was able to win bipartisan support for significant legislation. Even after the Democratic victory in the off-year election of 1982, Reagan won support for many of his key goals, especially increased **defense spending** and **tax reform.** However, this changed in the latter part of the Reagan years and in the Bush years, particularly after 1986 as the Democrats gained control of both houses and the **Iran-contra affair** unraveled.

Without a doubt, differences between Democrats, who regained control of the U.S. Senate in the 1986 election, and President Reagan helped produce this gridlock. However, some analysts argued that the inability of the federal government to enact needed reforms also reflected a much deeper malaise in the land. Specific examples of gridlock abounded. Presidents Reagan and Bush and Congress failed to enact several anticrime proposals, despite claims from both the White House and the capitol that they favored a **crime bill.** Neither **health care reform** nor **campaign finance reform** went anywhere, in spite of skyrocketing health care and campaign costs. Most important, year after year the government rolled up a large **budget deficit,** with each political party blaming the other for the government's inability to balance the budget.

During his four years as president, George Bush vetoed 41 bills. Only once, in the case of **cable television regulation,** did Congress override his veto. While the number of vetoes by the president during one term fell far short of the record—Grover Cleveland vetoed 414 bills in one term—he would have had to veto more had Republicans in the Senate not proven themselves able to block the passage of numerous other bills via obstructionist tactics, mostly the threat of filibuster. For example, Republican filibusters of Democratic anticrime measures killed bills that had been passed by the House of Representatives. (Technically, the Republicans did not even filibuster but only threatened to do so. Lacking the votes to demand cloture, which would kill a filibuster, Democratic leaders in the Senate did not even bother introducing certain legislation to the entire body.)

Many students of government note that the gridlock of the early 1990s was not due solely to the squabbling between President Bush and the Democratic Party. The growing power of special interest groups contributed to gridlock, as did the views of the public itself. Ironically, while American dissatisfaction with Washington grew, voters continued to split their votes, electing Republican presidents and Democratic members of Congress, which in turn underlay the lack of action by the federal government.

Suggested Readings: E. J. Dionne, Jr., *Why Americans Hate Politics* (1992); "President Bush's Vetoes . . . A Near-Perfect Record," *Congressional Quarterly Almanac* (1992), p. 6.

Related Entries: House of Representatives, United States; Senate, United States.

GUN CONTROL. One of the most controversial issues of the Ronald Reagan–George Bush years was gun control. In 1980, several prominent liberal senators, who were targeted by the National Rifle Association because of their advocacy of gun control, lost at the polls. Their defeat suggested that gun control legislation would gain little ground during the 1980s. To a certain extent, this proved true. In 1986, facing strong pressure from the National Rifle Association, Congress enacted, and President Reagan signed into law, a bill that weakened federal gun control legislation dating back to 1968, following in the wake of the assassinations of Martin Luther King, Jr., and Robert F. Kennedy.

However, the assassination attempt on President Reagan by **John W. Hinckley, Jr.,** gave the gun control movement new life. Even as the 1968 law was being modified, gun control advocates were gaining new important allies, most notably **James S. Brady,** Reagan's press secretary, who had been seriously wounded by Hinckley in the assassination attempt, and Ronald Reagan himself. Through most of the latter part of the 1980s and early 1990s, gun control advocates sought to gain the passage of legislation that demanded registration and waiting periods for buying handguns, as well as bans on assault weapons. They got a strong boost from Sarah Brady, Jim Brady's wife, who spoke in favor of the "Brady bill" (the name given to gun control legislation sponsored by Congress). Ironically, it was not the shooting of her husband but the discovery of a handgun by her five-year-old son that converted Sarah Brady to the gun control legislation. Initially, Jim Brady did not join the gun control crusade, refusing to differ with his boss, President Reagan, on this issue. However, by the end of the 1980s, he, too, had become a prominent advocate of gun control.

With the Bradys in the lead, the Democrats attempted time and time again to enact gun control legislation, usually attaching it to larger anticrime bills. Time and time again, however, filibusters in the Senate, or threats of filibuster, by the Republicans killed the **crime bill** itself. In 1991, Reagan gave the gun control movement a tremendous boost when he endorsed the Brady bill. Still, its passage was blocked in the Senate, and even if it had made it through the upper house it probably would have been vetoed by President Bush. Only with the election of **William (Bill) Jefferson Clinton** did gun control legislation pass in both houses of Congress. Clinton subsequently signed it into law.

Suggested Readings: *Congressional Quarterly Almanac* (1990); *Congressional Quarterly Almanac* (1993); *Historical Documents* (1993) p. 500.

Related Entry: Assassination Attempt (Ronald Reagan).

H

HABIB, PHILIP CHARLES. (February 25, 1920, Brooklyn, N.Y.– .) Diplomat.

Several times during the 1980s, President Reagan relied on Philip Habib, a veteran of the U.S. foreign service, to respond to international crises. Habib served as a special envoy for the president in Lebanon in 1981 and 1982. He held a similar post in the **Philippines** in 1986, responding to the turmoil surrounding Ferdinand Marcos's attempt to maintain power, and again in Central America, in response to an escalation of tensions in the region. Habib first earned national prominence as head of the U.S. delegation to the Paris peace talks with the North Vietnamese, nearly two decades before the Reagan presidency.

Habib worked at various blue-collar jobs before attending the University of Idaho (B.S., 1942). After graduating, he enlisted in the U.S. Army, rising to the rank of captain. In 1946 he left the military and enrolled in a Ph.D. program in economics at the University of California, Berkeley, graduating in 1952. Even before he completed his dissertation, Habib started his long career in the foreign service. Among his posts over the following thirty years were counselor for political affairs in South Korea, chief political adviser to Ambassador Henry Cabot Lodge in South Vietnam, deputy assistant secretary of state for East Asian affairs, ambassador to the Republic of Korea, and undersecretary of state for political affairs. Habib served admirably under both Democratic and Republican administrations.

In 1978 Habib suffered a massive heart attack, which kept him politically inactive until the spring of 1981, when President Reagan requested that he rush to Lebanon to help defuse the situation there, which

President Reagan and Secreary of State Alexander Haig. Reagan Library.

stemmed out of enmity between Israel and Syria as well as numerous Lebanese factions. Knowing himself to be well qualified due to his Lebanese descent, Habib accepted the assignment. While his shuttle diplomacy failed to end the civil war in Lebanon, it temporarily eased tensions in the region.

Habib is married to Marjorie W. Slightam. They have two children.

Suggested Readings: *Current Biography* (1981) p. 185; Philip C. Habib, *Diplomacy and the Search for Peace in the Middle East* (1985).

Related Entries: Latin America; Middle East; Philippines.

HAIG, ALEXANDER MEIGS, JR. (December 2, 1924, Bala Cynwyd, Pa.– .) Secretary of State, 1981–1982.

Alexander Haig had a long and distinguished career in public service, as a soldier, presidential adviser, and statesman, but his public career came to a disquieting close on June 25, 1982, when he was forced to resign following several policy disputes with Secretary of Defense **Caspar Willard Weinberger** and other Reagan advisers. Coming on top of revelations of some improper actions, on Haig's part, which followed the attempted assassination of President Reagan, these disputes forced Haig to give up his post as secretary of state. (Haig had incorrectly implied, following the attack on Reagan, that he was third in line to succeed the president. In fact, the speaker of the House becomes president should something incapacitate both the president and vice president.)

Haig was born in a Philadelphia suburb. His father, Philadelphia's city solicitor, died when Haig was ten. Afterward, his mother worked hard to keep the family solvent. Haig attended Notre Dame University for a year before transferring to the United States Military Academy at West Point in 1943. He graduated in 1947. For the next twenty-five years Haig moved up the ranks in the military. He served as commander in chief of the United States forces in the North American Treaty Organization (NATO) from 1974 to 1979. During the late 1960s and early 1970s, he was a top adviser and then chief of staff to President Richard Nixon. Many claim he played a key role in convincing Nixon to resign in 1974.

Double-bypass heart surgery did not deter him from becoming President Reagan's secretary of state. While in office, Haig adopted a "hawkish" position toward the **Soviet Union.** The United States became more aggressive against communism in the Western Hemisphere, supported the British in the **Falkland Islands War,** and invaded **Grenada.** While Haig's political views tended to dovetail with Reagan's, he did not get along with many other top Reagan officials. To make matters worse, Haig insisted that the administration speak with one clear voice on foreign policy—and that the voice be his. This demand did not please several of Reagan's other top aides, especially Weinberger and Central Intelligence Agency (CIA) Director **William Joseph Casey,** both of whom had known the president for longer than Haig. Hence, few were surprised when the president asked for Haig's resignation and replaced him with the less volatile and more amicable **George Pratt Shultz.**

Haig is married to the former Patricia Antoinette Fox. They have three children. Since his resignation Haig has worked for several think tanks, taught at various universities, and served on numerous boards and commissions.

Suggested Readings: *Current Biography* (1987) p. 230; Roger Morris, *Haig: The General's Progress* (1982).

Related Entries: Assassination Attempt (Ronald Reagan); Foreign Policy.

HAITI. In December 1990, Jean-Bertrand Aristide was elected president of Haiti in the first open and democratic elections in this poverty-ravaged

Caribbean nation since 1957. The election took place three years after the overthrow of Jean-Claude Duvalier, the son of Francois (Papa Doc) Duvalier, who had ruled the island with an iron hand for thirty years. Shortly after his election, Aristide informed the United Nations, "Democracy has won out for good." Despite the fact that the United States had provided economic and military backing for Duvalier, his downfall was applauded by the Reagan administration as part of the rising tide of democracy. The Bush administration doubled its direct aid to Haiti following Aristide's election.

Less than seven months after being elected, however, Aristide was thrown out of power by a coup d'etat, which forced him to flee the island and seek refuge in the United States. Because this came shortly after the **Persian Gulf War,** many expected that the United States would send forces to Haiti to restore Aristide to power. While President George Bush condemned the coup, he refused to commit American troops to the region. Rather, the United States imposed economic sanctions. (The sanctions were officially enacted by the Organization of American States.)

Some suggested that the Bush administration's lukewarm reaction to the coup stemmed from its dislike for Aristide, whom Republican Senator **Jesse A. Helms,** for one, termed a communist. Even though Bush supported economic sanctions, he argued that the situation was not analogous to that in the Persian Gulf since no outside invasion had taken place.

In 1992 the Bush administration's Haitian policy became the target of much sharp criticism, especially from the congressional black caucus. It condemned what it saw as Bush's double standard. Members of the caucus particularly criticized the administration's policy toward Haitian refugees. While the United States allowed Cubans to emigrate to the United States—terming them political refugees—it turned back Haitian migrants who sought asylum. (In February 1992 the U.S. Coast Guard forcibly repatriated 381 Haitian refugees in spite of their claims that they would be persecuted on their return.) Critics of the Bush administration's policies were further angered when the president relaxed existing trade sanctions against Haiti, despite a report by Amnesty International (an independent, nonprofit organization) that hundreds of murders and beatings had taken place there since the fall 1991 coup. They argued that the sanctions should have been tightened, not relaxed.

In general, **William (Bill) Jefferson Clinton** joined the chorus of critics of Bush's Haitian efforts during the 1992 campaign. He described the federal government's treatment of Haitian refugees as immoral and termed the Bush administration's overall policies toward Haiti a failure. Bush defended his policy, although not with great verve.

Suggested Readings: Pamela Constable, "Haiti: A Nation in Despair, A Policy Adrift," *Current History,* March 1994, p. 108; Brenda Gayle Plummer, *Haiti and the United States* (1992).

Related Entries: Caribbean Basin Initiative; Election of 1992.

HART, GARY W. (November 28, 1936, Ottawa, Kans.– .) U.S. Senator, 1977–1985; Candidate for Democratic Presidential nomination, 1984, 1988.

As the 1988 presidential campaign first began to appear on the horizon, Gary Hart, a two-term senator from Colorado, was the favorite to win the Democratic nomination. Polls showed that he was the Democratic front-runner and had the best chance of defeating George Bush. A late entrant into the 1984 presidential primary, Hart had defeated the eventual nominee, **Walter Frederick Mondale,** in several large states, including Florida, California, and Ohio. In 1985 he had retired from the Senate in order to concentrate on the presidential race, building up a sizable campaign fund and a cadre of devoted campaigners. Then, however, Hart's campaign self-destructed. On May 3, 1987, the Miami *Herald* accused Hart of "womanizing." Photographs appeared of Hart spending time with Donna Rice, an actress and model, while Hart's wife was in Colorado. Attempts to put a favorable spin on this and other alleged escapades failed. Hart withdrew from the race, only to reenter in early 1988, claiming that his wife was satisfied with his explanation of the affair. However, he proved unable to regain his earlier momentum. **Michael Stanley Dukakis,** the eventual nominee, was the prime beneficiary of Hart's decline.

Hart received his undergraduate degree from Bethany Nazarene College of Oklahoma and a law degree from Yale University. After working for the Justice Department and as special counsel for the Department of the Interior, he served as George McGovern's presidential campaign manager from 1970 to 1972. Four years later, he was elected to the U.S. Senate, where he earned high marks from environmentalists and among those who favored political reform. In the 1980s Hart also tried to develop a reputation as an innovator in defense and economic policy. He is married to the former Lee Ludwig. They have two children.

Suggested Reading: Gary Hart, *The Good Fight: The Education of an American Reformer* (1993).

Related Entry: Election of 1988.

HEAD START. One of the Great Society programs to survive the Reagan-Bush years intact was Head Start. Between 1981 and 1992, funding for this program increased over 70 percent after inflation, to about $2 billion per year. The Head Start program was first enacted during the mid-1960s to provide preschool education to disadvantaged children. Advocates of the program argued that it provided them with the foundation to succeed in school. They added that the program represented an investment in children that actually saved money in the long run by averting long-term social problems associated with poorly educated adults. While President Ronald Reagan was a fierce opponent of the Great Society programs in general and favored reduced federal spending for **education,** Head Start survived most attempts to cut it back. Even a twenty-year review of Head Start, which found that it did not produce significant long-term results, failed to harm the program. Under George Bush, funding for Head Start was increased even more, and during 1992 both candidates pledged to expand it further.

Suggested Readings: Susan Muenchow and Edward Zigler, *Head Start: The Inside Story of America's Most Successful Educational Experiment* (1992); Valora Washington, *Project Head Start: Past, Present and Future Trends in the Context of Family Needs* (1987).

HEALTH CARE REFORM. During early 1990s health care reform became a major issue on the political agenda, spurred in part by Democrat Harris Wofford's emphasis of the issue during a special election for the U.S. Senate in 1991. (Wofford upset **Richard L. Thornburgh,** a former governor of the state of Pennsylvania and President Bush's U.S. attorney general.) In 1991 health care costs consumed over 15 percent of the federal budget, up from 11.7 percent in 1980. The United States spent a much greater proportion of its gross domestic product (GDP) on health care than any other developed nation. Moreover, the costs of health care were rising every year and at a faster rate than the GDP.

In 1991 and 1992, Democrats in Congress introduced numerous proposals for health care reform. These plans aimed at attaining universal coverage—by 1991 there were an estimated 35 million uninsured Americans—and containing costs. None of these proposals made it through Congress, however, and even if they had passed, it is doubtful they would have been signed into law by President George Bush.

Despite growing public concern, the Bush administration remained silent on the health care issue until 1992. Even then, the president merely called for limited reform, namely, cutting malpractice insurance costs and increasing market incentives. Whether this proved a politically apt position remains unclear. **William (Bill) Jefferson Clinton** cited the lack of action on the issue by both Ronald Reagan or Bush as a main reason for supporting change. Indeed, his promise to break the **gridlock** on health care reform stood as one of the cornerstones of this campaign (and subsequent dilemmas as president).

Actually, the call for health care reform was an old one in the United States. Early in the twentieth century, labor groups had advocated national health insurance, and the American Medical Association (AMA) had lobbied for such a program during the Progressive Era. Momentum for such reform increased during Presidents Franklin Roosevelt and Harry Truman's tenures in office. However, by the post–World War II period, the AMA had become a fierce opponent of any type of national health insurance, seeing it as a threat to the private health care system itself. During the 1960s President Johnson gained passage of partial reform, establishing Medicare, which provided national health insurance for the elderly, and Medicaid, a national program for the poor. Richard Nixon briefly pushed for further reform, but his programs never got anywhere. As a result, by the time Reagan became president, the United States was one of the few developed nations in the world without some form of national health insurance.

Reagan's opposition to big government programs pushed health care reform off the political agenda for most of the 1980s, although rising costs did prompt him to appoint a commission to study ways for the government and the private sector to cover catastrophic illnesses. As a direct result of this commission's report, in 1988 he signed an act that expanded Medicare coverage for the elderly. However, the law, which raised monthly premiums, did not deal with the broader issues of containing general health care costs nor the increasing number of uninsured Americans.

Suggested Readings: *Congressional Quarterly Almanac* (1991); Eli Ginzberg, *The Road to Reform* (1994); Paul Starr, *The Logic of Health Care Reform* (1994).

HECKLER, MARGARET MARY. (June 21, 1931, Queens, N.Y.– .) Secretary of Health and Human Services, 1983–1985; Ambassador to Ireland, 1985–1989.

On October 1, 1985, President Ronald Reagan announced that Margaret Heckler would leave her post as the secretary of health and human services to become the ambassador to Ireland. The administration sought to suggest that this move was voluntary and represented a reward for Heckler's "fine job," to use the president's words, but in reality it grew out of conservative disenchantment with Heckler's leadership. During her tenure as the secretary of health and human services, she had not taken a lead in promoting the conservative agenda on **welfare.** Unlike secretary of education **William John Bennett** or attorney general **Edwin Meese III,** Heckler did not forcefully defend the administration's attempts to cut social spending. Rather, she acted within the administration as an advocate of the elderly and other groups. Ironically, Heckler had replaced **Richard Schultz Schweiker,** who similarly had not been in the forefront of the drive to bring down the welfare state, much of which was administered by the Department of Health and Human Services.

Margaret Mary O'Shaughnessy Heckler is the daughter of Irish immigrants. She received her B.A. from Albertus Magnus College in Connecticut, married John M. Heckler, and earned her law degree from Boston College (1956). Ten years later she was elected to Congress, a post she held until 1982, when she lost to Democrat Barney Frank. Throughout her tenure in Congress she was a strong supporter of women's rights. Even though she had never expressed any great interest in Irish affairs, on her nomination to become ambassador, she stated, "Every American of Irish ancestry can appreciate the special place that Ireland is to each of us."

She had three children. In 1986 her marriage to John Heckler ended in a divorce.

Suggested Reading: *New York Times,* October 2, 1985 p. II: 5.

HELMS, JESSE A. (October 18, 1921, Monroe, N.C.– .) U.S. Senator, 1972– .

Jesse Helms has represented North Carolina in the U.S. Senate since the early 1970s. Throughout his tenure he has earned a reputation as one of its most conservative members.

After graduating from Wake Forest College, Helms worked briefly as the city editor of the Raleigh *Times.* When World War II began he joined the United States Navy. Afterwards, he became the news program director of radio station WRAL in Raleigh. Then, for two years, he worked as the administrative assistant to Senator Willis Smith (Democrat), the conservative firebrand who had defeated Frank Graham in one of the most hard-

President Reagan and North Carolina Senator Jesse Helms. Reagan Library.

fought senatorial elections in American history. From 1953 to 1960, Helms was employed by the North Carolina Bankers Association. Then, from 1960 to 1972, he returned to radio (and television).

During this period Helms sharply criticized the liberal bias of the media. He gained particular notoriety for his sharp attacks on liberal academics and the federal government. In 1970 Helms switched from the Democratic to the Republican Party, and two years later he upset Nick Galifiankis to win a seat in the U.S. Senate. Although he has faced fierce competition in a number of his subsequent campaigns, he has been reelected four times. (Helms's senatorial races have become notorious for the amount of money spent in them, as both liberal and conservative groups from around the nation have poured funds into the state.)

An early supporter of Ronald Reagan, Helms is one of the best known spokesmen for several **New Right** causes, including constitutional amendments allowing for prayer in school, outlawing **abortion** and making it a crime to burn the American flag. Helms is also a vociferous opponent of **affirmative action** and multiculturalism, and an ardent proponent of so-called traditional **family values.** As a senator, Helms has earned a reputation for his obstructionism. He often launches filibusters to thwart the confirmation of judges or federal appointees whom he considers too liberal. Similarly, he consistently attacks federal programs for the **arts** and humanities.

Helms is married to the former Dorothy Coble. They have two daughters and a son.

Suggested Readings: *Current Biography* (1979) p. 165; Ernest B. Furguson, *Hard Right: The Rise of Jesse Helms* (1986).

Related Entries: Conservative Coalition; Constitutional Amendments (Proposed); Senate, United States.

HIGH TECHNOLOGY. The Ronald Reagan–George Bush years witnessed the spread of numerous high-technology products, from the personal computer and the facsimile ("fax") machine to the microwave oven and the videocassette recorder (VCR). Many of these high-technology developments were introduced before Reagan became president, but they seemed to blossom from the mid-1980s onward (see Figure 4). Some even suggested that the United States had entered a new age. Furthermore, supporters of Reagan and Bush cited the growth of high technology to prove that **Reaganomics** worked. President Reagan himself often pointed to breakthroughs in the world of high technology to show that the entrepreneurial spirit was alive and well in America and to argue that if the federal government would only unleash business from its regulatory grip, the economy would boom. Moreover, Reagan's supporters also justified the massive defense buildup of the 1980s on the grounds that it underlay many of the breakthroughs in the field of high technology.

The symbol of the expansion of high technology was the personal computer. In 1977 the Apple Computer Company Incorporated, which had been founded in a garage not far from San Francisco, introduced the Apple II, a computer for personal use. It sold for $1,298 and used a television monitor and audiocassettes to store data. Four years later, International Business Machines (IBM), the giant maker of mainframe computers as well as a host of other business machines, sold its first personal computer. By the end of the decade, nearly 7 million personal computers were being sold a year—and they were much more powerful and easier to use than any of those available earlier in the decade. The spread of the computer was so great that by the time President Bush left office, discussion of the "information highway," whereby individuals could communicate via their computers and gain access to billions of bits of infor-

Figure 4
High Technology (Sales of Selected Items)

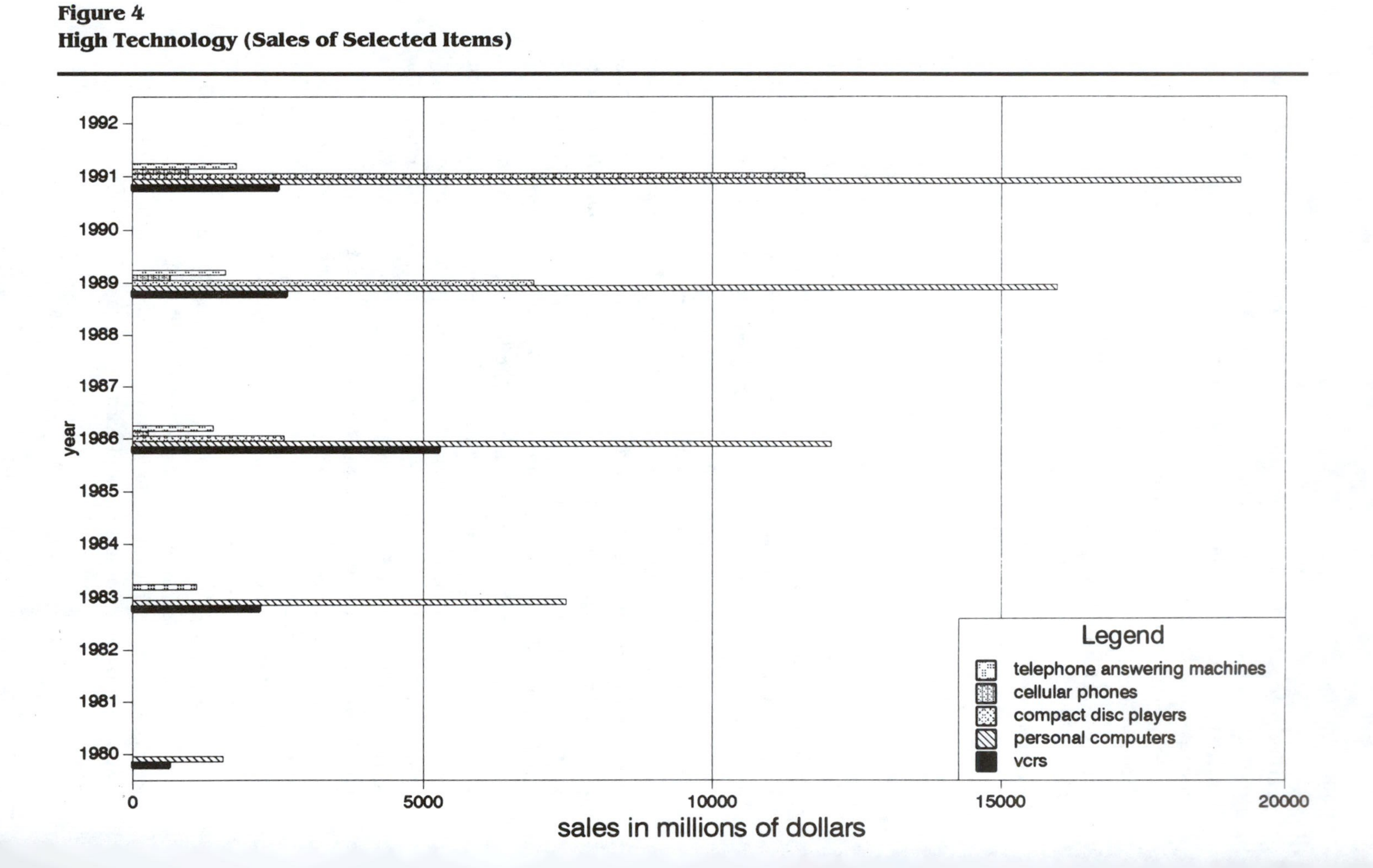

mation, was becoming a reality. Indeed, in 1993 President Clinton went online, accepting electronic mail (e-mail) messages and providing texts of his speeches and other information to personal computer users throughout the world. Although less spectacular than the computer, improvements in consumer electronics similarly altered the way people lived. The number of people with VCRs, microwave ovens, telephone message machines, cordless telephones, and even cellular car phones skyrocketed. Cellular phones, for instance, were first introduced in 1983. By 1993 there were over 16 million subscribers, with growth at a rate of 4.9 million new subscribers per year. The Sony Walkman portable cassette player, like Scotch tape earlier in the century, came to represent an entire new industry, in this case, that of portable radio and tape players.

The impact of high technology on the business world was just as great. By 1992 millions of employees had their own personal computers at work and enjoyed the benefits of voice mail and fax machines. Businesses made greater use of high technology in the products they built and the services they provided. Stores introduced scanning machines at the checkout counter to speed up service and improve accounting and inventory methods. Automakers added tiny computer chips to aid in everything from braking to steering. Banks began to utilize automatic tellers to improve access to their services.

One byproduct of the high technology revolution was that for the first time in years, the number of people who worked in their homes increased. With the use of personal computers and fax machines, many found that their home could be their office. At the same time, improvements in high technology did not resolve numerous problems and may have exacerbated some. The rate of poverty did not decrease during the 1980s, and some would argue that since high-technology products, like wealth in general, were poorly distributed, they have the potential of increasing the social and economic distances between rich and poor. Put simply, those with money have the greatest access to new innovations, which perhaps gives them an even greater advantage. The poor, in contrast, prove unable to purchase many new products, reinforcing their disadvantages.

This said, most economists agree that ultimately the benefits of these new high-technology products will improve the standard of living for all, just as older inventions, from the light bulb to the polio vaccine, improved the lives of nearly everyone over time. Cellular phones, for example, may allow people in undeveloped countries that have never enjoyed a traditional phone system (in part because of the capital costs of laying phone lines) to communicate with people around the globe. Even though cellular phones remain too expensive for this to take place at the present, rapid decreases in price make this a distinct possibility. (Calculators, for instance, cost upwards of $500 in the mid-1970s but dropped in price to less than $10 by the end of the 1980s.)

Suggested Readings: Electronic Industries Association, *The U.S. Consumer Electronics Industry* (1994); Tom Forester, *High-Tech Society: The Story of the Information Technology Revolution* (1987); Everett M. Roberts and Judith Larsen, *Silicon Valley Fever* (1984).

HILL, ANITA. See **THOMAS-HILL HEARINGS.**

HILLS, CARLA ANDERSON. (January 3, 1934, Los Angeles, Calif.– .) United States Trade Representative, 1989–1993.

In an era in which foreign trade took on increasing economic and political significance, Carla Edith (Anderson) Hills assumed a tough job when she became the chief U.S. foreign trade representative during the George Bush administration. However, Hills was accustomed to accepting responsibility. She had served as secretary of housing and urban development (HUD) from 1975 to 1977, under President Gerald Ford, and had years of experience as an attorney for both the federal government and private firms. Indeed, many had expected that she would become the first woman nominated to the Supreme Court, an honor that went instead to **Sandra Day O'Connor.**

The daughter of a socially prominent family in Los Angeles, Hills earned a bachelor's degree in history from Stanford University (1955), while simultaneously captaining the women's tennis team. She spent a year at Oxford University before heading to Yale Law School, graduating near the top of her class in 1958. Denied employment from private law firms because of her sex, Hills worked for three years for the U.S. Attorney General's Office. In 1962 she joined her husband's private law firm. Twelve years and four children later, she accepted a post as assistant attorney general in charge of the civil division of the Justice Department under Elliot Richardson, a post she held until she became secretary of HUD. (Hills ended up working under William Saxbe, who took over for Richardson when Richardson became one of the victims of the "Saturday Night Massacre," part of the Watergate scandal.)

Following President Ford's defeat by **James (Jimmy) Earl Carter,** she returned to the private sector, remaining there until 1989, when she was nominated as federal trade representative. Once confirmed, Hills took responsibility for negotiating trade agreements with Japan and the European Community. She represented the United States during the Uruguay Round of the General Agreement on Tariffs and Trade (GATT). During the 1992 campaign, Democratic candidate **William (Bill) Jefferson Clinton** and independent **H. Ross Perot** criticized the trade policies of the Bush administration, which favored free trade over protectionism and rarely moved beyond rhetorical threats in attempts to decrease the trade deficit with specific countries. However, supporters of Hills and Bush countered that American exports to **Japan** were increasing and that barriers to the trade of goods to other nations were falling. This, they added, boded well for the economy, especially in the long term.

Suggested Readings: Keith Bradsher, "Trade Warrior," *New York Times Biographical Service,* December 1992, p. 1624; *Current Biography* (1993) p. 240; Paul Magnusson, "Carla Hills, Trade Warrior," *Business Week,* January 20, 1990, p. 50.

Related Entries: Election of 1992; Trade Deficit; Women's Rights.

HINCKLEY, JOHN W., JR. (May 29, 1955, Ardmore, Okla.– .) Would-be assassin.

On March 30, 1981, John Hinckley, Jr. attempted to assassinate Ronald Reagan outside the Washington Hilton Hotel. Shots from Hinckley's revolver nearly killed the president and seriously wounded Reagan's press secretary **James S. Brady.** Hinckley also shot a Washington, D.C., policeman and a Secret Service agent. Newspaper and government investigators subsequently revealed that Hinckley had a troubled past. He was infatuated with actress Jodie Foster, having written numerous letters to her in which he described a make-believe romance with her. He had been arrested on October 9, 1980, at the Nashville, Tenn., airport for carrying concealed firearms, perhaps with the purpose of trying to assassinate **James (Jimmy) Earl Carter,** who was president at the time. He collected clippings on the murders of John F. Kennedy and John Lennon, the slain member of the famous Beatles. He was described by many as a troubled loner who had deep resentments against all sorts of people.

John W. Hinckley, Sr., was a successful oil engineer who was active in Christian affairs and a regular contributor to the Republican Party. Along with his older brother and sister, John Hinckley, Jr., grew up in an affluent Dallas neighborhood. He had a fairly normal childhood, being elected class president in junior high school, although he was always outshone by his older brother and sister. Hinckley enrolled at Texas Tech University in 1973. For the next seven years he took classes at the state university in Lubbock on an on-again, off-again basis. While not in school, he drifted through Hollywood and joined the National Socialist Party of America, even attending a 1978 rally in St. Louis, Missouri, to commemorate the birth of George Lincoln Rockwell, Jr., the founder of the American Nazi Party. Among the papers he wrote while at Texas Tech was one on Adolf Hitler's *Mein Kampf.*

Hinckley ultimately pleaded not guilty because of insanity. The court accepted this plea, and he was committed to a psychiatric facility for an indefinite period.

Suggested Readings: *Facts on File* (1981); "U.S. Agents Find Hinckley Had Recent Shift to Violent Emotion," *New York Times Biographical Service,* April 1991, p. 490.

Related Entry: Assassination Attempt (Ronald Reagan).

HODEL, DONALD PAUL. (May 23, 1935, Portland, Ore.– .) Secretary of Energy, 1982–1985; Secretary of Interior, 1985–1989.

In February 1985 Donald Hodel took over for **William Patrick Clark,** who himself had replaced **James Gaius Watt,** as head of the Department of Interior. Prior to becoming secretary of the interior, Hodel had served under Watt as the undersecretary of the Department of Interior and then, from 1982 to 1985, as secretary of energy, a new cabinet post. Ironically, Reagan had hoped that Hodel would dismantle the Energy Department, something Hodel did not do.

Hodel grew up in Oregon. In the early 1950s, he journeyed east to attend Harvard University, where he received a B.A. in government (1957). Upon graduation, he returned to his home state to study law at the University of Oregon, receiving his degree in 1960. After working briefly as an attorney in a private law firm, Hodel became an in-house counsel for Georgia Pacific, the lumber and paper conglomerate, and involved himself in Republican politics. From 1969 through 1977 he worked as the deputy administrator and then top administrator of the Bonneville Power Administration, a federal agency that markets electricity produced by dams in the region which were owned by the national government. Hodel's harsh criticism of environmental groups and advocacy of nuclear energy made his tenure as administrator of the Bonneville a stormy one and hinted at some of the battles he would face during the 1980s.

While serving as Watt's deputy, Hodel helped implement a number of very controversial policies. Environmentalists claimed that the Interior Department, which was entrusted with the responsibility of securing the public's resources, was involved in their wholesale "fire sale." As secretary of energy and interior, Hodel promoted Ronald Reagan's goal of selling off public lands for commercial use, developing nuclear power, and loosening environmental regulations. Since Hodel was less of a loose cannon than Watt, however, he got along much better with the press and proved less controversial than the latter.

Hodel is married to the former Barbara Beecher Stockman. They have one living son. An older son, Philip, died in the 1970s.

Suggested Readings: *Current Biography* (1987) p. 234; Donald Hodel, *Crisis in the Oil Patch* (1994).

Related Entry: Environment.

HOMELESSNESS. During the 1980s the number of homeless people grew dramatically, with some analysts arguing that it doubled nearly every year in several metropolitan areas. The causes of this rise in the number of people without a permanent residence were multiple. The recession of the early 1980s added to the homeless rolls, as did **deindustrialization** and the decline in the number of jobs in manufacturing. An increase in drug use as well as the deinstitutionalization of many men and women who had once been in psychiatric facilities worsened the problem. In addition, many advocates for the homeless claimed that President Ronald Reagan's social and economic policies, which cut funding for public housing and **welfare,** contributed to the rise in homelessness in America.

Homelessness in New York City and Los Angeles became particularly glaring during the 1980s, with Anna Kosof, an expert on the subject, estimating that in 1988, for example, there were about 30,000 homeless men and women in the former city alone. While the "average" homeless person was a nonwhite, middle-aged male, an increasing number of women and children joined the ranks of the homeless during the Reagan-Bush years.

In response to those who blamed homelessness on Reagan's policies, conservatives argued that the Great Society, Lyndon Johnson's welfare programs in particular, and a decline in traditional **family values** lay at the root of the problem. Permissive government policies and welfare encouraged irresponsible behavior, such as drug use, they argued. Less, not more, government would help resolve the problem. Conservatives also contended that liberals overestimated the number of homeless in America and argued that many of those who slept on the streets did so out of choice, not because they were forced to by the lack of a safety net.

Suggested Readings: Cheryl Gordar, *Homeless! Without Addresses in America* (1988); Mary Ellen Hombs, *Contemporary World Issues: American Homelessness* (1990); Anna Kosof, *Homeless in America* (1988).

Related Entries: Poverty; Recessions.

HORTON, WILLIE (COMMERCIAL). One of the most effective and controversial commercials of the 1988 presidential campaign was the Willie Horton television spot. Willie Horton was a convicted murderer and rapist. While serving a life sentence in Massachusetts, he was allowed to leave the prison for ten weekends as part of a special program in that state. **Michael Stanley Dukakis,** the Democratic presidential nominee, was governor of Massachusetts when Horton was released. On one of these occasions, Horton kidnapped a young couple, stabbing the man and raping the woman. A thirty-second, pro-Bush television commercial noted that George Bush favored the death penalty. Then, with a picture of Dukakis on the screen, a voice announced that, not only did the Democratic Party's presidential nominee oppose the death penalty, he had allowed "first-degree murderers to have weekend passes from prison." The commercial came to a climax with a mug shot of Willie Horton accompanied by the announcer summarizing his crime and Dukakis's leave program.

The Dukakis camp and many of his supporters described the advertisement as racist, since it presented a menacing picture of Horton, a black man. By implication, critics charged, Bush was seeking to win the support of white voters by appealing to their fear of crime and their latent racism. Since the commercial was produced by an independent group, Americans for Bush, not the official Bush campaign, the vice president was able to disavow it. At the same time, he benefited from its message. In addition, Bush used the controversy over the Horton commercial to reemphasize his support for the death penalty as opposed to Dukakis's "softness" on crime.

Several years later one of Bush's political advisers, **(Harvey) Lee Atwater,** admitted that the advertisement had been a cheap shot and that its producers had sought to appeal to white voters on their most base level. Atwater added that he regretted promoting the commercial. However, neither Atwater nor Bush ever retreated from the stance that Dukakis's plan, which provided leave for Horton, was wrong and that it symbolized the two candidates' differences on crime.

Suggested Readings: Michael Barone, *Our Country; Facts on File* (1988); Jack Germond and Jules Witcover, *Whose Broad Stripes and Bright Stars? The Trivial Pursuit of the Presidency* (1989).

Related Entries: Civil Rights; Election of 1988.

HOUSE OF REPRESENTATIVES, UNITED STATES. Throughout the Ronald Reagan–George Bush years, the Democratic Party retained control of the U.S. House of Representatives. During much of the time period, it checked many of the conservative initiatives of Presidents Reagan and Bush. Reagan proved unable to sweep Republicans into control of the House on his coattails, even during his landslide victory in 1984, and George Bush came to power in 1989 with more Democrats in Congress than at any time since the 1970s. This said, especially early in his administration, Reagan was able to put together a working majority in the House that joined with the Republican majority in the Senate to enact many of his **domestic policy** and **foreign policy** proposals. Southern Democrats joined with Republicans in support of tax cuts and increases in **defense spending.** They also backed Reagan's call for dismantling several Great Society programs (first enacted by President Lyndon Johnson in the mid-1960s) and whittling away others. (These Democrats were sometimes referred to as "boll weevils," which is a small beetle that infests cotton plants. In a political context, this term is used to identify Southern Democrats who ally themselves with Republicans.)

During the Reagan-Bush era, there were three Democratic speakers of the House (see Table 12). **Thomas (Tip) Philip O'Neill, Jr.,** a Democrat from Massachusetts, held the post until 1987. He was succeeded briefly by **James (Jim) Claude Wright,** a Democrat from Texas. After Wright

Table 12
Leaders and Party Makeup

Congress	Years	Majority Party	Minority Party	Speaker
97th	1981–83	D-243	R-192	Tip O'Neill
98th	1983–85	D-269	R-165	Tip O'Neill
99th	1985–87	D-252	R-182	Tip O'Neill
100th	1987–89	D-258	R-177	Tip O'Neill
101st	1989–91	D-259	R-174	Jim Wright
102nd	1991–93	D-258	R-176	Tom Foley

resigned due to questions about his ethics (which were raised by **Newton (Newt) Leroy Gingrich,** the leader of conservative Republicans in the House), **Thomas Stephen Foley,** a Democrat from the state of Washington, took the helm. Among the other prominent Democratic and Republican members of the House during this era were: **Jack French Kemp,** Republican, New York; **Richard Andrew Gephardt,** Democrat, Missouri; and Tony Coehlo, Democrat, California.

One of the main themes of the era was growing public disenchantment with the U.S. Senate and House of Representatives. Even though incumbents continued to be re-elected at a high rate, public opinion polls showed a growing dissatisfaction with politics as usual, as practiced by Congress. Anger over congressional pay raises led to ratification of the so-called **Madison Amendment (Twenty-Seventh Amendment to the U.S. Constitution),** which limited congressional ability to raise its members own salary. Several groups began to promote another constitutional amendment that would limit the number of terms for members of Congress.

Suggested Reading: E. J. Dionne, Jr., *Why Americans Hate Politics* (1992).

Related Entry: Senate, United States.

I

IACOCCA, LEE ANTHONY. (October 15, 1924, Allentown, Pa.– .) Former automobile executive.

The relationship between the Ronald Reagan and George Bush administrations and Lee Iacocca is a twisted and ambiguous one. Throughout the late 1970s and 1980s, Iacocca was one of the best-known and most personable business executives in the nation. He first gained fame in 1964 when, while with Ford Motor Company, he helped introduce the Mustang, one of Ford's most memorable cars. Subsequently, Iacocca rose through the ranks of Ford to the position of president until he was dismissed, at the relatively young age of fifty-four, in 1978. Afterward, Iacocca took over the reigns of the Chrysler Corporation and was credited with saving it from bankruptcy. This achievement, television commercials for Chrysler's automobiles featuring Iacocca himself, and his best-selling autobiography, made him into perhaps the most celebrated auto executive since Henry Ford.

Iacocca also gained fame and admiration through his chairmanship of the Statue of Liberty–Ellis Island Commission, a quasi-public organization that sought to raise funds for the restoration of these two national landmarks. Despite the fact that Reagan touted the recovery of Chrysler as evidence of the success of his economic policies, Iacocca himself clashed with the administration on several occasions. Most notably, in 1986, Secretary of Interior **Donald Paul Hodel** fired Iacocca from his position as chairman of the Statute of Liberty–Ellis Island Commission because, Hodel claimed, there was a possible conflict of interest between the auto executive's position as chairman of the private foundation entrusted with raising money for the monument's restoration and the public body charged with advising the government on the use of the restored site. It was considered a conflict of interest because Iacocca could have advised using the site in a way that would benefit one of the donors. Iacocca retorted that he had been fired because of his criticism of Hodel's plans to use much of Ellis Island for a private conference center and hotel complex, or what Iacocca called a "luxury project" paid for with "tax credits for the rich." Such populism on Iacocca's part garnered calls for him to run for president or to accept a spot as the vice presidential nominee from the Democratic Party. (He was a life long Democrat.) However, Iacocca never sought public office, nor was he ever nominated for a top government spot.

Iacocca has been married twice: first, to Mary McCleary, who died in 1956, and subsequently, to Darien Earle. He has two children. Iacocca received a B.S. from Lehigh University (1945) and a master's degree in engineering from Princeton University (1946).

Suggested Readings: *Current Biography* (1988) p. 259; Lee Iacocca, *Iacocca: An Autobiography* (1984); Peter Wyden, *The Unknown Iacocca: An Unauthorized Biography* (1987).

Related Entry: Statute of Liberty Celebration.

IMMIGRATION REFORM AND CONTROL ACT OF 1986. See **SIMPSON-MAZZOLI BILL.**

INF TREATY. See **INTERMEDIATE-RANGE NUCLEAR FORCES (INF) TREATY.**

INFLATION. As the Ronald Reagan–George Bush years began, inflation represented one of the nation's worst problems (see Figure 5). In 1979 and 1980, the consumer price index (the most common measure of inflation) rose 13.3 percent and 12.4 percent, respectively. This represented the first time since 1918–1919 that the nation had been plagued by double-digit inflation for two consecutive years. Although part of this rise was due to a sharp increase in oil prices in 1978–1979, a byproduct of the Iranian revolution, inflation had been a problem ever since the late 1960s. While not all goods and groups of Americans were affected equally by this rise in prices, a broad consensus existed among economists that the steep increase in prices had to be combated. Inflation made American goods less competitive against foreign products. It deterred businesses

Figure 5
Inflation

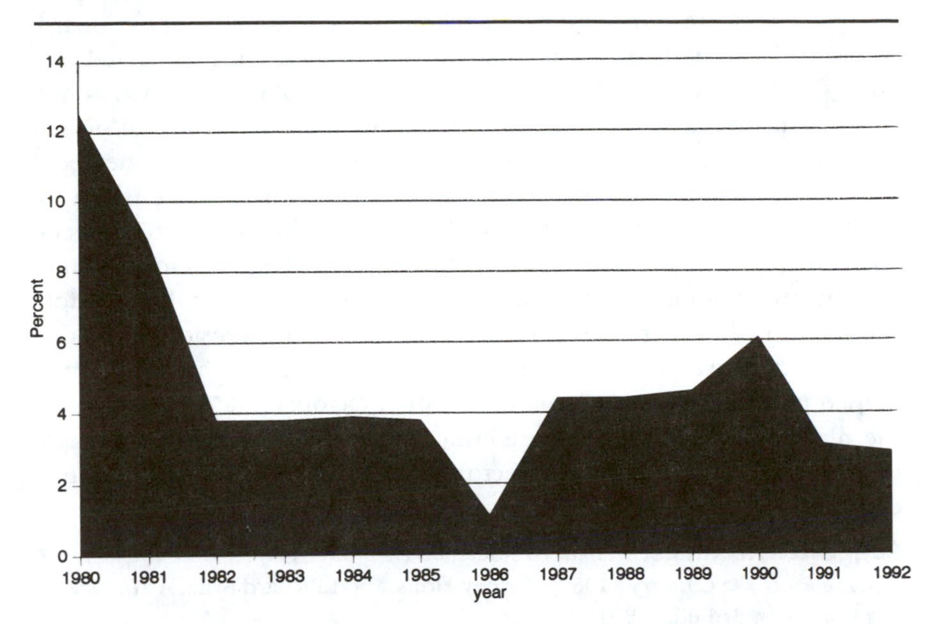

from investing in new equipment and sapped the savings of millions of Americans, especially those on fixed incomes.

Even before Reagan's inauguration, the **Federal Reserve Board,** headed by **Paul Volcker,** a **James (Jimmy) Earl Carter** appointee, had embarked on a "tight money" policy to rein in inflation. To do so the Federal Reserve Board (the Fed) raised interest rates (technically, the board raised the rate at which it loaned out money to banks). In May 1981 the Federal Reserve Board set its discount rate at a record 14 percent. Despite the fact that such high rates helped produce the worst recession and highest unemployment rates since the Great Depression, the Federal Reserve Board remained committed to a tight monetary policy. The Reagan administration supported the Fed's action, viewing it as complementary to its economic recovery program.

While the cost was high, nearly all economists give Volcker and the Federal Reserve Board credit for achieving its objective. Aided by decreases in the cost of oil, by March 1982 the rate of inflation had begun to decline. With the economic recovery of the mid-1980s, inflation gradually rose, but it never got close to the double-digit levels that had existed during Carter's last years in office. Whereas the consumer price index rose nearly 40 percent during Carter's four years as president, it rose at only about 20 percent during Reagan's eight years in office and at an even lesser rate during President Bush's tenure.

This said, some have wondered whether the Federal Reserve Board went too far in its fight. Even after inflation declined, it maintained relatively high interest rates. Only with the recession of the early 1990s did it lower its discount rate to levels once considered the historical norm. By and large, the Reagan administration supported this tight money policy, as evidenced by the president's nomination of **Alan Greenspan** to replace Volcker as chairman of the Federal Reserve Board in 1987. Greenspan sharply raised interest rates after taking over the board in response to renewed inflation. (In 1986 prices rose only 1.1 percent, but the following year, they increased 5.1 percent.) Neither the president nor the secretary of treasury criticized this action, despite the fact that rising rates helped precipitate the stock market crash of October 1987. Even though the market recovered, tempering criticism of Greenspan's actions, high interest rates were one of the factors that caused the recession of the early 1990s.

Suggested Readings: William Greider, *Secrets of the Temple: How the Federal Reserve Runs the Country* (1987); Sidney Homer and Richard Sylla, *A History of Interest Rates,* 3rd ed. (1991).

Related Entries: Economy, U.S.; Reaganomics; Recessions; Stock Marker Crash of 1987.

INTERMEDIATE-RANGE NUCLEAR FORCES (INF) TREATY. "May December 8, 1987, become a date that will be inscribed in the history books, a date that will mark the watershed separating the era of a mounting risk of nuclear war from the era of a demilitarization of human life." These were the words of **Mikhail Sergeyevich Gorbachev,** the leader of the **Soviet Union,** on the occasion of the signing of the Intermediate-range Nuclear Forces (INF) Treaty between the United States and the USSR. The agreement represented one of the most significant and somewhat ironic developments of Ronald Reagan's presidency. It set the United States and the **Soviet Union** on the course of relative demilitarization (and ultimately, the end of the cold war), at the end of a decade in which the United States had spent more on defense than at any time in its history.

The INF Treaty, signed on December 8, 1987, by President Ronald Reagan and Soviet leader Mikhail Gorbachev—it was subsequently ratified by the U.S. Senate—called for the scrapping of intermediate-range

President Reagan and Soviet leader Mikhail Gorbachev sign Intermediate-range Nuclear Forces (INF) Treaty, December 8, 1987. Reagan Library.

nuclear-force missiles. The treaty was signed on the final day of a three-day summit between the two leaders in Washington, D.C. The pact required the destruction of 830 U.S. and 1,752 Soviet missiles. In terms of nuclear warheads, the treaty was even more favorable toward the United States than it appeared (since many of the Soviet missiles had triple warheads, while most of the intermediate U.S. missiles had single warheads). The treaty represented the first time that the two nations had agreed to destroy an entire class of nuclear weapons.

The signing of the treaty followed years of arduous and often acrimonious negotiations, stretching back to late fall 1980. These negotiations reached a low point in November 1983 when Soviet negotiators walked out of talks in Geneva following the arrival of the first **Pershing II missiles** in West Germany. Talks between the two sides did not restart until November 1985 but were quickly given a boost by Reagan and Gorbachev's first summit in Geneva in November 1985. (Reagan did not meet with any of Gorbachev's predecessors.)

The key to the INF treaty was an unprecedented system for independent verification by both countries. On very short notice, experts were entitled to personally visit and inspect facilities in the other country. The treaty itself was nearly 200 pages long. The agreement did not cover "battlefield" or short-range nuclear missiles, nor did it affect nuclear-armed aircraft or submarine-launched ballistic missiles. At the time of its signing, negotiations between the two nations on strategic arms were in progress.

Suggested Readings: Raymond Garthoff, *The Great Transition: American-Soviet Relations and the End of the Cold War* (1994); George Rueckert, *Global Double Zero: The INF Treaty, from Its Origins to Implementation* (1993).

Related Entries: Arms Control; Strategic Arms Reduction Talks (START) Treaty; Summits, with Soviet Union.

IRAN-CONTRA AFFAIR. The Iran-contra affair was not just one incident, but a number of interrelated developments that came to haunt the Ronald Reagan administration during its last three years in office. The affair continued to linger on in a more muted manner throughout George Bush's tenure as president. It had two roots. First, the president authorized an attempt by the National Security Council to sell arms to Iran in exchange for the release of American hostages held in Lebanon. Second, top Reagan administration officials decided to divert some of the proceeds from these arms deals to contra rebels in **Nicaragua.** Both these activities were covert operations; the latter may have been illegal. The affair grew in significance when Reagan administration officials initially lied to Congress about specific details of each endeavor. To make matters worse, the president initially denied knowledge of these developments, although he later took responsibility for them. As the public learned from the press and mass media the details of the operations themselves and of possible lies to Congress, several investigations were launched, most prominently, a presidential investigation headed by former Texas Senator John Tower, joint congressional hearings, and a very long investigation headed by Special Prosecutor **E. Lawrence Walsh.**

The decision to trade arms to the Iranians for hostages was made in December 1985 by President Reagan. This action contradicted the administration's public policy of not acquiescing to the demands of terrorists. The arms deals were conducted through third parties and were initially denied by the president. Governmental officials subsequently testified that one of the goals of the arms deals was to improve relations with moderates in Iran. Millions of dollars of arms were sold without solid results. The hostages were either not released as promised or their release came only after additional dealings and negotiations. To make matters worse, there was no evidence that the exchange augmented the position of moderates in Iran. Furthermore, not all the money that was exchanged during the deals could be accounted for. Some disappeared from Swiss bank accounts where the money for the arms was funneled.

Even before Reagan approved of the arms-for-hostages deal, the administration had already solicited funds for the contras from foreign nations. This allowed the administration to claim that technically it was in compliance with the **Boland Amendment,** which banned federal funding for the contras except for humanitarian purposes. Whether President Reagan explicitly approved of a plan to take money derived from the arms-for-hostages deal and provide it to the contras is still unclear. Without a doubt, Colonel **Oliver North, Robert (Bud) McFarlane, William Joseph Casey,** and other top officials believed that the president approved of such a plan, at least in its broad outlines if not in fine detail. For instance, during congressional hearings, Oliver North admitted that he had negotiated a deal with the Iranians whereby they would receive 1,000 Tube-launched missiles (TOW) in exchange for the release of hostages in Beirut and about $6 to $10 million dollars. North then testified that he took these funds and gave them to Richard Secord, a retired army general, who bought weapons to trade for the hostages.

When rumors of such deals first surfaced, the administration had denied them. However, as more information was released, the administration's denials became less and less credible. Finally, in March 1987, President Reagan, in a public address, took full responsibility for his actions and those of his administration. However, this pronouncement only came after the **Tower Commission** had issued a report that chastised the administration for its lax control over the operations of the National Security Council and after Colonel Oliver North, a central figure in the affair, had been forced to resign. Indeed, various figures in the affair, from Presidents Reagan and Bush to Secretary of Defense **Caspar Willard Weinberger** and Colonel North, continued to present conflicting interpretations and testimony regarding the specific responsibility and culpability of individuals well into the 1990s. During nationally televised hearings before Congress, North gained fame by claiming that he simply was following the orders of the president, while at the same time arguing that the actions were justifiable. At the time, President Reagan denied that he knew of many of the specifics of the affair, including the decision to divert funds to the contras. Likewise, George Bush denied that he was privy to major policy decisions regarding the affair, although other parties involved claimed that he was. The sudden death of Central Intelligence Agency (CIA) director William Casey, who seemed to be at the center of the covert operations, complicated the situation.

Ultimately, North, **John Marlan Poindexter,** McFarlane, and General Richard Secord were indicted, tried, and convicted on charges stemming from the Iran-contra affair. Many of the convictions were subsequently overturned on technical grounds—namely, that the special prosecutor had relied on information obtained by congressional investigators while under grants of immunity to obtain the convictions. In his final report, Special Prosecutor Lawrence Walsh harshly criticized the President and many of his top aides. By the time the report was issued, however, public interest in the affair had died, Walsh himself had become a target of criticism for his overzealousness in the case, and North had become a champion of the **New Right** for his defiance of Congress and his patriotic zeal.

Perhaps the most difficult part of the Iran-contra affair to calculate is its political costs. To an extent, the affair damaged the Reagan administration, diminishing the president's image as a "teflon president" invulnerable to personal criticism. The affair certainly emboldened Democrats in Congress, as they overrode several of Reagan's vetoes of domestic reform bills. However, on his retirement, Reagan's approval ratings were very high, suggesting that he managed to survive the Iran-contra affair with his standing relatively untarnished. In addition, George Bush managed to deflect all attempts to turn Iran-contra into a political issue in 1988. Moreover, Oliver North managed to turn his commitment to the cause of the contras and open hostility toward congressional meddlers into a political asset. Thus, despite the fact that the affair involved numerous top Reagan administration officials, represented a possible violation of the law by the president, and achieved little in terms of **foreign policy** objectives, it had remarkably little long-term impact on the Reagan presidency, especially when compared to the effect that similar scandals, such as Watergate, had on previous presidents.

Brief Chronology of the Iran-Contra Affair

Dec. 1981. Executive order authorizing the CIA to covertly aid Nicaraguan contras signed by President Reagan.

Dec. 20–21, 1982. Congress passes Boland Amendment restricting funding of the contras.

Feb.–Aug. 1985. Colonel Oliver North arranges for purchase of arms for hostages by private and foreign sources. Reagan states that North and others are providing only military advice.

Nov. 19, 1985. North assumes responsibilities for plan to sell arms to Iran in exchange for hostages held in Lebanon.

Apr. 4, 1986. In memorandum to new National Security Adviser, John Poindexter, for Reagan's eyes, North proposes funneling profits from the arms-for-hostages deals to contras.

Oct. 5–9, 1986. Eugene Hasenfus, American CIA operative providing arms to contras, shot down over Nicaragua by Sandinistas.

Nov. 3–19, 1986. Reports of arms-for-hostages deal broken by press. Reagan ends exchange.

Nov. 25, 1986. North and Poindexter dismissed by Reagan after **Edwin Meese III** announces that some of profits from arms-for-hostages deal were diverted to the contras.

Dec. 19, 1986. Special prosecutor, Lawrence Walsh, appointed to investigate Iran-contra affair.

Feb. 16, 1987. Tower Commission issues report. It criticizes management of National Security Council but finds no criminal wrongdoing on the president's part.

Jul. 7–15, 1987. Congressional investigations of Iran-contra affair come to a climax with nationally televised testimony and questioning of Oliver North.

Nov. 18, 1987. Congressional report claims that President Reagan is ultimately responsible for Iran-contra affair. Republicans on committee reject this stern conclusion.

Apr. 7, 1990. Poindexter convicted of perjury.

May 4, 1990. North convicted of obstructing justice.

Jul. 20, 1990. North and Poindexter's convictions overturned on technical grounds.

Dec. 24, 1992. Former Defense Secretary Caspar Willard Weinberger is pardoned by President Bush. (He was under indictment for perjury.)

Jan. 18, 1992. Special prosecutor issues final report. While the report finds that neither Reagan nor Bush committed any criminal activities, it is sharply critical of the Reagan administration for deceiving Congress and the public about the affair.

Suggested Readings: Theodore Draper, *A Very Thin Line: The Iran-Contra Affairs* (1991); John Tower, Edmund Muskie and Brent Scowcroft, *Tower Commission Report* (1987); Lawrence Walsh, *Iran-Contra: The Final Report* (1994); Ann Wroe, *Lives, Lies, and the Iran-Contra Affair* (1991).

Related Entries: Iranian Hostages; "Teflon Presidency."

IRANIAN HOSTAGES. Twenty minutes after Ronald Reagan was sworn in as the fortieth president of the United States, fifty-two Americans who had been held hostage in Iran since November 1979 were released. For over fourteen months their captivity had plagued the Carter administration. In a sense **James (Jimmy) Earl Carter** was held hostage by the crisis. It came to symbolize his shortcomings as president, making him look inept and America weak. Their release, in contrast—even though arranged by President Carter—provided a fitting symbol of the new president's promise to make America strong again.

In November 1979, sixty-six Americans were captured by militant Islamic students. A few of them subsequently escaped, but the vast majority were held captive for 444 days. Throughout 1980 the Carter administration sought their release, including an unsuccessful rescue mission, in which three U.S. helicopters were disabled by desert sand and eight commandos were killed. Two days before the election, the Iranian parliament announced the conditions for return of the hostages. This included an agreement to unfreeze approximately $8 billion in Iranian assets, which had been frozen by the Carter administration and the lifting of trade sanctions against Iran. The Iranians also demanded that the United States pledge not to interfere in Iranian internal affairs. Working through Algerian intermediaries, on the day before Reagan became President, the Carter administration and representatives of the government of Iran sealed a deal that met all Iran's demands.

Gary Sick, a Carter administration official, later contended that President Reagan's campaign director, **William Joseph Casey**—who later served as Reagan's director of the Central Intelligence Agency—had secretly negotiated a deal with the Iranians that had ensured that they would not release the hostages before the election, in exchange for favorable treatment by Reagan when he became president. When Congress held hearings to investigate these allegations, however, Reagan unconditionally denied the charges (both as president and after leaving office). The hearings did not produce any conclusive evidence to substantiate Sick's charges of this so-called "October surprise."

Suggested Readings: James A. Bill, *The Eagle and the Lion* (1988); Paul Ryan, *The Iranian Rescue Mission* (1985); Gary Sick, *October Surprise* (1991).

IRAN-IRAQ WAR. The Iran-Iraq War was the longest and one of the most deadly wars to take place in modern times. It began in September

1980, when Iraqi troops invaded Iran, and did not end until August 20, 1988. The war had both immediate and long-term causes, ranging from border disputes to ethnic and intra-Islamic religious rivalries. The war widened to include attacks on civilian sites, the use of chemical weapons by Iraq, and the bombing of neutral ships in the Persian Gulf. While it is difficult to determine the number of lives lost in the war, experts estimate that there were in excess of a million casualties.

The official U.S. position toward the war was neutrality. Prior to the fall of the shah of Iran in 1979, the United States had been allied with Iran against Iraq, which was a Soviet ally. The rise of militant Islamic fundamentalists in Iran, capped by the **Iranian hostage** crisis, however, prevented the United States from supporting Iran. Long-standing antagonisms between the United States and Iraq, as well as its attacks on Iranian oil tankers and use of chemical weapons, kept the United States in the neutral corner.

One of the main policy objectives of the United States during the long Iran-Iraq War was to improve its relations with other Arab nations, especially Saudi Arabia and Kuwait, both of which feared that the war would spill over their borders. The United States did not wish for either Iran or Iraq to win the war, fearing the development of a single anti-American power in the region.

During the latter part of the war, the Reagan administration increased U.S. naval presence in the Persian Gulf so as to assure the safe movement of oil tankers in and out of the region. In 1988 this resulted in the downing of a civilian Iranian airliner, which was mistakenly identified as a warplane by crewmen on the warship USS *Vincennes.* All 290 passengers onboard the airliner were killed.

One of the legacies of the war was that when the **Persian Gulf War** erupted, Iran, which was the next largest Islamic military power in the region after Iraq, did not join Saddam Hussein when he called for a *jihad* (holy war) against the West. This made the U.S. task in the region easier to successfully complete.

Suggested Reading: Dilip Hiro, *The Longest War: The Iran-Iraq Military Conflict* (1991).

Related Entries: Foreign Policy; Middle East.

J

JACKSON, JESSE LOUIS. (October 8, 1941, Greenville, S.C.– .) Candidate for Democratic presidential nomination, 1984, 1988.

In the 1980s, Jesse Jackson, the son of a poor black cosmetologist and a former protégé of Dr. Martin Luther King, Jr., became the most prominent black man in the United States. Twice he ran for the Democratic presidential nomination. In 1988 he won more votes than many ever dreamed possible for a black man. Jackson, who was born out-of-wedlock—a point he often emphasized in his political campaigns to counter the Reagan administration's attacks on unwed mothers—grew up in Greenville, South Carolina. A star football, basketball, and baseball player, he won a sport's scholarship to the University of Illinois. After a year there he transferred to the University of North Carolina Agricultural and Technical State in Greensboro. Shortly before he arrived, four black students from the college had staged the first sit-ins, which in turn helped catalyze a new phase in the **civil rights** movement.

While pursuing his degree, Jackson became involved in the fight for racial equality, leaving college one semester short of graduation in order to work for Operation Breadbasket, a program organized by the Southern Christian Leadership Conference headed by Martin Luther King, Jr. Under Jackson's direction, Operation Breadbasket vigorously fought for more jobs for young blacks in Chicago. During this time period, Jackson worked closely with King and was at King's side at the time of his assassination. In the 1970s Jackson remained active in the fight for civil rights, most notably as director of Operation PUSH (People United to Save Humanity), which grew out of Operation Breadbasket. Jackson promoted self-esteem among blacks with his slogan, "I am somebody."

In 1984 Jackson mounted a somewhat disorganized campaign for the Democratic nomination for the presidency. Nonetheless, he did better than expected, winning more votes than former Democratic Presidential nominee George McGovern, the famed astronaut Senator John Glenn, and several other contenders. In 1988 Jackson mounted another campaign for the Democratic presidential nomination. Jackson won Democratic primaries in several Deep South states, including Alabama, Mississippi, Georgia, and Louisiana. Just twenty years earlier, it was next to impossible for a black person to vote, not to mention run for president, in these states. Even though Jackson failed to secure the presidential nomination, losing to **Michael Stanley Dukakis,** his campaign was inspiring to many. Jackson's outstanding oratory ability, in particular, won him the admiration of even some of his sternest critics. His "Keep Hope Alive" address to the Democratic convention was one of the highlights of the entire campaign.

Throughout the 1980s, Jackson was a sharp critic of the Reagan administration's **domestic policy** and **foreign policy,** arguing that both favored the elite over the downtrodden. Jackson's flamboyance and outspokenness, however, often led others to describe him as an extremist who could never really get elected to the presidency. At times, his outspokenness even offended individuals who might otherwise have supported him, as was the case when he referred to New York City as "Hymietown," a clear offense to many Jews, who had traditionally supported civil rights.

Jackson is married to the former Jacqueline Lavina Brown. They have five children. He is an ordained minister and did postgraduate studies at the Chicago Theological Seminary.

Suggested Readings: Frank Clemente and Frank Watkins, ed., *Keep Hope Alive: Jesse Jackson* (1989); Elizabeth O. Colton, *The Jackson Phenomenon* (1984); *Current Biography* (1986) p. 243; Adolph Reed, *The Jesse Jackson Phenomenon* (1986).

Related Entries: Election of 1984; Election of 1988.

JAPAN. Disputes over the growing **trade deficit** dominated relations between the United States and Japan during the Ronald Reagan–George Bush years. By 1985, about one-third of the United States record-high (near $150 billion) trade deficit grew out of a trade imbalance with Japan. To make matters worse, Japanese-made goods were very visible in the American market. Arguing that Japan restricted the entrance of American-made goods into Japan, many Democrats and Republicans alike called for retaliation against Japan. The Reagan administration convinced the Japanese to establish voluntary quotas on the export to the United States of automobiles and steel so as to reduce the trade deficit. At about the same time, the United States pushed for a devaluation of the dollar in relation to the Japanese yen, so as to make American goods cheaper abroad. This did lead to some decrease in the trade deficit but did not break the American consumers' near addiction to Japanese-made goods.

The declining trade deficit during the latter part of the 1980s, however, did not quench America's desire to get tough with Japan. Japanese investments in the United States, sensationalized by the media, heightened anti-Japanese feelings. In 1988 Congress enacted the Omnibus Trade and Competitiveness Act which gave the federal government the authority to retaliate against Japan—via high tariffs—if Japanese trade barriers did not come down. However, the ability to get the barriers down was hampered by several factors. Perhaps most important, the American appetite for Japanese-made products remained very high. By 1989 Honda had become the best-selling car in America, and Japanese electronic goods, from videocassette recorders (VCRs) to stereo components, gained an even greater share of the American market. Moreover, as many economists noted, the American and Japanese economies were so interdependent that any retaliation or trade war was bound to hurt them both.

In spite of tensions over trade, Japan and the United States remained strong allies. Japan supported the U.S. role in the **Persian Gulf War** and provided financial support to other allies in Southeast Asia. In addition, neither Reagan nor Bush wanted to risk alienating Japan, which they saw as the main keystone for stability in the Pacific Rim region.

Suggested Readings: Roger Buckley, *U.S.-Japan Alliance Diplomacy, 1945–1990* (1992); Akira Iriye and Warren Cohen, eds., *The United States and Japan in the Postwar World* (1984).

Related Entry: High Technology.

JAPANESE-AMERICAN INTERNEES, REPARATIONS FOR. On April 20, 1988, following intense and emotional debate, the U.S. Senate passed a bill to compensate the families of Japanese-Americans who were interned during World War II. Under provisions of the bill, the U.S. government would pay about 60,000 surviving family members up to $20,000 each. The House of Representatives had already passed a similar bill.

Even though President Ronald Reagan originally opposed paying reparations, terming them too costly, on August 10, 1988, he signed the bill into law. At the time, he called the decision to intern the Japanese during World War II a "mistake" that was finally being rectified. One of the chief opponents of reparations was North Carolina Senator **Jesse A. Helms.** He sought to hold up the bill by attaching an amendment that demanded that Japan pay reparations to the victims of the Japanese attack on Pearl Harbor in exchange for the reparations for Japanese-American citizens whose rights had been denied. Helms's amendment failed to gain congressional approval.

Two of the reparation bill's main sponsors were Senators Spark Matsunaga and Daniel Inouye, both Democrats from Hawaii and World War II veterans. Inouye had received the Bronze Star and two Purple Hearts for his service in Italy. Another sponsor was Congressman Normandy Y. Mineta, a Democrat from California who had been interned in a camp for Japanese-Americans during World War II. Only ten years old at the time, Mineta watched his family lose its property and freedom without having done anything wrong.

Suggested Readings: *Congressional Quarterly Almanac* (1988); *Facts on File* (1988); *Historical Documents* (1988) p. 287.

JOHN PAUL II (KAROL WOJTYLA). (May 18, 1920, Wadowice, Poland– .) Pope of Roman Catholic Church, 1978– .

One of the most important world figures during the Ronald Reagan–George Bush years was John Paul II, the Roman Catholic Pope. Born Karol Wojtyla, he became the first Pope of Polish descent on October 16, 1978. On May 13, 1981, less than two months after **John W. Hinckley, Jr.,** shot President Reagan, John Paul II was shot in an assassination attempt in St. Peter's Square. Like Reagan, he fully recovered.

Theologically, John Paul II is considered a very conservative man. He resisted reforms that would have further secularized the church, such as allowing women to become priests. He emphasized the Roman Catholic Church's opposition to **abortion** and all other forms of artificial birth control. He resisted calls to modernize the church any further than his post–World War II predecessors already had.

In spite of his conservative theology, John Paul II is extremely popular. He is a charismatic man who has traveled abroad widely, drawing enormous crowds wherever he goes. Among his many trips was one to North America in 1987. Before huge crowds in Miami, San Francisco, Detroit,

President Reagan with Pope John Paul II, Fairbanks, Alaska, May 2, 1984. Reagan Library.

and other American cities, he stressed the conservative views of the Roman Catholic Church and refused to offer concessions to American Catholics who want the Church to grant a greater role to women and the laity.

John Paul II has had an especially significant impact on Poland, his native country. During the 1980s, Poland was in the throes of a struggle between Solidarity, representing the forces of democracy, and the Communist Party. John Paul II supported the Solidarity movement, while at the same time mediating a peaceful resolution of the struggle. His efforts helped establish Solidarity as the new government in Poland.

Suggested Readings: John Paul II, *The Pope Speaks to the American Church* (1992); David Wiley, *God's Politician: John Paul at the Vatican* (1992).

"JUST SAY NO". A central part of the Reagan administration's **war on drugs** was its campaign to get drug abusers and potential abusers to "just say no" to drugs. First Lady **Nancy Davis Reagan** emphasized that the answer to drugs was individual responsibility, as embodied by this slogan. She associated herself with a youth-oriented "Just Say No" campaign, which was run by the Just Say No Foundation and established "Just Say No" clubs. As part of this campaign she prodded parents and community leaders to enforce zero tolerance for drug use. At the same time, she called for men and women around the globe to become involved in the war on drugs and help youth resist the pressure to use them.

While many experts in the field welcomed the first lady's interest in raising awareness about drugs in American society, they found her remedy naive. They argued that it oversimplified the problem by not examining why youths used drugs in the first place. As one critic, Richard Schwebel, argued: "With adolescents, the 'Just Say No' approach is entirely misdirected. Adolescents . . . do not necessarily benefit from the campaign nor take it seriously."

Suggested Readings: Nancy Reagan, "The War on Drugs Is Desperately Needed," in *Drug Abuse: Opposing Viewpoints* (1988) ed. by Julie S. Bach; Richard Schwebel, *Saying No Is Not Enough* (1989).

K

KEATING FIVE. On February 27, 1991, the Senate Ethics Committee rebuked five prominent senators for improper actions in connection with Charles H. Keating, a prominent figure in the **savings and loan crisis.** The five senators were Alan Cranston, Democrat from California; Dennis DeConcini, Democrat from Arizona; Donald Riegle, Democrat from Michigan; John Glenn, Democrat from Ohio; and John McCain, Republican from Arizona. Keating, who was later convicted on charges stemming from the savings and loan crisis, had contributed $1.5 million to the campaigns of these five senators. The ethics committee investigated charges that they had intervened improperly with federal regulators on his behalf in return for these contributions. Of the five, the ethics committee found "substantial credible evidence" of misconduct for only one, Cranston of California. The Republicans on the ethics panel wanted to censure Cranston, who was a one-time candidate for the Democratic nomination for the presidency. The Democrats on the panel, however, refused to go this far, and instead, a compromise statement of reprimand was read into the *Congressional Record,* which described Cranston's behavior as "improper and repugnant." In response to these charges, Cranston admitted no wrongdoing. On the contrary, he proclaimed that he was being used as a scapegoat. Cranston added that his actions "did not violate established norms" of the Senate, thus suggesting that the entire Senate was judging him by stricter standards than it would wish itself judged by.

The Keating Five scandal grew out of an investigation conducted by Common Cause, a nonpartisan, although generally liberal, public interest group. In October 1989, Common Cause had requested that the Senate and Justice Department examine ties between Charles Keating and Cranston. Keating, who headed Lincoln Savings and Loan Association in California (one of the largest savings and loan institutions in the nation to fail), had contributed over $1 million to Cranston's senatorial campaign over a five-year period from 1982 to 1987 and an additional $500,000 to the other four senators. The Senate hired a special counsel, Robert S. Bennett, to investigate charges of possible impropriety. The committee found that even though the five senators had not caused Lincoln Savings to fail or broken any law, Cranston "may have engaged in improper conduct which may reflect [badly] upon the Senate."

None of the five senators was charged with breaking the law. However, Cranston did not seek reelection in 1992 and in 1994, both DeConcini and Riegle chose not to run again. The Keating Five incidents added to the demand for **campaign finance reform,** with some arguing that it was the need to raise large sums of money that produced such semblances of impropriety. The Keating Five scandal also added to a growing disillusionment with the federal government, with polls showing that the public's faith in Congress falling to all-time lows.

Suggested Readings: Michael Binstein, *Trust Me: Charles Keating and the Missing Billions* (1993); *Facts on File* (1991).

Related Entries: House of Representatives, United States; Senate, United States.

KEMP, JACK FRENCH. (July 13, 1935, Los Angeles, Calif.– .) U.S. Congressman, 1971–1989; Secretary of Housing and Urban Development, 1989–1992.

During the 1980s Jack Kemp was one of the most noteworthy young Republicans in Washington, D.C. He cosponsored the Kemp-Roth tax bill (**Economic Recovery Act of 1981**), which cut taxes by 25 percent over three years. This was one of the cornerstones of the Ronald Reagan administration's domestic agenda. While in Congress, and later, as secretary of housing and urban development, he promoted numerous other "neoconservative" ideas, from school vouchers to empowerment or enterprise zones. The former would provide tax credits to those who chose to send their children to private schools. This, according to its proponents, would ease the burden of paying for private education for middle- and working-class families while at the same time spurring public schools to compete in order to improve their product. The latter would offer tax credits or other inducements to businesses to locate in poor urban neighborhoods, thus boosting economic growth in areas of the greatest need. Both proposals reflected Kemp's faith in the free market.

President Reagan with Jack Kemp. Reagan Library.

Kemp's significance, however, went beyond the specifics of his proposals. His youth and charisma led many to deem him the heir to Ronald Reagan. The fact that he represented a working-class district in the Buffalo, New York, region demonstrated that he would be able to win votes among the so-called Reagan Democrats, blue-collar, urban Catholic or ethnic Americans who had traditionally allied themselves with the Democratic Party. Kemp's concentration on urban problems, even if he offered a conservative solution that ran counter to those favored by most African-American representatives, also suggested that he might be able to garner black votes for the Republican Party, something few other Republican candidates could promise.

However, Kemp's not-so-subtle interest in higher office, as well as his lukewarm endorsement of much of the **New Right**'s social and cultural agenda, put him at odds with other Republican notables. In 1992, Kemp clashed with Bush's top aides following the **Los Angeles riot.** Kemp rushed off to Los Angeles following the outbreak of violence, offering his help in regenerating South Central Los Angeles. This decisive action made Bush, who responded slowly to the events, appear uncaring and out-of-touch.

Kemp is married to the former Joanne Main. They have four children. He earned his B.A. from Occidental College (1957). After spending a year in the U.S. Army, he became a professional football player, one of the biggest stars in the fledgling American Football league. In 1970, shortly after his retirement from football, he successfully ran for Congress. Many thought he would run for president in 1996. However, in 1995 he announced that he would not seek the Republican nomination.

Suggested Readings: Fred Barnes, "Notes on Kemp," *New Republic,* May 9, 1994, p. 18; *Current Biography* (1980) p. 181. David Frumm, "Happy Warrior," *National Review,* August 1, 1994, p. 38.

KEMP-ROTH TAX ACT. See **ECONOMIC RECOVERY ACT OF 1981.**

KENNEDY, ANTHONY MCLEOD. (July 23, 1936, Sacramento, Calif.– .) U.S. Supreme Court Justice, 1988– .

Throughout his presidency, Ronald Reagan sought to move the **courts** in a more conservative direction, including the **Supreme Court.** His last nominee to the Supreme Court, Anthony M. Kennedy, fit this pattern.

As a youth Kennedy worked as a page for the state legislature in California. He earned his B.A. (1958) from Stanford University, studied abroad for a year at the London School of Economics, and then gained his law degree from Harvard University (1961). For two years he worked at Thelen, Marrin, John & Bridges, a private law firm in San Francisco. On his father's death, he returned to Sacramento to start his own law firm. For twenty-three years he taught law on a part-time basis, earning fame for his imaginative lectures. He helped draft tax-reduction legislation for Governor Reagan and became involved in state politics in a variety of other ways.

In 1975, Kennedy became a judge of the U.S. Court of Appeals for the Ninth Circuit. As a judge, he earned a reputation as a conservative, especially on **civil rights,** civil liberties, and criminal law. Unlike **Robert Heron Bork** or **Antonin Scalia,** however, he was not a dogmatic or ideological conservative. As he told the Senate judicial committee during his Supreme Court confirmation hearings: "I do not have an overarching theory, a unitary theory of interpretation. I am searching, as I think many judges are, for the correct balance in constitutional interpretation." Among his more controversial rulings as an appellate court judge was one that upheld the right of the U.S. Navy to dismiss a serviceman due to his homosexuality (*Beller* v. *Middendorf,* 1980).

Unlike Bork, Kennedy won the unanimous support of the American Bar Association. While he faced some tough questioning during his confirmation hearings, he was unanimously confirmed by the entire Senate. Since joining the Supreme Court, he has tended to occupy a middle ground, sometimes siding with **William Hubbs Rehnquist,** Scalia, and Clarence Thomas, but just as often siding with **Sandra Day O'Connor** and **David Souter,** who have resisted reversing some of the more famous decisions of the Earl Warren and **Warren Earl Burger** Courts, most notably the *Roe* v. *Wade* decision, which provides women with the right to have an **abortion.**

Kennedy is married to Mary Jeanne Davis. They have three children.

Suggested Readings: *Current Biography* (1988) p. 289; Ann McDaniel, "The Court Spins Right," *Newsweek,* June 28, 1989, p. 16; Robert Reinhold, "Restrained Pragmatist," *New York Times Biographical Service,* November 1987, p. 1181.

Related Entries: Thomas-Hill Hearings; Women's Rights.

KEYWORTH, GEORGE ALBERT, 2ND. (November 30, 1939, Boston, Mass.– .) Science Adviser to President Ronald Reagan and Director, Office of Science and Technology, 1981–1985.

George Keyworth served as President Ronald Reagan's science adviser from 1981 until 1985. From the moment of his confirmation, he committed himself to acting as a "team player," promoting Reagan's broader agenda of increasing **defense spending** and cutting the size of the federal government. He called for decreasing government's involvement in research projects. At the same time he fought hard to increase government grants for basic research which, as he argued, kept the United States at the "frontier of knowledge" and ahead of the **Soviet Union** in terms of defense. To bolster support for his views, Keyworth formed an advisory panel, the Science Council, comprised largely of other conservative scientists (most prominently Edward Teller, the father of the Hydrogen bomb and a long-time adviser to Ronald Reagan on defense matters). When President Reagan announced his intention to develop a space-based anti–nuclear weapons system, the **Strategic Defense Initiative**

(Star Wars), Keyworth became one of its chief advocates. When two members of the Science Council resigned in objection to the initiative, Keyworth defended the president, declaring that their criticism was "without substantiation and politically motivated."

Keyworth was born and raised in Massachusetts. He attended Deerfield Academy, received his B.A. in physics from Yale University (1963), and earned his Ph.D. in nuclear physics from Duke University (1968). On graduation he went to work at the Los Alamos laboratory in New Mexico, moving up the ranks from research scientist to head of the experimental physics division in 1978. After four years as President Reagan's chief science adviser, he resigned from his post, as planned, and formed his own private firm with former Central Intelligence Agency director **William Joseph Casey** and Herbert Meyer, the vice president of the National Intelligence Council.

Keyworth is married to Polly Lauterbach (Keyworth). They have two children.

Suggested Readings: *Current Biography* (1986) p. 265; "George Keyworth Looks Back," *Chemical and Engineering News,* May 26, 1986, p. 7; Irwin Goodwin, "Keyworth: Parting Shots," *Physics Today,* February 1986, p. 57.

KIRKPATRICK, JEANE JORDAN. (November 19, 1926, Duncan, Okla.– .) U.S. Ambassador to the United Nations, 1981–1985.

In 1981 Jeane Kirkpatrick, a Republican professor of political science (and a former Democrat), became the first woman ambassador to the United Nations in U.S. history. In addition to her specific responsibilities at the United Nations, she was one of the chief architects of Reagan's **foreign policy,** especially during his first four years in office.

Kirkpatrick was born in a small town near the Texas border. An outstanding student, she spent two years at Stephens College, in Columbia, Missouri, and then received her B.A. from Barnard College in New York City and her M.A. from Columbia University. From the mid-1950s through the late 1960s she worked for the Defense Department, raised three children, taught political science at Trinity College, and completed her Ph.D. at Columbia (1968). Shortly before finishing her doctorate she joined the faculty of Georgetown University, where she remained for over a decade.

Reared as a New Deal Democrat, she worked for former vice president Hubert Humphrey in his unsuccessful presidential bids in 1968 and 1972. However, as the Democratic Party moved to the left, she drifted out of the party. Like other neoconservatives, she disagreed with the human rights emphasis of President Carter's foreign policy. Her article in *Com-*

President Reagan with UN Ambassador Jeanne Kirkpatrick. Reagan Library.

mentary (November 1979), "Dictatorships and Double Standards," caught the attention of Ronald Reagan and, in turn, landed her a position as one of his foreign policy advisers during the 1980 presidential campaign. Soon after Reagan won the election, he nominated her to the post of ambassador to the United Nations. The Senate unanimously confirmed her nomination.

In her writings and while ambassador she argued, in what some labeled the "Kirkpatrick doctrine," that the United States should support authoritarian regimes that were friendly to the United States but should vigorously oppose totalitarian regimes that were not. Like President Reagan, she favored establishing a strong defense and aiding anticommunist insurgents, such as the contras in **Nicaragua.** The Reagan administration by and large followed this doctrine, particularly in **Latin America** and, to a lesser extent, in **South Africa.** This position contrasted sharply with President **James (Jimmy) Earl Carter**'s emphasis on human rights and put her at odds with those who sought to democratize various nations around the globe. Because of her views and persona, which appeared tough, she became a target of liberal criticism.

While ambassador to the United Nations she was often critical of the organization for its anti-American bias. She did not believe it was proper to allow small nonaligned nations to bash the United States without repercussions, and she prompted Congress to link foreign aid to the voting records of these nations. While her first year in office was filled with difficulties, things improved when **George Pratt Shultz,** whom she got along with better than **Alexander Meigs Haig, Jr.**, became secretary of state.

In 1985 Kirkpatrick returned to teaching. She remained active politically, writing a syndicated column and speaking on a regular basis. Her departure from the Reagan administration coincided with the ascendancy of **Mikhail Sergeyevich Gorbachev** in the **Soviet Union** and the improvement in relations between the two superpowers. By and large she favored a cautious attitude toward the Soviet Union. While she continued to promote conservative foreign policy views in her writings and lectures, at times she openly disagreed with the Republican Party on social issues.

Kirkpatrick is married to Evron Kirkpatrick. Together they have raised three sons. She is the author of numerous articles and books.

Suggested Readings: Pat Harrison, *Jeane Kirkpatrick* (1991); Jeane J. Kirkpatrick, *Dictatorships and Double Standards: Rationalism and Reason in Politics* (1982); Jeane J. Kirkpatrick, *The Reagan Doctrine and U.S. Foreign Policy* (1985).

Related Entries: Election of 1980; Reagan Doctrine.

KOOP, C. (CHARLES) EVERETT. (October 14, 1916, Brooklyn, N.Y.–) Surgeon General of the United States, 1981–1990.

While most expected that C. Everett Koop, M.D., like most surgeon generals before him, would be merely a figurehead in Washington, D.C., he quickly distinguished himself as the best-known surgeon general in years and perhaps the most effective one ever. His experience as a practicing physician earned him respect within the medical and public health professions. His willingness to use his position as a bully pulpit and his tireless advocacy of public education on various health issues made him a favorite with the press and public at large. Even when his views conflicted with those of conservatives, including President Ronald Reagan, his personality, which was akin to that of an old New England minister, made him one of the most-liked members of the administration.

Ironically, Koop almost did not become surgeon general as critics stalled his confirmation for nine months. Many liberals attacked him as an religious zealot, even calling him Dr. Kook, because of his stance against **abortion** and his religious evangelicalism. Koop defended his views by pointing to his experience as a pediatric surgeon for thirty-three years, which included saving the lives of numerous deformed infants who went on to live productive lives. By the end of Reagan's term, Koop had become a favorite with many liberals, not because he changed his stance on abortion—which he did not—but because he openly broke with the conservative orthodoxy on numerous other medical and public health issues.

Most important, from early on he took on the cigarette industry. He called for a "smoke-free society" by the year 2000, describing the tobacco industry's claims that cigarettes did not cause cancer, "flat-footed lies." He castigated the United States as a nation of "fatsoes" and demanded that Americans give up red meat in favor of a high-fiber diet. Furthermore, while the Reagan administration and conservatives in general sought to portray **acquired immunodeficiency syndrome** (AIDS) as a homosexual disease and responded slowly to the growing epidemic, Koop took a much more open and controversial stance. In a report that he released in 1986, Koop refused to preach abstinence as the only cure. Rather he promoted sex education and safe-sex with condoms. As he stated, "The White House doesn't like the C word. But if you don't talk about condoms, people are going to die." Koop further angered conservatives by stating that abortion was not psychologically harmful, which they had contended for years.

Koop grew up in New York City, earning his B.A. from Dartmouth and his M.D. from Cornell University. In 1948 he became the chief surgeon at Children's Hospital in Philadelphia, gaining fame when he separated Siamese twins who had been joined at the abdomen and pelvis. He established the nation's first neonatal unit.

He is married and has four children, the youngest of whom, David, died while mountain climbing in 1968.

Suggested Readings: Margaret Carson, "Profile: A Doctor Prescribes Hard Truth," *Time,* April 24, 1989, p. 82; C. Everett Koop, *Koop: The Memoirs of America's Family Doctor* (1991).

KOREAN AIRLINES FLIGHT 007. On September 1, 1983, the news media reported that a Soviet jet fighter had shot down Korean Airlines flight 007, killing all 269 passengers and crew members, including Georgia Congressman Larry McDonald. Initially, the Soviets denied the incident. After the United States released radio tapes that documented the attack, the Soviets proclaimed that the commercial Boeing 747 jet had strayed over its airspace and had been warned to return to international airspace or risk attack. Only when it had refused to change course, according to the Soviets, had a Soviet fighter shot down the plane. Soviet authorities added that the refusal of the plane to alter its flight route demonstrated that it was involved in an intelligence-gathering mission. The very fact that U.S. aircraft were monitoring the radio conversation in the first place, the Soviets noted, demonstrated the nature of the flight.

The Ronald Reagan administration and most world leaders argued that this was preposterous. President Reagan described the action as barbaric, ordered the closing of the offices of the Soviet airline Aeroflot in the United States, and suspended negotiations on cultural and scientific exchanges with the **Soviet Union.** The United States sponsored a United Nations (UN) Security Council resolution that condemned the Soviet action and called for a UN investigation of the incident—the Soviets vetoed the resolution. When the governors of New York and New Jersey refused to allow Soviet Foreign Minister Andrey Gromyko to land at the airports in their states, so he could attend a UN meeting, the State Department supported their action. (However, it did allow Gromyko to land at a military airport.)

While the Reagan administration did not suspend grain shipments to the Soviets nor walk out of recently convened arms negotiations, the Korean Airline shooting clearly worsened tensions between the two superpowers. Earlier in the spring relations had reached a new low, as displayed by President Reagan's comment that the Soviet Union was an evil empire. Under the counsel of Secretary of State **George Pratt Shultz,** it had looked as if relations might improve. However, the dispute over the shooting set back whatever steps had been made toward improved relations and a genuine thaw did not develop until **Mikhail Sergeyevich Gorbachev** took power two years later.

Suggested Readings: Seymour Hersh, *The Target Is Destroyed* (1987); Marilyn Young, *Flights of Fancy, Flight of Doom* (1990).

L

LABOR MOVEMENT. The labor movement in the United States suffered from a decline in membership and political clout during the Ronald Reagan years, especially during the first half of the 1980s (see Figure 6). In 1970, unions represented just short of 21 million workers, or about 28 percent of the workforce. Economic stagnation in the 1970s left the total number of unionized workers about the same but reduced the percentage of Americans who belonged to unions to 23 percent of the workforce. During the 1980s, both the total number of men and women and the percentage of workers who belonged to unions declined, the first time in over half a century that both these figures had dropped. By 1986 there were only 17 million unionized workers, representing less than 18 percent of the workforce. By 1992 there were about 16.3 million unionized workers, representing 15.8 percent of the workforce. Not since the 1930s had organized labor been so weak.

The causes for the labor movement's demise were multiple, but nearly all analysts agreed that President Reagan's policies played a part. They noted that Reagan set the tone for labor-management relations very early in his presidency by firing striking air traffic controllers, members of the Professional Air Traffic Controllers Organization (PATCO). Reagan stacked the National Labor Relations Board with probusiness appointees. He also blamed labor for the United States' economic travails. For example, in 1984, following early endorsement by the American Federation of Labor and Conference of Industrial Organizations (AFL-CIO) of **Walter Frederick Mondale,** Reagan described organized labor as a large, selfish, special interest group that sought to unravel the economic recovery.

The decline of labor had a complex political and economic impact on

Figure 6
Labor Union Membership (as Percentage of Labor Force)

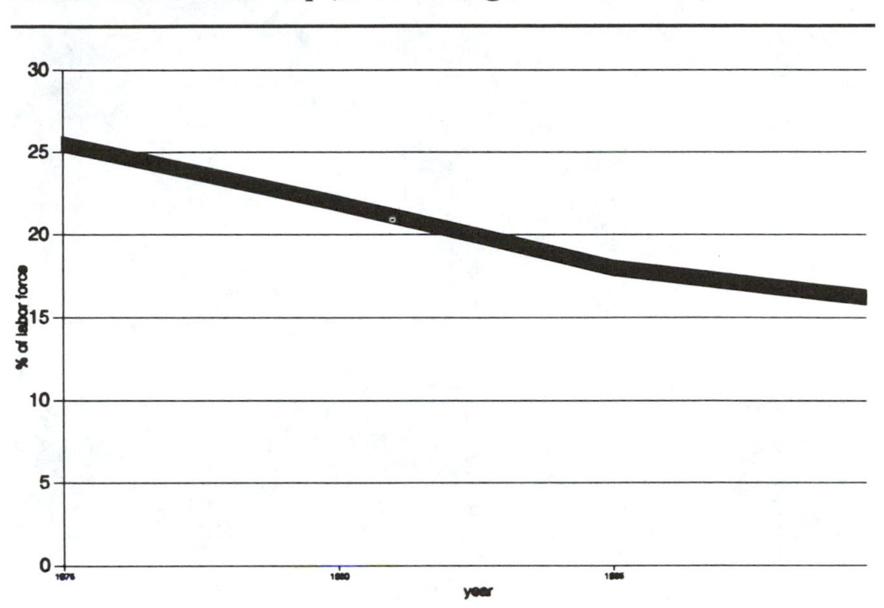

the nation. On the one hand, due to their smaller numbers, labor unions lost political clout. On the other hand, Reagan provided organized labor with a convenient central target. Put another way, he helped solidify the labor movement—this was seen in 1984 when the AFL-CIO endorsed Walter Mondale even before the primaries began. On the economic front, the decline of labor arguably had a ripple effect on the broader middle class. When corporations forced labor unionists to take wage and benefit concessions, nonunion workers often saw their situations worsen as well. Since many Americans did not understand the relationship between labor's decline and their own hard times, however, they did not side with labor in its disputes with the Reagan administration.

Suggested Readings: Gordon Clark, *Unions and Communities under Seige* (1991); Thomas Geoghegan, *Which Side Are You On?* (1991).

Related Entry: Air Traffic Controllers (PATCO) Strike.

LATIN AMERICA. Based on its overall human rights orientation, the **James (Jimmy) Earl Carter** administration pursued a comparatively radical course toward Latin America, at least in comparison to the Ronald Reagan and George Bush administrations. Under Carter, the United States

The invasion of Panama. Still Media Center, Department of Defense.

had negotiated a treaty to sell the Panama Canal to Panama, supported the Sandinista revolution against Anastasio Somoza in **Nicaragua,** and sought improved relations with Cuba. When Reagan became President, the United States took a much different course.

Viewing Carter's policy as a form of appeasement that was too soft on communism, Reagan shifted attention away from human rights to the goal of fighting communism. Shortly after his election, Reagan focused national attention on the communist threat in Nicaragua and **El Salvador.** Over the course of the next two terms, the administration pursued military aid for the right-wing government of El Salvador and for the contras, or anti-Sandinista forces, in Nicaragua. Citing a threat to the lives of American medical students and the danger of a growing communist presence, Reagan ordered the invasion of **Grenada** in 1983. Unlike Carter, Reagan did not seek the ouster of right-wing governments in Argentina, Chile, Brazil, or other South American nations. Moreover, at least until the end of his presidency, Reagan paid little heed to Central American attempts to negotiate a peace settlement for the region.

By the time George Bush became president, Latin America represented a region wrought with contradictions. The Reagan administration had won few friends south of the U.S. border. The **war on drugs** and antiimmigrant fervor in the United States, aimed especially at Mexican-Americans, did little to improve the situation. Matters were also worsened by the **foreign debt crisis,** in which the United States prodded banks to pursue a tough policy rather than put forth a massive aid package. However, in the late 1980s and early 1990s, relations improved somewhat. Clearly, the **collapse of communism** in Europe, combined with Bush's less ideological style, contributed to this change. It paid off via peace accords in Central America, a diminishing of the debt crisis, and a number of democratic elections in the region.

There were exceptions to this change, however. The United States invasion of Panama reinvigorated Latin American distrust of the United States. The Organization of American States even censured the United States for the invasion, with Peru's president, Alan Garcia Perez, terming it a "criminal act." The Bush administration also did not relax its opposition to Fidel Castro in Cuba, which remained a target of U.S. economic sanctions and rhetorical barbs. Moreover, Bush's Latin American policy did not signal a return to Carter's human rights orientation, as became apparent in the last two years of Bush's term. During this period the government continued to allow Cubans to migrate to the United States with relative ease but simultaneously turned back Haitian refugees on the grounds that the Haitians, unlike the Cubans, were not political refugees.

Suggested Readings: Walter Lafeber, *Inevitable Revolutions* (1993); Gaddis Smith, *The Last Years of the Monroe Doctrine* (1994); Howard J. Wiarda, *American Foreign Policy toward Latin America in the '80s and '90s* (1992).

Related Entries: Falkland Islands War; Haiti; Latin America; Panama Canal Treaty; Panama Invasion; Reagan Doctrine.

LAVELLE, RITA MARIE. (September 8, 1947, Portsmouth, Va.– .) Official, Environmental Protection Agency, 1981–1983.

On February 7, 1983, Rita Marie Lavelle was dismissed from her position as assistant administrator for solid waste and emergency response at the Environmental Protection Agency (EPA) amid allegations of perjury and conflict of interest. While **Anne McGill (Gorsuch) Burford,** head of the EPA, told the press that Lavelle's departure grew out of personal, not political, concerns, few believed her statement. In December 1982, the House of Representatives had voted in favor of bringing contempt charges against Lavelle for her failure to provide subpoenaed documents to a House subcommittee investigating the cleanup of toxic waste sites that were under her oversight. Lavelle had refused to do so on the order of EPA director Gorsuch who, herself, was acting on the orders of President Ronald Reagan. A year after she departed from her EPA post, Lavelle was convicted on perjury charges, sentenced to six months in prison with an additional five years of probation, and fined $10,000.

Lavelle spent much of her youth in California. She received her bachelor's degree in biology and mathematics from the College of Holy Names in Oakland, Calif., and an M.B.A. from Pepperdine University. She worked for Governor Reagan, first as a publications assistant and then as part of the state's Department of Consumer Affairs. During the latter half of the 1970s she was employed by various private companies, including Aerojet Liquid Rocket Company. It was her work for this firm, which was one of the companies under investigation by the EPA, that ultimately led to conflict-of-interest charges. Congressional investigators claimed that she lied to them and to other EPA officials about the point at which she discovered that her former employer was under investigation. She also was accused of seeking the dismissal of another EPA employee, Hugh Kaufman, who had complained about the inaction of the environmental agency. While Lavelle was the only EPA employee to be convicted of committing a crime, over twenty other agency officials resigned as a result of the scandal, including EPA director Anne (Gorsuch) Burford.

Suggested Readings: David Burnham, "Reagan Dismisses High E.P.A. Official," *New York Times,* February 8, 1983, p. 1; Irvin Molotsky, "Dismissed E.P.A. Aide: Rita Marie Lavelle," *New York Times,* February 10, 1983, p. II: 10; Philip Shavecoff, "Rita Lavelle Gets 6-Month Term and Is Fined $10,000 for Perjury," *New York Times,* January 10, 1984, p. 1.

Related Entry: Environment.

LAXALT, PAUL DOMINIQUE. (August 2, 1922, Reno, Nev.– .) Governor of Nevada, 1967–1970; U.S. Senator, 1975–1987; Chairman, Ronald Reagan's Campaign Committees, 1976, 1980, 1984; General Chairman, Republican National Committee, 1983–1987.

Paul Laxalt was one of the least known but most influential Republicans of the Ronald Reagan–George Bush years. A Governor, and then Senator, from Nevada, Laxalt was an early supporter of Ronald Reagan. In the mid-1970s, when other Republican (GOP) officials lined up behind the GOP incumbent, Gerald Ford, Laxalt formed Citizens for Reagan. At the 1976 convention, Laxalt nominated Reagan for president, and after Ford lost the general election, he became one of the first supporters of Reagan's 1980 presidential bid.

Laxalt and Reagan shared a common political and ideological orientation. Both advocated a strong defense and were staunch critics of big federal government. In addition, both had a likable and graceful style. As a senator, chairman of Reagan's presidential campaigns, and head of the GOP during the mid-1980s, Laxalt gained a reputation as a staunch conservative with class. He was the first Republican to win a seat to the U.S. Senate from Nevada in twenty years. He retired with high approval ratings in 1987.

Laxalt grew up in Nevada. He enrolled at Santa Clara University in Santa Clara, Calif., but, before he could complete his degree, he joined the U.S. Army to fight in World War II. After the war ended, he earned his bachelor's and law degrees from the University of Denver. Upon graduation he returned to Carson City to open a private law practice. He quickly entered politics, winning the lieutenant governorship in 1962. In 1967 he became the governor of Nevada. As governor he initiated a crackdown on organized crime and prodded big businesses to buy out the casinos—this included investments by multimillionaire Howard Hughes. In 1974, in the wake of the Watergate scandal, when most Republicans were losing at the polls, Laxalt eked out a 626 vote victory in his run for the U.S. Senate. He was reelected by a much wider margin in 1980.

Laxalt is married to Carol Wilson (Laxalt). They have five children.

Suggested Readings: Fred Barnes, "Easy Does It," *New Republic,* August 25, 1986, p. 13; Paul Laxalt, *Venue at the Crossroads* (1982); Amy Wilentz, "I Have Paid My Dues," *Time,* September 2, 1985, p. 18.

Related Entry: Election of 1980; Senate, United States.

LEBANON. See **BEIRUT, LEBANON (BOMBING OF U.S. MARINE BARRACKS).**

LIBYA. Several times during the 1980s, the United States clashed with Libya, a North African nation headed by Muammar Qaddafi. Libya became a target of American military actions for several reasons. Under the leadership of Qaddafi, Libya built up an arsenal of Soviet-made weapons, championed the cause of Islamic fundamentalism in the **Middle East,** and, according to the Reagan administration, sponsored terrorism around the globe. In addition, Qaddafi became the target of American venom because he openly taunted the United States.

In 1982, shortly after **George Pratt Shultz** became secretary of state, U.S. naval forces were deployed to the Gulf of Sidra along Libya's northern coast. Proclaiming that the gulf was Libyan, not international, territory, Qaddafi dared Americans to cross the "line of death." When U.S planes did they encountered Libyan planes. A brief air battle ensued with losses on the Libyan side, but none by U.S. forces. Similar skirmishes and results occurred in January 1989.

In 1986, three years before this second skirmish, Reagan had ordered American planes to bomb Libya following a terrorist attack on a Berlin nightclub. Describing him as "the mad dog of the Middle East," Reagan justified the bombing of Qaddafi's headquarters by arguing that he had sponsored this terrorist attack as well as others. One of Qaddafi's daughters was killed in the attack; the Libyan leader himself survived. Not only was public support for the bombing high, it seemed to have its desired effect. In the wake of the bombing, Qaddafi muted his criticism of the United States.

Suggested Readings: Peter J. Schraeder, *Intervention in the 1980s* (1989); Mahmoud G. El Warfally, *Imagery and Ideology in U.S. Policy toward Libya* (1988).

LOS ANGELES RIOT. On April 29, 1992, four Los Angeles policemen were acquitted of beating Rodney King, a middle-aged black man. Months earlier, an amateur photographer had videotaped King's arrest for drunken driving and his vicious beating by the four policemen. The video tape of the beating was shown nationwide on television and convinced almost everyone who had viewed it that the police would be found guilty of brutality. When the jury returned with a not-guilty verdict, many Americans were shocked. Even more important, the verdict sparked a violent riot in Los Angeles. By the time it ended, fifty-three people lay dead, thousands had been injured and thousands more arrested, and over 1,200 businesses had been destroyed by fires. All told, there was over $1 billion in property damage. It was, by some estimates, the worst riot of the century. To make matters worse, some smaller riots took place in other American cities following the eruption of violence in Los Angeles.

The riots began in South Central Los Angeles, a mostly black section of the community, where approximately 50 percent of all of the residents aged sixteen and over were unemployed and gangs were rampant. Between the hours of 4:00 and 5:35 P.M. on April 29 there were reports that a liquor store had been looted and that youths had begun to smash car windows in the area. Police responded to the calls, crowds gathered, and tensions began to rise. Finding themselves outnumbered, the police retreated and the looting and rioting spread. While the rioting began in South Central Los Angeles, incidents of looting and arson occurred in other parts of the city. Statistics compiled after the riots showed that only one in five of those arrested during the riots, in fact, came from South Central Los Angeles.

Meanwhile the nation watched with horror as video crews aboard helicopters beamed pictures of fires all across Los Angeles. One incident that particularly horrified the nation took place near the spot where the rioting started. Reginald Denny, a white truck driver, was dragged from the cab of the truck by several black youths and beaten into unconsciousness. To make matters worse, Los Angeles Police Chief Robert Gates, who was already a target of sharp criticism growing out of the King beating and other alleged incidents of brutality by members of the Los Angeles police force, was nowhere to be seen. Ultimately, state troopers were dispatched to Los Angeles to help control the riots.

The riots proved a major test of the Bush administration and, some contended, served as a turning point in its history. Prior to the riots, Bush's popularity was riding high. However, in combination with the recession, the riots suggested to the public that Bush was too concerned with **foreign policy** matters and lacked solutions to domestic problems. Bush responded to the riots by demanding law and order. Despite the fact that he, too, was surprised by the verdict in the Rodney King case, he defended the jury's action. Presidential spokesman **Marlin (Max) Fitzwater** added that the deeper cause of the riots was the failed policies of the liberal Great Society, especially the welfare programs established by President Lyndon Johnson during the mid-1960s. Subsequently, in his famous "Murphy Brown" speech, **Danforth (Dan) James Quayle** blamed the riots on declining moral values, themselves rooted in the 1960s.

In contrast, many Democrats argued that the riots grew out of years of ignoring the problems of the poor in urban areas on the part of the Reagan and Bush administrations. They added that the Reagan and Bush administrations had exacerbated racial divisions in America through their **civil rights** policies, from opposing **affirmative action** to appointing conservatives to the federal courts. Bush's use of the infamous Willie Horton commercial during the 1988 presidential campaign, to many liberals, symbolized the Republicans' complicity in the riots.

The four policemen were subsequently tried on federal charges for having violated King's civil rights. Two of them, Officer Lawrence Powell and Sergeant Stacey Koons, were convicted on these charges and sentenced to two and a half years in prison; two other officers were acquitted of the same charges.

Suggested Readings: Mark Baldassare, ed., *The Los Angeles Riots: Lessons for the Urban Future* (1994); Pam Hazen, ed., *Inside the L.A. Riots* (1992); Robert Gooding Williams, ed., *Reading Rodney King/Reading Urban Uprising* (1993).

Related Entries: Horton, Willie (Commercial); Recessions.

M

MADISON AMENDMENT (TWENTY-SEVENTH AMENDMENT TO THE U.S. CONSTITUTION.) On May 27, 1992, the state of Michigan ratified the "Madison Amendment." Named for James Madison, who wrote the amendment in 1789, it prohibited Congress from raising its own salary during the middle of its term: "No law varying the compensation for the services of the Senators and Representatives shall take effect until an election of Representatives shall have intervened." The amendment, which had fallen short of ratification by the states when Madison had first proposed it, was revived in the late 1970s as public faith in Congress and government in general declined. Between 1978 and 1992, thirty-three states approved it. When added to the five original states that had ratified the amendment nearly two hundred years earlier, these votes made it part of the Constitution. While some questioned the validity of the amendment since it had been written so long before it was ratified, it was not challenged in the courts. Most modern amendments include a time limit during which they must be ratified, but the "Madison Amendment" had not included such a clause. It was added to the constitution by the National Archivist shortly after ratification by the state of Michigan.

Suggested Readings: *Congressional Quarterly Almanac* (1992); *Facts on File* (1992).

Related Entry: Constitutional Amendments (Proposed).

MCFARLANE, ROBERT (BUD). (July 12, 1937, Washington, D.C.– .) National Security Adviser to President Ronald Reagan, 1983–1985.

When Robert McFarlane succeeded **William Patrick Clark** as President

Robert McFarlane briefs President Reagan and Secretary of State Shultz on Grenada. Reagan Library.

Ronald Reagan's national security adviser, many felt that the post had been turned over to a less visible and controversial figure. Unlike Clark, McFarlane was not an old associate of the president. Rather, he was a long-time military man, known more as a technocrat than as a policy maker. By the end of the 1980s, however, McFarlane had become perhaps the most visible and infamous national security adviser in U.S. history. For his early role in the **Iran-contra affair,** he stood at the center of charges that the National Security Council was unaccountable to the president or Congress. In the midst of congressional hearings he attempted suicide, and in 1988 he pleaded guilty to breaking the law.

McFarlane is the son of William McFarlane, a Democratic congressman from Texas. He grew up in Texas and earned his B.S. in engineering from the U.S. Naval Academy in 1958. After spending nearly seven years on military duty in the Far East, he furthered his education at the Graduate Institute of International Studies at the University of Geneva, receiving his M.A. in 1967. He returned to active duty in Vietnam and Korea and then accepted a post as a White House fellow (a type of paid internship) in 1971, moving up to military assistant to Henry Kissinger in 1973. McFarlane kept the same job under **Brent Scowcroft,** President Gerald Ford's national security adviser. During the Carter presidency, McFarlane taught at the National Defense University in Washington, D.C. In 1979 he resigned from the Marines and accepted a position on the professional staff of the Senate Armed Services Committee. Upon Reagan's inauguration, McFarlane went to work for Secretary of State **Alexander Meigs Haig, Jr.,** as a counsel to the State Department. When William Clark became national security adviser in 1982, he brought McFarlane with him to serve as his deputy assistant for national security affairs. A year later, when Clark became secretary of the interior in the wake of scandals involving **James Gaius Watt,** McFarlane became Reagan's third national security adviser. Much of McFarlane's attention was immediately focused on the Middle East, particularly Beirut, Lebanon, the scene of a terrorist attack on a U.S. Marine barracks in Lebanon just six days after McFarlane assumed his new position. His tenure as national security adviser also coincided with the continuing arms buildup and, as became apparent following his departure, with efforts to aid the contras.

By the time the Iran-contra scandal emerged, McFarlane had already handed over the national security adviser job to Admiral **John Marlan Poindexter.** News reports and subsequent investigations quickly showed, however, that he had played a key role in efforts to raise funds for the Nicaraguan rebels. Upon his recommendation, Colonel **Oliver North** had come to work at the White House. Along with North, McFarlane worked out the details of the arms-for-hostages deal. In testimony before Congress, McFarlane claimed that Reagan had approved of this exchange, on the grounds that it would improve the position of moderates in Iran, in spite of the fact that U.S. law banned arms sales to Iran. (Technically, McFarlane got around this prohibition by going through a third party.) Even after he left his post as national security adviser, McFarlane continued to work on the arms-for-hostages deal, although his connection to the decision to divert funds to the contras was less clear. On March 16, 1988, McFarlane pleaded guilty to misdemeanor charges growing out of the affair, namely, withholding information from Congress. He was sentenced to two years' probation and fined $20,000.

McFarlane is married to Jonda Riley. They have three children.

Suggested Readings: *Current Biography* (1984) p. 265; Lawrence Walsh, *Iran-Contra: The Final Report* (1994).

Ed Meese. Reagan Library.

Related Entry: Beirut, Lebanon (Bombing of U.S. Marine Barracks).

MEESE, EDWIN, III. (December 2, 1931, Oakland, Calif.– .) Adviser to President Reagan, 1981–1985; U.S. Attorney General, 1985–1988.

Edwin Meese was one of President Reagan's most influential and controversial aides and cabinet members. Meese's connections with the president went back to Ronald Reagan's years as governor of California. Along with **Michael Keith Deaver** and **James (Jim) Addison Baker III,** he was part of Reagan's "troika," or top team of aides, which played a very important role in developing policies and political strategies during Reagan's first term in office. In 1985, when this team was broken apart, with Baker swapping jobs with Secretary Treasurer **Donald Regan,** Meese became the U.S. attorney general. Meese's nomination and his subsequent tenure as director of the Justice Department, however, were fraught with controversy, and in August 1988 he resigned.

Meese earned his B.A. from Yale University (1953) and his law degree from the University of California, Berkeley (1958). He first came to Ronald Reagan's attention for his condemnation of student protestors at Berkeley while a deputy district attorney in Alameda County, California. From 1967 to 1969, he served as Governor Reagan's legal affairs secretary. From 1969 until 1975 he served as his chief of staff. In 1980 Meese worked as one of President Reagan's top campaign advisers. Many, in fact, were surprised when Reagan chose James Baker, George Bush's campaign manager and a Washington insider, rather than Meese, to be his chief of staff. However, if Meese harbored any anger over this decision he did not display it, instead working with Baker and Deaver to form one of the most efficient "kitchen cabinets" in recent presidential history.

Considered more of a conservative ideologue than Baker or Deaver, Meese assumed responsibility for policy issues. He headed the National Security Council and participated in numerous other councils or groups created by the president as a means to more efficiently develop and implement Reagan's programs. Along with Baker and Deaver, Meese controlled outside access to the president. Although Baker was the chief of staff, Meese was the only one of the three to hold cabinet rank. More so than Deaver or Baker, he was a target of criticism. Meese's harsh attacks on various liberal groups and issues earned him few friends in Washington, D.C. When President Reagan nominated him to head the Justice Department, liberals challenged Meese's legal qualifications. They also raised questions about his connections to the **Wedtech scandal,** in which a close friend of his had improperly sought military contracts. As a result of these objections, Meese's confirmation was held up for nearly a year. Ultimately, he was confirmed for the post. Nevertheless, Meese never escaped from doubts about his behavior. His direct involvement in the selection of federal judges, many of them controversial themselves, did nothing to improve his position among liberals. Meese drew further fire for his resistance to appointing a special prosecutor to investigate the **Iran-contra affair,** his early denials that the president had anything to do with the scandal, and his claim that no laws had been broken. To make matters worse, insiders reported that morale within the Justice Department among the hundreds of nonpolitical appointments had reached new lows while Meese was their boss. Finally, on July 5, 1988, under pressure from Democrats and Republicans alike, Meese resigned. Although Meese claimed no wrongdoing in the Wedtech scandal and was never charged with breaking any laws, the independent counsel for the case wrote, that "simply avoiding criminal conduct is not the mark of public service."

Meese is married to Ursula Herrick (Meese). They have three children. He is the author of one of the better known memoirs of the Reagan years. Unlike many other similar works, Meese offered little criticism of the president. Rather, what stands out in Meese's autobiography is his unbending loyalty to Ronald Reagan, a characteristic that stood out during Meese's years as a gubernatorial and presidential aide, as well.

Suggested Readings: "Adieu: E. Meese," *Economist,* July 9, 1988, p. 20; *Current Biography* (1981) p. 274; Edwin Meese, *With Reagan: An Inside Story* (1992).

MIDDLE EAST. One of the most troubled regions of the world during the Ronald Reagan–George Bush years, and one in which both administrations experienced some of their greatest difficulties, was the Middle East. The Reagan administration's greatest foreign policy setbacks, the **Iran-contra affair** and the car-bombing of a marine barracks in Beirut, Lebanon, involved this region of the world. Neither the Reagan nor Bush administrations proved able to build upon the momentum established by the peace accord signed by Anwar Sadat, president of Egypt, and Menachem Begin, the leader of Israel, in 1979 at Camp David, while **James (Jimmy) Earl Carter** was president. While the Bush administration triumphed during the **Persian Gulf War,** Bush left office with Saddam Hussein still in power. This said, the United States did not suffer from any oil crises during the Reagan-Bush years. Both administrations used diplomacy and the military to keep oil flowing to the rest of the world and prices relatively stable, to the benefit of the American public.

While the Reagan administration pledged to overcome the Vietnam syndrome, symbolized by the **Iranian hostages,** by early 1982 it found itself drawn into the turmoil of the Middle East. In late 1981 Israel annexed the Golan Heights and bombed Palestinian Liberation Organization (PLO) camps in Lebanon. The Reagan administration responded by condemning these actions and suspending a military agreement with Israel. When continued strife in Lebanon further jeopardized Israeli security, Israel invaded its neighbor, with the aim of rooting out the PLO. The United States responded to this action by negotiating an agreement whereby PLO and Israeli forces left Beirut and U.S. marines entered as peacekeepers. This arrangement unraveled, however, in the face of terrorist attacks on Americans in Beirut, most notoriously with the car-bombing of a U.S. Marine barracks, which killed over 241 marines on October 23, 1982. Shortly after the attack, Secretary of State **George Pratt Shultz** declared, "If I ever send in the Marines again, somebody shoot me." Early in 1984

President Reagan withdrew U.S. troops from Lebanon with the region still in turmoil.

Between 1984 and 1986 relations between the United States and Israel improved, but they were tested once again when Palestinians who lived on the West Bank of Israel and the Gaza Strip launched an uprising, called the Intifada, which was aimed at gaining a homeland. Secretary of State Shultz called for an international conference to resolve the long-standing dispute, an idea that both sides rejected. When PLO leader Yasir Arafat sought to speak before the United Nations in New York, the State Department denied him a passport to enter the United States.

Turmoil in other sections of the Middle East affected the United States as well. When the **Iran-Iraq War** resulted in attacks on oil tankers in the Persian gulf, the Reagan administration sent U.S. naval vessels to the region to protect neutral vessels. On May 1987 two missiles fired by Iraqi aircraft hit the USS *Stark*, killing 37 Americans. Ironically, the United States was supporting Iraq at this point in the war. Shortly after this incident, U.S. aircraft attacked an Iranian oil platform in retaliation against attacks against a Kuwaiti tanker. In July 1988 sailors on the USS *Vincennes* shot down a civilian Iranian airplane after mistaking it for a military plane, killing all 290 passengers. The United States apologized for this mistake and later paid limited reparations, but this did not appease most Iranians.

The Middle East also occupied much of the Bush administration's attention, especially during the Persian Gulf War. Critics of the Reagan and Bush administrations argued that they encouraged Hussein to invade Kuwait by providing him with military and economic aid (or ignoring illegal transfers of high technology). Just a week before Iraq invaded Kuwait, April Glaspie, the U.S. ambassador to Iraq, stated that the United States had no "opinion on inter-Arab disputes," which Hussein took as a reference to its long-standing border dispute with Kuwait. Regardless of his culpability in encouraging the attack, Bush responded quickly and decisively to the invasion itself. He and Secretary of State **James (Jim) Addison Baker III** rounded up regional and global support for American intervention. Baker also prodded Israel to refrain from entering the war after it was attacked by Iraqi scud missiles. The U.S. military overwhelmed the Iraqi forces, and Kuwait was regained with minimal American casualties.

Ironically, it was the American public that displayed the greatest long-term disappointment with Bush's policy in the Middle East. They second-guessed the Bush decision not to invade Baghdad and seek Hussein's overthrow during the war and found his pronouncement that the war signaled the dawn of a **new world order** relatively hollow and unfulfilling. Nonetheless, encouraged by the successful military operation in the Persian Gulf War, Bush and Baker revived efforts to broker a peace accord between Israel and the Palestinians in its wake. Baker pleaded with Israel to stop settlement on the Western Bank. The decision of Saudi Arabia to quit funding the PLO—partly because the PLO supported Hussein's invasion of Kuwait—strengthened Baker's hand. When Yasir Arafat agreed to negotiate, the Bush administration pressured Israel to meet with him by withholding a $10 billion loan guarantee. However, meetings between the Palestinians and Israel did not produce any concrete results during this time period.

Suggested Readings: George Ball, *Error and Betrayal in Lebanon* (1984); Lawrence Freedman and Efraim Kursh, *The Gulf Conflict* (1993); George Lenczowski, *American Presidents and the Middle East* (1984); William R. Polk, *Peace Process* (1993).

Related Entry: Beirut, Lebanon (Bombing of U.S. Marine Barracks).

MILKEN, MICHAEL. (1946, Encino, Calif.– .) Financier.

During the 1980s, Michael Milken was one of the world's most famous financiers. Some compared him to J. P. Morgan, the titan of finance at the turn of the century. His fame derived from his development of the "junk" (high-risk) bond, which gave rise to one of the greatest merger movements in American history. He earned hundreds of millions of dollars a year through his financial wizardry, making him one of the richest men in the world, and perhaps in history. At the end of the decade, however, his fortune took a turn for the worse when he was implicated in various insider-trading scandals, for which he was ultimately convicted and sentenced to jail. To many, Milken's rise and fall symbolized the highs and lows of Wall Street and the **U.S. economy** during the Ronald Reagan–George Bush years.

Michael Milken grew up in southern California. He attended the University of California at Berkeley during the mid-1960s. While protest dominated campus life, Milken concentrated on his studies, hitting upon the idea that high-risk bonds, later dubbed junk bonds, could prove a very lucrative investment for those who bought them. He noted that the high interest rates on these bonds tended to compensate for their relatively high rate of default. Put another way, an investor with a sizable portfolio of high-risk bonds would make more in interest than he or she would loose through bonds that failed. After graduating from Berkeley, Milken earned his M.B.A. from the Wharton School of the University of Pennsylvania, where he focused further attention on the performance of these bonds. In the 1970s he went to work for Drexel Firestone, an old, conservative investment banking firm in Philadelphia. He worked extremely hard and began to develop a market for junk bonds.

It was not until the mid-1980s, however, that others took notice of Milken's innovation. Then he began to use junk bonds as a source to finance **corporate takeovers.** His junk bond department at Drexel Burnham, which Milken operated near his original home in southern California, became the engine for the merger movement of the 1980s and helped finance some of the largest takeovers of the era. Even though Milken was officially only a senior vice president at Drexel, he became the firm's most dominant figure. He earned enormous bonuses and did pretty much what he pleased.

In 1987, he was indicted on charges of fraud and racketeering. A year later, he pleaded guilty to improper trading. (In exchange for a plea bargain, the government dropped several more severe charges.) He was sentenced to ten years in prison and fined $600 million, the largest individual fine in history. His fall from grace prefigured the collapse of Drexel Burnham and troubled times for numerous other investment banking firms.

Milken is married to Lori Milken. They have three children.

Suggested Readings: Fenton Bailey, *Fall from Grace: The Untold Story of Michael Milken* (1992); Connie Bruck, *The Predator's Ball* (1988); Robert Sobel, *Dangerous Dreamers: The Financial Innovators from Charles Merrill to Michael Milken* (1993).

Related Entry: Boesky, Ivan Frederick.

MINIMUM WAGE. On November 17, 1989, President George Bush signed HR 2710, a measure to raise the minimum wage from $3.35 to $4.25 over a period of two years. His signing of the bill represented the end of a decade-old battle between Democrats and Republicans. President Ronald Reagan had blocked all attempts to raise the minimum wage, arguing that such a hike would backfire by increasing unemployment among those groups most at risk, especially young blacks. Bush ultimately signed the legislation but only after Congress agreed to include a subminimum or training wage in the measure, which allowed employers to pay new workers below the minimum wage for a period of up to six months. Prior to signing HR 2710, Bush had vetoed a bill that had included a training wage but mandated raising the minimum wage to $4.45 an hour. The House of Representatives had failed to override his veto of this bill. Following the veto, rather than wait for the next term to resubmit the bill, a coalition of organized labor, **civil rights,** and other liberal groups lobbied Congress to push through a minimum wage hike at $4.25 rather than $4.45. Feeling vulnerable on the issue, many moderate Republicans joined the majority of Democrats in favor of this proposal. Subsequent studies cast doubt on the value of the subminimum wage, showing that few people were hired to work for so little. Still, the debate over the impact of raising the minimum wage continued into **William (Bill) Jefferson Clinton**'s presidency.

Suggested Readings: *Congressional Quarterly Almanac* (1989); John Schacter, "House Panel Clears Wage Bill, Overriding Bush Demands," *Congressional Quarterly Weekly Report,* March 18, 1989; Paul Starobin, "GOP Members Pressuring Bush to Deal on Minimum Wage," *Congressional Quarterly Weekly Report,* September 23, 1989.

MISERY INDEX. During the 1976 presidential campaign, **James (Jimmy) Earl Carter** utilized the "misery index" as a means to measure and display the weaknesses of the economy during President Gerald Ford's tenure. The index consisted of the sum of inflation and unemployment (see Figure 7). While economists considered the misery index too simplistic to provide a true sense of economic performance, it proved a powerful political tool. Carter was able to show that the index had climbed to dangerous levels. (Many suggested that any rating over ten portrayed particularly tough times.) Ironically, in 1980 the index came to haunt Carter himself.

One of the main points that Ronald Reagan made on the campaign trail was that the **U.S. economy** had worsened during Carter's presidency. During a crucial debate with Carter, Reagan turned to the television audience and stated: "Ask yourself, are you better off than you were four years ago?" Based on Carter's own index, Reagan's campaign team pointed out, the answer was no. In addition, during his presidency, Reagan pointed to the misery index to document the improvement of the economy. Not surprisingly, Bush did not refer to the index during his reelection campaign in 1992, as it increased during his presidency.

Suggested Reading: Martin A. Asher, "The Misery Index: Only Part of the Story," *Challenge,* March/April 1993, p. 58.

Related Entries: Debates, Presidential; Election of 1980; Recessions.

Figure 7
Misery Index, 1980–1992 (Inflation Plus Unemployment)

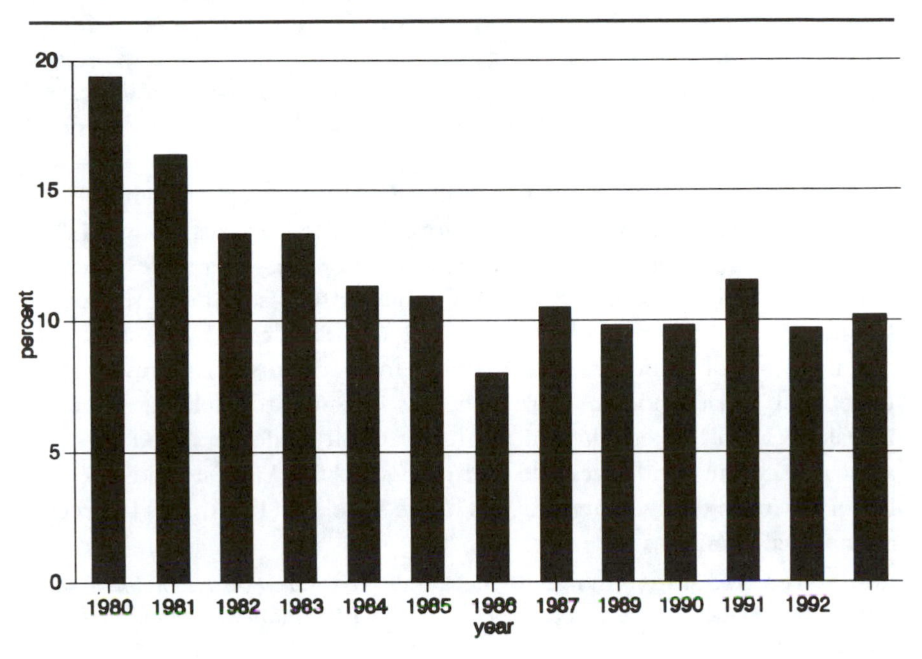

MONDALE, WALTER FREDERICK. (January 5, 1928, Ceylon, Minn.–) U.S. Senator, 1965–1976; Vice President of the United States, 1977–1981; Democratic nominee for President, 1984.

Walter Mondale is a lifelong liberal who, first as **James (Jimmy) Earl Carter**'s vice president and then as the Democratic Party's presidential nominee in 1984, ran against Ronald Reagan and George Bush. Both times he lost. His political career, in many ways, paralleled that of the liberal wing of the Democratic Party. A protégé of former Minnesota Senator Hubert H. Humphrey, Mondale became a Minnesota senator when Humphrey became Lyndon Johnson's vice president in 1964. Elected in his own right in 1966 and reelected in 1972, Mondale earned a reputation as a advocate of child welfare, civil rights, and other liberal programs. As vice president, he worked closely with Jimmy Carter and proved a vigorous campaigner in both 1976 and 1980.

In 1984 he secured the Democratic presidential nomination, but only after a bitter and drawn-out campaign, which weakened the Democratic Party. Partly in an attempt to heal wounds between different factions of the party, he nominated **Geraldine Anne Ferraro**, a Congresswoman from New York, as his running mate. She was the first woman to be nominated to such a post in history. During the campaign, Mondale attacked Reagan's record on the **budget deficit,** the **Strategic Defense Initiative Plan (Star Wars),** civil rights, the **environment,** and **women's rights.** In addition, Mondale sought to cast the Democrats as the party of fairness versus the Republicans, whom he described as the party of greed.

However, Mondale was unable to close the gap between himself and President Reagan. Mondale's declaration: "He'll raise taxes, so will I. He won't tell you, I just did," probably lost him votes, as public concern about the deficit had not yet peaked, while antitax sentiment remained strong. While Reagan exuded optimism, Mondale could not shirk the gloom-and-doom label that the Republicans had stuck to Jimmy Carter. Except for a brief moment during the first presidential debate, in which Ronald Reagan looked old and unprepared, Mondale appeared the less attractive of the candidates. He lost in one of the biggest landslides in history, winning only Minnesota, his home state, and less than 41 percent of the total popular vote.

Suggested Readings: Thomas Byrne Edsall, *The New Politics of Inequality* (1984); Steve Gillon, *The Democrats' Dilemma: Walter Mondale and the Liberal Legacy* (1992).

Related Entries: Debates, Presidential; Election of 1984.

MORAL MAJORITY. The Moral Majority was a fundamentalist, conservative religious organization created by the Reverend **Jerry Falwell** in June 1979. The organization consisted of four divisions, covering education, lobbying, endorsement of political candidates, and legal aid. At its high point in the mid-1980s, the Moral Majority's membership stood near 2 million.

The Moral Majority endorsed free enterprise, a balanced budget, and prayer in school. It opposed **abortion,** for any reason whatsoever, as well as homosexuality and the Equal Rights Amendment. According to the Moral Majority, society should live by God's laws and should not sanction practices that violate Scripture or the Ten Commandments.

The growth of the Moral Majority as a powerful political organization paralleled Falwell's rise to prominence. By the early 1980s Falwell had written a best-selling book, hosted a weekly television show, and wrote regular newspaper and magazine articles. His "fire and brimstone" speeches inspired hundreds of thousands of men and women in America to join the Moral Majority. The Moral Majority became adept at fund-raising, with Falwell cajoling followers to contribute to the "war against sin," which, he added, could not be fought with an empty bank account. By 1985 the Moral Majority had raised over $11 million and Falwell's television show had an audience estimated at about five million.

Although Falwell denied that the Moral Majority was tied to any one political party or candidate, nearly all experts agreed that it was strongly in President Ronald Reagan and the Republican Party's corner and that it contributed considerably to the conservative triumphs of the early 1980s. The Moral Majority distributed "Moral Report Cards" on candidates, which generally criticized Democratic candidates. The organization also undertook a massive voter registration drive among fundamentalists, which added close to four million new voters to the voting roles.

In June 1987, the fortunes of the Moral Majority began to unravel as a series of scandals involving many prominent televangelists took place. Jim and Tammy Bakker, who had built an evangelical empire associated with the Moral Majority, and Jimmy Swaggart, another prominent fundamentalist, saw their reputations collapse in the midst of accusations of sexual and financial misdeeds. Many followers felt betrayed and left the Moral Majority. At the same time, the end of President Reagan's term suggested that the Moral Majority's tangible gains were not as great as they had expected. Abortion remained legal; the women's movement was fighting back against attacks from the right. However, even if the power of the Moral Majority itself had waned, fundamentalist Christians remained a prominent political force, with many of the Moral Majority's members transferring their allegiance to **Marion Gordon (Pat) Robertson**'s Christian Coalition.

Suggested Readings: Alan Crawford, *Thunder on the Right* (1984); John C. Green and James L. Guth, "The Moralizing Minority: Christian Right Support among Political Contributors," *Social Science Quarterly* 68 (1987): 7; James D. Hunter, *American Evangelicalism: Conservative Religion and the Quandry of Modernity* (1983); Lee Sigelman, Clyde Wilcox, and Emmett H. Buell, "An Unchanging Minority: Popular Support for the Moral Majority, 1980 and 1984," *Social Science Quarterly* 68 (1987): 4.

Related Entries: Conservative Coalition; New Right.

"MORNING IN AMERICA". The slogan, "It is Morning in America," was Ronald Reagan's campaign theme in 1984. In contrast to the pessimistic message of the Democrats, personified by President **James (Jimmy) Earl Carter**'s "malaise" speech and **Walter Frederick Mondale**'s argument that the U.S. government had to raise taxes, it depicted Reagan's optimistic vision that America's best days lay ahead, rather than the notion that the country was in the state of decline. The slogan meshed with the overall upbeat and patriotic image that Reagan's advisers and campaign team emphasized time and time again in 1984, from his D-Day commemoration speech at Normandy to the Los Angeles Olympics. Viewers of his campaign commercials heard an announcer declare: "It's morning again in America. In a town not too far from where you live, a young family has just moved into a new home. Three years ago, even the smallest house seemed completely out of reach. Right down the street, one of the neighbors has just bought himself a new car, with all the options. The factory down the river is working again. . . . Life is better, America is back. And people have a sense of pride they never felt they'd feel again. And so it's not surprising that just about everyone in town is thinking the same thing. Now that our country is turning around, why would we ever turn back?"

Suggested Readings: Paul D. Erickson, *Reagan Speaks: The Making of an American Myth* (1985); Kathleen Hall Jamieson, *Packaging the Presidency* (1992); Gary Wills, *Reagan's America: Innocents at Home* (1987).

Related Entries: Election of 1984; Gergen, David Richmond; Great Communicator, The; Normandy, France, D-Day Celebration.

MOTOR VOTER BILL. The Motor Voter Bill was designed with the goal of easing the process of voter registration and increasing voter participation in elections. The bill required states to provide voter registration forms at motor vehicle departments and at other public offices, such as those that provide public assistance. Applicants for these services or licenses would automatically be registered to vote on completion of voter registration forms. The bill also required states to offer registration opportunities at military recruitment offices and to develop standard mail-in registration forms.

The bill was first introduced by Senator Wendell H. Ford, a Democrat from Kentucky, in 1989. It immediately became a subject of heated debate and criticism. Senator Ted Stevens, a Republican from Alaska, the leading opponent of the measure, argued that the voter turnout at elections would not necessarily rise with an increase in registration. He and other Republican critics of the bill complained that the bill's requirements would financially burden states and would lead to increased fraud. Democratic supporters of the bill countered that politics, not costs or concerns about fraud, lay at the bottom of the Republican Party's objections.

Many experts believed that the bill would increase registration primarily among individuals who could be expected to vote for the Democratic Party.

For three years Republicans blocked the bill from coming to a vote. In 1991, Democrats failed to gain enough votes to invoke cloture, which was necessary to bring the bill to a vote before the full Senate, where it would have been passed. President George Bush supported his party's position on this matter. In the late spring of 1992 Democrats gained enough votes to invoke cloture and the bill (S. 250) was passed by both houses of Congress. President Bush vetoed the legislation, calling it burdensome and constitutionally questionable. Unable to override his veto, Congress had to let the measure die until **William (Bill) Jefferson Clinton** became president, at which point Congress passed it again and Clinton signed it into law.

Suggested Readings: *Congressional Quarterly Almanac* (1992); *Congressional Quarterly Almanac* (1993).

MX (MISSILE, EXPERIMENTAL) MISSILE. Dubbed the "Peacekeeper" missile by President Ronald Reagan, the MX missile was one of the most controversial weapon programs that the Reagan administration promoted during the first half of the 1980s.

Research and development of the MX missile began well before Reagan became president. Initially, it was designed to carry multiple warheads and be deployed in mobile launchers. By the early 1980s, however, many questions regarding the ability to deploy it in a mobile manner—the main advantage of such a missile—had arisen. As a result, many in Congress sought to kill the MX missile program.

Reagan largely ignored these criticisms. Based on the recommendations of a bipartisan commission, which he appointed, he proposed placing them in existing Minuteman missile silos. He battled with Congress when it complained about the expense and utility of the new missiles. When the Senate and House both voted against appropriations for research and development, Reagan continued to push for deployment. These efforts paid off as Congress reversed itself, voting for appropriations of a modified MX missile package. In 1984 Congress again dealt the Reagan administration a setback, reducing the number of MX missiles to be built and deployed from forty, as requested by the president, to twenty-one. However, Reagan remained determined to overcome this opposition. In 1985, following his landslide reelection, Reagan requested more funds for the MX and Congress granted the Defense Department another $1.5 billion to build and deploy twenty-one more missiles. All together, at least fifty missiles were deployed. Reagan's critics pointed to the MX missile to emphasize the financial waste of the era. In contrast, Reagan's supporters contended that Reagan's determination to build up American defenses, despite objections at home and from the Soviets, drove the latter to the bargaining table which ultimately produced arms reductions.

Suggested Readings: Noble Frankland, ed., *The Encyclopedia of Twentieth Century Warfare* (1989); William Kaufmann, *A Reasonable Defense* (1986); Scott D. Sagan, *Moving Targets* (1989).

Related Entries: Defense Spending; Foreign Policy; Intermediate Nuclear Forces (INF) Treaty; Summits, with Soviet Union.

N

NAFTA. See **NORTH AMERICAN FREE TRADE AGREEMENT.**

NATO. See **NORTH ATLANTIC TREATY ORGANIZATION.**

NEW FEDERALISM. In his second State of the Union Address, President Reagan proposed shifting numerous federal government programs and taxes to the states. He called his plan, the "new federalism." Reagan had laid the groundwork for this 1982 announcement in spring 1981 by appointing two committees, the Presidential Advisory Committee on Federalism and the Coordinating Task Force on Federalism. Stacked with conservatives and headed by his former campaign manager, Nevada Senator **Paul Dominique Laxalt**, the committees provided ammunition for Reagan's criticism of the growth of the federal government and augmented his claim that large federal bureaucracies stifled economic growth and initiative. Building on their reports, Reagan contended that the new federalism would renew America's economy.

According to the plan, an exchange would take place in which state governments would assume responsibility for dozens of programs, ranging from **welfare** and healthcare to transportation, while the federal government would assume responsibility for Medicaid. "In a single stroke," President Reagan declared, "we will be accomplishing a realignment that will end cumbersome administration and spiraling costs at the federal level, while ensur[ing] [that] these programs will be more responsive to both the people they are meant to help and the people who pay them."

President Reagan's new federalism plan received a mixed response and ultimately met with mixed results. After being announced with much gusto in 1982, the plan quickly lost steam. Some governors initially favored the swap, but the National Governors Association proclaimed that it would hurt state governments in the long run. The plan was additionally hurt by other issues, from the recession to the cold war, which took precedence over it.

Ultimately, only a limited part of the new federalism plan was implemented. Some federal grant programs to the states were increased, and states were granted increasing the authority over them. However, these changes hardly produced a radical shift in power. Most programs continued to be paid for and administered by the federal government. At times it seemed hard to believe that any shift had ever taken place.

Suggested Readings: D. R. Beam, "New Federalism, Old Realities: The Reagan Administration and Intergovernmental Reform," in *The Reagan Presidency and the Governing of America,* ed. L. M. Salamon and M. S. Lund (1984); Dilys M. Hill, "Domestic Policy in an Era of 'Negative' Government," in *The Reagan Presidency: An Incomplete Revolution?* ed. Dilys M. Hill, Raymond A. Moore and Phil Williams (1990).

Related Entries: Domestic Policy; Economy, U.S.; Recessions.

NEW RIGHT. The New Right emerged as a major political force with the **election of 1980.** It stood for traditional conservative goals, most notably a dislike for a strong central government, and contained an evangelical Christian edge. The New Right also used modern political techniques to recruit members and raise money. Its leaders included Richard Viguerie, a master at raising funds through direct mail; Jerry Falwell, the founder of the **Moral Majority;** and Phil Gramm, a Democrat-turned-Republican Senator from Texas. Some analysts have suggested that the New Right contained contradictory aims, on the one hand libertarian and on the other hand authoritarian. In terms of economic policies it tends toward libertarian views, yet in the cultural arena, it favors regulation and restrictions on behavior. George Nash, author of one of the best studies of modern conservatism, has argued that anticommunism provided the glue that kept the New Right together. Its greatest impact was on the nation's economic policies, most notably the enactment of tax cuts. It also had a considerable impact on the Republican Party, moving it in a more conservative direction.

Suggested Readings: George Nash, *The Conservative Intellectual Movement in America since 1945* (1976); Gillian Peele, *Revivial and Reaction: The Right in Contemporary America* (1984).

Related Entries: Election of 1984; Senate, United States.

NEW WORLD ORDER. The phrase, "new world order," is an old one, which has been used in many contexts and at different times in world history. George Bush revived the concept at the end of the cold war and during the offensive against Iraq in the **Persian Gulf War.** "We have in this past year," President Bush declared in an address to the nation on January 16, 1991, "made great progress in ending the long era of conflict and cold war. We have before us," Bush continued, "the opportunity to forge for ourselves and for future generations a new world order." In his State of the Union Address of January 29, 1991, he repeated this phrase. After describing the Persian Gulf War as a "defining hour" in American history, Bush declared: "What is at stake is more than one small country. It is a big idea: a new world order."

For those who found the meaning of this phrase vague, Bush sought to add some specificity to it. This new world order, Bush stated, translated into a world where "the rule of law, not the law of the jungle, governs the conduct of nations." Further, it denoted a world "where diverse nations are drawn together in common cause to achieve the universal aspirations of mankind: peace, security, freedom."

Bush's pronouncement did not receive universal applause. The *New York Times* described the phrase as "unfortunate . . . reminiscent of Nazi sloganeering." Former Secretary of State Henry Kissinger contended that President Bush would have a difficult time attaining a new world order in the **Middle East,** not to mention other areas of the world. Indeed, Kissinger warned against selling or describing American **foreign policy** objectives in such idealistic terms. Still others argued that the new world order sounded a lot like old-fashioned American global hegemony or domination rather than something new.

Regardless of the debate, Bush's announcement of a new world order signified an important change in history. Since the end of World War II, the cold war had served as the focal point of American foreign policy. With the cold war over, Americans found themselves grappling to develop a new focus for their role in the world. American actions in the wake of the victory in the Persian Gulf War suggested that this would not be easy to do. Bush did not intervene in **Haiti** or Yugoslavia when the rule of law was broken. Moreover, as the recession worsened, American isolationism and the desire to focus on domestic problems increased.

Suggested Readings: Richard Barnett, "Reflections: After the Cold War," *New Yorker,* January 1, 1990, p. 65; Michael Hogan, ed., *The End of the Cold War* (1992).

Related Entries: Bosnia and Herzegovina; Communism, Collapse of; Foreign Aid.

NICARAGUA. One of the cornerstones of President Ronald Reagan's **foreign policy** was his focus on the threat of communism in the Western Hemisphere and the need to take forceful actions against it. While the president did not launch an invasion of Cuba, the most significant communist nation in the region, he did authorize the invasion of **Grenada,** sought to further isolate Cuban leader Fidel Castro, supported the government of **El Salvador** against left-wing insurgents, and backed anticommunist rebels in and around Nicaragua.

Even before becoming president, Reagan had signaled that if elected, his foreign policy would not be based on the philosophy of human rights, as had Carter's, but rather on the more stringent cold war doctrine of anticommunism. He sharply criticized President **James (Jimmy) Earl Carter** for deserting long-time Nicaraguan leader Anastasio Somoza, who had been overthrown by Sandinista rebels. Early in 1981, Secretary of State **Alexander Meigs Haig, Jr.,** accused the Soviets of seeking to expand their power in the Western Hemisphere. President Reagan added that the Sandinistas were providing the **Soviet Union** with a "safehouse" in America's backyard. Proclaiming that the Sandinista government was providing aid to El Salvadoran leftist rebels, on April 1, 1981, the Reagan administration suspended $15 million in aid to Nicaragua.

Moving beyond economic pressures, President Reagan subsequently instructed Central Intelligence Agency (CIA) director **William Joseph Casey** to help build up anti-Sandinista forces. Before long, Reagan was describing these counterrevolutionaries, called *contras,* as "freedom fighters." In 1982, when asked about the effort, William Casey informed Congress that the contras did not aim at overthrowing the Sandinistas. Rather, he insisted, they sought the limited objective of blocking the Nicaraguan government from aiding leftist El Salvadoran rebels. However, news reports suggested otherwise.

Not wanting a repeat of the Vietnam War and finding President Reagan's description of the communist threat in Central America a bit exaggerated—after all, Nicaragua's population was only about 4 million and its military included only about 20,000 soldiers—Congress enacted the

Boland Amendment in September 1982. Named after Edward P. Boland, a Democrat from Massachusetts, it limited aid to the contras and prohibited attempts to overthrow the Sandinistas.

For several years the Reagan administration sought to get around the Boland Amendment by having the Pentagon or Defense Department provide the contras with weapons and other supplies. In response, Congress tightened the Boland Amendment, banning direct or indirect aid to the contras from the CIA or any other intelligence agency. House Speaker **Thomas (Tip) Philip O'Neill, Jr.,** felt the law was so well written that he declared the contras "dead."

However, the Reagan administration was not to be deterred. A coterie of top officials, including Casey, **Robert (Bud) McFarlane,** and **Oliver North,** raised funds for the contras from private sources and from foreign countries. Part of this scheme to support the contras led to the decision to divert funds from the arms-for-hostages deal with the Iranians to the Nicaraguan rebels, in an episode better known as the **Iran-contra affair.**

At the same time it was soliciting funds for military aid from private sources, the Reagan administration requested that Congress provide humanitarian aid for the contras. After first turning down this request, Congress changed course and appropriated humanitarian aid. (A trip to the Soviet Union by Nicaraguan president Daniel Ortega helped turn the tide on this request in the president's favor.)

At no time did the Reagan administration soften its economic sanctions against Nicaragua. In April 1984 reports emerged that the CIA had secretly planted mines in Nicaraguan harbors. This action angered even conservative Republicans such as Arizona Senator Barry Goldwater, since it took place without congressional oversight. When Nicaragua announced that it would sue the United States in the World Court for this illegal action, the Reagan administration declared that the international court lacked jurisdiction in this matter, a position that many legal scholars contested.

In 1987, with the Iran-contra scandal dominating the headlines, President Oscar Arias of Costa Rica helped broker a five-nation Central American peace plan. President Reagan opposed the plan, proclaiming that it would undermine the contras. Instead, he continued to push for nonmilitary U.S. aid. In 1988 Congress again approved providing humanitarian assistance to the contras while at the same time offering its support for the Arias-led peace talks.

By the time he left office, Reagan spoke less often about Nicaragua than he had when he first assumed power. Whereas he once warned of the dangers of a communist invasion emanating from Central America, improved relations with the Soviet Union as well as the Iran-contra scandal led him to downplay the importance of the region.

During his first two years in office, President George Bush called for, and received, humanitarian aid for the contras. He also supported the Arias peace process. In February 1990, these talks culminated in a democratic election in Nicaragua in which Daniel Ortega was ousted in favor of Violeta Barrios de Chamorro. The contras and Sandinistas agreed to a cease-fire in their civil war, and the United States lifted economic sanctions against Nicaragua. Interpretations of this course of events vary, with conservatives proclaiming it a victory for the policies of the Reagan administration, while others argued that the administration had overreacted to the Sandinista threat in the first place, wrongly opposed the peace process initiated by Arias, and through its hard-line policies in the early 1980s, worsened civil strife and crippled the Nicaraguan economy.

Suggested Readings: Roy Gutman, *Banana Diplomacy* (1987); Walter LaFeber, *Inevitable Revolutions* (1993); Thomas W. Walker, ed., *Reagan vs. the Sandinistas* (1987); Thomas W. Walker, *Revolution and Counterrevolution in Nicaragua* (1990).

Related Entries: Caribbean Basin Initiative; Latin America.

NITZE, PAUL. (January 16, 1907, Amherst, Mass.– .) Arms negotiator.

From 1981 to 1984 Paul Nitze headed U.S. **arms control** talks with the **Soviet Union.** These were years in which few serious discussions took place, as the Ronald Reagan administration concentrated on building up American military forces. Nitze stepped down as chief U.S. delegate on nuclear force talks at about the same time that relations between the two superpowers began to thaw, which ultimately led to the **Intermediate-range Nuclear Forces (INF) Treaty** in 1987. During this latter period, Nitze continued to serve as a special adviser to the president and secretary of state **George Pratt Shultz** on arms control matters.

Nitze earned his A.B. from Harvard University (1928) and received additional education at the New School for Social Research and Pratt Institute (in New York City). During World War II, Nitze held various government positions within the War Department and other war-related agencies. He continued to work for the government during the Harry Truman administration. In the 1960s, when the Democrats returned to power, Nitze served as an assistant secretary in the Department of Defense (1961–1963) and then as secretary of the navy (1963–1967). He was also deputy secretary of defense (1967–1969). When Richard Nixon became president, Nitze served as a member of the U.S. delegation that negotiated the first Strategic Arms Limitation Treaty (SALT I), the first arms control agreement between the superpowers.

Nitze is married to Phyllis Pratt (Nitze), and they have four children. He has received numerous awards and honors, including the Presidential Medal of Freedom and the George C. Marshall Award.

Suggested Reading: Strobe Talbott, *The Master of the Game* (1988).

Related Entry: Summits, with Soviet Union.

NOFZIGER, LYN. (June 8, 1924, Bakersfield, Calif.– .) Political consultant to Ronald Reagan.

From the mid-1960s through mid-1980s, Lyn Nofziger served as an important political consultant to Ronald Reagan. He was considered one of the president's old confidants, who provided campaign and political advice.

Nofziger grew up in southern California, served in the army for three years during World War II, temporarily attended the University of California at Los Angeles and earned a B.A. from San Jose State in 1950. For the next fifteen years he worked in the newspaper business as a reporter and editor. His conservative views and idiosyncracies, however, hampered his rise through the ranks. Through James S. Copley, the owner of a chain of conservative newspapers, Nofziger obtained a position as Reagan's press secretary in January 1966. After Reagan's election, Reagan hired him as his director of communications.

In 1968 Nofziger left his press secretary post to become an independent political consultant. From 1969 through 1974 he worked in various capacities for President Richard Nixon. He rejoined the Reagan team shortly after the 1976 election, establishing Citizens for the Republic, a political action group aimed at aiding conservative candidates and preparing Reagan's 1980 presidential bid. By the time of the general election campaign, Nofziger was once again working as Reagan's press secretary and communications director. Toward the end of the campaign, however, Nofziger repeatedly raised the ire of important members of Reagan's team, including **Nancy Davis Reagan,** and thus found himself demoted and stripped of certain responsibilities.

Following Reagan's election Nofziger was hired as the assistant to the president for political affairs and given a virtual veto over subcabinet appointments. For about a year he played a key role in promoting Reagan's domestic goals. However, Nofziger was not a good insider or organizational man. Nofziger's irreverence, disdain for conventional dress, and unkempt appearance often set him apart from other members of the Reagan administration. Early in 1982 he left his post as an assistant to the president to work again as an independent political consultant. He continued to provide President Reagan with advice, especially as Reagan's reelection bid neared.

In 1987, Nofziger was indicted for illegally lobbying senior White House officials in connection with the **Wedtech scandal.** The following year, he was convicted of violating the 1978 Ethics and Government Act. A federal Appeals Court overthrew his conviction, in a 2–1 vote, on the grounds that Nofziger did not know that his lobbying efforts violated the 1978 law. The two judges who voted to overturn the earlier conviction were Reagan appointees, while the dissenter had been appointed by Jimmy Carter.

Nofziger is married to the former Bonnie Foster. They have two daughters.

Suggested Readings: *Current Biography* (1983) p. 269; *Facts on File* (1988).

Related Entry: Election of 1980.

"NO NEW TAXES". One of the highlights of the 1988 presidential campaign was George Bush's oft-repeated line: "Read my lips: no new taxes." Stated with simplicity and firmness, this pledge, more than any other campaign promise, came to personify Bush and helped him defeat **Michael Stanley Dukakis.** Two years later, however, the pledge came to haunt Bush, as a mounting **budget deficit** prompted him to renege and support a tax hike. While Bush lost in his bid to be reelected in 1992 for many reasons, the one that stands out in the minds of many people is his breaking of that pledge, which alienated him from conservative Republicans while winning him little support with Democrats or independents.

Bush's campaign pledge rested, to a large degree, on vastly inaccurate economic forecasts. He claimed that he could meet budget targets established by the **Gramm-Rudman-Hollings Act (Balanced Budget and Emergency Deficit Control Act of 1985)** without raising taxes. However, as the **U.S. economy** slowed to a crawl, reducing revenues to the federal government, his forecasts proved too rosy. The **savings and loan crisis** worsened the situation, mushrooming the federal budget deficit. As a result, whereas in January he predicted that the budget for fiscal year

1991 would meet the deficit target of just under $65 billion, by July the administration was estimating a budget deficit closer to $230 billion, and some in Congress claimed even this estimate was too low.

On June 26, in a brief memorandum, President Bush retreated from his "no new taxes" pledge. Congressional leaders and aides to the president developed a revised budget plan that sought to reduce the deficit by $500 billion over five years. To do so, Bush proposed increasing gasoline taxes by 12 cents a gallon and cutting Medicare by almost $60 billion. Conservative Republicans objected to the tax hike, and Democrats criticized the cuts in Medicare.

On September 30, 1990, Bush delivered a personal televised plea for support for his budget plan. It was, he proclaimed, the result of "eight months of blood, sweat and fears—fears of the economic chaos that would follow if we fail to reduce the deficit." Just a few months before Bush delivered this address, he had been standing sky-high in the polls—so high that many thought he would be unbeatable in 1992. However, his popularity began to fall in the face of the recession and a rebellion in Republican ranks over Bush's decision to go back on his pledge.

As the fall of 1990 approached, the situation worsened. **Gridlock** in Congress over the budget almost shut down the government. Bush actually had to temporarily suspend nonessential services for the Columbus Day weekend until Congress passed an emergency appropriations measure. Ultimately, Congress devised its own budget package—one that deviated in many of its details from Bush's proposal. It raised the top income bracket from 28 to 31 percent, limited tax deductions for the wealthy, increased gasoline taxes by 5 cents per gallon, and cut Medicare by $42.5 billion. Bush reluctantly accepted this plan.

Some conservatives claimed that the tax hike caused the recession of the early 1990s, further arguing that it proved the validity of supply-side economics (also called **Reaganomics**), which was built on tax cuts. However, most economists disagree with this contention, noting that the economy had already begun to retreat before the tax hike went into effect. Gross domestic product declined nearly 4 percent in the last quarter of 1990 and 3 percent in the first quarter of 1991. The income tax hike did not go into effect until April 15, 1991.

Suggested Readings: *Congressional Quarterly Almanac* (1990); Dilys M. Hill and Phil Williams, eds., *The Bush Presidency: Triumphs and Adversities* (1994); Charles Kolb, *White House Daze: The Unmaking of Domestic Policy in the Bush Years* (1994).

Related Entries: Election of 1988; Recessions.

NOONAN, PEGGY. (September 7, 1950, Brooklyn, N.Y.– .) Speechwriter for Presidents Ronald Reagan and George Bush.

Peggy Noonan was perhaps the best known speechwriter of the Ronald Reagan–George Bush years. Noonan, who was working for CBS Broadcasting when Reagan was elected, did everything she could to obtain a job with the president in the early 1980s. Her efforts paid off when, in March 1984, she was hired as a writer in the speech department, working under Bentley T. Elliot. Only a few months later, she crafted one of Reagan's best-known orations, the speech he gave at Normandy on the occasion of the fortieth anniversary of D-day. Ironically, she was lucky to have been allowed to write this speech, as some insiders thought it was inappropriate for a woman who had never donned a military uniform to be entrusted with commemorating one of the greatest battles in history. Other well-known Reagan speeches that Noonan wrote included one that followed the ***Challenger* disaster** and another regarding the Nicaraguan contras, in which Reagan termed them "the moral equal of our Founding Fathers." Despite her success, she left the Reagan administration in 1986, largely due to her disagreements with **Donald Regan** and several of the president's other top aides.

In 1988, following George Bush's poor showing in the Iowa caucus, she rejoined the world of political speech writing, working on Bush's presidential campaign. During this stint she helped write his Republican nomination acceptance speech, in which she coined the phrase, **"A Thousand Points of Light."** Many called this speech the best of Bush's career. She also helped write President Reagan's farewell address and Bush's inaugural address.

Noonan was reared in the working-class neighborhoods and suburbs of New York City and its environs. She received her B.A. from Fairleigh Dickinson College in 1974. While at college, according to her autobiography, *What I Saw at the Revolution* (1990), in reaction to the extremism of the New Left she became a conservative. Before joining Reagan's staff she worked for CBS radio and television. Her personal account of her life and years at the White House became a best-seller. In it she presented a flattering picture of Ronald Reagan while at the same time providing insight into the conservatives' disillusionment with George Bush.

Noonan married Richard Rahn in 1985. They were divorced six years later. She has one son.

Suggested Readings: *Current Biography* (1990) p. 394; Peggy Noonan, *What I Saw at the Revolution* (1990).

Related Entries: Farewell Address (Ronald Reagan); Great Communicator, The; Nicaragua; Normandy, France, D-Day Celebration.

NORIEGA, MANUEL. See **PANAMA INVASION.**

NORMANDY, FRANCE, D-DAY CELEBRATION. On June 6, 1984, during a ten-day trip to Europe, President Reagan visited Normandy to participate in the fortieth anniversary celebration of the World War II D-Day invasion of Europe by the Allied forces. At the ceremonies Reagan delivered one of his most powerful speeches. Written by **Peggy Noonan,** the speech championed the American G.I. who had helped liberate Europe from Nazism. Reagan was at his best with the delivery of the address. The setting, the Pointe du Hoc, jutting out from Omaha Beach where U.S. troops had landed forty years earlier, was perfect. The speech invoked patriotism and reminded Americans of a simpler day. Even though Reagan himself had not fought in Normandy—he made movies during the war—he linked himself to the sacrifice embodied by the war effort, and especially the D-Day invasion. Just as important, the event meshed perfectly with Reagan's broader message, "America Is Back." During the 1984 presidential campaign, his campaign team highlighted the occasion, showing footage of him at the Normandy commemoration. As much as any event during his presidency, it showed the extent to which Reagan excelled at conducting ceremony.

Suggested Readings: Lou Cannon, *The Role of a Lifetime* (1991); Peggy Noonan, *What I Saw at the Revolution* (1990); Gary Wills, *Reagan's America: Innocents at Home* (1987).

Related Entries: Election of 1984; Great Communicator, The; "Morning in America."

NORTH, OLIVER. (October 7, 1943, San Antonio, Tex.– .) Colonel, U.S. Marine Corps; staff member, National Security Council.

Colonel Oliver North was the central figure in the **Iran-contra affair.** For six days in July 1987 the nation focussed its attention on North's televised testimony before Congress. Throughout the hearings, North maintained his innocence of any wrongdoing, claiming that he acted under the direction of his superiors, while at the same time testifying that he was not sure whether President Ronald Reagan knew of the specifics of the diversion of funds obtained from Iran to the Nicaraguan contras.

Nancy and Ronald Reagan at Omaha Beach Memorial, Normandy, France, June 6, 1984. Reagan Library.

Four years later, in *Under Fire,* North told a different story, proclaiming that Reagan "knew everything" about the diversion of funds.

In March 1988, North was indicted on sixteen different counts of violating the law. On May 4, 1989, North was found guilty on three charges: obstructing Congress, destroying documents, and accepting an illegal gratuity. He was sentenced to two years' probation and 1,200 hours of community service and was fined $150,000. Slightly over a year later, the U.S. Court of Appeals overturned one of the convictions and set aside the other two, directing the special prosecutor, **E. Lawrence Walsh,** to prove that North's testimony before Congress, in 1987, which North had delivered while under immunity, had not unduly influenced any of the witnesses. Unable to prove this, Walsh dropped the remaining charges.

North was born in the midst of World War II. As the son of a lieutenant colonel, who had served under George Patton during the war, North's vocation as a soldier seemed preordained. North briefly attended the State University of New York at Brockport but then transferred to the U.S. Naval Academy in Annapolis. After graduation, he shipped off to Vietnam, where he received both the Bronze and Silver Stars. Through the 1970s he rose through the ranks of the U.S. Marines, facing only one serious setback, a 1974 bout with depression, believed to be triggered by marital difficulties. During his work at the U.S. Navy Staff and Command College in Newport, Rhode Island, he attracted the attention of John F. Lehman, the secretary of the navy, who recommended North for a position with the National Security Council (NSC). For the next six years he worked for the NSC, becoming an expert on Central America. During this time he became one of the best-known proponents of the Nicaraguan contras, even delivering addresses on their behalf at various conservative functions. North played a key role in the exchange of arms for hostages and with the diversion of funds to the contras.

Throughout the period of the hearings and trials, North was a hero to many conservatives. They celebrated his unabashed patriotism, commitment to his superiors, and devotion to a "just cause." They also saw him as an underdog, defying pompous senators and members of Congress. In the midst of the scandal, North resigned from the Marine Corps. In 1994 he ran for the U.S. Senate in the state of Virginia. He won the state Republican Party nomination, but not the support of Republicans nationwide. Ronald Reagan, for one, refused to endorse him. Others supported an independent candidate for the office. On Election Day, North narrowly lost to the Democratic incumbent, Charles Robb.

North is married to the former Frances Elizabeth Stuart. They have a son and three daughters.

Suggested Readings: Ben Bradlee, Jr., *Guts and Glory: The Rise and Fall of Oliver North* (1988); *Current Biography* (1992) p. 419; Oliver North, *Under Fire: An American Story* (1991).

Related Entries: Latin America; Nicaragua.

NORTH AMERICAN FREE TRADE AGREEMENT (NAFTA). In the waning days of his presidency, on December 17, 1992, President George Bush signed the North American Free Trade Agreement. This treaty with Canada and Mexico aimed at eliminating tariffs and other trade barriers over a period of fifteen years. On ratification by Congress, during Clinton's presidency, it created a huge free-trade zone covering all North America. At the time when Bush signed the treaty it was unclear whether Congress would ratify it. Ironically, as a Democrat, Clinton was in a better position to gain ratification than Bush, since he proved able to sway a minority of Democrats to join with a majority of Republicans in the Senate in favor of the treaty.

Since the early 1970s every president—Richard Nixon, Gerald Ford, Jimmy Carter, Ronald Reagan, and then Bush—had supported the principle of decreasing tariffs and promoting free trade with other nations. However, efforts to develop a free-trade pact with Mexico were strongly opposed by organized labor, which feared losing industrial jobs. NAFTA also faced considerable opposition from environmentalists who feared it would undermine efforts to curb pollution. In the weeks leading up to the signing of the agreement, the House of Representatives unanimously passed a resolution declaring that it would not tolerate a pact that weakened U.S. health, safety, or labor laws. During the signing ceremony President Bush insisted that NAFTA did not threaten such protections, and he countered Democratic opposition by arguing that it would generate economic growth. Subsequently, Bush and the Republican Party sought to use the agreement as a weapon against the Democrats, claiming that they hindered economic growth. However, Bill Clinton's endorsement of the treaty weakened this attack and paved the way for bipartisan enactment of it in 1993.

Suggested Readings: *Congressional Quarterly Almanac* (1992); Robert A. Pastor, *Integration with Mexico* (1993); Sidney Weintraub, Luis Rubio and Alan D. Jones, *U.S.-Mexican Industrial Integration* (1991).

Related Entries: Environment; Trade Deficit.

NORTH ATLANTIC TREATY ORGANIZATION (NATO). NATO was established in 1949 by the United States and most of its northern European allies. Throughout the cold war it stood as the bulwark of the policy of containment of communism in Europe. NATO was a very important component of the Ronald Reagan administration's **foreign policy,** while simultaneously experiencing some of its most trying times.

Early in Reagan's presidency, massive protests took place against NATO's plans to deploy **Pershing II missiles** in Western Europe. Many Europeans felt the U.S. military buildup, of which these weapons were part, unduly jeopardized their safety. President Reagan and the leaders of the European NATO states, however, refused to bow to protestors' demands and deployed the missiles in 1983. British Prime Minister, **Margaret Hilda Thatcher (Roberts),** and German Chancellor, Helmut Kohl, in particular, stuck with Reagan's strategy despite tremendous pressure at home to do otherwise.

As the cold war came to an end, NATO faced a challenge of different sorts. The rapid reunification of Germany and the **collapse of communism** in other Eastern European states, including the **Soviet Union,** called into question the rationale for NATO's existence. Consistent with his general conservative approach to foreign policy, Bush resisted calls for disbanding NATO and advocated a cautious approach toward including Eastern European states into NATO.

Suggested Readings: Jonathan Haslam, *The Soviet Union and the Politics of Nuclear Weapons in Europe, 1969–87* (1990); David M. Schwartz, *NATO's Nuclear Dilemma* (1983); Steven K. Smith and Douglas A. Wertman, *U.S.-Western European Relations during the Reagan Years* (1992).

NUCLEAR FREEZE MOVEMENT. Massive increases in **defense spending** and increasing tensions between the United States and the **Soviet Union** gave rise to a grass-roots nuclear freeze movement in the United States and Europe in the early 1980s. The movement aimed to freeze or stop the construction and deployment of new nuclear weapons. This movement became particularly active in 1982 and 1983 as relations between the Soviet Union and the United States deteriorated and as the Ronald Reagan administration implemented plans to deploy medium-range **Pershing II missiles** in Europe.

On June 12, 1982, the American wing of the nuclear freeze movement presented its most significant display of its size and power when upward of 700,000 people assembled in New York City's Central Park to demonstrate for a freeze on the production and deployment of nuclear weapons. The protest, which by some estimates was the largest in the nation's history, was reminiscent of those that took place against the Vietnam War during the 1960s and early 1970s. It attracted well-known celebrities and representatives from a wide variety of political groups. Its basic message was that the United States should unilaterally freeze production and deployment of new nuclear weapons so as to alleviate the building pressures of the cold war.

President Reagan, who saw the nuclear freeze movement as a threat to one of his most basic policies, counterattacked it. At best, he argued, its participants were naive for favoring a policy that history had demonstrated had failed in the past, namely appeasement. At worst, he claimed, the nuclear freeze movement was infiltrated by communist agents. Rather than accede to movement demands, Reagan maintained the military buildup, insisting that peace would be gained through strength alone.

However, Reagan's criticism of the nuclear freeze movement did not stop it from growing. In May 1983, the National Conference of Catholic Churches issued a pastoral letter that condemned nuclear war as immoral and called for a nuclear freeze. In Europe, hundreds of thousands of men and women in West Germany, Britain, and Italy protested against the deployment of cruise and Pershing II missiles. In 1983, the House of Representatives passed a resolution that called on both the United States and the Soviet Union to cease building new weapons of mass destruction. Toward the end of the same year, one of the largest television audiences ever watched a special television docudrama, "The Day After," which depicted the devastating effects of a nuclear war.

Whether all this had an impact on the president remains problematic. Reagan continued to call for more arms, and Congress granted most of his demands. In 1984, **Walter Frederick Mondale** sought to win popular support by criticizing President Reagan's **Strategic Defense Initiative (Star Wars),** but to little avail. This said, the size of the nuclear freeze movement and its ability to strike a respondent chord among other Americans may have prodded Reagan to develop a more flexible approach to **arms control.** His call for arms reduction by both sides was timed to steal some of the wind from the sails of the nuclear freeze movement. In addition, the movement's existence kept the pressure on President Reagan to remain flexible and keep his options open.

Suggested Readings: David S. Meyer, *A Winter of Discontent* (1990); Jerome Price, *The Antinuclear Movement* (1989); Douglas C. Waller, *Congress and the Nuclear Freeze* (1987).

O

O'CONNOR, SANDRA DAY. (March 26, 1930, El Paso, Tex.– .) Associate Justice, U.S. Supreme Court, 1981– .

On July 7, 1981, President Ronald Reagan nominated Sandra Day O'Connor to the U.S. **Supreme Court.** On September 21, 1981, the U.S. Senate unanimously confirmed her for the post. Four days later she was sworn in as the first woman justice in the history of the highest court of the nation. O'Connor, who was Reagan's first nominee to the Court, gained confirmation with relative ease. In her years on the Court she developed a reputation as a moderate, siding with Justice William Brennan and the other liberal judges some of the time and with Reagan's more conservative appointees at other times. Although Reagan had hoped that the Supreme Court would overturn *Roe* v. *Wade,* O'Connor sided with those on the Court who maintained that women had a constitutional right to have an **abortion.** At the same time, O'Connor allowed for more restrictions on that right than did some of the more liberal justices.

Sandra Day, the oldest of three children, grew up on a ranch in Arizona and in El Paso, Texas, where, in her own words, she did "all the things boys did," except that she attended a private, all-girls school. After graduating from high school at age sixteen, she enrolled at Stanford University, earning a B.A. in economics (1950). Two years later she graduated third in her class from Stanford University Law School. One of her classmates was **William Hubbs Rehnquist,** who graduated first in the class. Shortly after graduating she married John Jay O'Connor, another Stanford law student. Unable, as a woman, to attain employment at leading firms in either San Francisco or Los Angeles, O'Connor went to work in the public sector, first for the county of San Mateo (California), and then for

Sandra Day O'Connor sworn in as Supreme Court justice. Reagan Library.

the military. With her husband she relocated to Arizona in 1957. Two years later she gave birth to the first of three sons.

While her children were small she worked for herself and became active in Republican Party politics. In 1965 she took a position as assistant attorney general for the state of Arizona, leaving the job only when she was nominated to replace a retiring member of the state legislature. Subsequently, she was elected to the legislature and became its majority leader. She was the first woman to hold such a post in American history. In 1975 she became a judge for the Maricopa County Superior Court. Six years later she was nominated to the Supreme Court.

O'Connor's nomination fulfilled one of Reagan's campaign pledges, to nominate a woman to the court, but angered the **Moral Majority,** which objected to her support for the Equal Rights Amendment and to several of her proabortion votes while a member of the Arizona State Legislature. In contrast, she won strong support from a wide range of senators, including both Arizona Republican Barry Goldwater, the standard-bearer of conservatism and Massachusetts Democrat Edward Kennedy, one of the best-known liberals in the nation.

Suggested Readings: *Current Biography* (1982) p. 297; Carol Greene, *Sandra Day O'Connor: First Woman on the Courts* (1982).

Related Entries: Courts; Women's Rights.

O'NEILL, THOMAS (TIP) PHILIP, JR. (December 9, 1912, Cambridge, Mass.–January 5, 1994, Boston, Mass.) Speaker, U.S. House of Representatives, 1977–1986.

For the first six years of Ronald Reagan's presidency, Tip O'Neill, a Democratic from Massachusetts, was the speaker of the House of Representatives. In many ways O'Neill was the epitome of a New Deal Democrat. He defended the liberal ideal that the government should stand up for the little guy. As speaker, he sought to defeat many of Reagan's domestic proposals. He met with mixed results. Enjoying about a 100-seat majority, House Democrats were able to resist many of Reagan's domestic spending cuts. However, Reagan often gained the support of the southern Democrats or "boll weevils," especially for increased **defense spending** and tax cuts, in spite of O'Neill's objections. (Boll weevils are small beetles that attack cotton plants. The term was first used in the 1950s to identify southern Democrats who allied with northern Republicans.)

Even though O'Neill and Reagan held different political views, with O'Neill representing the liberal wing of the Democratic Party and Reagan the conservative wing of the Republican Party, and even though the two clashed frequently over Reagan's proposals, they came to respect and like each other. As Reagan recalled in his memoir, *An American Life* (1990), O'Neill once stated to him that "after six o'clock we can be friends; but before six, it's politics."

O'Neill grew up in an Irish-Catholic family in Boston. He received his A.B. from Boston College (1936). Later that same year he was elected to the Massachusetts State Legislature, rising to the post of speaker in 1948. He held that post until 1952, when he was elected to the House of Representatives, filling the seat left vacant by John F. Kennedy, who had won election to the U.S. Senate. Over the following thirty-four years, O'Neill became a fixture in Congress, proving himself to be one of the leading supporters of President Lyndon Johnson's Great Society and other liberal programs. During the terms of Presidents Richard Nixon, Gerald Ford, and Ronald Reagan (all times when the Democrats maintained control of the House of Representatives), he served as one of the leading opponents of their conservative programs. This said, O'Neill was probably best known, not for his ideology but for his wit, charm, and political know-how. He was a consummate political insider who made sure to serve his constituents in his home district. Most of his colleagues considered him a strong majority leader (1973–1977) and speaker of the House, in the tradition of Sam Rayburn.

O'Neill was married to the former Mildred Anee Miller. They had five children. Upon retirement, he wrote a best-selling autobiographical account of his days in Congress, *Man of the House* (1987). He died of a heart attack in Boston, Massachusetts, on January 5, 1994. Over two thousand men and women attended his funeral, including former presidents Jimmy Carter and Gerald Ford.

Suggested Readings: Paul R. Clancy, *Tip: A Biography of Thomas P. O'Neill* (1980); Tip O'Neill, *Man of the House* (1987).

P

PANAMA CANAL TREATY. In 1977 the United States and the nation of Panama signed a treaty in which the United States agreed to transfer ownership of the Panama Canal to Panama in the year 2000. In addition, Panama agreed to the neutral operation of the canal. The U.S. Senate ratified the treaty in 1978, but even after it was ratified, it remained a hot political topic. Conservatives condemned it, with Ronald Reagan arguing that Panamanian control of the canal threatened American national security interests. Linking the treaty to the growing communist presence in the region, during the 1980 campaign Reagan attacked President **James (Jimmy) Earl Carter** for his support for it. Reagan added that the decision to relinquish control of the canal symbolized our declining will to stand up for American interests. "We bought it, we paid for it, it's ours, and we're going to keep it." Despite such rhetoric, while in office, neither Reagan nor George Bush sought the repeal of the treaty.

Suggested Readings: J. Michael Hogan, *The Panama Canal in American Politics* (1986); Walter LaFeber, *The Panama Canal* (1989).

Related Entries: Election of 1980; Foreign Policy; Latin America.

PANAMA INVASION. At 1 A.M. on December 20, 1989, a force of 12,000 American soldiers, led by U.S. paratroopers, invaded Panama. They were joined by an additional 10,500 troops already stationed in that country. Within seventy-two hours they took command of Panama City and the surrounding countryside. The objective of this invasion, according to President George Bush, was to depose Panamanian leader General Manuel Noriega. At first this objective was not achieved, as Noriega gained

U.S. troops in action during Panama Invasion. Still Media Center, Department of Defense.

temporary refuge in the Vatican embassy. On January 3, 1990, following diplomatic talks with Vatican officials and an assault on the embassy with rock music, which Noriega was known to hate, the general surrendered. Prior to this, Guillermo Endara had been installed as president—Endara had won an election the previous year but was denied power by Noriega. After the surrender, Panamanian authorities agreed to extradite Noriega to the United States, where he was wanted on drug trafficking charges. Twenty-three U.S. soldiers lost their lives in the invasion.

Noriega had raised the ire of the Bush administration through a series of abusive actions. Most important, he participated in the trafficking of drugs to the United States, for which he was indicted by a federal grand jury in Miami. To make matters worse, in May 1989, when Panamanian voters did not elect his hand-chosen candidate, Noriega brazenly voided the election and then executed military officers who sought to depose him in a coup. By December 1989, Americans viewed Noriega as a ruthless villain and a thug.

While polls at first showed that the American public widely supported the invasion, as time passed the public view of the Panamanian invasion dimmed. Noting that Noriega had served as a long-time Central Intelligence Agency informant, critics emphasized that Noriega had gained power, in part, because of American backing. They also observed that the invasion was condemned throughout **Latin America** as an unjustifiable violation of international law and sovereignty. Reports that thousands of Panamanian citizens had been killed or wounded during the invasion raised doubts about the military efficiency of the invasion, which initially was perceived as a remarkably clean expedition. To make matters worse, as money for rebuilding Panama failed to materialize, many Panamanians, who at least initially cheered U.S. forces, began to harass those who remained.

Meanwhile, Noriega lingered in an American jail awaiting his trial on drug charges. One of the things that stalled the case for eighteen months was Noriega's threat that he would implicate U.S. officials in various illegal activities. In April 1992, Noriega was convicted on drug charges and sent to a federal prison.

Suggested Readings: Kevin Buckley, *Panama* (1992); Jolin Dinges, *Our Man in Panama* (1990); Frederick Kempe, *Divorcing the Dictator* (1990).

PATCO STRIKE. See **AIR TRAFFIC CONTROLLERS (PATCO) STRIKE.**

PC. See **POLITICALLY CORRECT.**

PEROT, H. ROSS. (June 27, 1930, Texarkana, Ark.– .) Businessman, independent candidate for President, 1992.

H. Ross Perot, a multimillionaire businessman from Texas, shook up the political world with his independent candidacy for the presidency in 1992. During the campaign (one of the most bizarre in history, in which Perot first entered the race, then withdrew, and then reentered), the wealthy Texan, with a net worth estimated at approximately $2 billion, sought to portray himself as a man of the people who opposed Washington, D.C., and politics as usual. Although he failed to win a single electoral college vote, his 18.9 percent of the total popular vote established him as the most successful third-party candidate since Teddy Roosevelt in 1912.

Perot grew up in Texarkana, a town on the Texas-Arkansas border. He did not leave his hometown until he was nineteen, when he entered the U.S. Naval Academy in Annapolis. Perot did fairly well in school and was elected senior class president. However, in 1956, after only three years of active service, he left the navy and went to work for International Business Machines (IBM, or "Big Blue"). Perot rose quickly through the ranks of Big Blue, becoming one of the corporation's top salesmen. Six years later, in 1962, he left IBM to establish his own company, Electronic Data Systems (EDS). Over the next two decades he built EDS into a Fortune 500 company, becoming one of the richest men in America.

Perot was a big supporter of President Richard Nixon, raising money for prowar advertisements and spending much of his own time and money trying to get Vietnam War prisoners of war (POWs) released. Throughout the 1970s and 1980s, he remained active in politics, although working behind the scenes. Perot added to his image as an iconoclast and patriot by personally trying to win the release of several hostages in Iran and also by quitting General Motors (with compensation) because, as he claimed, of his inability to shake up its stoic corporate culture. (Perot had sold EDS to General Motors in 1984 for $2.5 billion. As part of the deal, he also gained a seat on the General Motors board of directors. Two years later, General Motors paid Perot $700 million for his shares of stock in the company and removed him from the board.) During the 1992 campaign, as antigovernment and anti-Washington fervor grew, he emphasized that he was not a politician but a businessman. He claimed he could make government work and contended that America needed to elect representatives with business experience who would "return the government to the people." He chastised both Republicans and Democrats for making a mess of things, from the federal budget to the economy. Using charts and graphs in half-hour infomercials, which he paid for largely through his own money, he showed that American wages were stagnating while the federal **budget deficit** kept rising.

Even more important than the points Perot made was the manner in which he made them. In an era in which politicians were groomed for office by advertising experts, Perot packaged himself as the antipolitician, making fun of his own appearance, from his big ears to his squeaky voice. A superb salesman, Perot displayed a knack for developing catchy slogans and for making sweeping promises to improve things. However, Perot's critics claimed that his plans were full of contradictions. They also complained about Perot's unpredictable personality.

In the summer of 1992 Perot seemed to shake these attacks. Polls showed him nearly even with the Democratic and Republican frontrunners. Then, however, faced with even sharper criticism by the press, attacks by the major candidates, and desertions among his supporters, he quit the race—only to officially rejoin it about a month before the elections. During several presidential debates Perot distinguished himself with his candor and wit. Nonetheless, he proved unable to win back some of his earlier supporters, who felt betrayed by his earlier departure from the race.

Suggested Readings: Jack Germond and Jules Witcover, *Mad as Hell: Revolt at the Ballot Box* (1993); Molly Ivans, "The Billionaire Boy Scout," *Time,* May 4, 1992, p. 38; *New York Times Magazine,* June 28, 1992, pp. 20–40; H. Ross Perot, *United We Stand* (1992).

Related Entries: Economy, U.S.; Election of 1992.

PERSHING II MISSILES. The Pershing II missiles were very accurate intermediate-range nuclear missiles that were first deployed in Europe in 1983. They were a weapon of great controversy, with supporters of the **nuclear freeze movement** arguing that they further endangered Europe and further escalated the arms race between the two superpowers. In 1981 President Ronald Reagan offered to stop the planned deployment of the Pershing IIs if the **Soviet Union** would stop deploying its own new generation of nuclear missiles. The Soviets rejected this offer, arguing that its missiles did not threaten the United States, while the missiles aboard U.S. bombers and submarines and those controlled by U.S. allies in Europe did. As the date for deployment of the Pershing II missiles neared, mass protests erupted in Europe. Backed by British Prime Minister **Margaret Thatcher** and German leader Helmut Kohl, however, Reagan carried through with his pledge to deploy the missiles. Many were later removed under the terms of the **Intermediate-range Nuclear Forces (INF) Treaty,** which Reagan and **Mikhail Sergeyevich Gorbachev** signed in 1987.

Suggested Readings: Jonathan Haslam, *The Soviet Union and the Politics of Nuclear Weapons in Europe* (1990); Druid N. Schwartz, *NATO's Nuclear Dilemma* (1983); Leon V. Siegal, *Nuclear Forces in Europe* (1984).

Related Entries: Arms Control; North Atlantic Treaty Organization (NATO); Thatcher (Roberts), Margaret Hilda.

PERSIAN GULF WAR. On August 2, 1990, a force of 140,000 Iraqi troops invaded Kuwait and quickly overran it. The invasion followed two weeks of Iraqi troop buildup along its border with Kuwait and years of border disputes between the two nations. While Saddam Hussein, Iraq's leader, had a history of aggression—Iraq had just completed a long war with Iran—the George Bush administration did not expect him to invade

Burning Oil Field during Operation Desert Storm (Persian Gulf War). Still Media Center, Department of Defense.

Kuwait. This belief was based, in part, on meetings that U.S. diplomats had held with Hussein, including one that later became a point of embarrassment for the administration. On this occasion, April Glaspie, the U.S. ambassador to Iraq, seemed to encourage Hussein to pursue his claims to certain disputed Kuwaiti landholdings.

Regardless of the causes of Hussein's actions, the United States and most of its allies quickly and firmly condemned the invasion. On August 2, the United Nations (UN) passed resolution 660 demanding an immediate withdrawal of Iraqi troops from Kuwait. Four days later the United Nations imposed stiff trade sanctions on Iraq (resolution 661) for refusing to abide by resolution 660. On the same day, King Fahd of Saudi Arabia informed President Bush that he would accept U.S. troops in his country to ward off further Iraqi aggression. Within two days, American troops began to arrive in the Saudi desert. At the same time, Secretary of State **James (Jim) Addison Baker III** crisscrossed the globe building a broad alliance in support of "Desert Shield," the name given to the military operation in Saudi Arabia and eventually in support of implementation of all of the UN resolutions. This included endorsement by many Arab

Operation Desert Storm (Persian Gulf War). Still Media Center, Department of Defense.

states, the **Soviet Union,** and the United States' traditional allies in Europe and Asia. By the end of the fall, over thirty nations had sent troops to the region. This included over 500,000 Americans. During the same time period, economic sanctions against Iraq were further tightened by the United Nations, so that only humanitarian aid was allowed into the country.

By October 30, however, President Bush had become convinced that economic sanctions would not convince Hussein to withdraw from Kuwait—or the alliance would fall apart by the time he did. Hence, Bush made a private decision to change the military plan in Saudi Arabia from a defensive to an offensive one. To further this end, Bush won approval from the United Nations (resolution 678) to use force against Iraq if its troops did not leave Kuwait by January 15, 1991. He ordered the military to ready a plan of attack and appealed for support at home. While many in America, including a large number of Democrats, favored sticking to economic sanctions, three days before the January 15 deadline, Bush secured congressional approval for using force against Iraq. (Bush insisted that he had the authority to use force even without congressional approval but preferred to obtain it.)

President Bush authorized the commencement of Operation Desert Storm, the military name for the military campaign against Iraq, on the 15th itself. The armed coalition, which included troops from Egypt, Saudi Arabia, and several European nations, began massive air and missile strikes against Iraq and occupied Kuwait, some of which were witnessed live, on television, via cameras actually stationed in Baghdad. On average, two to three thousand sorties were conducted by coalition forces daily. It soon became clear that the U.S.-led coalition had complete control of the air. The most frightening moments of the war, at least from the American perspective, came when Iraq began to fire scud missiles at Israel. Hussein hoped to provoke Israel into retaliating via these attacks, which in turn, he believed, would split the coalition, perhaps even enabling him to lead a *jihad* (holy war) of Islamic states versus the West. Despite heavy losses, Israel did not retaliate, instead leaving its security to American air forces, which sought to destroy the scud launchers. In addition, Israel secured from the United States two batteries of Patriot missiles (anti-missile defense systems) to ward off scud attacks.

After over a month of punishing air attacks, on the morning of February 24, coalition forces launched their ground attack on Iraqi positions in Kuwait. U.S. General **H. (Stormin') Norman Schwarzkopf,** the commander in the region, devised a two-front strategy, whereby U.S. and allied forces attacked directly from Saudi Arabia and drove toward Kuwait City. Simultaneously, other troops hit the Iraqis' flank, with the goal of cutting them off from their supply lines and reinforcements. Predictions of high casualties and difficult fighting, especially against several of Iraq's armored forces, proved unfounded. Almost all the Iraqi army in the region was routed. By January 28, Kuwait City had been secured by coalition forces and over 30,000 Iraqi troops had been captured. One hundred hours after launching the ground attack, President Bush declared a cease-fire.

The incredibly low number of casualties—only 148 American soldiers were killed in action—and the ease of the military victory, however, were not enough to provide President Bush with enough political clout to win reelection two years later. General Schwarzkopf and General **Colin Lu-**

Tomahawk Missile. Persian Gulf War. Still Media Center, Department of Defense.

ther Powell, the head of the Joint Chiefs of Staff at the time, became overnight heroes in America. The American soldiers were given a series of victory parades, the likes of which the Vietnam War veterans often complained that they had never received. Even those who had fought hard for a large military buildup during the 1980s felt vindicated as their new high technology weapons seemingly performed to perfection. (Later investigations cast some doubt on the performance of some of the most sophisticated weaponry.)

Nonetheless, many Americans felt ill at ease with the ultimate outcome of the war. Saddam Hussein remained in power in Iraq. Not only did internal revolts against him fail, he openly crushed the most serious ones by Shiites in the south and Kurds in the north. Moreover, some who had criticized the military action all along pointed out that the war, even though it produced few American casualties, resulted in extremely high death rates in Iraq (estimated by some as close to 300,000). Nor was it clear, at least immediately, that the war would produce peace in the Middle East. Last, the United States' refusal to appease Hussein did not deter other individuals from taking part in aggressive actions in other regions of the world. Perhaps this accounts for Bush's inability to capitalize on the victory in the Persian Gulf at the polls in 1992.

Suggested Readings: Thomas B. Allen, et al., *War in the Gulf* (1991); Lawrence Freedman and Efraim Karsh, *The Gulf Conflict* (1993); Michael J. Mazarr, Don M. Snider and James A. Blackwell, Jr., *Desert Storm* (1993); Michael L. Sifry and Christopher Cerph, eds., *The Gulf War Reader* (1992).

Related Entries: Election of 1992; High Technology; Iran-Iraq War; Middle East.

PHILIPPINES. For years Ferdinand Marcos ruled over the Philippines—an important ally of the United States—with a dictatorial hand. In 1981, just a few days before Ronald Reagan was inaugurated, Marcos ended seven years of martial law. However, he kept in place all the restrictive decrees that he had promulgated during this time period. While the Reagan administration might have preferred that Marcos promote reforms at a faster pace, it did not push hard due to its larger strategic goals. The Philippines was the home to large U.S. naval and air force bases, and Reagan did not want to jeopardize them. In addition, Marcos was an ardent anticommunist, who promised to aid Reagan in his broader goal of combating communism around the globe.

Internal developments in the Philippines during the mid-1980s, however, tested the Reagan administration's policy toward that nation. In August 1983, Benigno Aquino, a longtime opponent of Marcos, returned to the Philippines following three years of self-exile. He hoped to lead the reform movement that had begun to develop since the end of martial law in 1981. Upon his arrival at Manila airport, however, he was killed while in the custody of Marcos' security guards. The United States labeled his murder a "despicable act" and President Reagan postponed plans to visit the Philippines.

However, the Reagan administration did not back out of its agreement to give the Philippines $900 million over a period of five years in exchange for the use of air and naval bases. Nor did President Reagan personally condemn President Marcos. Moreover, in late October 1985, when a panel that Marcos had appointed to investigate Aquino's murder reported that the chief of staff of the Philippine military was partly responsible for Aquino's murder, the Reagan administration praised Marcos for his handling of the case.

However, the investigation did not placate reformers in the Philippines, who saw Marcos as partially responsible for Aquino's death and for other problems that beset the nation. In 1984 and 1985, as protests against the Marcos regime escalated, the Reagan administration continued to offer its public support for him. Increasingly, however, this position became less tenable. In December 1984, Corazon Aquino, Benigno Aquino's widow, declared that she would oppose Marcos in the upcoming presidential election. A groundswell of support developed around her candidacy. On the day of the election, Marcos declared himself the winner, despite much evidence of voter fraud. This resulted in mass protests against Marcos, but still, Reagan was reluctant to break with him. Only after leaders of the military joined the protests did the Reagan administration change course. In late February 1985, it announced that it would be best for Marcos to resign. Shortly afterward, Marcos fled the Philippines aboard a U.S. military aircraft and sought and received safe haven in the United States.

Following Marcos's departure, the United States recognized the new government headed by Corazon Aquino. Shortly thereafter, the Reagan administration put together an emergency aid package for the Philippines. Later in the year, Corazon Aquino traveled to the United States. In a public address to Congress she requested an even larger aid package than the one originally offered by the Reagan administration, emphasizing the democratic nature of the revolution that had just taken place in the Philippines. In part moved by her charisma and by the remarkable success of the revolution, Congress agreed to provide an addition $200 million in aid.

In the late 1980s, U.S. relations with the Philippines were complicated by court battles over the Marcos's assets, which the Aquino government claimed Marcos had stolen from his people. Not wanting to offend either an old ally or a new one, the Reagan administration tried to appear neutral. It refused to deport Marcos back to the Philippines, despite cries for his return. A bit short of a year after George Bush assumed the presidency, segments of the Filipino military sought to topple Aquino in a military coup. Supported by masses of people in the streets, other segments of the military, and two U.S. jet fighters that flew cover for government forces, she triumphed. President Bush also had to decide what to do with U.S. naval and air bases in the Philippines, for which the Filipino government was demanding ever-increasing sums of money (as part of new lease agreements). Aquino also wanted tighter control over the types of weapons located at the bases. With communism collapsing and the rivalry between the United States and the **Soviet Union** diminishing, the bases became less important to the United States. On top of this, volcanic eruptions in the Philippines made one of the bases virtually inoperable. As a result of all these factors, on December 7, 1991, the United States announced it would leave the naval base at Subic Bay and relocate its fleet to Singapore.

Suggested Readings: David Bain, *Sitting in Darkness* (1984); Raymond Bonner, *Waltzing with a Dictator* (1987); H. W. Brands, *Bound to Empire* (1992); Stanley Karnow, *In Our Image* (1989).

Related Entries: Communism, Collapse of; Foreign Aid; Foreign Policy.

PIERCE, SAMUEL RILEY, JR. (September 8, 1922, Glen Cove, N.Y.–) Secretary of Housing and Urban Development, 1981–1989.

Samuel Pierce was the highest-ranking black in the Ronald Reagan administration. For eight years he headed the Department of Housing and Urban Development (HUD).

During the mid-1960s, President Lyndon Johnson saw HUD as a key player in the war on poverty. Conservatives, like Reagan, however, saw this massive agency as representative of the excesses of liberalism. Accordingly, during Reagan's administration, HUD saw its funds decline 75 percent. Pierce generally agreed with Reagan's philosophy of scaling back HUD's objectives. However, at the same time, as its chief administrator, he was charged with doing as good a job as possible with whatever funds were provided. Rather than make the best of a bad situation, however, HUD, under Pierce's leadership, fell into further disrepute, as top aides milked the agency for their own personal profit.

Samuel Pierce grew up on Long Island, the son of a successful small businessman. In high school, Pierce was a star athlete, which earned him an athletic scholarship to Cornell University. Prior to graduation, he left school, to serve in the army (1943–1946). After completing his service, he returned to Cornell, earning a B.A. (1947) and a law degree (1951). He then earned an L.L.M. in taxation from New York University law school. He went to work for the Manhattan District Attorney's Office and then became an assistant U.S. attorney. In 1955 he joined the Dwight Eisenhower administration. Subsequently, he barely lost an election to become a top criminal judge in New York. Throughout the 1960s, Pierce was in private practice, even assisting in Martin Luther King, Jr.'s, defense in the famous *New York Times* v. *Sullivan* case. In 1970 he accepted a top subcabinet post in the Richard Nixon administration. In 1981 he became President Reagan's Secretary of Housing and Urban Development.

While secretary of HUD, Pierce insisted that blacks needed to cut their reliance on government programs. He championed President Reagan's policies, including large domestic spending cuts, claiming they would revive the economy. Pierce was not a very visible member of the cabinet. Ironically, only at the end of his years of service did most Americans come to know him, and they did so because of a corruption scandal involving HUD. Investigators revealed that Pierce and his top aides at HUD had awarded contracts to their friends and political cronies. Billions of dollars over a period of years had been improperly spent. Funds went to build golf courses, luxury apartments, and swimming pools, rather than low-income housing. Even though Pierce himself was never charged with violating the law, several of his aides were, including Deborah Gore Dean, his assistant, who was charged and convicted for committing fraud.

Pierce is married to Barbara Penn Wright. They have one child.

Suggested Readings: *Current Biography* (1982) p. 318; *Facts on File* (1994).

Related Entry: Economy, U.S.

PLANT-CLOSING BILL. In 1988 President Ronald Reagan and the Democratically controlled Congress went to battle over the "plant-closing bill" part of the Omnibus Trade and Competitiveness Act of 1988. Reagan opposed the measure; the Democrats favored it. Ultimately, Reagan lost, as Congress passed legislation mandating that employers provide advance notification of layoffs to their employees.

In response to the growing **trade deficit** and the decrease in manufacturing jobs, Congress passed the Omnibus Trade and Competitiveness Act of 1988. Among the bill's provisions were protection for the textile and shoe industry, increased power for the Office of the U.S. Trade Representative, and the requirement that companies with more than one hundred employees provide sixty days' advance notice before closing any plant or laying off any of their workers.

While President Reagan disagreed with several provisions of the trade bill, he found the plant-closing section particularly objectionable and stated so when he vetoed the act on May 24. He declared that he believed that companies should provide advance notice but added that they should do so on a voluntary basis. He stated: "I object to the idea that Federal Government would arbitrarily mandate, for all conditions and under all circumstances, exactly when and in what form the notification should take place." The House of Representatives quickly overrode his veto, but in the Senate, where the Democratic majority was smaller, the override vote fell short.

However, the bill's sponsors did not give up. Rather, they developed a compromise measure that was more acceptable to the White House. The plant-closing section of the bill was separated from the trade bill, and Reagan signed the trade bill into law. At the same time, Democrats, with the support of a number of Republicans, passed a separate plant-closing bill. Since it received more than a two-thirds vote in both houses, President Reagan decided not to veto it. It became law without his signature.

The ability of Democrats to enact this measure suggested that Reagan's power was waning. As a lame duck president, and perhaps because of the **Iran-contra affair,** he was no longer able to push through his agenda or block the Democrats from enacting part of theirs. This boded poorly for George Bush who, as president, would have to contend with a Democratically controlled Congress.

Suggested Readings: *Congressional Quarterly Almanac* (1988); Jane Mayer and Doyle McManus, *Landslide: The Unmaking of a President, 1984–88* (1988); "Trade Bill Vetoes," *Historic Documents* (1988) p. 213.

POINDEXTER, JOHN MARLAN. (August 12, 1936, Washington, Ind.–) National Security Adviser, 1985–1987.

In fall 1987, John Poindexter resigned from the U.S. Navy and relinquished his post as national security adviser. His resignation came on top of testimony before the U.S. Congress in which he took full responsibility for the **Iran-contra affair.** He was subsequently convicted on charges of obstructing justice. These events brought a tragic ending to a life of public service and achievement. Ironically, many felt he was simply the fall man for higher officials in the scandal.

Poindexter grew up in a small midwestern farm community in Indiana. In high school he was the valedictorian and class president, achievements which helped earn him admission to the U.S. Naval Academy. In 1958 he graduated top in his class from the academy. Six years later he was awarded a Ph.D. in nuclear physics from the California Institute of

Technology. Throughout the 1960s and 1970s he rose through the ranks in the navy.

In 1981, when Ronald Reagan became president, Poindexter won a promotion to rear admiral and became the military assistant to **Richard Vincent Allen,** Reagan's first national security adviser. As Allen's assistant, he played a key role in planning the military invasion of **Grenada,** which in turn led to another promotion, this time to the position of deputy national security adviser under **Robert (Bud) McFarlane.** For two years he worked as McFarlane's deputy, until December 1985, when he assumed McFarlane's responsibilities.

A very hard worker, Poindexter continued to pursue a hard-line policy toward left-wing Central American regimes and to promote a continued buildup of American arms. After less than six months on the job, he developed and implemented the policy of "proportional response," whereby the United States staged air strikes against **Libya** for its alleged sponsoring of terrorist attacks. By the end of 1986, Poindexter's role in the Libyan affair had been overshadowed, however, by the Iran-contra affair, in which he allegedly played a key role. In November 1986 Poindexter refused to cooperate with Congress in its investigation of the affair. He resigned the following summer and, after being granted limited immunity, he testified that he had helped divert money for arms. He admitted having expanded the policy handed down to him by Robert McFarlane. Not long afterward, he was indicted and then convicted on several charges. They were later overturned on technical grounds.

Suggested Readings: *Current Biography* (1987) p. 435; Lawrence Walsh, *Iran-Contra: The Final Report* (1994).

Related Entry: Defense Spending.

POLITICALLY CORRECT (PC). In the early 1990s, the term, "politically correct," or "PC," became part of the American lexicon. Although originally coined by scholars on the left as a phrase of self-criticism, it was usually used by conservatives to condemn what they saw as a narrowing of political discourse. Put differently, conservatives and some liberals used the term *PC* as a shorthand way to attack the growth of multiculturalism, which insisted that greater attention and sensitivity be paid to women, minorities, and other disadvantaged groups, both in substance and in everyday language, and against other liberal trends.

Multiculturalism had grown out of the social movements of the 1960s. It demanded a broader interpretation of history and an expansion of the traditional curriculum. During the 1980s, several leading conservatives, from **William John Bennett,** head of the National Endowment for the Humanities, to Alan Bloom, a professor at the University of Chicago and author of the best-seller, *The Closing of the American Mind* (1988), sharply criticized multiculturalism, arguing that it watered down American education and downplayed or misrepresented the significance of classical Western thought. Lynne Cheney, Bennett's successor at the National Endowment for the Humanities, as well as conservative and neoconservative newspaper columnists and talk radio hosts, joined the fray in the latter part of the 1980s and early 1990s. They pointed to incidents where student activists or other pressure groups had limited freedom of expression. This included pressuring universities to enact speech codes that limited allegedly racist and sexist speech by whites, while at the same time allowing black radicals and feminists to denigrate white males.

Supporters of multiculturalism or variants of it countered that conservatives were the ones who actually sought to narrow political discourse. Rather than engage new scholarly developments, they chose to dismiss them in a simple and publicly popular way. Debate over what was politically correct was further complicated by the fact that some who called themselves feminists or radicals condemned certain brands of multiculturalism; moreover, the media exaggerated the extent of limitations on speech. For instance, claims that traditional authors were no longer read on college campuses, that all schools had restrictive speech codes, or that espousing sensitivity in language was akin to censorship simply were not the case.

It may be years before historians can sort out the winners and losers in the culture wars of the 1980s and 1990s. Both multiculturalism and the politically correct—and the backlash against them—seemed to grow each year. During the 1992 election, the Republican Party sought to emphasize the Democratic Party's association with multiculturalism and the PC. Ironically, at the same time, conservatives seemed to root out moderate Republicans who did not hold the politically correct line on conservative issues such as **abortion.**

Suggested Readings: Lawrence Grossberg, *We Gotta Get Out of This Place: Popular Conservatism and Postmodern Culture* (1992); James Davison Hunter, *Culture Wars* (1991).

Related Entries: Arts; Election of 1992; Popular Culture.

POPULAR CULTURE. To a degree, popular culture reinforced the conservative message of the Ronald Reagan–George Bush years. Reagan sought to invoke a nostalgia for the past, for a better and simpler time. Many of the top movies, television shows, and other forms of entertainment did so as well. However, it would be an overstatement to suggest that the entire entertainment world reflected a conservative yearning for the past. Indeed, popular culture of the 1980s contained many elements of the counterculture of the 1960s.

The most blatantly conservative movies were those produced by Sylvester Stallone, who had gained fame during the 1970s for his portrayal of *Rocky,* the story of a mythical white boxer. Stallone's blockbuster *Rambo* films of the 1980s returned Americans to Vietnam, except that this time, the superhero, Rambo, is freed from the restraints of the press and Congress, and so prevails. Steven Spielberg continued to produce one blockbuster film after another, including *Back to the Future,* which captured a simpler era while at the same time suggesting that high technology, à la Reagan's **Strategic Defense Initiative (Star Wars),** offered a means to solving contemporary problems.

On the television screen, "Dallas" and "Dynasty," two prime-time soap operas about the rich and famous, dominated the airwaves. Other top shows included "The Cosby Show" and "Family Ties," updated versions of the 1950s and early 1960s family sitcoms. Perhaps the most notable aspect about television was the disappearance of shows involving strong female characters, such as the "Mary Tyler Moore Show," which had arisen with the women's movement during the 1970s. Particularly with the spread of cable television and videocassette recorders (VCRs), viewers had more choices and television offered a greater variety than in the past. Moreover, several perennial favorites, from "60 Minutes," the CBS news journal, to sports, continued to draw the largest audiences, just as they had before Reagan's ascension to power.

The music world was one of contradictions, displaying both conservative trends and cannon fodder for conservatives who railed at it. Country Western music gained in popularity, yet at the same time, within the African-American community, soul and disco gave way to rap and hip-hop, a decidedly antiestablishment trend. Likewise, rock stars from Madonna to Michael Jackson assaulted traditional values. Just as important, the young now watched their favorite rock stars on the MTV cable channel, which played music videos saturated with sex, drugs, and violence. The 1980s also witnessed one of the largest "political" concerts ever, "Live Aid," a massive international fund-raiser for famine-stricken **Africa,** which featured the song, "We Are the World," sung by an all-star cast of rock performers, from Stevie Wonder to Bob Dylan.

Theater, the world of fiction, and other forms of entertainment offered up a mixed message as well. Revivals of older Broadway musicals or musicians appeared with regularity, yet the 1980s also saw new, innovative musicals and dramas, from *Cats* (1982) to *M. Butterfly* (1988). Similarly, Tom Wolfe's *Bonfire of the Vanities* (1988), a critique of the culture of greed during the Reagan years, closed out the 1980s on the best-seller list, yet through much of the decade, more Americans read thrillers by Stephen King and Tom Clancy than books like Wolfe's.

In sum, popular culture displayed the themes of change and continuity side-by-side with conservatism and the permanence of modern art forms. One final reflection of this theme came from the advertising world, as Mick Jagger, the singer of the Rolling Stones rock group, and one of the icons of rebellion of the 1960s, helped sell Budweiser beer. For some observers, this represented a sellout, the final collapse of the counterculture, yet for others, this represented its triumph.

I. TOP-RATED TELEVISION SHOW, 1980–1992

1980–81	"Dallas"
1981–82	"Dallas"
1982–83	"60 Minutes"
1983–84	"Dallas"
1984–85	"Dynasty"
1985–86	"The Cosby Show"
1986–87	"The Cosby Show"
1987–88	"The Cosby Show"
1988–89	"Roseanne"
1989–90	"Roseanne"
1990–91	"Cheers"
1991–92	"60 Minutes"
1992–93	"60 Minutes"

II. ACADEMY AWARD FOR BEST PICTURE, 1980–1992

1980	*Ordinary People*
1981	*Chariots of Fire*
1982	*Gandhi*
1983	*Terms of Endearment*
1984	*Amadeus*
1985	*Out of Africa*
1986	*Platoon*
1987	*The Last Emperor*
1988	*Rain Man*
1989	*Driving Miss Daisy*
1990	*Dances with Wolves*
1991	*The Silence of the Lambs*
1992	*Unforgiven*

III. GRAMMY AWARD FOR BEST RECORD, 1980–1992

1980	Christopher Cross, *Sailing*
1981	Kim Carnes, *Betty Davis Eyes*
1982	Toto, *Rosanna*
1983	Michael Jackson, *Beat It*
1984	Tina Turner, *What's Love Got to Do with It*
1985	USA for Africa, *We Are the World*
1986	Steve Winwood, *Higher Love*
1987	Paul Simon, *Graceland*
1988	Bobby McFerrin, *Don't Worry Be Happy*
1989	Bette Midler, *Wind Beneath My Wings*
1990	Phil Collins, *Another Day in Paradise*
1991	Natalie Cole with Nat "King" Cole, *Unforgettable*
1992	Eric Clapton, *Tears in Heaven*

IV. PULITZER PRIZE IN FICTION, 1980–1992

1980	Norman Mailer, *The Executioner's Song*
1981	John Kennedy O'Toole, *A Confederacy of Dunces*
1982	John Updike, *Rabbit Is Rich*
1983	Alice Walker, *The Color Purple*
1984	William Kennedy, *Ironweed*
1985	Alison Lurie, *Foreign Affairs*
1986	Larry McMurtry, *Lonesome Dove*
1987	Peter Taylor, *A Summons to Memphis*
1988	Toni Morrison, *Beloved*
1989	Anne Tyler, *Breathing Lessons*
1990	Oscar Hijuelos, *The Mambo Kings Play Songs of Love*
1991	John Updike, *Rabbit at Rest*
1992	Jane Smiley, *A Thousand Acres*

Suggested Readings: E. Ann Kaplan, *Rocking around the Clock* (1987); Nicolaus Mills, ed., *Culture in the Age of Money* (1990); Celeste Olalquiaga, *Megalopolis: Contemporary Cultural Sensibilities* (1992).

POVERTY. During the Ronald Reagan–George Bush years, poverty remained a significant aspect of the American scene. Pointing to growing disparities between the rich and poor and the further disintegration of America's inner cities, liberal critics of the Reagan administration argued that the president's policies had made things worse for the poor. Conservatives countered by suggesting that liberals overestimated the number of Americans who were poor. In addition, rather than blaming Reagan's policies for the persistence of high levels of poverty, they claimed that long-standing liberal programs were responsible.

Based on government statistics, poverty increased slightly during the Reagan-Bush years, in both absolute and relative terms (Table 13). As in the past, the percentage of blacks who were poor remained much higher

Table 13
Poverty by Race, 1970–1990

Year	Total (mils.)	% of Pop.	Percent Living in Poverty	
			Black	White
1970	25.4	12.6%	7.5 (33.5%)	17.5 (9.9%)
1980	29.3	13.0%	8.6 (32.5%)	19.7 (10.2%)
1990	33.6	13.5%	9.8 (31.9%)	13.5 (10.7%)

than the percentage of whites who were. Nonetheless, despite popular myth, the average poor person was not an inner-city black man, but a white woman. Throughout the 1980s and early 1990s, more whites were poor than blacks and poverty became increasingly feminized, meaning that a growing percentage of those considered poor were women, and often unmarried or divorced women with children.

While the causes of poverty were multiple, among the factors that contributed to the persistence of poverty in the United States was the decline in manufacturing jobs. In addition, most new jobs created during the 1980s were located outside the highest concentration of poor people in inner cities, and they often demanded higher levels of skill than in the past. Rates of poverty were particularly high among young black and white men without at least a high school education. Liberal critics added that President Reagan's policies, which cut back on expenditures for job training and public housing and decreased payments for food stamps and other **welfare** programs, exacerbated the problems faced by the poor. While tax cuts, they contended, substantially boosted the income of the elite, little "trickled down" to the lower levels. Liberals also observed that although an increasing number of poor people were working, the Reagan administration's refusal to increase the minimum wage delegated them to poverty.

Supporters of President Reagan's policies argued that liberals misunderstood the causes and levels of poverty in America. Rather than blaming cuts in welfare programs on the economy, they focused on the changes in American culture and values. As **Danforth (Dan) James Quayle** suggested in his famous "Murphy Brown" speech, a decline in values that resulted in a growing number of unwed mothers accounted more for high poverty rates than did cuts in welfare. Some conservative intellectuals, such as Charles Murray, argued that welfare was the cause of poverty. It trapped the poor in a state of dependency, encouraging them to act irresponsibly. In addition, many conservative politicians and economists claimed that government figures on poverty presented a distorted picture, noting that the poverty level rose from $8,414 in 1980 to $13,359 in 1990. Put differently, today's poor people were better off than the poor of the past. Moreover, conservatives argued, such figures did not take into account aid that the poor received from the government, from food stamps to medicaid, which lifted the real earnings of many above the poverty line.

Regardless of the debate, poverty rates in the United States remained much higher than in most other developed countries, and they underlay many of America's social problems, such as high crime and drug abuse. In addition, the concentration of poverty in many inner cities was said to create a permanent "underclass," a group of Americans born into poverty and bound to replicate itself. The existence of an underclass contradicted the American pattern of social mobility. It appeared to represent a permanent segment of the American population that was not affected by economic growth.

Suggested Readings: Sar Levitan and Issac Shapiro, *Working But Poor, American Contradiction* (1987); Charles Murray, *Losing Ground: American Social Policy, 1950–1980* (1984); Harell R. Rogers, Jr., *Poor Women, Poor Families and the Economic Plight of America's Female Headed Households* (1986); William Julius Wilson, *The Truly Disadvantaged* (1987).

Related Entries: Civil Rights; Deindustrialization; Economy, U.S.; Recessions.

POWELL, COLIN LUTHER. (April 5, 1937, New York, N.Y.– .) Deputy National Security Adviser, 1987–1989; Chairman, Joint Chiefs of Staff, 1989–1993.

During the **Persian Gulf War,** General Colin Powell, the chairman of the Joint Chiefs of Staff, became one of the best-known and most admired men in America. The highest-ranking black man in American military history, Powell was born in Harlem, the son of two Jamaican immigrants who worked in the garment industry. Powell attended New York City public schools and graduated with a B.A. from the City College of New York, with a major in geology, in 1958. While in college he joined the Reserve Officers' Training Corps (ROTC), and on graduation he became a second lieutenant in the United States Army. During the 1960s he distinguished himself during his service in Vietnam, rising through the army ranks. Following his second tour of duty, he received his M.B.A. from George Washington University, after which he

General Colin Powell. Still Media Center, Department of Defense.

became a White House fellow, working under **Frank Charles Carlucci, 3rd,** Richard Nixon's director of the Office of Management and Budget. In 1973 Powell returned to active duty, and in 1975 he enrolled at the National War College before being given command of the Second Brigade of the 101st Airborne Division. He continued to alternate between military and political posts from 1976 though 1983, when he accepted a post as Defense Secretary **Caspar Willard Weinberger**'s senior military assistant. Even though he was one of the top military advisers during the **Iran-contra affair**, he emerged from the scandal unscathed. In 1987, when his former boss, Frank Carlucci, took over from **John Marlan Poindexter** as President Ronald Reagan's National Security Adviser, Powell became Carlucci's deputy, a post he held until President George Bush nominated him to become chairman of the Joint Chiefs of Staff.

As the top general during the Persian Gulf War, Powell assumed responsibility for the failure or success of the military attack—known as Operation Desert Storm. The tremendous success of the invasion, along with Powell's cool and professional demeanor, made him one of the nation's most admired men. Along with General **H. (Stormin') Norman Schwarzkopf,** who directed the fighting, Powell gained credit for the victory. Indeed, his retirement in 1993 led many to suggest that he could become the first black president in U.S. history a view reinforced by strong showings in the public opinion polls.

Powell is married to Alma V. Johnson. They have three children.

Suggested Readings: *Current Biography* (1988) p. 455; Howard B. Means, *Colin Powell: Soldier/Statesman* (1992); David Roth, *Sacred Honor: A Biography of Colin Powell* (1993).

PROFESSIONAL AIR TRAFFIC CONTROLLERS (PATCO) STRIKE. See **AIR TRAFFIC CONTROLLERS (PATCO) STRIKE.**

Q

QUAYLE, DANFORTH (DAN) JAMES. (February 4, 1947, Indianapolis, Ind.– .) Vice President of the United States, 1989–1993.

George Bush's choice of Dan Quayle, a relatively unknown senator from Indiana, to serve as his running mate in 1988 surprised many Americans. Few political pundits had given Quayle much chance of gaining the nomination, although in retrospect, Bush's biographers could point to a few hints made by Bush while on the campaign trail to the effect that he would choose Quayle. By choosing Quayle, Bush solidified conservative support for his candidacy—historically, conservatives had distrusted Bush, while Quayle was one of their favorite politicians. By not selecting as his running mate a well-known Republican such as **Robert Joseph Dole,** Bush was able to stand out as a candidate, whereas he had been overshadowed by Ronald Reagan for many years.

Dan Quayle enjoyed a privileged youth. His maternal grandfather, Eugene C. Pulliam, was a multimillionaire, owner of five newspapers, and champion of conservatism. Quayle's father's family owned the Chicago Dowel Company, best known for its production of the popular toy, Lincoln Logs. In addition to enjoying the benefits that came with wealth, Dan Quayle was reared into a very conservative tradition. His father and mother belonged to the John Birch Society and were early and strong supporters of Barry Goldwater, the Republican presidential nominee, in 1964.

In 1965 Quayle enrolled at DePauw University. After four years of undistinguished study, he graduated with a B.A. in political history. Following graduation he joined the National Guard and worked for the state government. In 1974 he received his law degree from Indiana University

The Reagans, Bushes, and Quayles. Reagan Library.

and then joined his family business as a publisher and general manager of the Huntington *Herald Press.* Two years later, he surprisingly defeated Edward Roush in a race for Congress by attacking the Democratic incumbent's liberal record, and four years later, he became the youngest senator in Indiana history. Despite an insider reputation as an undistinguished legislator, he displayed a knack for winning elections.

During the 1988 campaign, Quayle championed conservative views, to the delight of Ronald Reagan's long-time supporters, many of whom distrusted Bush because of his moderate past. As vice president, Quayle became a spokesman for continuing the Reagan agenda. He earned special notoriety following the **Los Angeles riot** when, in his "Murphy Brown" speech (referring to the television character becoming a single mother), he attacked the cultural decline that, he claimed, lay at the root of the riots—and of much of what was wrong with America. Even before this address, which much of the media derided, he had become a favorite target of liberals, who especially relished making fun of his gaffs and misstatements. Although many political pundits continued to insist that he was a liability to President Bush, detailed studies did not show that he ever cost Bush votes. After the 1992 election, many thought that

Quayle was one of the leading candidates for the 1996 Republican nomination, but after testing the political waters, he decided not to seek the presidency.

Suggested Readings: *Current Biography* (1989) p. 448; Dan Quayle, *Standing Fast* (1994).

Related Entries: Election of 1988; Election of 1992.

R

REAGAN, NANCY DAVIS. (July 6, 1923, New York, N.Y.– .) First Lady, 1981–1989.

Nancy Davis Reagan was President Ronald Reagan's biggest fan and his closest confidante. Like Reagan, she came from show business roots. Shortly after she was born, her father left and later divorced her mother, an actress. Since her mother was busy performing on the Broadway stage, Nancy spent much of her early childhood in the care of her aunt, Virginia Galbraith, in Bethesda, Maryland. Her mother's remarriage to Dr. Loyal Davis, a prominent Chicago physician, markedly improved her life. Economic worries disappeared and her family life became more stable. (Nancy was formally adopted when she was fourteen.) She enrolled in Girls' Latin School in Chicago and later, Smith College (B.A., 1943). At both institutions she became involved with drama. This led to roles on Broadway and, in 1949, a contract with MGM Studios in Hollywood. Altogether she acted in eleven movies.

In 1949 she met Ronald Reagan, who had recently divorced his first wife, Jane Wyman. They were married in a small ceremony in 1952. Two years later she gave birth to their first child, Patricia Ann (Patty). They had a second child, Ronald, in 1958. Although Nancy had a few more movie roles after her marriage, she concentrated on raising her children.

When Ronald Reagan became more active in politics during the early 1960s, Nancy became one of his most avid campaigners. As the wife of the governor of California for eight years, she earned a reputation for high style and elegance, which she carried with her as first lady. Both as the governor's wife and as first lady, Nancy Reagan focused much of her time and attention on troubled youths, promoting the Foster Grandparent Program and fighting drug and alcohol abuse. She made famous the **"Just Say No"** campaign against drugs. Especially during Ronald Reagan's second term, she also gained a reputation as a protector of her husband. The resignation of several of Reagan's old California aides, including **Michael Keith Deaver** and **Edwin Meese III,** probably pushed her in this direction.

While public opinion polls showed that most Americans admired her, they also revealed that the public felt she was too ostentatious during economic hard times. Nancy Reagan's lowest political moment came after the couple left the White House with the simultaneously publication of several books and articles that described her as a fervid follower of **astrology** and a dangerous meddler in political affairs. In *My Turn* (1989), her autobiography, she aggressively defended herself from accusations made in these works. Otherwise, she seemed to relish retirement on the Reagan farm in Santa Barbara, California.

Suggested Readings: *Current Biography* (1982) p. 338; Joan Quigley, *"What Does Joan Say?" My Seven Years as the Astrologer to Nancy and Ronald Reagan* (1990); Nancy Reagan, *My Turn* (1989).

REAGAN, RONALD WILSON. (February 6, 1911, Tampico, Ill.– .) Fortieth President of the United States, 1981–1989.

On January 20, 1989, following George Bush's inaugural address, the new President and Barbara Bush accompanied Ronald and Nancy Reagan to a waiting helicopter on the first stop of their journey to their new home in Bel Air, California. The Reagans bid one last farewell, the helicopter provided them with one last glimpse of the White House; then, they faded off into the horizon, like cowboys riding off into the sunset in a Hollywood movie. This scene culminated a storybook-like eight years in Washington, D.C., barely interrupted by one of the worst **recessions**— and also, one of the worst scandals—in U.S. history.

Reagan ended his presidency with some of the highest popular opinion approval ratings of any president in U.S. history. Not since Herbert Hoover took office had the Republican Party succeeded itself through a presidential election, and not since Andrew Jackson handed over the reins to his vice president, Martin Van Buren, had any president served two complete terms and then watched his vice president win the presidency in an election.

Ronald Wilson Reagan was born in the small town of Tampico, Illinois, in 1911 in the midst of the Depression. His family moved often, as his father, an on-again, off-again shoe salesman, struggled to stay employed.

His mother, a deeply religious and pious women, helped hold the family together during this trying time. As a youth, Ronald worked as a lifeguard and at other odd jobs. He attended Eureka College, a small, private Protestant institution. He had mediocre grades but excelled at sports and drama. He was a devoted New Deal Democrat—his father benefited from a Works Progress Administration (WPA) job—and admired President Franklin D. Roosevelt's leadership skills and policies.

After graduation Reagan worked as a radio announcer, broadcasting Chicago Cub baseball games to an Iowa audience. In 1937 he took a screen actor's test in Hollywood, which won him a contract with Warner Brothers. For nearly thirty years he worked as an actor, in the movies and then in television. He married Jane Wyman, a Hollywood star, divorced her eight years later, and then, in 1952, married Nancy Davis, a budding Hollywood starlet. His most famous films were *Knute Rockne—All American* and *King's Row.* Most of his roles were in "B" movies, westerns, war films, or comedies, such as *Bedtime for Bonzo,* in which he costarred with a chimpanzee.

Even before his acting career came to a close, Reagan had become involved in politics. He was the president of the Screen Actors Guild during the critical post–World War II red scare or anticommunist hysteria and worked for eight years for General Electric (GE), hosting its television show, "Death Valley Days." His work for GE included touring the nation as its public relations spokesman. While on tour he developed a stump speech that criticized big government and high taxes and warned of the dangers of communism. This was a message that he would repeat throughout the rest of his career. During the 1950s and early 1960s, Reagan also drifted away from his ties to the Democratic Party.

In 1964, Reagan delivered a lengthy televised fund-raising address for Republican presidential nominee Barry Goldwater, which was very well received by conservatives across the nation. It elicited more positive mail than had Goldwater's appearances. He displayed in this address, perhaps not for the first time, his ability to reach the public, a skill that would later earn him the title, **"the Great Communicator."** The speech also convinced many political pundits and Republican Party insiders that Reagan himself should run for office.

In 1966, Ronald Reagan mounted a vigorous campaign against Edmund (Pat) Brown, the two-term Democratic governor of California. Reagan promised to cut wasteful government spending and criticized liberals for coddling lawbreakers who participated in urban riots and campus disturbances. Attempts to portray Reagan as an extremist—a tactic that had helped produce Lyndon Johnson's landslide victory against Goldwater—failed. In contrast to many other conservative candidates, Reagan exuded a feeling of warmth and optimism. He won in a landslide—by nearly a million votes—and went on to serve as governor of the largest state of the nation for eight years.

While governor, Reagan actually had a fairly moderate record. State spending increased during his eight years in office. He even signed an **abortion** bill into law. However, at the same time, Reagan continued to deliver conservative speeches in which he railed at big government and promoted traditional values. He gained considerable notoriety for his attacks on student and antiwar protestors.

In 1976 Reagan mounted a campaign for the Republican (GOP) presidential nomination. Despite his popularity among conservatives, he was unable to defeat the incumbent, Gerald Ford. After Ford's loss in the general election, Reagan and several of his long-term aides turned their attention to 1980. Drawing on the support of a growing number of conservative organizations, he developed a solid political organization. By 1980 he was the clear front-runner, and he captured the Republican nomination with relative ease. Throughout, he reiterated his basic message: the need to cut taxes, reduce the size of the federal government, and rebuild American military strength. He also made President **James (Jimmy) Earl Carter** the issue. Without much difficulty he won the election in November, sweeping Republicans on his coattails into the majority in the U.S. Senate.

Following the advice of his Chief of Staff, **James (Jim) Addison Baker III** (George Bush's former campaign manager), Reagan maintained his focus on gaining passage for his economic and military promises, pushing aside divisive social and cultural issues. While he continued to speak out against abortion and for school prayer and other traditional values, he gave priority to winning a tax cut and increasing **defense spending.** By and large, only through his nominations to the federal **courts** did Reagan have a significant impact on these social and cultural issues.

When he left office, Reagan counted as his greatest accomplishments the creation of millions of new jobs, over five years of economic expansion, and an **arms control** agreement with the Soviet Union. Ironically, in the early years of his administration, the nation suffered from one of the most severe recessions in modern history and American relations with the **Soviet Union** reached one of their worst points of the entire cold war. Most agreed that his biggest failure was his inability to shrink the federal **budget deficit** or government spending. Reagan had argued that his economic policies, known as **Reaganomics** or supply-side economics, would simultaneously reduce taxes and the deficit, yet this did not take place.

A final area in which Reagan had a mixed record was that of the prestige of the office of the presidency and of the federal government itself. The Vietnam War, Watergate, and the **Iranian hostages** crisis, among other things, had reduced Americans' faith in the federal government and their respect for the president. In his 1980 campaign Reagan had ridden this anti-Washington wave into the White House. However, as president, partly through his appeals to patriotism, he helped rebuild the esteem of the office. Then came the **Iran-contra affair** which, even though it did not considerably diminish his personal popularity, reinvigorated public distrust of Washington. A series of autobiographies by his aides and associates, along with unauthorized biographies that were published toward the end of his term and immediately afterward, added to his checkered legacy. In the final analysis, it will probably be awhile before historians determine whether Reagan restored Americans' faith in their nation or just provided them with a "quick fix" of nostalgia that faded after he left office.

Suggested Readings: Larry Berman, ed., *Looking Back on the Reagan Presidency* (1990); Lou Cannon, *President Reagan: The Role of a Lifetime* (1991); Ronald Reagan, *An American Life* (1990); Gary Wills, *Reagan's America: Innocents at Home* (1987).

Related Entries: Election of 1980; Senate, United States; Summits, with Soviet Union.

REAGAN DOCTRINE. The term *Reagan Doctrine,* which is usually credited to journalist Charles Krauthammer, refers to the overall **foreign policy** approach of the Reagan administration. According to the Reagan Doctrine, the United States' military and foreign policy should be determined by national security interests rather than concerns about human rights. Since the United States was committed to containing communism and liberating those who lived under communist rule, it should provide support for anticommunist regimes, even if they were not democratically run, and to anticommunist insurgents in the developing world. The Reagan Doctrine underlay the decision to aid the contras in **Nicaragua** and the right-wing government of **El Salvador.** Similarly, it provided the basis for supporting anticommunist rebels in Angola while practicing "constructive engagement" with **South Africa.** It helped account for the Reagan administration's willingness to support Ferdinand Marcos in the

Philippines but not to seek détente with Fidel Castro in Cuba. Among the chief architects and proponents of the Reagan Doctrine was **Jeane Jordan Kirkpatrick,** Reagan's ambassador to the United Nations. Liberals criticized the Reagan Doctrine as a simplistic approach to world problems. They felt it exaggerated the communist threat and underestimated the dangers of supporting undemocratic anticommunist regimes.

Suggested Readings: Jeane Kirkpatrick, *The Reagan Doctrine and U.S. Foreign Policy* (1985); David Kyvig, ed., *Reagan and the World* (1990); Jeff McMahan, *Reagan and the World: Imperial Policy in the New Cold War* (1986).

REAGANOMICS. Throughout the 1980s, the term *Reaganomics* was widely used to describe President Ronald Reagan's and his administration's economic policy and vision. It was also used interchangeably with the more technical term, *supply-side economics.*

During the 1980 campaign, Reagan had pledged to get the economy going again by cutting government spending and taxes. He argued that such cuts would increase savings, investments and productivity. In turn this would boost government revenues which would lead to a decreased federal **budget deficit** and diminished **inflation.**

On February 18, 1981, in a speech to Congress, President Reagan spelled out the specifics of Reaganomics, or what he called his "program for economic recovery." He requested $41.4 billion dollars in budget cuts, affecting 83 federal programs, and a 30 percent personal income tax cut spread over three years. At the same time, he called on Congress to eliminate unnecessary regulations and for a tight monetary policy aimed at maintaining the value of the dollar and stopping inflation.

Reagan's economic vision was based on the theory of supply-side economics, whereby tax and spending cuts lead to economic growth, increased federal revenues, and the eradication of federal budget deficits. However, Reagan deviated from a strict application of supply-side economics by promising to dramatically increase **defense spending** at the same time that he pursued deep federal tax cuts. In his speech to Congress, he pledged to save $28.2 billion in defense spending by cutting waste in military savings, yet overall, between 1980 and 1985, spending by the defense department nearly doubled.

When Reagan had argued during the 1980 presidential campaign that the government could simultaneously cut taxes, increase defense spending, and balance the federal budget deficit, George Bush, his opponent at the time, claimed that this was impossible. Indeed, Bush described Reaganomics as "**voodoo economics.**" After being nominated as Reagan's running mate, however, Bush quit making this argument. Instead, like most other Republicans, he became a firm champion of Reagan's policies.

While President Reagan did not win the full implementation of his economic recovery plan of 1981, Congress enacted most of it. Taxes were cut 25 percent over three years; the fiscal budget of 1982, originally proposed by President **James (Jimmy) Earl Carter,** was reduced by $34.2 billion dollars; and defense spending was increased. He did not, however, cut the largest "entitlement" programs, namely medicaid, **Social Security** and civilian and military pensions. Nor did he scale back defense spending in the face of the recession of the early 1980s.

The success or failure of Reaganomics is still a hotly debated subject. Reagan's supporters focus on the fact that the **U.S. economy** grew significantly from 1983 though 1988, that inflation was brought under control, and that tax revenues increased. His critics counter that yearly budget deficits consistently were much worse than those projected by the administration, rising from a little over $73 billion in 1980 to $155 billion in 1988. Moreover, the gross federal debt tripled during President Reagan's eight years in office and continued to climb precipitously during President Bush's years in the White House. Put another way, whatever growth Reaganomics produced during the 1980s jeopardized America's future economic prosperity. In addition, Reagan's critics noted that the wealthy gained the most from Reaganomics, while the middle and lower classes enjoyed nominal benefits, at best.

Suggested Readings: Marlin Anderson, *Revolution* (1988); Michael Boskin, *Reagan and the Economy* (1987); Paul Craig Roberts, *The Supply Side Revolution* (1984); Anandi P. Sahu and Ronald L. Tracy, eds., *The Economic Legacy of the Reagan Years* (1991).

Related Entries: Economic Recovery Act of 1981; Election of 1980.

RECESSIONS. The Ronald Reagan–George Bush years witnessed two recessions, one that was one of the steepest in American history in the early 1980s and one that hit during President Bush's term. Ironically, although the first recession was more severe than the second, President Bush suffered much more politically from the economic downturn than did President Reagan.

The first recession began in the fall of 1981 and lasted until early 1983. During this period, unemployment rose from a yearly rate of 7 percent in 1980 to 9.5 percent in 1982 and 1983. The recession reached its depth in December 1982, with unemployment hitting 10.8 percent for the month. For the year, the economy contracted 1.8 percent. Workers in heavy industry and construction were hit particularly hard by this recession, and male workers tended to be affected more than female workers. For example, in 1983, the unemployment rate stood at 14.2 percent for the construction trades and at 15.4 percent for machine operators, assemblers, and inspectors. In spring 1983, the **U.S. economy** began to rebound, and it continued to grow for the next five years.

Despite the severity of the recession, Reagan was easily reelected in 1984. This was due to several factors. For one, the recession hit relatively early during his first term in office, and by 1984, the recovery was well on its way. Second, Reagan fairly effectively argued that the recession of the early 1980s had been caused by the economic policies of his Democratic predecessor and cast his economic policies, including his budget cuts (which hurt many who were in need), as the medicine necessary for long-term growth.

The second recession of the Reagan-Bush years began in July 1990. Unemployment climbed from a yearly average of 5.3 percent in 1989 to 7.4 percent in 1992. The gross domestic product (GDP) contracted for three consecutive quarters, from July 1990 through March 1991. Even though the GDP began to rise in the second quarter of 1991—meaning that the recession was technically over—the weakness of the recovery and the persistence of high unemployment led many to insist that it did not really end until **William (Bill) Jefferson Clinton** became president.

One way to measure the differences between the two recessions is to compare data on economic growth in the immediate quarters following each one. In the second quarter of 1983 the gross national product (GNP) grew at a phenomonal rate of 9.7 percent. In comparison, in the second quarter of 1991, it grew at an anemic 1 percent. The recession of the early 1990s also hit a broader spectrum of the workforce than did the recession of the early 1980s. White-collar as well as blue-collar workers and middle-level managers as well as autoworkers, faced layoffs, furloughs, and financial insecurity. Unaccustomed to feeling the brunt of recessions and already feeling the pinch of years of stagnating wages and rising costs, many middle-class Americans blamed President Bush for their woes.

To make matters worse for Bush, unlike Reagan, he lacked a comprehensive program to combat the recession and could not, for political reasons, blame his predecessor for the economy's downturn. This left him blaming the Democrats and piecing together a number of uncon-

James Baker and Don Regan. Reagan Library.

nected programs—from capital gains cuts to delayed withholding taxes—as his response. In contrast, Democrats argued that **Reaganomics,** which Bush refused to condemn for obvious reasons, had caused the recession of the early 1990s. Conservatives disagreed but were of little help to Bush since they argued it was his decision to renege on his **"no new taxes"** pledge that caused the recession.

Suggested Readings: Alberto Alesina and Geoffrey Carliner, eds., *Politics and Economics in the Eighties* (1991); Anandi P. Sahu and Ronald L. Tracy, eds., *The Economic Legacy of the Reagan Years* (1991).

REGAN, DONALD. (December 21, 1918, Cambridge, Mass.– .) Secretary of the Treasury, 1981–1985; White House Chief of Staff, 1985–1987.

In 1946, following nearly six years in the navy, Don Regan, a graduate of Harvard University (B.A., 1940), accepted a post as a stockbroker with Merrill Lynch. For the next thirty-five years he rose through the ranks of what became the largest brokerage house in the nation. From 1971 until 1980, when President Ronald Reagan nominated him to the post of secretary of the treasury, he served as Merrill Lynch's chairman, directing its expansion into new types of business and continued growth.

At first, due to his lukewarm support for the theory of supply-side economics (also called **Reaganomics**), many conservatives viewed Regan with a wary eye. Regan's ties to Wall Street also put him at odds with a number of those on the **New Right.** However, by 1982 Regan had won over conservatives by taking the lead in getting Congress to adopt President Reagan's tax cut proposals, which were the cornerstone of supply-side economics. Indeed, by 1984 Regan often sounded much more like a full-fledged supply-sider than a traditional economic conservative by suggesting that cutting taxes, which he proclaimed would revitalize the economy, was much more important that balancing the budget. Regan's fervid advocacy of **deregulation** also endeared him to the New Right.

In 1985 Regan swapped positions with **James (Jim) Addison Baker III.** Baker became secretary of the treasury and Regan took Baker's post as President Reagan's chief of staff. Regan encountered tougher going in this post than he had expected. He did not get on as well with many long-time Reagan advisers, and he had difficulty matching Baker's genius for accommodating the different factions and personalities that allied themselves with the president. He bore much of the blame for the **Iran-contra affair,** with **Nancy Davis Reagan** contending that the affair would not have taken place or been nearly as severe had Baker still been the chief of staff. As a result of these troubles, in February 1987, Don Regan resigned as chief of staff. Afterward he wrote *For the Record* (1988), an insider's account of the Reagan years. While Regan tended to defend the president, he was not nearly as kind to the Reagan insiders with whom he had feuded, including the first lady.

While Regan's record as a businessman is enviable, his legacy as secretary of the treasury is more ambiguous. Advocates of supply-side economics credit him, along with the president, for reviving the economy of the 1980s via sharp tax cuts. However, critics of the president and Regan note that the **budget deficit** increased dramatically during the latter's tenure and that the deficit, in turn, created long-term economic problems that President Reagan's successors had to face.

Regan is married to the former Ann G. Buchanan. They have four children.

Suggested Readings: *Current Biography* (1981) p. 342; Don Regan, *For the Record* (1988); Marcia Lynn Wicker, "Managing and Organizing the Reagan White House," in *The Reagan Presidency,* ed. Dilys M. Hill, Raymond A. Moore and Phil Williams (1990).

Related Entry: Economic Recovery Act of 1981.

William Rehnquist being sworn in as chief justice of the Supreme Court, September 26, 1986. Reagan Library.

REHNQUIST, WILLIAM HUBBS. (October 1, 1924, Milwaukee, Wis.– .) Associate Justice, U.S. Supreme Court, 1971–1986; Chief Justice, U.S. Supreme Court, 1986– .

When President Ronald Reagan ran for president in 1980 he promised to reverse the liberal drift of the U.S. **Supreme Court,** symbolized by the decisions of the Warren Court but including, in many conservative minds, the direction of the court through much of the twentieth century, both before and after Earl Warren. In 1986 the president took his most dramatic step in this direction by nominating Associate Supreme Court Justice William Hubbs Rehnquist to replace the retiring **Warren Earl Burger** as chief justice of the court and appointed **Antonin Scalia** to the vacancy created by Rehnquist's promotion. By 1986 Rehnquist had earned a reputation as a very conservative jurist. During his tenure on the Court, he had written numerous dissents of liberal opinions, including criticisms of the court's actions in the area of civil law, criminal law, and **women's rights.** While liberals disagreed with Rehnquist's views, they generally respected his intelligence and admired his writing skills. Nonetheless, Rehnquist did not easily win confirmation. Thirty-three Senators voted against him, the highest number of negative votes against a judge up for confirmation by the Senate in U.S. history.

As chief justice, Rehnquist sought to move the court in a conservative direction. Through the Ronald Reagan–George Bush years, he experienced a mixed record in this regard. He was part of the majority in *Richmond* v. *J. A. Croson Co.* (1989), which ruled against minority set-aside programs, the most important **affirmative action** case of the late 1980s, and he also sided with the majority in a number of cases that limited the reach of the civil rights law, including *Ward's Cove* v. *Atonio* (1989) and *Patterson* v. *McClean Credit Union* (1989). However, he was unable to convince the court to prohibit affirmative action or to overturn *Roe* v. *Wade,* which established a woman's constitutional right to obtain an **abortion**. A number of older justices often resisted taking the court in such conservative direction. Also resistant—to the president's surprise—were several Republican nominees.

Rehnquist grew up in the Midwest and attended Kenyon College for a year before enlisting in the U.S. Army. Following World War II, he attended Stanford University, receiving a B.A. (1948) and law degree (1952). One of his classmates was **Sandra Day O'Connor,** President Reagan's first appoi–ntment to the Court. (Ironically, O'Connor became part of the moderate majority on the Court, which often resisted Rehnquist's conservative lead.) After serving as a law clerk to Supreme Court Justice Robert H. Jackson, Rehnquist worked as a lawyer in Phoenix, Arizona. While there he became active in Republican Party politics. From 1969 to 1971 he served as President Richard Nixon's assistant attorney general, leaving this post when he was nominated to the Supreme Court by Nixon.

Rehnquist is married to the former Natalie Cornell. They have three children. Rehnquist is the author of several books on legal and political issues, including *Grand Inquests: The Historic Impeachments of Justice Samuel Chase and President Andrew Johnson* (1992).

Suggested Readings: Donald E. Boles, *Justice Rehnquist, Judicial Activist* (1987); *New York Times,* June 18, 1986, p. 31; David G. Savage, *Turning Rights: The Making of the Rehnquist Supreme Court* (1992).

Related Entry: Courts.

REYNOLDS, WILLIAM BRADFORD. (June 21, 1942, Bridgeport, Conn.– .) Assistant Attorney General, Civil Rights Division, U.S. Department of Justice, 1981–1988.

During Ronald Reagan's presidency, William Bradford Reynolds headed the civil rights division of the Justice Department. From this position he led the administration's attacks on what it saw as leftward drift of the nation in terms of **civil rights,** as symbolized by **affirmative action,** which the administration viewed as a form of reverse racism. Reynolds's critics, including most civil rights groups, accused him of failing to enforce a number of civil rights laws. Reynolds countered that he believed in a color-blind society and that it was the civil rights groups who had betrayed the ideals of the civil rights movement of the 1960s. Reynolds's attacks on affirmative action were not fully successful. The **Supreme Court** repeatedly upheld affirmative action, although it narrowed its reach and scope during the Ronald Reagan–George Bush years.

Reynolds grew up in Delaware, marrying into the DuPont family. He went to Phillips Academy and then Yale, graduating from the latter in 1964. He attended Vanderbilt Law School, where he served as editor of the law review and graduated second in his class in 1967. (His father had graduated first in his class at Vanderbilt Law School.) After a brief stint with Sullivan & Cromwell, a large, prestigious New York law firm, he went to work in the solicitor general's office. In 1973 he joined Shaw, Pittman, Potts & Trowbridge, a well-known Washington, D.C., law firm, where he stayed until he was offered the post as assistant attorney general.

Very early in his tenure, Reynolds sided with **Bob Jones University** in its battle with the Internal Revenue Service. Reynolds sought to convince the court to reverse an eleven-year-old sanction against the University that was based on its discriminatory practices. Over 100 of the 176 lawyers of the Justice Department's civil rights division protested against Reynolds's decision to take this step. The university and the Justice Department lost the case. He initially argued against extending the 1965 Voting Rights Act and opposed tightening the 1964 Civil Rights Act in favor of plaintiffs.

In 1987 Reynolds and Lynn Morgan divorced after twenty-three years of marriage. They had four children. Following his departure from the Justice Department, Reynolds went back to work in the private sector.

Suggested Readings: *Current Biography* (1988) p. 476; Steven A. Shull, *A Kinder, Gentler Racism* (1988).

ROBERTSON, MARION GORDON (PAT). (March 22, 1930, Lexington, Va.– .) Evangelical minister and candidate for Republican presidential nomination, 1988.

President Reagan and Pat Robertson, September 20, 1985. Reagan Library.

Pat Robertson is one of the best-known evangelical ministers in the nation, the founder of the Christian Broadcasting Network, and from 1968 to 1986, host of "The 700 Club," a conservative television show. Throughout his career he has used the pulpit to promote his conservative views, including strong opposition to **abortion** and homosexuality and support for prayer in the schools. Much more so than many other influential conservative ministers of the period, such as Jim Bakker or even **Jerry Falwell,** Robertson organized the religious or **New Right** into a powerful, grass-roots political force. In 1980 and again in 1984, Robertson mobilized these forces in support of Ronald Reagan. However, in 1988, distrusting Vice President George Bush's commitment to "traditional values," Robertson decided to mount his own campaign for the presidency. With the help of very committed and well-organized supporters, Robertson won early, surprise victories in nonbinding caucuses in Michigan and South Carolina. In spring 1988, however, Robertson was unable to build on these early "victories" to sustain a serious challenge to Vice President Bush for the Republican nomination. Ultimately, he endorsed the George Bush–Dan Quayle ticket.

Robertson grew up in a family with a long tradition of religion and politics. Both his paternal and maternal grandfathers were Baptist ministers. His mother was a born-again Baptist who urged her son to "surrender his life to Jesus." His father served in Congress for thirty-four years (both in the House of Representatives and Senate), gaining a reputation as a fervid, anti–New Deal, southern Democrat and a fierce opponent of the liberal drift of his party. Robertson's distant relatives included presidents William Henry Harrison and Benjamin Harrison.

Robertson attended Washington and Lee University, graduating with honors in 1950. After serving in the marines and briefly studying economic at the University of London, he enrolled at Yale University Law School in 1952. After graduating from Yale with a J.D., he took a job with W. R. Grace Company in New York City, working as a financial analyst. Then he became a partner with Curry Sound Company, an audio components firm. During the mid-1950s he campaigned for Adlai Stevenson and imbibed in some of the social amenities that New York had to offer.

However, following a meeting arranged by his mother with Cornelius Vanderbreggan, a Baptist minister, Robertson took a new direction in his life. He reenrolled in college, received his M.A. in divinity from New York Theological Seminary (1959), and was ordained as a minister by the Southern Baptists. He quickly became involved in televangelism, building a small ultra-high frequency (UHF) television station into the Christian Broadcasting Network, the biggest distributor of religious television and radio programs in the nation. He gained his own audience through the widely watched 700 club, which he hosted. Robertson is married to the former Adelia Elmer. They have four children.

Suggested Readings: *Current Biography* (1987) p. 475; John B. Donovan, *Pat Robertson: The Authorized Biography* (1988); Pat Robertson, *A Date with Destiny* (1986).

Related Entries: Election of 1988; Family Values; Moral Majority.

RUDMAN, WARREN BRUCE. (May 18, 1930, Boston, Mass.– .) U.S. Senator from New Hampshire, 1980–1992.

Warren Rudman was elected to the U.S. Senate in 1980, defeating Democrat incumbent John Durkin. He owed his victory, in part, to Ronald

Reagan's coattails. However, by the time he retired from the Senate following his second term, Rudman had earned a reputation as one of the most independent and nonpartisan politicians in Congress.

Rudman was born in Boston and grew up in New Hampshire. He received a B.S. from Syracuse University, served in the army during the Korean War, and then enrolled in law school, receiving his degree from Boston College in 1960. For ten years he practiced in a private law firm in New Hampshire before taking a job as the legal counsel to Governor Walter R. Peterson, a moderate Republican. Within a year Peterson named Rudman state attorney general, a post he held until 1976. Shortly before leaving office, Gerald Ford nominated Rudman to be chairman of the Interstate Commerce Commission, but New Hampshire's Senator Durkin blocked the appointment. Four years later, following a tough primary campaign, Rudman won the right to oppose Durkin in the 1980 senatorial election.

As a senator, Rudman became best known for his cosponsorship of the **Gramm-Rudman-Hollings Act** (Balanced Budget and Emergency Deficit Control Act of 1985), a bill that promised to balance the budget by 1993. Rudman gained further note for his role as the ranking Republican on the congressional committee that held nationally televised hearings on the **Iran-contra affair.** Both his authorship of the budget amendment and conduct during these hearings, in which he criticized the Reagan administration, earned him a reputation as an independent politician who did not always tow the party line. During most of his twelve years in the Senate, Rudman supported Presidents Reagan's and Bush's economic and **foreign policy** measures, although he regularly opposed their social agenda. In 1992 Rudman announced that he would not seek reelection. Along with Paul Tsongas, he helped found the Concord Alliance, an organization committed to cutting the federal **budget deficit** and to political reform. Rudman is married to the former Shirley Wahl. They have three children.

Suggested Readings: Richard L. Berke, "Combative New Hampshire Senator Evokes Colleagues Fear and Respect," *New York Times Biographical Service,* June 1980, p. 608; *Current Biography* (1989) p. 485 (1989); Hays Gorey, "The Iconoclast of Capitol Hill," *Time,* September 3, 1990, p. 14.

S

SALT-II. See **STRATEGIC ARMS LIMITATION TREATY II (START-II).**

SAVINGS AND LOAN CRISIS. In the late 1980s the United States experienced an economic catastrophe that had few, if any, equals in all U.S. history, namely, the collapse of hundreds of banks and thrifts. In total, approximately 1,000 savings and loan institutions failed between 1980 and 1991, most of them at the tail end of this time period.

The significance of this failure was multiple. Since the savings and loans were an important part of the financial infrastructure of the United States, their failures in the late 1980s created a dent or drag on the money supply, which in turn increased interest rates, dampened economic growth, and helped produce a recession. In addition, the cost of bailing out the savings and loans was very high, increasing the federal **budget deficit** and compelling George Bush to call for a tax hike. The bailout covered both federally insured deposits and, since the government adopted a strategy of not allowing the largest banks to fail, guaranteeing the deposits of noninsured customers (in many cases). Some estimated that the total costs of this bailout would eventually total about $500 billion. The failure of the savings and loans also cast doubt on the efficacy of **deregulation,** one of the main goals of the "Reagan Revolution."

The causes of the savings and loan crisis included the deregulation of the banking industry, which began under President **James (Jimmy) Earl Carter** and continued during Ronald Reagan's presidency. Among other things, deregulation put the savings and loans at a competitive disadvantage against other financial institutions which could offer investors a much higher rate of return than could be earned with a typical account at a savings institute. In response, many savings and loans began to make riskier loans, especially in commercial real estate. As long as the values of commercial properties rose, the savings and loans turned a profit, but later, when real estate values began to stagnate and decline, the balance sheets of savings and loan institutions took a turn for the worse. At the same time, in order to retain customers, savings and loans began to offer higher-than-usual interest rates to depositors, which reduced their profit margins. To make matters worse, many investigators uncovered numerous occasions of fraud and deception by the managers of various savings and loan institutions. Loose banking regulations made it easier for these officers to defraud their associations. Of the over 1,000 savings and loans that failed, up to 40 percent allegedly were involved in some form of criminal conduct.

In response to the savings and loan crisis, Congress enacted the Financial Institutions Reform, Recovery and Enforcement Act. This measure established the Resolution Trust Corporation to supervise the sale and liquidation of failed savings and loans. The law tightened regulations, while at the same time allowing bank-holding companies to purchase stable institutions.

By the time President Bush left office, the savings and loan crisis had largely passed. Indirectly, it contributed to his defeat by inflating the deficit, adding to the tax burden, and raising doubts about the conservative campaign for deregulation. The crisis even more directly affected the careers of several prominent senators, the so-called **Keating Five** (including Alan Cranston, a senior Democrat from California), who were implicated in the collapse of one of the biggest thrifts. However, for most Americans, the causes and effects of the crisis remained a mystery, something that they did not understand and did not associate with either political party or any particular political views. Paradoxically, the federal government's response to the savings and loan crises demonstrated one of the ways in which a strong central government could effectively intervene in the economy. Even if the cost of the bailout was high, few, if any, argued that the American public would have been better off had the government simply allowed all the savings and loans to fail. Nor was there any evidence that the states could have effectively dealt with the crisis on their own.

Suggested Readings: Martin Mayer, *The Greatest-Ever Bank Robbery* (1990); Lawrence J. White, *The S & L Debacle: Public Policy Lessons for Bank and Thrift Regulators* (1991).

Related Entries: "No New Taxes"; Recessions.

SCALIA, ANTONIN. (March 11, 1936, Trenton, N.J.– .) Associate Justice, U.S. Supreme Court, 1986– .

In 1986 President Ronald Reagan nominated Antonin Scalia, a U.S. Court of Appeals judge and former law professor at the Universities of Chicago and Stanford, to a seat on the U.S. **Supreme Court,** which had been left vacant by the retirement of Chief Justice **Warren Earl Burger.** (**William Hubbs Rehnquist,** a sitting associate justice, was appointed to Burger's post as chief justice.) Scalia's conservative views, from his opposition to **affirmative action** and federal funding of **abortion** to his strong support of the executive branch in cases where it conflicted with the legislative or judicial branches, meshed well with President Reagan's. Scalia's judicial philosophy won him few friends among liberals, yet even his opponents acknowledged the power of his intellect and strong scholarly record.

Scalia was born in an Italian-American section of Trenton, N.J., the son of an Italian immigrant, Eugene Scalia, a professor of literature and languages at Brooklyn College. Scalia spent most of his youth in Queens, where he attended Catholic grade and high school. He earned his B.A. at Georgetown University in 1957, graduating first in his class, and then attended Harvard Law School. Once again he distinguished himself, serving as an editor of the *Harvard Law Review.* Following his graduation, he joined the Cleveland law firm of Jones, Day, Cockley & Reaves, gaining a reputation for his very conservative views. In 1967 he turned down an offer to become a partner at Jones, Day, instead accepting a post at the University of Virginia Law School. In the early 1970s, Scalia held several posts with the Richard Nixon administration, including offering legal advice to the president during the Watergate scandal. (He contended that Nixon's Watergate tapes belonged to the president alone, a position the Supreme Court rejected.) With Jimmy Carter's election, Scalia returned to academia where he augmented his reputation as one of the leading conservative legal scholars in the nation, although his advocacy of judicial restraint produced differences between himself and several prominent conservative scholars at the University of Chicago.

In 1982 Reagan appointed Scalia to the U.S. Court of Appeals in the District of Columbia. Among his decisions was one upholding the U.S. Navy's ban against homosexuals in the military. During his years on the Supreme Court he has generally aligned himself with Chief Justice William Rehnquist, steering the court in a conservative direction. Scalia often

General Norman Schwarzkopf. Still Media Center, Department of Defense.

issues biting opinions that, among other things, not-so-subtly attack the contrary views expressed by his fellow, more-moderate judges on the court.

Scalia is married to the former Maureen McCarthy. They have nine children (five boys and four girls).

Suggested Readings: *Current Biography* (1986) p. 502; *New York Times,* June 19, 1986, p. 27.

SCHWARZKOPF, H. (STORMIN') NORMAN. (August 22, 1934, Trenton, N.J.– .) Commander, U.S. forces, in Persian Gulf War.

In 1991 General H. Norman Schwarzkopf retired from the U.S. Army after over thirty years of service. Unlike other soldiers, Schwarzkopf did not "fade away"; rather, he left the military a war hero, acclaimed for his command of the U.S. and allied forces in the **Persian Gulf War.** Based on this, many Democrats and Republicans sought to convince him to run for public office—on their party ticket.

Schwarzkopf had an unusual background and childhood. Shortly before he was born, Schwarzkopf's father, a graduate of West Point, had directed the New Jersey State Police investigation into the kidnapping of Charles Lindbergh's son (one of the most famous crimes in U.S. history). Afterward, the family moved to Tehran, where his father helped the Shah of Iran establish his own police force. In 1952 Norman enrolled at the U.S. Military Academy at West Point, graduating in 1956. For the next thirty years he rose in the ranks, serving two tours of duty in Vietnam. After the war's end he held several posts in Washington, D.C., and abroad. In 1983 he was promoted to general, playing a lead role in the invasion of **Grenada.** By 1988 he had risen to the rank of four-star general and taken on the responsibility for drawing up contingency plans for a major war in the **Middle East.** That war came in 1991, following Iraq's invasion of Kuwait in August 1990.

Headquartered in Riyadh, Saudi Arabia, Schwarzkopf watched over the massing of close to three-quarters of a million troops and laid plans for an extensive air attack, to be followed by a ground assault. Many credited Schwarzkopf (along with General **Colin Luther Powell**) for the tremendous success of the allied invasion, which resulted in few American casualties and the rapid removal of the Iraqi forces from Kuwait. Schwarzkopf's down-to-earth personality, his accessibility, and his apparent close relationship with his troops won him the admiration of the American public. Upon his return from Saudi Arabia and retirement from the service, he was offered many jobs, ranging from university president to chief executive officer of several large corporations, all of which he turned down. His autobiography, published in the fall of 1992, became an overnight best-seller.

Schwarzkopf is married to the former Brenda Holsinger. They have three children.

Suggested Readings: Jack Anderson and Dale Van Atta, *Stormin' Norman* (1991); *Current Biography* (1991) p. 506; H. Norman Schwarzkopf and Peter Petre, *It Doesn't Take a Hero* (1992).

SCHWEIKER, RICHARD SCHULTZ. (June 1, 1926, Norristown, Pa.– .) U.S. Senator, 1969–1980; Secretary of Health and Human Services, 1981–1983.

Richard Schweiker, a moderate Republican senator from Pennsylvania, first joined forces with Ronald Reagan during Reagan's unsuccessful bid for the presidency in 1976. As a means of gaining support from the moderate wing of the party, Reagan pledged to nominate Schweiker as his running mate if he secured the presidential nomination. Many moderates criticized Schweiker at the time for agreeing to link arms with Reagan. Four years later, Reagan and Schweiker renewed their ties when the president nominated the Pennsylvania senator to the post of secretary of health and human services. As one of the most moderate members of his administration and a well-liked senator on Capitol Hill, Schweiker easily won confirmation. However, his task as secretary of the agency responsible for many **welfare** programs proved a difficult one. Reagan's promise to reduce government and reform welfare put Schweiker in the unenviable position of having to propose cuts in the program administered by his office. As a result, he won few friends among either liberals or moderates. At the same time, Schweiker never overcame conservative distrust, based on his liberal past.

Schweiker grew up in eastern Pennsylvania, enlisted in the U.S. Navy at the tail end of World War II, graduated with a B.A. from Penn State University (1950), and then joined his father's construction business. He quickly became involved in local Republican politics, running for office for the first time in 1960. In a surprise win, he defeated John A. Lafore, the conservative incumbent, and joined Congress with a reputation as a moderate-liberal Republican. Eight years later he ran successfully for the U.S. Senate, a post he held until nominated to serve in President Reagan's cabinet. In Congress, he earned an 89 percent rating from the liberal Americans for Democratic Action. More conservative groups gave him a much lower rating, however.

In 1983 Schweiker resigned as secretary of health and human services. Schweiker is married to the former Claire Joan Coleman. They have five children.

Suggested Readings: Richard Brownstein, *Reagan's Ruling Class* (1984); *Current Biography* (1977) p. 377.

SCOWCROFT, BRENT. (March 19, 1925, Ogden, Ut.– .) Member, Tower Commission, 1986–1987; National Security Adviser to President George Bush, 1989–1993.

Brent Scowcroft was one of the three members of the **Tower Commission,** the panel appointed by President Ronald Reagan to investigate the **Iran-contra affair.** Even though Scowcroft drew some political fire due to the commission's relatively tame findings, the Senate confirmed his nomination to be President George Bush's national security adviser, a post he held until the end of Bush's term.

Scowcroft had spent many years within the military and as an adviser to presidents. Born in Ogden, Ut., in 1925, Scowcroft received his B.S. degree from the U.S. Military Academy in 1947. Injured in a fighter plane crash in 1948, Scowcroft continued to work for the Air Force while at the same time pursing an advanced degree in international relations at Columbia University. After earning his M.A., in 1953 he landed a job as an assistant professor at West Point. Following further training and a post oversees, he returned to academia as an associate professor and then full professor of political science at the U.S. Air Force Academy in Colorado Springs, Colo. He received his Ph.D. from Columbia in 1967 and then worked at the Naval War College, at the Department of Defense, and as an adviser to President Richard Nixon. In January 1973 Scowcroft became deputy assistant to the president for national security affairs and then succeeded Henry Kissinger in 1975 as President Gerald Ford's national security adviser. At the time he had risen to the rank of lieutenant general.

Partly because of his involvement in the second round of **Strategic Arms Limitation Treaty II (SALT-II),** under President Ford, which conservatives opposed, Scowcroft was not offered a post in the Reagan administration, although he was appointed to various committees on military weaponry and readiness. Based in part on this work, which was well received by members of the Reagan administration, the president asked him to join former Senators John Tower and Edmund Muskie as a member of the Tower Commission in 1986.

While national security adviser for President Bush, Scowcroft figured prominently in negotiations with the Soviets on strategic nuclear arms. He played a prominent role during the **Persian Gulf War** and was involved in difficult decisions regarding defense department cuts in the wake of the end of the cold war. While some criticized Scowcroft and other Bush appointees for reacting too slowly to the Soviet Union's demise, most analysts admitted that the National Security Council under his direction was a much improved body. Unlike the National Security Council under Reagan, which drew the ire of even the Tower Commission for its lack of accountability and direction, Scowcroft ran a tight ship and worked directly with the President. Unlike Henry Kissinger and Zbigniew Brzezinski (Presidents Richard Nixon's and Jimmy Carter's national security advisers, respectively), Scowcroft brought with him military experience and a lack of interest in the limelight. He did not perceive his role as that of policy maker, but rather as a technical adviser. This fit well with the **foreign policy** approach of the Bush administration, which was directed by the president himself and by his long time friend, **James (Jim) Addison Baker III.**

Scowcroft is married to Marian Horner. They have one daughter.

Suggested Readings: Larry Berman and Bruce W. Tentleson, "Bush and the Post–Cold-War World: New Challenges for American Leadership," in *The Bush Presidency: First Appraisal,* ed. Colin Campbell and Bert A. Rockman (1991); *Current Biography* (1987) p. 500.

SEARS, JOHN PATRICK. (July 3, 1940, Syracuse, N.Y.– .) Campaign Manager for Ronald Reagan, 1979–1980.

Shortly after the straw vote at the Republican Party caucus in Iowa, in mid-January 1980, which George Bush won over Ronald Reagan (33,530 to 31,348), John Sears, Reagan's campaign manager, was forced out of his top job. Sears had headed Reagan's campaign efforts ever since the former California governor had made a decision to run for the White House, not long after Gerald Ford's defeat in 1976. Sears had crafted a strategy that cast Reagan as the Republican front-runner. Assuming that Reagan would need to win the support of moderates within the Republican Party and the electorate at large to win both the nomination and the general election, Sears had urged Reagan adopt a low profile during the campaign. This entailed refusing to debate Bush, **Robert Joseph Dole,** and other Republican contenders, and toning down his rhetoric. However, this strategy backfired when Bush aggressively campaigned for the presidency in Iowa. After the Iowa loss, Reagan's longtime aides convinced him to dump Sears. (Officially, Sears did not resign until the day after Reagan's landslide victory in the New Hampshire primary.) Moreover they convinced him to adopt a different strategy: to go on the attack, participate in televised debates, and stake out a clear position on the political right. This tactic worked, as Reagan went on to win both the Republican nomination and the general election.

Sears was raised in upstate New York and attended the University of Notre Dame (B.A., 1960). He earned his law degree from Georgetown University in 1963 and then went to work for Richard Nixon's law firm in New York City. He was a member of Nixon's campaign staff and White House team. His professional experience made him attractive to Reagan after his 1976 loss to Gerald Ford, but it also alienated him from many of Reagan's closest aides. After leaving the Reagan team in the early 1980s he continued to work as a political analyst for NBC News and to write and teach courses on politics.

Sears is married to Carol Jean Osborne. They have three children.

Table 14
U.S. Senate

Congress	Years	Majority Party (Net Gain or Loss)	Minority Party (Net Gain or Loss)
97th	1981–83	R-53 (+12)	D-46 (−12)*
98th	1983–85	R-54 (+1)	D-46 (−1)
99th	1985–87	R-53 (−1)	D-77 (+1)
100th	1987–89	D-55 (+8)	R-45 (−8)
101st	1989–91	D-55	R-45
102nd	1991–93	D-56 (+1)	R-44 (−1)

*One independent.

Suggested Readings: Lou Cannon, *Reagan* (1982); Jack W. Germond and Jules Witcover, *Blue Smoke and Mirrors: How Reagan Won and Carter Lost the Election in 1980* (1981).

Related Entry: Election of 1980.

SENATE, UNITED STATES. In 1980, riding on Reagan's coattails, Republicans gained control of the U.S. Senate for the first time since 1955. Not only did they gain a 53-to-47 majority, Republican candidates defeated several very prominent Democratic incumbents, most notably, Warren Magnuson, Frank Church, and Birch Bayh. The Republicans maintained control of the Senate in the 1982 and 1984 elections. However, they lost control in 1986, as the Democrats won in a big way in an off-year election, gaining eight seats. The Democrats maintained control of the Senate for the remainder of the Reagan-Bush years (Table 14).

Tennessee Senator **Howard (Henry) Baker, Jr.,** a moderate, served as the Senate majority leader until 1985. Upon his retirement, Kansas Senator **Robert Joseph Dole** assumed the top post. When the Democrats regained control of the Senate in 1987, Dole became the Senate minority leader and Robert Byrd, from West Virginia, who had been the Democratic minority leader from 1981 though 1986, took over as the majority leader. Byrd later relinquished this post to George Mitchell of Maine. Among the other Republican and Democratic leaders in the Senate during this period were: Alan Cranston (Calif.), Democratic whip from 1977 to 1991; Ted Stevens (Ark.), Republican whip from 1977 to 1985; and Alan K. Simpson (Wyo.), Republican whip from 1985 to 1992.

The Senate supported most of Reagan's tax and defense proposals during his first six years in office. It also tended to confirm most of his appointees. During his last two years, however, Reagan experienced tougher going in the Senate. It passed the **plant-closing bill** by a wide enough margin to make it veto proof, rejected **Robert Heron Bork**'s nomination to the **Supreme Court,** and embarked, with the House of Representatives, on tough investigations of the **Iran-contra affair.**

During his four years as president, Bush was in constant battle with the Democratically controlled Senate. **Gridlock,** referring to the inability of the federal government to enact legislation, became the operative term in Washington, D.C. The Democrats lacked a large enough majority to pass most bills over Bush's veto. However, unlike Reagan, Bush rarely was able to muster a coalition of Republicans and Democratic conservatives to enact his proposals. (He did manage to put together such a coalition in support of the **Persian Gulf War.**)

Suggested Reading: Robert C. Byrd, *The Senate, 1789–1993* (1993).

Related Entry: House of Representatives, United States.

SESSIONS, WILLIAM STEELE. (May 27, 1930, Fort Smith, Ark.– .) Director, Federal Bureau of Investigation, 1987–1993.

In 1987, William Sessions, a United States district court judge and a former U.S. attorney, was nominated by Ronald Reagan to become the director of the Federal Bureau of Investigation. Due to his experience in the criminal justice system and reputation as a tough but fair judge, his nomination was received warmly by both Democrats and Republicans.

Sessions's father, a minister with the Disciples of Christ, worked as an army chaplin. Shortly after enrolling in college, the Korean War erupted and Sessions joined the United States Air Force. After four years of service (1951–1955), Sessions enrolled at Baylor University, receiving his B.A. and law degrees in 1956 and 1958, respectively. During the 1960s he practiced law in Waco, Texas, and became active in politics. When Richard Nixon was elected president, Sessions moved to Washington, D.C., to head the government operations section of the Justice Department. Two years later Nixon nominated him to the post of U.S. attorney for the western district of Texas. In 1974 he left this job to become a United States district court judge. In general, Sessions was seen as a conservative, though not ideologically driven, judge. He gained the general respect of Democrats and Republicans alike.

Ironically, by the time Sessions was forced to resign in 1993, he had

President Reagan and Secretary of State George Shultz, December 31, 1982. Reagan Library.

earned the enmity of both Democrats and Republicans and the public at large. In October 1992, a scandal emerged regarding Sessions's unethical use of public planes for private purposes. Even after the Justice Department initiated an investigation of his abuse of his office—which Sessions declared was politically motivated—it was reported that he had taken a public plane to the ballet in Atlantic City, N.J. Sessions fought to keep his job after Bush lost the election. He pledged to complete his ten-year term, but finally, on July 20, 1993, **William (Bill) Jefferson Clinton** forced him to step down. As a result, the *New York Times* (July 21, 1993) observed that Sessions, who was once a "symbol of integrity," ended his public career a "kind of comic-opera figure."

Suggested Readings: *Current Biography* (1988) p. 518; *New York Times,* July 21, 1993.

SHULTZ, GEORGE PRATT. (December 13, 1920, New York, N.Y.– .) Secretary of State, 1982–1989.

For nearly a quarter of a century, George P. Shultz was one of the most important public officials in the United States. He held three cabinet posts under two separate Republican presidents. During the Richard Nixon administration he served as secretary of labor (1969–1970), director of the Office of Management and Budget (1970–1972), and secretary of the treasury (1972–1974). Following the resignation of **Alexander Meigs Haig, Jr.**, he became Ronald Reagan's secretary of state and maintained this post until Reagan left the White House.

George P. Shultz spent most of his youth in the affluent suburb of Englewood, N.J. His father had a Ph.D. in history and was the founder of the New York Stock Exchange Institute. Shultz received his B.A. from Princeton University in 1942. Following graduation he enlisted in the U.S. Marine Corps, rising to the rank of captain. After the war he resumed his education, earning a Ph.D. in industrial economics from the Massachusetts Institute of Technology (MIT), specializing in labor relations. Following a brief stint teaching at MIT, Shultz went to work for the Dwight Eisenhower administration as a senior staff economist on the Council of Economics. In 1957 he left government, to become a professor of industrial relations at the University of Chicago. Eventually he rose to dean of the University of Chicago's Graduate School of Business. Throughout this time period, Shultz worked as a consultant for various government agencies and committees. His nomination, by Richard Nixon, to the post of secretary of labor in 1969 was received warmly by both Democrats and Republicans. Shultz was one of the more influential cabinet members during the Nixon presidency. He was also one of Nixon's few longtime advisers not to be implicated in the Watergate scandal.

From 1974 until 1982 Shultz worked as an executive for the Bechtel Corporation, one of the largest privately held firms in the world. He also taught part-time at Stanford University. He easily won Senate confirmation as secretary of state, ninety-seven to zero. Many welcomed him to his new post due to his reputation for integrity and because of his low-key style, which contrasted sharply with that of Haig or Nixon's former secretary of state, Henry Kissinger. He was also viewed as being much less ideological than many others within the administration, including Secretary of Defense **Caspar Willard Weinberger** and several of Reagan's national security advisers.

While Shultz did not publicly clash with hawks within the administration, over time he gained a reputation as a pragmatist who pushed President Ronald Reagan toward a more conciliatory direction toward the **Soviet Union.** Shultz opposed the scheme to use funds gained from the trade of arms to Iran as a means to support the contras. His crowning moments came in the last years of the Reagan administration with the general thaw in relations with the Soviet Union and, even more important, with the negotiation of the **Intermediate-range Nuclear Forces (INF) Treaty.** While the administration made little progress toward achieving peace in the **Middle East** and its initiatives in **Latin America** and **Africa** received mixed reviews, overall many considered Shultz an exemplary secretary of state. Ironically, he succeeded in spite of the administration's general dislike for the State Department and traditional diplomacy. While the **collapse of communism** in Eastern Europe took place after he left office, he should be remembered for the key role he played at the tail end of the cold war.

Shultz is married to the former Helena Maria O'Brien. They have three daughters and two sons.

Suggested Readings: *Current Biography* (1988) p. 525; George Shultz, *Turmoil and Triumph: My Years as Secretary of State* (1993).

SIMPSON-MAZZOLI BILL (IMMIGRATION REFORM AND CONTROL ACT OF 1986). On November 6, 1986, President Reagan signed into law the Simpson-Mazzoli bill, the most comprehensive immigration act passed by Congress in years. Named after its chief sponsors, Senator Alan K. Simpson, a Republican from Wyoming, and Congressman Romano L. Mazzoli, a Democrat from Kentucky, the law sought to limit illegal immigration into the United States, particularly from **Latin America.** Its enactment followed years of battles and negotiations between various parties. For five years, bills seeking to limit illegal immigration had worked their way through Congress, only to be killed by one of the two Houses or in conference committees established to work out differences between separate bills. Finally, in 1986 a compromise was reached. The Senate approved the bill, 63–24, on October 17. Reagan signed the Immigration and Control Act of 1986 shortly thereafter.

The new law contained several crucial parts. For the first time in U.S. history, it became a federal crime to knowingly hire illegal aliens. Employers who violated this provision were subject to fines ranging from $250 to $10,000, per illegal alien, and in flagrant cases, to six months in jail. (Although the law became effective on Reagan's signing, the penalties did not take effect until May 1988.) The law stiffened the penalties for those involved in efforts to smuggle aliens into the United States. It also contained an amnesty provision that granted legal status to illegal aliens who could prove that they had entered the United States since January 1, 1982. The new immigration law sought to alleviate the concerns of western **farmers,** who traditionally relied on illegal workers, by establishing a program that granted temporary resident status for up to 350,000 foreigners as long as they could show that they had worked for at least ninety days in agriculture in the United States between May 1985 and May 1986.

While the bill was passed and signed into law with much fanfare on the part of some and trepidation on the part of others, its impact on illegal immigration was unclear. By the mid-1990s, immigration had once again become a very hot political topic, especially in the border states.

Suggested Readings: *Congressional Quarterly Almanac* (1986); George Vernez, ed., *Conference on the International Effects of the 1986 Immigration Reform and Control Act* (1990).

SKINNER, SAMUEL KNOX. (June 10, 1938, Chicago, Ill.– .) Secretary of Transportation, 1989–1991; President George Bush's Chief of Staff, 1991–1992.

Samuel Skinner earned his bachelor's degree in accounting from the University of Illinois (1960) and then joined the army. On leaving the military, Skinner went to work for International Business Machines (IBM), becoming one of its top salesmen. At the same time he campaigned for Barry Goldwater for president and attended the evening division of DePaul University Law School. Shortly after earning his law degree he went to work for the U.S. Attorney's Office in northern Illinois, a job that paid about one-quarter what he had earned at IBM. He quickly became a protégé of James R. Thompson, the U.S. attorney general for the northern district of Illinois. When Thompson resigned to campaign for governor of Illinois, Skinner became the U.S. attorney. In 1977 Skinner joined the private law firm of Sidley and Austin. He simultaneously worked on various governmental commissions, including President Ronald Reagan's Commission on Organized Crime. In 1988, Skinner played a key role in George Bush's campaign. Not long after Bush was elected, Skinner was nominated and subsequently confirmed as the secretary of transportation.

Although the post was generally not a very high-profile one, Skinner quickly gained public attention through his calls for federal government intervention in an Eastern Airlines strike. He helped coordinate cleanup activities that followed the **Exxon *Valdez*** oil spill. Moving away from the Reagan administration's efforts to foster **deregulation** in virtually all aspects of life, Skinner favored tougher fuel efficiency standards for automobiles, as mandated under the **Clean Air Act of 1990,** and called for greater federal action to ensure against alcohol abuse by members of the merchant marine—an alleged cause of the *Valdez* spill.

In 1991, when **John Henry Sununu** resigned as President Bush's chief of staff, Skinner took his place. His relationship with the president was generally good. However, as Bush's popularity fell in the polls, Skinner received some of the blame.

Skinner is married to Susan Ann Thomas. They have three children.

Suggested Readings: John Cushman, "A Model of Competence, Composure and Savy," *New York Times Biographical Service,* December 1991, p. 1312; *Current Biography* (1989) p. 531; Dirk Johnson, "Portrait of Bush's New Chief of Staff," *New York Times Biographical Service,* December 1991, p. 1412.

Related Entry: Election of 1988.

SMITH, WILLIAM FRENCH. (August 26, 1917, Wilton, N.H.–October 29, 1990, Los Angeles, Calif.) U.S. Attorney General, 1981–1985.

Of Ronald Reagan's entire original cabinet, William French Smith, his attorney general, had the longest and closest relationship with the president. Smith and Reagan's ties went back to 1963 when Smith became Reagan's personal lawyer. In the mid-1960s Smith helped convince Reagan to run for governor, and during Reagan's eight years in the California statehouse, Smith was a member of Reagan's kitchen cabinet.

Smith came from old New England stock. He was the direct descendant of Uriah Oakes, the fourth president of Harvard University. His father, who died when he was six, had been president of the Mexican Telephone and Telegraph Company, headquartered in Boston. Drawn by the open spaces of the West, Smith attended the University of California at Berkeley, receiving his B.A. in 1939. On graduation he returned to the east coast, to study law at Harvard (J.D., 1942). During World War II Smith joined the naval reserves and then settled in California, where he became an attorney with the prominent Los Angeles firm of Gibson, Dunn & Crutcher.

Smith and Reagan shared similar conservative political views. Both disliked the growing influence and size of the federal government, and both lashed out at antiwar protesters. As chair of the University of California Board of Regents (a post to which Reagan nominated him in 1970), Smith played an instrumental role in cracking down on student demonstrations at Berkeley and other California state schools. Once confirmed as attorney general, Smith moved the Justice Department in a conservative direction, particularly in the areas of **civil rights** and antitrust law. Smith called for stiffer federal anticrime legislation, which would increase the number of capital crimes. He sought to restrict the reach of the Freedom of Information Act, which had been passed after the Watergate scandal and provided for greater access to federal records and documents.

In January 1984 Smith announced his resignation, claiming that he wished to devote his time to President Reagan's reelection bid and to return private life. However, he did not step down from office for over a year due to the long battle over confirmation of his successor, **Edwin Meese III.** At the time of his death, Smith was married to the former Jean Webb. He was survived by four children (all from his first marriage, which had ended in divorce), two stepchildren, and seven grandchildren.

Suggested Readings: *Current Biography* (1982) p. 402; *New York Times,* October 30, 1990, p. B6.

SOCIAL SECURITY DISABILITY INSURANCE. One of the ways in which the Reagan administration sought to reduce federal spending was by cutting back on Social Security Disability Insurance (SSDI) expenditures. It did so by tightening rules for eligibility and by reviewing the eligibility of those already receiving insurance payments. These actions proved highly controversial. They resulted in numerous court cases which challenged the government's new policies on social security.

In response to changes in the payment of SSDI, Democrats in Congress sought to enact new regulations that limited the administration's ability to cut off benefits. According to these new rules, the burden of proof to establish that a recipient no longer depended on SSDI was shifted to the government, rather than the beneficiary. The Reagan administration, however, refused to follow these new regulations. This resulted in more legal challenges and increasing political pressure on the administration to rescind its changes. As a result, in 1985 the Reagan administration decided to quit reviewing and cutting off disability payments. (By this time, 160,000 individuals had already had their benefits restored through a burdensome appeals process.) The SSDI cuts did little to reduce the mounting federal **budget deficit** or to affect the larger problem of the rising costs of much bigger entitlement programs, nor were they very popular politically.

Suggested Reading: Deborah Stone, "No Longer Disabled," *American Political Science Review* 84, no. 1 (1990): 317–18.

Related Entries: Courts; Social Security Reform Act; Welfare.

SOCIAL SECURITY REFORM ACT. On April 20, 1983, President Reagan signed into law the Social Security Reform Act. It authorized a significant overhaul of the old-age and survivors' insurance trust fund—most commonly known as Social Security. A two-year battle between Republicans and Democrats in Congress, and also between Congress and the White House, over the best way to keep the social security system in sound financial shape, preceded its enactment. By and large, the final bill followed recommendations made by a bipartisan national commission that President Reagan had created early in his presidency.

The act raised the retirement age from sixty-five to sixty-seven for those who wanted full benefits and delayed for a half year the cost-of-living increase scheduled to take place on July 1, 1983. Both these changes were to be implemented in stages and completed by 2027. As of January 1, 1984, according to the mandate of the new law, all employees of private nonprofit organizations and of the government had to join the social security system. (Both groups had been exempted previously.) In addition, the new law sped up increases in the payroll tax for social security, which had already been enacted by Congress. Beginning on January 1, 1984, some social security benefits were to be made taxable. To further guarantee the solvency of the fund, a "stabilizer" provision was added that sought to make sure that its reserves never fell below 20 percent. Other reforms affected the benefits of early retirees, divorcees, widows and widowers.

In spite of these reforms, public confidence in social security waned in the latter half of the 1980s and the early 1990s. During the 1984 presidential campaign, the Democrats argued that President Reagan and his economic policies posed a threat to social security recipients. Reagan responded with a pledge that he would never reduce social security benefits. While this may have appeased senior citizens, whose political clout was great, it further alienated younger voters from the government, who feared an impending crisis in the social security system as the number of senior citizens increased proportionate to the rest of the population. Defenders of the social security system countered that the fund was in no danger except for the fact that the government kept borrowing from its reserves; that if government simply left the fund alone, it would be in no trouble. However, fiscal and political constraints inhibited Congress and the president from pushing through this change or from enacting even more significant reforms—such as a cutback in cost-of-living increases or means testing of the amount to be received by beneficiaries, as senior citizens were well organized and prone to vote against politicians who reduced their benefits.

U.S. Troops in Somalia. Still Media Center, Department of Defense.

Suggested Readings: Edward D. Berkowitz, *America's Welfare System* (1991); Michael Boskin, *Too Many Promises: The Uncertain Future of Social Security* (1986).

Related Entries: Election of 1984; Welfare.

SOMALIA. One of President Bush's last actions as president was his decision to send U.S. troops to Somalia. He called this action "Operation Restore Hope," and it involved American forces joined by soldiers from other nations, who landed in Mogadishu, the capital of Somalia, with the purpose of ensuring that emergency food supplies were delivered to the starving Somalis. The intervention followed years of famine and civil strife and unsuccessful international efforts to aid the famine-stricken.

The first 1,800 U.S. Marines arrived in Mogadishu on December 9, 1992, about a month after Bush lost his bid for reelection to President **William (Bill) Jefferson Clinton** and about a month before the inauguration. The marine landing was like no other in history. It was met by the media, with television cameras and blaring lights, and by Somalis who eagerly sought to touch the Marines and to offer their thanks for providing relief.

Ironically, it was this warm reception and the ease of entry that presented the greatest threat to the endeavor—mission creep. Many Somalis hoped that the troops might do more than simply open a corridor through which the United Nations (UN) and other groups could provide medical supplies and food to the famine-stricken populace. In addition, they wanted U.S. forces (and their allies) to stabilize the nation, restore peace, and even initiate a new Marshall Plan, which had helped rebuild Europe after World War II.

Shortly after the troops arrived, Robert Oakley, the U.S. special envoy to the region, met with Somalia's rival warlords and arranged for a cease-fire between them. While this made the immediate military operation safer, it also legitimized the position of the warlords who had been previously blamed for the starvation and whose long-term aspirations of supremacy remained unaffected. For example, the cease-fire did not force the warlords to surrender their weapons, which seemed to suggest that they intended to use them in the future.

As long as Bush was president, support for the operation in Somalia and the United States remained strong. Even the Congressional Black Caucus, a long-time foe of Reagan's and Bush's foreign policies, approved of the effort. In the long run, however, support was tempered by sporadic gunfights between American (or French) troops and Somali gunmen and by the apparent slowness of the forces to move into the countryside and establish a secure route for relief workers. By the time American troops left and relinquished control to UN troops in the spring of 1993, support for the effort had virtually eroded in the United States. Even though the intervention had accomplished its primary objective of averting starvation for thousands of Somalis, the United States had not avoided mission creep. By May 1993, it was clear that the U.S. attempt to establish a permanent peace and to build a new, more democratic government had failed. To make matters worse, by this time gunmen aligned with Somali warlord Mohammed Farrah Aidid had killed American marines, augmenting the American demand that the troops be brought back home.

Former President Bush argued that the mission creep, which eroded public support for the operation and others like it, took place under President **William (Bill) Jefferson Clinton.** Others, who previously had argued that President Clinton lacked foreign policy experience, concurred. Regardless of whether this criticism was correct—Oakley's negotiations with the warlords suggest a more complicated interpretation of events—the operation did not add considerably to Bush's reputation as a strong leader in foreign affairs nor stand as a shining example of the so-called **new world order.**

Suggested Readings: John R. Bolton, "Wrong Turn in Somalia," *Foreign Affairs,* January/February 1994, p. 56; George J. Church, "Somalia: Mission Half Accomplished," *Time,* May 17, 1993, p. 42; Peter J. Schraeder, *United States For-*

eign Policy toward Africa (1994); Jill Smolowe, "Operation Restore Hope," *Time*, December 21, 1992, p. 28.

Related Entries: Africa; Foreign Policy.

SOUTER, DAVID. (September 17, 1939, Melrose, Mass.– .) Justice, U.S. Supreme Court, 1990– .

On July 25, 1990, George Bush nominated David Souter, a federal appellate judge and a former justice of the Supreme Court of New Hampshire, to the United States **Supreme Court** to fill the seat left vacant by the retirement of Justice William Brennan. Bush expected that Souter would move the Court in a more conservative direction and would vote with Chief Justice **William Hubbs Rehnquist** and Reagan's four Supreme Court nominees to make up a conservative majority on the court. While Souter sided with Rehnquist 86 percent of the time in his first year in office, by the mid-1990s he was identified with a more moderate block, which tended to hold the balance of power on the court. For instance, while Souter sided with the majority to uphold a state ban on nude dancing in *Barnes* v. *Glen Theater* (1991), he also joined the majority in the case of *Casey* v. *Planned Parenthood,* which allowed the state of Pennsylvania to restrict abortions but also reaffirmed the Court's support for a woman's right to have an **abortion.**

Souter was born to a family with deep Yankee New England roots. He attended public schools, where he excelled in his studies. He received his B.A. from Harvard University in 1961, writing his senior thesis on the judicial philosophy of Oliver Wendell Holmes, Jr., one of America's most noted Supreme Court justices. He studied at Oxford University from 1961 to 1963 on a Rhodes scholarship, returning to the United States to obtain his law degree from Harvard (1966). After obtaining a military draft deferment because one of his legs is shorter than the other, he went to work for a private law firm, Orr & Reno, in Concord, New Hampshire, not far from his family's farm. After a couple of years in private practice he took a post in the public sector, first as an assistant district attorney general and then as deputy attorney general, working under **Warren Bruce Rudman,** the future Republican senator from the state of New Hampshire. In 1976 Souter became attorney general of the state. While at this post he pursued several cases that displayed his conservative views, including prosecuting Jehovah's Witnesses for obscuring the state's motto, "Live Free or Die." In 1978 he became an associate justice of the Superior Court of New Hampshire, where he earned a reputation as a conservative but fair and impartial judge.

Souter, who is unmarried, is known for his plain and frugal dress; love for classical music, history, and literature; and quiet, reserved demeanor.

Suggested Readings: *Current Biography* (1991) p. 543; *New York Times,* July 24, 1990, p. 1.

SOUTH AFRICA. Throughout the Ronald Reagan–George Bush years, the white regime of South Africa faced opposition from abroad and, increasingly, from within its own nation. Even before President Reagan took office, an antiapartheid movement had arisen in the United States which demanded that the country place sanctions on South Africa. Demands for such sanctions, most notably divestment by U.S. corporations—in other words withdrawing investments or removing American businesses from South Africa—grew in the 1980s, especially as protests against apartheid within South Africa escalated.

In spite of the growing antiapartheid movement, the Reagan administration balked at the call to "get tough" with South Africa. Instead, it pursued a policy it termed "constructive engagement," which favored quiet diplomacy over sanctions. This approach dovetailed with the broader foreign policy views favored by **Jeane Jordan Kirkpatrick, Chester Arthur Crocker,** and other conservative foreign policy aides. It conflicted, however, with the strategy pursued by President **James (Jimmy) Earl Carter,** which emphasized the need to push for human rights around the globe, even among America's allies.

Regardless of the arguments in favor of or against constructive engagement, as time passed it became increasingly difficult for the Reagan administration to stave off all calls for sanctions. Protests in South Africa prompted South African prime minister Pieter Botha to declare a state of emergency in July 1985. This led to greater cries for sanctions against South Africa from antiapartheid activists in the United States and Europe. In response, in late summer 1985 Reagan announced limited trade and financial sanctions against South Africa. At the same time, the Reagan administration claimed that it would not impose stiffer restrictions, claiming that these would only backfire and produce a worse situation for black South Africans.

During the remainder of his presidency, Reagan and antiapartheid activists continued to debate this point. Bishop Desmond Tutu, one of South Africa's most prominent black leaders and an eventual recipient of the Nobel Peace Prize, called for broad economic sanctions. This helped convince Congress to pass a bill to establish stiff sanctions against South Africa.

President Reagan, sticking to his faith in constructive engagement, vetoed the bill. However, in one of the biggest setbacks of his administration, both the House and Senate overrode his veto.

Unlike President Reagan, President Bush did not fight sanctions. Nor did Bush shy away from meeting with controversial black South African leaders. In 1990, Nelson Mandela, the head of the African National Congress (who had spent twenty-seven years in prison), met with President Bush and spoke to a joint session of Congress, an event that had seemed impossible during the Reagan presidency. In July 1991, in response to the dismantling of apartheid, Bush issued an executive order that terminated sanctions against South Africa. Throughout this period, U.S. **foreign policy** toward South Africa was one of the issues that affected domestic politics. The Congressional Black Caucus made punishing the white minority regime in South Africa one of its top priorities. The Reagan administration's policy of constructive engagement hurt it among black voters and with some other groups, which flocked to the antiapartheid cause. Whether Reagan's opposition to the demands of the antiaparthied movement gained him votes from some whites is difficult to determine.

Suggested Readings: Pauline H. Baker, *The United States and South Africa* (1989); James Barber and John Barrett, *South Africa's Foreign Policy* (1990); Michael Clough, *Free at Last?* (1992).

Related Entries: Africa; Reagan Doctrine.

SOVIET UNION. Even before Ronald Reagan became president, tensions between the United States and the Soviet Union had begun to increase, as symbolized by President **James (Jimmy) Earl Carter**'s decision to impose a grain embargo on the USSR and to boycott the 1980 Olympics in Moscow in retaliation for its invasion of **Afghanistan.** With Ronald Reagan's election, whatever chances existed for détente to be revived disappeared rapidly. Reagan had made campaign promises to take a tough stance toward the Soviet Union. He criticized the **Strategic Arms Limitation Treaty II (SALT-II),** which Carter had signed but which had not yet been ratified in the U.S. Senate. Reagan pledged to dramatically increase **defense spending** so as to counter the Soviet Union's buildup—and he vowed to combat Soviet-sponsored communist insurgencies around the globe.

During his first term in office, Reagan lived up to every one of these campaign promises. Relations between the two superpowers reached a new low. Despite Soviet objections, Reagan went ahead with plans to deploy cruise missiles in Europe, the **MX (missile, experimental) missile** in the United States, and many other new weapon systems. **Arms control** talks with the Soviet Union came to a standstill, and in 1983 Reagan announced plans to construct a space-based missile system, the **Strategic Defense Initiative,** dubbed Star Wars by its critics. Reagan also stepped up his rhetoric, referring to the Soviet Union as the "evil empire." Unlike his predecessors, he held no summits with any Soviet leaders during his first term in office.

Meanwhile, the Soviet Union entered a period of economic decline and political turmoil. Following Leonid Brezhnev's death, a series of leaders took power. Not until **Mikhail Sergeyevich Gorbachev** assumed power did the Soviet Union regain some sense of political direction, and the direction it took under his lead was radically different from what it had taken in the past. Gorbachev called for *perestroika,* internal reform, and *glasnost*, a new openness to the global community. He whittled away the powers of the Communist Party, promoted a move away from state control of the economy, fostered cultural exchanges with the rest of the world, and ended the Soviets' iron grip on the nations of Eastern Europe.

Undoubtedly, the economic crisis in the Soviet Union, perhaps spurred by its attempts to match the military buildup of the United States and by its embroglio in Afghanistan, motivated Gorbachev to call for a change of course. Regardless of the causes (and there were many), Gorbachev's rise to power provided President Reagan with the opportunity to alter his Soviet policy, which he did in his second term. Meeting with Gorbachev four times between 1985 and 1988, Reagan ended up signing the **Intermediate-range Nuclear Forces (INF) Treaty,** the most significant arms control agreement of the post–World War II era. Reagan also traveled to the Soviet Union, where he held friendly talks with the Soviet leader and lectured Russian students on the virtue of the free-market economy.

The improvement in relations between the United States and the Soviet Union continued during the George Bush administration. The two nations signed another major arms agreement, the **Strategic Arms Reduction Treaty (START).** Even more important, by the end of President Bush's term in office, the cold war had come to an end, the two powers had joined together as allies in the **Persian Gulf War,** and the Communist Party's rule had come to an abrupt end in the Soviet Union and in most of Eastern Europe. Underlying this remarkable turn of events was the collapse of the Soviet Union's economy and the disintegration of the USSR. (Some of the Soviet states, most notably the nations of Latvia, Lithuania, and Estonia, separated completely from Russia, while others remained tied to Russia via the new confederation.) In reaction to the dramatic events in the Soviet Union and Eastern Europe, Bush declared that we were witnessing the creation of a so-called **new world order.** Exactly how Russia and the former Soviet states fit into this order remained unclear.

Suggested Readings: John Lewis Gaddis, *Russia, the Soviet Union and the United States* (1990); David Shavit, *The United States' Relations with Russia and the Soviet Union* (1993); Robert W. Tucker and David C. Henrickson, *The Imperial Temptations* (1992).

Related Entry: Senate, United States.

SPEAKES, LARRY. (September 13, 1939, Cleveland, Oh.– .) Principal Deputy Press Secretary and Assistant to President Ronald Reagan, 1981–1987.

Larry Speakes served as President Reagan's principal liaison to the press from 1981 to 1987. Even though **James S. Brady** maintained the official title of press secretary to the president, Speakes essentially worked as Reagan's press secretary from the moment when Brady was shot by **John W. Hinckley, Jr.,** in 1981. While Speakes experienced rough moments, overall his colleagues in the press and in government praised his work and conduct.

Speakes was reared in Mississippi. He received his B.A. in journalism from the University of Mississippi in 1961. On graduation he went to work for the Oxford *Eagle,* after which he became editor of the *Bolivar Commercial.* He also worked for several other Mississippi newspapers. In 1968, Speakes became the press secretary for Mississippi Senator James O. Eastland, a post he held until 1974. He worked for a brief stint as an assistant press secretary for President Richard Nixon, advising one of the president's legal counselors. When Gerald Ford became president, Speakes maintained his post as assistant press secretary.

From 1977 to 1981 Speakes went to work in the private sector for the well-known public relations firm of Hill and Knowlton. However, his heart lay in the political world, and he welcomed a chance to work as one of President Ronald Reagan's press aides. Speakes's debut as press secretary, following the shooting of Brady and Reagan, proved to be one of the toughest moments of his career. When he stated in response to a question that U.S. forces were not on special alert due to the shooting, Secretary of State **Alexander Meigs Haig, Jr.,** took over the microphone in order to assure the public that everything was under control.

At first Speakes shared many of his duties with **David Richmond Gergen,** the White House director of communications. In 1984 he assumed responsibility for all daily briefings of the press. Despite his long years of service for the president, Speakes never became part of Reagan's inner circle of advisers and at times was forced to respond with incomplete information to press queries regarding the administration's policies. Since 1987 Speakes has worked in the private sector. He wrote one of the first insider accounts of the Reagan administration, *Speaking Out* (1987).

Speakes is married to Laura Christine Crawford. They have one son. Speakes has two other children from his first marriage, which ended in divorce.

Suggested Readings: *Current Biography* (1985) p. 397; Larry Speakes, *Speaking Out: The Reagan Presidency from inside the White House* (1987).

START. See **STRATEGIC ARMS REDUCTION TALKS (START) TREATY.**

STAR WARS. See **STRATEGIC DEFENSE INITIATIVE (STAR WARS).**

STATUE OF LIBERTY CELEBRATION. In 1986 the United States celebrated the one hundredth birthday of the Statue of Liberty. The celebration capped the refurbishment of the statue, which was designed by Frederic Auguste Bartholdi and given to the United States by France in 1886. Over the years, the statue had come to symbolize America's openness to foreign immigrants. Hence, the celebration was as much about America's ideals as it was about the monument itself. Coming in the midst of several years of economic growth and before the **Iran-contra affair** unfolded, the celebration marked one of the high points of the Reagan administration, which did its best to link the president's policies and achievements to the symbolic celebration. Plans for the restoration and celebration began to unfold in 1983. Efforts were made to restore "Lady Liberty" to her original greenish color; her torch was redone in gold leaf and her structure was reinforced. In addition, the statue was made more accessible to visitors and an American Museum of Immigration was added to the site. In spring 1986, hundreds of American and French workers labored tirelessly to complete the statue's refurbishment in time for festivities.

The celebration, on July 4, 1986, was a grand affair, put together by

Nancy Reagan and President Reagan at Statue of Liberty Celebration, July 4, 1986. Reagan Library.

Hollywood producer David Wolper. Over 6 million people crowded into New York to watch a procession of tall ships and catch a glimpse of celebrities, some of whom were part of a more select group of 4,000 who paid $5,000 each to sit in an amphitheater at the center of the day's events. The grand finale consisted of music, fireworks, and the symbolic lighting of the torch by President Reagan.

Bernard Weintraub of the *New York Times* described the event as "one of the most exuberant days of [Reagan's] Presidency." During the day, Reagan met with French President François Mitterrand and delivered numerous speeches that evoked the new spirit of patriotism, one of the cornerstones of the Reagan administration's appeal. Amid the euphoria of the celebration, it was generally forgotten that the statue's actual birthday was October 28. A much smaller festivity was held on Liberty Island on this day, attended by Interior Secretary **Donald Paul Hodel.** Also at the time, few noted the irony that while the president was celebrating the ideals represented by the statue, Congress was putting the finishing touches on a new immigration restriction bill, which was signed into law just over a week after the statue's actual birthday.

David Stockman, director of Office of Management and Budget, and President Reagan, October 6, 1981. Reagan Library.

Suggested Readings: David Gates, "Lady Liberty's Real Birthday," *Newsweek*, November 10, 1986, p. 8; Paul Goldberger, "For Miss Liberty, A New Grandeur," *New York Times*, May 27, 1986, p. II:1; Bernard Weintraub, "For Ronald Reagan, The Ceremonies Stir Pride and Patriotism," *New York Times*, July 5, 1986, p. I:1.

Related Entry: Simpson-Mazzoli Bill.

STOCKMAN, DAVID ALAN. (November 10, 1946, Camp Hood, Tex.–) Director, Office of Management and Budget, 1981–1985.

Traditionally, the position of director of the Office of Management and Budget (OMB) has not been a high-profile one. It is not a cabinet post and it deals with a subject matter that in the past drew little public attention, the details of the federal budget. During the early years of the Ronald Reagan administration, however, David Stockman, the director of the OMB, became one of the president's best-known and most controversial appointees.

Stockman spent most of his youth on a family farm in Michigan. Politics was part of his upbringing: his grandfather was the county chairman of the Republican party, and Stockman worked for Barry Goldwater's unsuccessful presidential campaign at the age of seventeen in 1964. While attending Michigan State University in the mid-1960s, his political views swung to the left. He worked for Vietnam Summer, a national antiwar organization, in 1967. In 1968, after graduating from college, he enrolled at Harvard University Divinity School, with thoughts of becoming a minister. While at Harvard, Stockman befriended Daniel Patrick Moynihan who, soon after Stockman got to Harvard, went to work for President Richard Nixon. With Moynihan's help, Stockman got a job with congressman **John Bayard Anderson,** a moderate Republican from Illinois. After several years of working for Anderson and the Republican Conference, in 1976 Stockman ran for a seat in the House of Representatives and won. While in Congress he allied himself with **Jack French Kemp** and other advocates of supply-side economics. He called for cutting taxes and decreased federal spending.

When Reagan was elected president in 1980, Stockman, as director of the OMB, took the lead in calling for the adoption of the Kemp-Roth tax cut (the **Economic Recovery Act of 1981**) and **deregulation.** He testified before Congress on the benefits of **Reaganomics,** including the specific budget cuts proposed by the administration. Stockman's role and his fervid advocacy of the Reagan program, however, often made him the target of liberals, who doubted that Reaganomics would work and considered it unfair. Stockman even clashed with other members of the administration who sought to protect the agencies they headed from the OMB director's budget-cutting knife.

In December of 1981, *Atlantic Monthly* published an article in which Stockman contended that the Reagan program would not work because it did not go far enough, that the failure to cut entitlement programs and insistence on increased **defense spending** and decreased taxes would lead to a mounting **budget deficit.** (Several years later, after leaving the administration, Stockman developed this argument in his 1986 book, *The Triumph of Politics: Why the Reagan Revolution Failed.*) While Reagan reprimanded Stockman for his *Atlantic Monthly* article, he refused to demand his resignation. As a result, Stockman remained an important adviser and advocate of further cuts until 1985, when he finally resigned. His critique ended up being accurate but also alienated him from many Republicans, who saw him as a poor team player and an opportunist.

Suggested Readings: *Current Biography* (1981) p. 400; William A. Niskanen, *Reaganomics: An Insider's Account of the Policies and People* (1988); David Stockman, *The Triumph of Politics: Why the Reagan Revolution Failed* (1986).

STOCK MARKET CRASH OF 1987. On October 19, 1987, the stock market suffered one of its worst collapses in history. The Dow Jones Industrial Average fell 508 points (a 22.6 percent loss) in a single session. While the loss was greater in absolute terms than the Great Stock Market Crash of 1929 ("Black Tuesday"), it was smaller in percentage terms and, unlike the former, did not lead to a long-term depression. In fact, following a period of tremendous volatility, in which stocks swung up and down with very high trading volume, the stock market resumed its general upward climb, which had begun shortly after Reagan took office. In addition, while the stock market crash of 1987 put a brief halt to the flurry of mergers and acquisitions that had helped drive up stock prices, the corporate takeover movement resumed in 1988.

Even with its subsequent recovery, the stock market crash of 1987 stood as an important signpost during the Ronald Reagan–George Bush years. Between 1983 and 1987 the stock market grew at a very steady pace, enjoying some of its best years ever. This bull market paralleled the economic recovery of the mid-1980s. While the stock market rebounded in 1988, its crash did portend tougher times ahead. A presidential task force, headed by **Nicholas Brady,** made suggestions, which the New York Stock Exchange generally followed so as to prevent future stock market crashes. This included limiting computer-initiated trading and establishing a circuit breaker mechanism to automatically halt trading if the market fell too fast in a short period of time.

However, the stock exchange reforms did not alleviate some of the concerns that had helped spark the crash in the first place. The federal **budget deficit** continued to mount, the **savings and loan crisis** was getting worse, the economy was losing steam, and **inflation** was creeping upward. Indeed, signs of inflation had prompted the **Federal Reserve Board** to hike interest rates, which may have precipitated the stock market crash. In sum, while the 1987 stock market crash did not cause the recession of the early 1990s, it hinted that weaknesses in the economy had begun to accumulate and that the boom of the mid-1980s was coming to an end.

Suggested Readings: Mark Fadiman, *Rebuilding Wall Street: After the Crash of '87* (1992); Jan Joporowski, *The Economics of Financial Markets and the 1987 Crash* (1993).

Related Entries: Corporate Takeovers; Economy, U.S.

STRATEGIC ARMS LIMITATION TREATY II (SALT-II). In June 1979 President **James (Jimmy) Earl Carter** and Soviet President Leonid Brezhnev signed the SALT-II Treaty, which limited the number of nuclear launchers each of the superpowers could deploy. However, Carter was unable to gain ratification for the treaty. He could not even get the Democratically controlled Senate Armed Service Committee to endorse it. In January 1980, following the **Soviet Union**'s invasion of **Afghanistan,** Carter withdrew the treaty from consideration by the Senate. Nonetheless, he hoped to gain ratification for it at a future date.

During the 1980 presidential campaign, Ronald Reagan made clear his opposition to SALT-II, calling it a "very dangerous and disturbing thing." He challenged the premise of the treaty—that the Soviets could be trusted to abide by its arms agreements—and during the presidential debate Reagan emphasized his differences with Carter over SALT-II.

Once Reagan became president, however, he and his advisers had to decide what to do with the treaty—seek ratification, renegotiation, or simply to ignore it. He refused to call for ratification of SALT II, yet moderates convinced him to abide by it, at least as long as it did not constrain American options and as long as the United States deemed the Soviets in compliance with it. In 1986, Reagan changed course. He declared that the Soviets were no longer in compliance with the treaty and the United States would no longer observe it either. (The Reagan administration pointed to the Soviet deployment of SS-25 mobile missiles as proof of their specific transgression of treaty.) The fact that SALT-II hindered the U.S. ability to continue its buildup and modernization clearly influenced the administration's decision to declare the treaty invalid. While the president had contended that SALT-II did not stop the United States from going ahead with the **Strategic Defense Initiative (Star Wars)** program, this was not a view shared by the Soviets or many other Americans.

Ironically, at the same time that the administration made its announcement, it was engaged in serious **arms control** negotiations with the Soviets which shortly thereafter produced the **Intermediate-range Nuclear Forces (INF) Treaty,** which went beyond the SALT-II treaty, mandating arms reductions rather than limitations.

Suggested Readings: Dan Caldwell, *The Dynamics of Domestic Politics and Arms Control* (1991); Phil Williams, "The Reagan Administration and Defense Policy," in *The Reagan Presidency: An Incomplete Revolution?,* ed. by Dilys M. Hill, Raymond A. Moore and Phil Williams (1990); Thomas W. Wolfe, *The SALT Experience* (1979).

Related Entries: Debates, Presidential; Election of 1980; Summits, with Soviet Union.

STRATEGIC ARMS REDUCTION TALKS (START) TREATY. While one of the cornerstones of the Reagan presidency was a military buildup, from early on he faced pressures from the **nuclear freeze movement** and supporters of the **Strategic Arms Limitation Treaty II (SALT-II)** to revive **arms control** negotiations with the **Soviet Union.** Presidents Richard Nixon, Gerald Ford, and **James (Jimmy) Earl Carter** all conducted such talks, but Ronald Reagan suspended them early in his presidency. Partly as a response to these pressures, in May 1982, in a major speech that he delivered at his alma mater, Eureka College, President Reagan called for new negotiations on strategic and long-range weapons, aimed at reducing, rather than simply controlling, the number of arms held by the superpowers.

Initially, few serious negotiations took place, and tensions between the superpowers actually increased in 1983 and 1984. Following **Mikhail Sergeyevich Gorbachev**'s assumption of power, however, they were given a fresh start. For President Reagan, these talks culminated in the negotiation, signing and ratification of the **Intermediate-range Nuclear Forces (INF) Treaty,** which Reagan and Gorbachev signed in December 1987.

During his last years in office, the Reagan administration also initiated discussions over strategic arms, called the Strategic Arms Reduction Talks (START for short). These proceeded slowly and did not produce any firm results during Reagan's presidency. During Bush's presidency, START talks continued to take place. The **collapse of communism** in Eastern Europe and reform in the Soviet Union dovetailed with the aims of these negotiations (namely, to reduce or eliminate strategic ballistic missiles).

In May 1990 Gorbachev and President Bush signed a treaty that agreed to end production and reduce stockpiles of chemical weapons. In July 1991, the two leaders went further, signing the START I treaty, which required that both nations reduce their strategic nuclear holdings by about 25 percent. Symbolically, they signed the START I treaty with pens made from scrap metal from missiles that had been destroyed under the INF treaty. The START treaty, as much as the fall of the **Berlin Wall,** depicted that the cold war had come to an end.

Suggested Readings: Michael R. Beschloss and Strobe Talbott, *At the Highest Levels* (1993); Richard Dean Burns, ed., *Encyclopedia of Arms Control and Disarmament* (1993); Michael Hogan, ed., *The End of the Cold War* (1992).

Related Entry: Summits, with Soviet Union.

STRATEGIC DEFENSE INITIATIVE (STAR WARS). In a nationwide television address on March 23, 1983, President Ronald Reagan announced a major new research program to develop an antiballistic missile defense system based in outer space. Dubbed "Star Wars" because it reminded many of the hit movie by the same name, Reagan declared that the Strategic Defense Initiative (SDI) would defend the United States from attacks from Soviet intercontinental ballistic missiles. Reagan claimed that space-based lasers and other high-technology weapons would intercept Soviet launched missiles in midflight. At the least, proponents of the plan claimed that SDI would effectively deter potential Soviet attacks. Even if it was imperfect, they added, it would provide more protection against a nuclear attack than no system at all.

Critics of Star Wars countered that the plan had numerous flaws. It would further escalate the arms race and might even prompt the Soviets to launch a preemptive, or first, strike, before Star Wars became operational. Furthermore, most of the scientific community doubted the viability of the plan, arguing that current technology did not allow for anything close to what Reagan proposed. On top of this, critics noted that Star Wars was extremely expensive and could easily jeopardize ongoing **arms control** negotiations. Despite these concerns, Congress approved a five-year, $26 billion funding package for the development and testing of the system.

During the 1984 presidential campaign and afterward, "Star Wars" remained very controversial. Democratic presidential candidate **Walter Frederick Mondale** was sharply critical of the program. **Mikhail Sergeyevich Gorbachev** initially insisted that scrapping Star Wars was a fundamental precondition to any arms agreement. Nonetheless, President Reagan refused to kill the program, agreeing only to a moratorium on testing in order to keep the arms talks going. Congress continued to fund SDI, although at lower levels than Reagan requested. Ultimately, arms accords between the Soviet Union and the United States as well as the end of the cold war made the Star Wars project moot. Some funding for research continued, but it did not remain a top priority as the government looked for ways to cut **defense spending.**

Suggested Readings: Donald C. Baucom, *The Origins of SDI, 1944–1983* (1992); Sidney D. Drell, Philip J. Farley and David Holloway, *The Reagan Strategic Defense Initiative* (1985); Edward J. Linethal, *Symbolic Defense* (1989).

Related Entries: Election of 1984; High Technology; Summits, with Soviet Union.

SULLIVAN, LOUIS WADE. (November 3, 1933, Atlanta, Ga.– .) Secretary of Health and Human Services, 1989–1993.

Louis Sullivan, the secretary of health and human services from 1989 through 1993, was the highest ranking black member of the George Bush administration. Sullivan and Bush met in the early 1980s when Vice President Bush was invited to a ceremony at Morehouse School of Medicine in Atlanta, where Sullivan was dean. Shortly thereafter, Sullivan joined Vice President Bush in a state visit to seven African nations, and **Barbara Pierce Bush** was named to the board of trustees of Morehouse Medical School. By 1988 Sullivan had developed such a close relationship to Barbara Bush that he was asked to introduce her to the Republican National Convention. Following the election she actively pushed her husband to nominate Sullivan to the post of secretary of health and human services. His confirmation ran into some trouble, however, from conservative antiabortion groups, who distrusted Sullivan due to his pro-choice views. However, Sullivan appeased conservatives by insisting during the confirmation hearings that he opposed **abortion** except in cases of rape, incest, or when the life of the mother was in jeopardy. As a result, he was confirmed by the Senate by a vote of ninety-eight to zero.

Sullivan, the son of an undertaker and a teacher, spent his early years in rural Georgia. His father, who headed the local chapter of the National Association for the Advancement of Colored People (NAACP), was nearly killed for his activism. Sullivan received his B.A. from Morehouse in 1954 and an M.D. from Boston University Medical School 1958, the only black member of his class. After completing his residency and performing postdoctoral work in New York and Boston, he became an assistant professor of medicine at New Jersey College of Medicine. After a couple of years there he returned to Boston University (BU), rising to the rank of professor. Rather than stay at BU, however, he returned to Atlanta to build a medical program at Morehouse, becoming its first dean in 1981. His reputation as a scholar and teacher helped Morehouse win research grants and private funding, allowing him to build Morehouse into a strong program.

Under his direction at Health and Human Services, the costs of many of the social and **welfare** programs continued to grow. He followed the president's lead, advocating a middle course—proving himself less ideologically opposed to federal help than Reagan but also opposed to new social programs. Neither he nor the president promoted major **health care reform,** despite skyrocketing costs. Nor did he pursue new regulations limiting smoking in public places, despite growing public clamor for such restrictions.

He is married to Eve Williamson. They have three children.

Suggested Readings: *Current Biography* (1989) p. 560; "Louis Sullivan Tries to Gore Health Care," *Economist,* December 1, 1990; "Nailing Dr. Sullivan," *Economist,* February 4, 1989; Julie Rovner, "HHS's Sullivan Criticized for Inaction on Tobacco," *Congressional Quarterly Weekly Report,* May 26, 1990.

SUMMITS, ECONOMIC (G-7). Throughout the Ronald Reagan–George Bush years the seven largest non-communist nations (known as the G-7) held economic summits. The G-7 nations were the United States, West Germany, Japan, Great Britain, Italy, France, and Canada. The summits were held in the following locations:

1981	Ottawa, Canada
1982	Versailles, France
1983	Williamsburg, Virginia
1984	London, England
1985	Bonn, West Germany
1986	Tokyo, Japan
1987	Venice, Italy
1988	Toronto, Canada
1989	Paris, France
1990	Houston, Texas
1991	London, England
1992	Munich, Germany

The summits, which began in 1975, allowed the leaders of the G-7 nations to meet and discuss a variety of concerns.

Several themes from these conferences stood out. First, while the nations often had significant differences over particular economic issues, they tended to maintain a spirit of cooperation and friendliness. For example, at his first summit, in Ottawa, Canada, President Reagan held firm to the policy of taming **inflation,** which included supporting high interest rates. This policy conflicted with the goal of revitalizing the economies of Europe, which high interest rates in the United States hindered. Still, at the end of the summit, the conferees issued a 2,000-word communiqué that displayed the common goal of fighting unemployment and inflation and moving toward free trade.

Second, although the summit was supposed to focus on economic is-

World leaders at G-7 economic summit, Williamsburg, Virginia, May 29, 1983. Reagan Library.

sues, **foreign policy** concerns, particularly those involving the **Soviet Union,** often received a good deal of attention. In 1982, for instance, President Reagan and Secretary of State **Alexander Meigs Haig, Jr.,** implored European nations to withhold credit from the Soviet Union and other Eastern Bloc nations. The following year, the summit provided the occasion for the release of a statement by the United States and Western European nations, in which they reaffirmed the U.S. commitment to deploy intermediate-range **Pershing II missiles** in Western Europe. Paradoxically, from 1989 onward, much of the discussion revolved around ways to provide economic aid to Eastern European nations. This culminated with an appearance by **Mikhail Sergeyevich Gorbachev** at the

1991 summit in which the Soviet leader described his plans for economic reform in his nation and called for aid for his efforts from the seven noncommunist nations. While the G-7 nations expressed support for Gorbachev's plan, they did not provide financial assistance until a year later, by which time communism had collapsed in the Soviet Union and **Boris Nikolayevich Yeltsin** had assumed power.

Presidents Reagan and Bush also used the summits to consolidate support around other foreign policy initiatives. Most notably, President Bush got the G-7 to take a strong position against Iraq, following the end of the **Persian Gulf War.** Over the years, statements regarding the common commitment to cooperatively fight **terrorism** were issued. Just as important, the summits were an occasion of high ceremony, which allowed the presidents to look and appear presidential, thus enhancing their international prestige.

Suggested Readings: *Historic Documents* (1981) p. 591; *Historic Documents* (1982) p. 469; *Historic Documents* (1983) p. 507; *Historic Documents* (1984) p. 439; *Historic Documents* (1985) p. 347; *Historic Documents* (1986) p. 437; *Historic Documents* (1987) p. 525; *Historic Documents* (1988) p. 391; *Historic Documents* (1989) p. 424; Robert D. Putnam, *Hanging Together* (1987).

SUMMITS, WITH SOVIET UNION. During President Ronald Reagan's first term the United States and the **Soviet Union** did not hold a single summit meeting between the heads of the two superpowers. In contrast, in Reagan's second term, after **Mikhail Sergeyevich Gorbachev** came to power, the two nations held regular summits, a trend that George Bush continued when he became president.

Reagan and Gorbachev held their first summit in Geneva, Switzerland, from November 19 through 21, 1985. The most important issue raised during these meetings involved nuclear **arms control,** with Gorbachev insisting that the United States had to shelve the **Strategic Defense Initiative (Star Wars)** if a broader agreement was to be reached. While President Reagan refused to accept this condition and the summit did not produce any concrete reductions in nuclear arms, it was nonetheless a very significant event. Discussions between the two men, in Reagan's words, were "frank and useful." An accord was reached to increase cultural exchanges. The two leaders agreed to accelerate discussions aimed at reducing intermediate-range missiles. Most important, simply by sitting down with Gorbachev and holding amicable talks, Reagan signaled that the cold war, which had heated up during his first term, was cooling down.

Ronald Reagan and Mikhail Gorbachev during Moscow Summit. Reagan Library.

On October 13 and 14, 1986, Reagan and Gorbachev met for a second time, in Reykjavik, Iceland. Expectations going into the summit were high, with many people hoping it would produce a major arms agreement. None was forthcoming, however, as President Reagan continued to refuse to scrap Star Wars, a concession that Gorbachev continued to insist was a necessary precondition to any arms agreement. Nonetheless, both leaders left Iceland committed to further arms negotiations. The third summit between Reagan and Gorbachev took place in Washington,

D.C., from December 8 through 10, 1987. It signaled a breakthrough in relations between the two superpowers and was the beginning of the end of the cold war. On the first day of the summit the two leaders signed the **Intermediate-range Nuclear Forces (INF) Treaty.** While the two exchanged barbs on the merits of their respective political systems, they also appeared more relaxed and warm toward one another than at previous meetings. The summit included a colorful ceremony with a twenty-one-gun salute to Gorbachev on the South Lawn of the White House. Reflecting the new mood, Gorbachev declared that the meeting marked "a new phase of Soviet-American bilateral relations."

Reagan and Gorbachev met for a last time in Moscow from May 29 to June 1, 1988. While this summit produced no new major accords, it represented the distance that the two nations had traveled in less than a decade. Reagan and Gorbachev held a joint press conference, the first ever conducted by a Soviet leader within the Soviet Union, and they toasted one another at state dinners. Moreover, when Reagan was asked about his earlier description of the Soviet Union as an "evil empire," he replied, "I was talking about another time, another era." Even Reagan's controversial meeting with Jewish refuseniks, his visit to the Danilov Monastery, and his address to students at Moscow University, during which he criticized the Soviet Union's human rights record, could not detract from the overall warm feeling that existed between him and Gorbachev. Indeed, in search of a story to highlight differences between the two nations, the press focused on allegedly tense relations between **Nancy Davis Reagan** and Raisa Gorbachev.

George Bush held four conferences with Gorbachev, twice in the United States, once in Malta, and the last time in Moscow. Technically, not all the meetings were summits, with the one in Malta in early December 1989 being termed a "nonsummit" aimed at preparing the two nations for a full-scale summit to be held in Washington in June 1990. Regardless of the name given to the meetings, however, they solidified the improving relations between the two superpowers. Disagreements over the specifics of arms control no longer dominated the discussions. Rather, talks about further reductions in nuclear arms were placed within a broader context of bolstering economic reform in the Soviet Union and cooperation in other parts of the globe.

Suggested Readings: John Lewis Gaddis, *The United States and the End of the Cold War* (1992); Raymond Garthoff, *The Great Transition* (1994); Michael Mandlebaum and Strobe Talbott, *Reagan and Gorbachev* (1987).

Related Entries: Arms Control; Foreign Policy.

SUNUNU, JOHN HENRY. (July 2, 1939, Havana, Cuba– .) Chief of Staff to President George Bush, 1989–1991; Counselor to President Bush, 1991–1992.

Many political pundits were profoundly surprised when President-elect George Bush named John Sununu, the former governor of New Hampshire, to serve as his chief of staff. Sununu was neither a longtime friend or aide to Bush nor a Washington, D.C. insider. However, he had provided critical help to the president during the campaign and had a strong reputation as a no-nonsense, take-charge governor. This helped convince Bush that he would make a good chief of staff. By naming Sununu, Bush was also stealing a page from the Reagan playbook. Eight years earlier Reagan had surprised many people by nominating **James (Jim) Addison Baker III,** who, like Sununu, was not a longtime aide, and Baker was considered by many to be one of the best chiefs of staff in modern history.

Unfortunately for Bush, Sununu's tenure was much more rocky than had been James Baker's under Reagan. Sununu seemed to irritate people both inside and outside the administration. For a while, when Bush's approval ratings remained high, Sununu weathered the storm, but when the economy and Bush's approval ratings headed downward, calls for Sununu's resignation increased. On December 3, 1991, Sununu stepped down. He was replaced by Secretary of Transportation **Samuel Knox Skinner.**

Sununu was born in Cuba while his parents were there on a business trip. He grew up in Queens, New York, and earned his B.A. (1961), M.S. (1962), and Ph.D. (1966) in engineering from the Massachusetts Institute of Technology. Until the early 1980s, Sununu worked in the private sector, primarily for JHS Engineering Company and Thermal Research, Inc., which he founded just before receiving his Ph.D. During much of the same period he taught, and ultimately served as dean of the College of Engineering, at Tufts University. In the 1970s he became active in New Hampshire politics, first as a state legislator and then as a member of several advisory councils and committees. In 1980 he lost to **Warren Bruce Rudman** in the Republican senatorial primary. Afterwards, as Rudman's campaign manager, he helped his old foe win the general election. Two years later, running as a staunch conservative opposed to any tax increases, Sununu defeated the Democratic incumbent, Hugh Gallen, in the gubernatorial election. He was reelected to two more two-year terms in 1984 and 1986. During his years as governor, New Hampshire's economy thrived. Sununu claimed that this proved the validity of conservative programs. His critics argued that the state's economy grew due to the boom in the defense industry and **high technology** and warned that a bust would follow. During the latter part of the 1980s and early 1990s, the state's economy did, in fact, start to bust.

Sununu is married to the former Nancy Hayes. They have eight children.

Suggested Readings: *Current Biography* (1989) p. 563; Ann McDaniel, "The Man Called 'Nunu,' " *Newsweek,* December 2, 1991, p. 30; Ann McDaniel, "The Reign of King John," *Newsweek,* May 13, 1991, p. 31.

SUPPLY-SIDE ECONOMICS. See **REAGANOMICS.**

SUPREME COURT. A central theme of the Ronald Reagan–George Bush years was the attempt of the presidents to reverse the liberal drift of the federal **courts.** Both sought to remake the Supreme Court into a bulwark of conservativism, as opposed to an engine of liberal reform as it had been during Earl Warren's and, to a lesser extent, **Warren Earl Burger**'s direction. During their twelve years in office, Reagan and Bush nominated five new justices, **Sandra Day O'Connor, Antonin Scalia, Anthony McLeod Kennedy, David Souter,** and Clarence Thomas. In addition, President Reagan elevated **William Hubbs Rehnquist,** a Richard Nixon appointee, to the Supreme Court to be chief justice, upon Warren Burger's retirement in 1986. As of the end of Bush's term in office, only one justice (of nine) had been nominated by a Democratic president (Table 15).

While the Supreme Court clearly became more conservative over time, it did not affect a counterrevolution in the law during the Reagan-Bush years. The court still upheld the right to an **abortion,** sanctioned **affirmitive action** as long as it was narrowly constructed, maintained a wall between church and state, and defended other first amendment rights. The court's vote on *Planned Parenthood* v. *Casey* (1992) reflected its views in general. In that case, the majority of the court upheld a Pennsylvania law that restricted abortions while simultaneously upholding the right to an abortion. Chief Justice Rehnquist, Antonin Scalia, and Anthony Kennedy ruled in favor of overturning *Roe* v. *Wade* in the case, but two Reagan-Bush nominees, O'Connor and Souter, joined with four other holdovers from the pre-Reagan-Bush years to uphold the landmark abortion decision. In other controversial cases, Anthony Kennedy sometimes joined with O'Connor and Souter to make up a middle ground between

Table 15
The Supreme Court during the Reagan-Bush Years

Name	Dates of Term	Appointed by
Warren E. Burger (Chief)	June 23, 1969–Sept. 26, 1986	Nixon
Byron White	Apr. 16, 1962	Kennedy
Thurgood Marshall	Oct. 2, 1967–June 17, 1991	Johnson
Harry A. Blackmun	June 9, 1970	Nixon
Lewis F. Powell, Jr.	Jan. 7, 1972–June 26, 1987	Nixon
William H. Rehnquist+	Jan. 7, 1972	Nixon
John Paul Stevens	Dec. 19, 1975	Ford
Sandra Day O'Connor	Sept. 25, 1981	Reagan
Antonin Scalia	Sept. 26, 1986	Reagan
Anthony Kennedy	Feb. 18, 1988	Reagan
David H. Souter	Oct. 9, 1990	Bush
Clarence Thomas	Oct. 23, 1991	Bush

+Appointed Chief Justice by President Reagan on Sept. 26, 1986.

the arch-conservatives on the court—Rehnquist, Scalia, and Thomas—and the more liberal members, John Stevens, Harry Blackmun, and Byron White. Perhaps if the nomination of **Robert Heron Bork** to the Supreme Court had been confirmed—it was rejected by the U.S. Senate—Reagan and Bush might have achieved a conservative majority, but this is unlikely since Kennedy assumed the post left vacant by Burger's resignation, instead.

Even though Reagan and Bush did not achieve a counter revolution, the court, especially under Rehnquist's lead, clearly became more conservative and no longer stood as an agent of liberal reform. Homosexuals found their attempts to gain greater protection generally rebuffed, and rights gained by criminals during the 1960s were slowly taken away. For instance, in *Nix* v. *Williams* (1984) the Supreme Court ruled that evidence obtained despite police misconduct was admissible in court. Likewise, it became easier to gain and carry out the death penalty during the Reagan-Bush years.

Most important, the views of the Reagan and Bush appointees were bound to affect the direction of the Supreme Court for years to come. In 1992 Clarence Thomas was aged 43, Scalia was 56, Souter was 62, Rehnquist was 68, Kennedy was 56, and O'Connor was 62. Given that federal

President Reagan and Supreme Court, September 25, 1985. Reagan Library.

judges are appointed for life, it is likely that the Supreme Court will remain a bastion of conservativism, if not an agent of counterrevolution, well into the twenty-first century.

Related Entry: Thomas-Hill Hearings.

T

TAILHOOK SCANDAL. The Tailhook Association is a group of retired and active naval aviators that takes its name from the hook on naval airplanes that grabs hold of the landing cable on aircraft carriers. In late 1991 and 1992, however, *Tailhook* became synonymous with one of the worst scandals in the history of the U.S. Navy. Along with the Anita Hill–Clarence Thomas hearings, Tailhook also raised the general awareness of the prevalence of sexual harassment in American society.

In September 1991 the Tailhook Association held its annual convention at the Las Vegas Hilton, the convention site for the organization for the previous nineteen years. The wild parties and festivities of the Tailhook group were legendary, and this one, which was attended by five thousand people, was little different from those in the past. Scheduled events included talks on aviation safety, aircraft technology, and military personal management. However, an unscheduled event took place on the third floor of the hotel, dubbed the "third deck" by navy men. There a drunken gauntlet of men pawed at women, leading to charges of sexual assault.

According to Navy Lieutenant Paula Coughlin, a helicopter pilot, she was grabbed from behind by a Marine Corps captain who nearly lifted her off the ground by her posterior. The same man, Coughlin contended, forced his hands into her shirt as another man grabbed her from behind. After an investigation was launched stemming from Coughlin's charges, other women, including fourteen officers, filed similar complaints.

Rear Admiral John Snyder, to whom Coughlin originally expressed her grievances, initially dismissed the complaint, stating, "That's what you get when you go to a hotel party with a bunch of drunk aviators." After other complaints were raised, however, the Naval Investigative Service

(NIS) launched a broader investigation—and Snyder was later demoted for his failure to take action. The NIS did not enjoy an easy time, as it was routinely stonewalled by interviewees. NIS uncovered the fact that Navy Secretary H. Lawrence Garrett and the Navy's top admiral, Frank B. Kelso, had both been on the third floor. Even though both men claimed that they did not witness the alleged incident, Garret resigned on June 26, 1992, and Kelso took early retirement.

As a result of the investigation, 140 cases were brought before the navy and marine corps. However, not one serviceman was tried because, according to investigators, of insufficient evidence. President George Bush offered sympathy to the victims of the assault, inviting them to the White House, but he refused to intervene any further. In 1993, the Defense Department criticized the investigation, but still no one was charged with committing any crimes. The only significant change was that the navy began to require sexual-harassment prevention training.

Suggested Readings: Jean Ebbert, *Navy Women: Crossed Currents: From WWI to Tailhook* (1993); U.S. Department of Defense, Office of the Inspector General, *The Tailhook Report* (1993).

Related Entry: Thomas-Hill Hearings.

TAXES. See **ECONOMIC RECOVERY ACT OF 1981; "NO NEW TAXES."**

TAX REFORM ACT OF 1986. On May 28, 1985, President Reagan unveiled a sweeping tax reform proposal which called for overhauling the tax code. Describing the plan as a "Second American Revolution," the president promised that it would make taxes lower, fairer, simpler, and more productive. The proposal called for reducing the number of tax brackets to three—15, 25, and 35 percent of income, raising the personal exemption, ending the deduction for state and local taxes, and limiting the deduction on interest payments except for those on home mortgages.

Despite his resounding victory in 1984, at least initially Reagan gained little support for his plan. Spokespersons for the administration blamed the press for the proposal's lukewarm reception, but concern over the budget and trade deficits probably had more to do with its reception. As time passed, however, interest in the proposal grew. In December 1985 Reagan made an unusual personal visit to Capitol Hill to lobby Congress to enact tax reform. The following spring, the U.S. Senate started work on a measure that resembled the president's initial proposal. Subsequently, the House developed its own bill. U.S. House and Senate conferees met and approved a compromise acceptable to both houses of Congress. On October 22, 1986, President Reagan signed the Tax Reform Act of 1986 into law.

While the final bill differed in several ways from Reagan's initial proposal, it also contained a number of similarities. Tax burdens on individuals and the number of tax brackets were reduced—this would be phased in over time, ultimately producing two brackets, of 15 and 31 percent. Personal exemptions and standard deductions were increased, while a number of itemized deductions, such as for state and local income taxes and interest payments on credit cards, were eliminated.

However, the final product hardly represented a second revolution. Filing taxes remained a burdensome task for millions of Americans, and the new tax code continued to have tens of exceptions and rules that proved difficult to follow. Moreover, the tax reform act did not quell public demand for lower taxes or animosity toward the Internal Revenue Service or the federal government.

Suggested Readings: *Congressional Quarterly Almanac* (1986); *Facts on File* (1986).

Related Entry: Budget Deficit.

TECHNOLOGY. See **HIGH TECHNOLOGY.**

"TEFLON PRESIDENCY". The phrase, "teflon presidency" (coined by Colorado Congresswoman Patricia Schroeder) referred to Ronald Reagan's ability to overcome adversity and remain popular in spite of scandals and disapproval of some of his key policies. As Walter Cronkite, the dean of the television news, observed, "I'm amazed at this Teflon Presidency. This Administration has had scandals, rumors of major influence-peddling and the like, yet it has no effect on the popularity of the President. Reagan is even more popular than [Franklin] Roosevelt, and I never thought I'd see anyone that well-liked. . . . Nobody hates Reagan. It's amazing." While some experts on Reagan, such as Reagan's biographer Lou Cannon, have argued that Reagan was not impervious to criticism and that his popularity did rise and fall with the times, most of his biographers have acknowledged that there was at least a kernel of truth to this characterization of Reagan. Even Cannon admits that most people felt that Reagan was "one of them." Hence, they tended to accept his interpretation of events more readily than they did those of other presidents in recent times.

Suggested Readings: Lou Cannon, *The Role of a Lifetime* (1991); Alan F. Pote, *What They Said in 1986* (1987).

Related Entry: Great Communicator, The.

TERRORISM. Among the most serious terrorist acts against the United States during Ronald Reagan's presidency was the suicide truck-bombing of an American marine barracks in Beirut, Lebanon, in 1983. Several years later, several Americans were kidnapped in Beirut, leading ultimately to the **Iran-contra affair** as President Reagan, despite his promises, authorized government officials to negotiate with the terrorists (or their associates) for their release. In both instances, Reagan's rhetoric that he would make the terrorists "pay for their actions" proved empty. In the latter incident, he broke his promise never to negotiate with terrorists and traded arms with Iran with the goal of obtaining the hostages' release. In the former instance, Reagan withdrew American troops from Beirut despite initial claims that to do so would be to send the wrong message to the bombers.

On other occasions, however, Reagan's actions meshed better with his words. In particular, Reagan took aim at Muammar Qaddafi, the leader of **Libya** and the alleged sponsor of numerous terrorist attacks. In 1986, Reagan ordered an aerial bombing of Libya, aimed at Qadaffi's headquarters, in retaliation for a terrorist attack on a Berlin nightclub in which American servicemen were killed, which was allegedly organized by Libyan terrorists. The bombing killed one of Qaddafi's daughters, but not the Libyan leader himself. In another instance, Reagan ordered American fighter planes to force to the ground an Egyptian airliner which was carrying Palestinian terrorists who were responsible for the murder of an American passenger on the cruise ship *Achille Lauro.* "You can run, but you cannot hide," Reagan declared upon their capture. These actions suggested that Reagan could actually end terrorist attacks through a "get tough" policy. They reinforced his image as a strong leader and his claim that his policies had revived American pride. It did not really matter that in many ways these counterattacks were the exception to the rule. Few if any Americans tabulated the number of terrorist attacks during the 1980s. They did not care if the numbers showed that terrorism had not really diminished. Rather, they credited Reagan with making them feel less vulnerable, even if the real reason they felt this way is that they had become more accustomed to living in an imperfect world in which terrorism did take place.

During the **Persian Gulf War,** concern about terrorism increased as Saddam Hussein threatened to bring the war to the United States. The failure of these threats to materialize, at least during the conflict, diminished concerns about terrorism. Even the bombing of the World Trade Center in New York City, which took place in February 1993 not long after **William (Bill) Jefferson Clinton** became president, did not bring back the level of fear that existed during the late 1970s and early 1980s. However, the bombing of the federal building in Oklahoma City in the spring of 1995 once again reminded Americans of their vulnerability, especially since the terrorists in this case were Americans rather than foreigners.

Suggested Readings: Marc Celmer, *Terrorism* (1988); Michael Ledeen, *Grave New World* (1985).

Related Entry: Beirut, Lebanon (Bombing of U.S. Marine Barracks).

THATCHER (ROBERTS), MARGARET HILDA. (October 13, 1925, Grantham, England– .) Prime Minister of Great Britain, 1979–1990.

Margaret Thatcher, the prime minister of Great Britain from 1979 to 1990, was one of President Ronald Reagan's strongest allies during his presidency. Although Thatcher's personality was virtually the opposite of Reagan's—she was stiff and intensely interested in detail, while he was effervescent and detached from the particulars of public policy—the two enjoyed an especially close relationship. They shared a common conservative ideology and, in their political careers, they paralleled each other. She became the leader of the conservative political party in Britain in 1975 and was elected prime minister in 1979. Both supported a military buildup, with Thatcher offering crucial backing for deployment by the **North Atlantic Treaty Organization (NATO)** of **Pershing II missiles** in Europe. Both pursued a policy of slashing liberal government programs and the **welfare** state. Together they helped revive a special bond between England and the United States that had diminished since the end of World War II. Just as important, her favorable view of **Mikhail Sergeyevich Gorbachev** helped convince Reagan to support the Soviet leader's reform efforts and work towards **arms control.**

After World War II, Thatcher earned a Bachelors of Science and Master's degree from Sommerville College of Oxford University. She married Dennis Thatcher in 1951, and they had a son and two daughters. She

President Reagan and Margaret Thatcher at Camp David, November 6, 1986. Reagan Library.

worked as a research chemist and as an attorney until 1959, when she became a member of Parliament. In 1975 she rose to the top position in her conservative party, and in 1979 she was elected Prime Minister of the United Kingdom.

Suggested Reading: C. J. Bartlett, *The Special Relationship* (1992).

Related Entry: Falkland Islands War.

THOMAS, CLARENCE. See **THOMAS-HILL HEARINGS.**

THOMAS-HILL HEARINGS. In the summer of 1991 President Bush nominated Clarence Thomas, an African-American U.S. Court of Appeals judge, to replace Thurgood Marshall, the first and only black on the **Supreme Court.** Marshall had announced his retirement earlier in the year, and it came as little surprise that Bush sought to fill the empty seat on the court with another African-American. However, Thomas's nomination proved especially controversial, first because of Thomas's conservative views and relatively short experience on the bench, and second, because of accusations of sexual harassment leveled at him by one of his former colleagues, Anita Hill.

The Thomas-Hill hearings—the name given to the segment of Thomas's confirmation hearings before the Senate Judiciary Committee that dealt with Hill's accusations—captured the nation's attention. Without a doubt they were the most followed confirmation proceedings in recent history. Presented live on television, they were compared to the famous Alger Hiss–Whitaker Chambers confrontation in the late 1940s before the House Committee on Un-American Activities.

Anita Hill and Clarence Thomas shared a great deal in common. Both were black Yale Law School graduates. She had worked for Thomas during the 1980s, first when he was at the **civil rights** department of the U.S. Department of Education and then when he served as chairman of the federal Equal Employment Opportunity Commission. After the Judiciary Committee had already questioned Thomas about his controversial legal views—Thomas was a well-known black conservative in a world in which there were few such individuals—charges arose that Thomas had sexually harassed Hill while she had worked for him. The context in which these charges first became public made the issue even more explosive, as the all-male committee had first ignored them as insignificant. Only after they became public did the committee pursue the charges with any vigor.

Under extreme scrutiny from Republicans on the Judiciary Committee, who favored Thomas's confirmation, Hill answered a barrage of questions on topics from her motivation for making the charges to inquiries into the alleged harassment incidents themselves. Though treated as an unfriendly witness, she withstood the questions, answering calmly and in great detail. As a result, by the time she had finished her testimony, many believed that Thomas, in fact, had sexually harassed her. Even if there were doubts about the legality or ethics of Thomas's treatment of Anita Hill, it seemed that if any of what she said was true, he had lied to the committee in the first place by denying the charges.

After Hill was questioned, Thomas returned to testify again. Even though he admitted that he had not watched Hill testify, he categorically denied all her charges. "I would like to start by saying unequivocally, uncategorically, that I deny each and every single allegation against me today." Moreover, he compared the hearings to a lynch mob, which put the committee on the defensive. Whereas the Republicans had thrown Hill one difficult question after another, both Republicans and Democrats treated Thomas in a much more friendly manner. Not only did Thomas deny Hill's charges of sexual harassment, he claimed that he was hurt and shocked by them, suggesting that she had leveled them because he had once spurned her advance on him.

After hearing the contradictory testimony of both Hill and Thomas, the committee called other witnesses to testify. Each side was just as forthright and assured of its version of the truth as were the principals involved. Several witnesses added weight to Hill's charges, but others made it seem virtually impossible that Thomas could have sexually harassed Hill. Pennsylvania Senator Arlen Specter and Utah Senator Orrin Hatch, the leading Republicans on the panel, claimed that Hill's charges did not ring true: they could not understand why she had followed Thomas when he changed jobs and why she had remained silent for so long. The reply from Hill and her supporters, that she did so because her career was tied to his and because she did not want to air the charges, which had emanated from independent sources, failed to convince them.

Polls showed sharp divisions in the public over who was telling the truth. *Time* magazine's cover story (October 21, 1991), "An Ugly Circus," captured the ambivalence in the nation: "As the nation looks on, two credible articulate witnesses present irreconcilable views of what happened nearly a decade ago." Following the hearings, the Judiciary Committee voted, largely along party lines, to support Thomas's nomination. More debate followed in the Senate. Thomas narrowly won confirmation, fifty-two to forty-eight, becoming the youngest (he was forty-three) member of the Supreme Court.

While Hill's charges did not derail Thomas, many analysts argue that they had an important after effect on the public. They raised awareness about the issue of sexual harassment and galvanized women's groups into action. At the least, women's groups demanded greater female representation in government so that similar charges would be taken more seriously in the future. In 1992, a number of women were elected to high office, including Carol Mosely Braun, the first black female senator in history.

For President Bush, his nomination of Clarence Thomas did little to help politically. Few believed him when he argued that he had nominated Thomas because he was the best-qualified individual in the land. It is doubtful that Bush won any black votes by nominating Thomas, and the Thomas-Hill hearings probably lost him some women's votes.

Suggested Readings: Robert Chrisman and Robert L. Allen, *Court of Appeal: The Black Community Speaks Out* (1992); Toni Morrison, ed., *Race-ing Justice, En-Gendering Power: Essays on Anita Hill, Clarence Thomas and the Construction of Social Reality* (1992); Timothy Phelps, *Capitol Games* (1992).

Related Entries: Courts; Women's Rights.

THORNBURGH, RICHARD L. (July 16, 1932, Pittsburgh, Pa.– .) U.S. Attorney General, 1988–1991.

In August 1988, Richard (Dick) Thornburgh, the former governor of Pennsylvania (1978–1986), succeeded **Edwin Meese III** as the attorney general of the United States. He took over a Justice Department whose morale was low, having been racked by years of scandal and politicization. Thornburgh remained the top public attorney for the next four years. In 1991, he resigned to run in a special election for a vacant seat in the U.S. Senate (left vacant by the tragic death of Pennsylvania Senator Joe Heinz in an airplane crash). Many considered him a shoe-in for the post. However, in an upset that portended poorly for the Republican Party in 1992, he lost to Democrat Harris Wofford.

Thornburgh was born in Rosalyn Farms, a suburb of Pittsburgh. While the Depression ravaged Pittsburgh, it hardly affected his family. He earned his engineering degree from Yale University (1954) and law degree from the University of Pittsburgh (1957). After graduation, he joined the private law firm of Kirkpatrick, Pomeroy, Lockhart & Johnson and seemed headed for a quiet life of corporate law. The sudden death of his wife and injury of his two sons in a car crash, however, turned his attention to public life.

Coming from a staunchly Republican family, Thornburgh had watched the rise of the conservative Barry Goldwater with dismay. In 1966, he ran for Congress as a moderate Republican, expressing his concern over the Vietnam War—he lost. He joined the National Association for the Advancement of Colored People (NAACP), became a director of the American Civil Liberties Union (ACLU), and supported New York Governor Nelson Rockefeller for president in 1968. A year later, Richard Nixon appointed him U.S. attorney for western Pennsylvania, a post he held until 1975 when President Gerald Ford named him assistant attorney general, in charge of the Criminal Division of the Justice Department.

In 1978 Thornburgh was elected governor of Pennsylvania. Shortly after being sworn in, he won fame for his handling of the Three Mile Island nuclear accident. He also earned admiration for his fight against corruption in the state and his efforts to limit the impact of the recession of the early 1980s on his highly industrial state.

As attorney general, he sought to reestablish morale within the Justice Department. Many considered him a potential vice presidential or even presidential candidate. In the 1991 special senatorial campaign, Wofford won by emphasizing Thornburgh's association with Bush, whose popularity rating was falling rapidly, and by emphasizing his own pledge to fight for **health care reform.** Afterward, Thornburgh returned to private practice.

Suggested Readings: *Current Biography* (1988) p. 560; *Facts on File* (1992).

Related Entry: Recessions.

"A THOUSAND POINTS OF LIGHT". In his acceptance speech at the Republican (GOP) convention in 1988, George Bush explained his and the GOP's differences with the Democratic Party's views. Among the differences, the presidential nominee contended, were their attitudes on the role of government. He argued that government should play only a partial role—that it was just part of a larger whole that sought to address America's problems and needs. The American tradition, Bush asserted, emphasized the participation of the community and voluntary associations, rather than relying only on the government. This tradition was strong. It included "the Knights of Columbus, the Grange, Hadassah, the Disabled American Veterans[,] . . . the union hall, the Bible study group[;] . . . a brilliant diversity spread like stars, like a thousand points of light in the broad and peaceful sky." During the campaign, in his inaugural address, and periodically during his presidency, Bush again invoked this metaphor. As he stated in his inaugural address, his administration intended to promote community and voluntary action. "I will go to the people and the programs that are the brighter points of light, and I'll ask every member of Government to become involved."

Suggested Readings: Alan F. Pote, *What They Said in 1989* (1990); *New York Times,* August 19, 1988, I:1.

TIANANMEN SQUARE INCIDENT. In spring 1989, protestors in Tiananmen Square in Beijing, **China,** captured the world's attention. Hundreds of thousands of students amassed to demand democracy and further economic reform. Many Americans naively thought that they were on the verge of achieving a nonviolent end to the Communist Party's rule in the People's Republic of China. However, then, on June 4, Chinese troops moved into Tiananmen Square and crushed the reform movement. They arrested some protestors, killed others, and squelched hope that the Communists' rule of China had come to an end.

The George Bush administration responded by suspending arms sales and delaying the extension of new loans to China. President Bush and other leaders sharply criticized the violent crackdown. Despite calls for stiffer actions, however, the Bush administration went no further, arguing that stiffer penalities would backfire and jeopardize the newly improved relations with China. Bush refused to revoke most-favored nation trading status or suspend diplomatic relations with China. Later in the year, former President Richard Nixon journeyed to China to assure Chinese leaders that the United States did not intend to renew its adversarial relation with it. At the end of 1991, National Security Adviser **Brent Scowcroft** visited China to reinforce Nixon's message. Even though many Democrats sharply criticized Bush's reaction to the crackdown at Tiananmen Square, it remained unclear what they would have done differently had they held power.

Ever since Richard Nixon had traveled to China in early 1970, U.S. relations with the nation had improved. Even President Ronald Reagan, a fervid anticommunist, took a moderate stance toward the communist regime in China and encouraged economic exchanges with the United States. One reason why the United States chose not to take a tougher position following the crackdown was that economic reform in China was continuing to take place. By the early 1990s China had become one of the United States' largest trading partners, and expectations were that trade would continue to grow. Furthermore, China supported the United States during the **Persian Gulf War.** Put another way, the Bush administration's reaction to Tiananmem Square depicted its realistic **foreign policy** approach. It was not about to sacrifice billions of dollars of trade in order to make a point, especially when it was not clear that stiffer sanctions against China would have altered the situation there.

Suggested Readings: Churyuan Cheng, *Behind The Tiananmen Massacre* (1990); Harry Harding, *A Fragile Relationship* (1992); Robert B. Ixbanm, "Asia/Pacific Challenges," *Foreign Affairs,* January 1993, p. 58.

Related Entries: Communism, Collapse of; Foreign Policy.

TOWER COMMISSION REPORT. On November 26, 1986, one day after the Ronald Reagan administration acknowledged that funds obtained from arms sales to Iran had been diverted to the Nicaraguan contras (something it had previously denied), the president appointed a bipartisan, three-member panel to investigate the affair. Headed by John Tower, a former Republican senator from Texas, the panel also included former secretary of state Edmund Muskie and former national security adviser, Retired Lieutenant General **Brent Scowcroft.**

On February 27, 1987, the commission issued its report. Based on interviews with eighty individuals, the commission criticized the Reagan administration for lacking full control over its top advisers, whom the commission blamed for the improper diversion of funds to the contras. The commission, however, did not find President Reagan personally culpable in the decision to divert money and argued that it did not even have definitive evidence that he had approved of the shipment of arms for hostages that had generated the funds in the first place. By and large the report faulted President Reagan's management style and overwillingness to delegate authority and criticized his top advisers for poorly serving the president. The report suggested that congressional oversight of the National Security Council should be augmented, but it did not call for any major institutional changes or legal action.

While Republicans largely applauded the Tower Commission for its investigation, the Democrats in Congress had almost the opposite reaction. Noting that the commission had lacked subpoena power and had not enjoyed the assistance of Special Prosecutor **E. Lawrence Walsh,** they contended that it had failed to get to the root of the matter. They vowed, in spite of the Tower Commission's report, to press on with their own investigations.

The day after the Tower Commission issued its report, **Donald Regan,** President Reagan's chief of staff, resigned. Regan had been criticized by the Tower Commission and was often blamed for the scandal by other longtime presidential advisers, as well as **Nancy Davis Reagan.** On March 4, 1987, President Reagan delivered a nationally televised address on the **Iran-contra affair,** in which he took "full responsibility" for the incident. Although "undertaken without my knowledge," Reagan declared, "I am still accountable for those activities."

Suggested Readings: Theodore Draper, *A Very Thin Line: The Iran-Contra Affair* (1991); John Tower, Edmund Muskie and Brent Scowcroft, *The Tower Commission Report* (1987); Lawrence Walsh, *Iran-Contra: The Final Report* (1994).

TRADE DEFICIT. One of the most notable economic trends of the Ronald Reagan–George Bush years was the persistence of relatively high trade

Table 16
Foreign Trade (billions of dollars)

Year	Merchandise Trade Deficit	Exports	Imports
1980	−24.2	220.6	244.9
1981	−27.3	233.7	261.0
1982	−31.8	212.3	244.0
1983	−57.5	200.5	258.0
1984	−107.9	217.9	325.7
1985	−132.1	213.1	345.3
1986	−152.7	217.3	370.0
1987	−152.1	254.1	406.2
1988	−118.6	322.4	441.0
1989	−109.6	363.8	473.4
1990	−101.7	393.6	495.3
1991	−65.4	421.7	487.1
1992	−84.3	448.2	532.5

Source: Statistical Abstracts (1993), p. 808.

deficits. For much of the twentieth century, the United States enjoyed a trade surplus, exporting more goods (in total value) than it imported. This situation changed in the mid-1970s and became progressively worse in the mid-1980s (see Table 16).

President Reagan's critics claimed that the mounting trade deficit threatened America's standard of living and represented the declining competitiveness of American businesses. At least initially, President Reagan countered that, on the contrary, the record trade deficits of the mid-1980s signified the strength of the American economy. It was a sign of the confidence of American consumers. Flush with more money, they were buying more goods. Nonetheless, to counter mounting trade deficits, the Treasury Department fostered a decline in the value of the dollar, which they hoped would make American goods more attractive abroad and boost exports. Between September 1985 and February 1987, the dollar dropped 40 percent against other major currencies.

Despite these efforts, the trade deficit remained high, peaking at $152 billion in 1987. To make matters worse, the rapid decline of the dollar helped create uncertainty in financial markets and indirectly contributed to inflationary pressures. In addition, Democrats argued that high trade deficits, especially with **Japan,** depicted Reagan's (and later, Bush's) lack of concern with the plight of the American worker whom, Democrats argued, was hurt the most by the growth of imports. Such attacks helped prompt President Reagan to prod the Japanese to agree to voluntary limits of automobile exports to the United States from 1981 to 1985.

When trade deficits began to fall during the late 1980s, President Bush took credit for their decline. Ironically, economists noted that the decline had more to do with the onset of the recession than with any new agreements negotiated by the Bush administration. Not surprisingly, Bush remained politically vulnerabile on trade issues in spite of the declining trade deficit.

While the trade deficit remained an important political issue, some economists downplayed its significance. They argued that it constituted only a small fraction of the total gross national product and added that more attention should be paid to the overall expansion of international trade, which historically produced economic benefits to all the parties involved, than to the deficit alone. From 1980 to 1992, exports doubled and promised to increase at an even faster pace in the near future. This expansion of foreign trade allowed for greater consumer choice, better prices and quality of goods, and hence, a higher standard of living. Revisionist economists disagreed with this interpretation, emphasizing that neverending trade deficits spelled a decline in America's standard of living relative to those nations that enjoyed a trade surplus.

Suggested Readings: Michael Bernstein and David Adler, eds., *Understanding American Economic Decline* (1994); Paul Klugman, ed., *Trade with Japan* (1992); Henry Nau, *The Myth of American Decline* (1990).

Related Entries: Deindustrialization; Economy, U.S.; Recessions.

TRUMP, DONALD JOHN. (August, 1946, Queens, N.Y.– .) Business tycoon.

During the Ronald Reagan–George Bush years, Donald Trump, a real estate developer in New York City and New Jersey, became one of the most famous businessmen in America. Like the robber barons of the Gilded Age, Trump symbolized the aura of the era. He built grand hotels and office buildings, each one more glitzy and embellished than the last. Several of his most famous buildings were Trump Tower on Fifth Avenue in New York City and Trump Castle in Atlantic City. During the peak of his wealth and fame, Trump owned an airline, the Trump Shuttle, and a football team (the New Jersey Generals of the United States Football League); he was also the author of a best-selling book, *Trump: The Art of the Deal* (1987). Much more so than others who gained financial fortunes in the decade, such as **Ivan Frederick Boesky** and **Michael Milken,** Trump lived a life of celebrity, often appearing with beautiful and famous women and on the covers of *People* magazine and the tabloid press.

As the economy slid into a recession, however, so, too, did Trump's fortunes. In the same way that his success seemed to depict the glory of the mid-1980s, his troubles came to represent those of the early 1990s. In 1990, unable to meet payments on approximately $2 billion in loans, he had to dismantle his empire in order to avoid bankruptcy. Apropos of his entrepreneurial genius, Trump managed to turn even this adversity into a money-making venture by writing another best-seller, *Trump: Surviving the Top* (1990).

Suggested Readings: *Current Biography* (1984) p. 400; Donald Trump, *The Art of the Deal* (1987); Donald Trump, *Trump: Surviving the Top* (1990).

Related Entry: Recessions.

TUTWILER, MARGARET DEBARDELEBEN. (December 28, 1950, Birmingham, Ala.– .) Special Assistant to President Ronald Reagan, 1981–1985; Assistant Secretary of the Treasury, 1985–1988; Assistant Secretary of Public Affairs, 1989–1992.

Margaret Tutwiler served as an adviser to both President Ronald Reagan and President George Bush. After working as the director of scheduling for George Bush during his unsuccessful 1980 presidential bid, she joined the Reagan White House. There she worked with **James (Jim) Addison Baker III** as a special assistant to the president, a post she held through Reagan's first term. When Baker moved to the Department of Treasury, she moved with him, serving as the assistant secretary of the Department of the Treasury. In 1988 she worked as the deputy chairman of the George Bush–**Danforth (Dan) James Quayle** campaign. After Bush's election, she continued to work with Baker, this time in the State Department. She became especially prominent during the **Persian Gulf War,** making many press releases. When Baker returned to the White House at the tail end of Bush's presidency, Tutwiler moved with him.

Tutwiler attended Finch College from 1969 to 1971 and then transferred to the University of Alabama, where she received her B.A. From a young age she was active in the fledgling Alabama Republican Party. In

1976 she worked on President Gerald Ford's 1976 campaign and then worked for the National Association of Manufacturers in Alabama.

Suggested Readings: Margaret Carlson, "As State Department Spokesperson, Margaret Tutwiler Has Won Even the Press's Respect," *Vogue,* October, 1989, p. 276; Peter Kilborn, "The Political Key to the Treasury," *New York Times Biographical Service,* December 1985, p. 1448.

Related Entries: Election of 1980; Election of 1988.

V

VESSEY, JOHN W., JR. (June 24, 1922, Minneapolis, Minn.– .) Chairman, Joint Chiefs of Staff, 1982–1985.

General John W. Vessey, Jr., spent forty-six years in the American military, rising to its top post, chairman of the Joint Chiefs of Staff, in 1982. Unlike most of America's other top commanders, he was not a graduate of West Point nor one of the other military academies. He did not even attend the Virginia Military Academy (VMI), the Citadel, or one of the other private academies. Rather, he won his first commission on the battlefield during World War II and advanced his career through service and hard work over the following decades. Indeed, Vessey even got into the army in an unusual way, by lying about his age at the outbreak of World War II. Still an underage boy from Crow Wing County when Pearl Harbor was bombed, he claimed he was old enough to enlist. He was the last chairman of the Joint Chiefs of Staff to have fought in World War II.

The main criticism Vessey encountered was that he was not visible or vocal enough while chairman. However, Vessey considered this one of his greatest strengths. He sought to depoliticize his job and, to a large degree, succeeded in doing so. He oversaw the largest peacetime buildup of the United States military in its history. This included massive expenditures on new arms, an expansion of America's strategic mobility, and improvements in the living standard and morale of America's servicemen and -women. While the president and Secretary of Defense **Caspar Willard Weinberger** maintained official command of the military, Vessey won from them a significant concession—that the military would enjoy the control of operations once troops had been committed to action. During the invasion of **Grenada,** in fact, military commanders enjoyed unprecedented freedom from civilian meddling. Many credited Vessey with restoring the reputation and prestige of the armed forces, which had fallen during the Vietnam War and afterward.

When Vessey retired at the age of sixty-three, President Ronald Reagan, who at the time was seventy-four, kidded him that he was old enough to run for president. Vessey chuckled, but he never showed an interest in politics. Vessey is married to Avis C. Funk. They have three children.

Suggested Readings: *New York Times,* October 1, 1985, I:14; *New York Times Magazine,* July 15, 1984, p. 18.

Related Entry: Defense Spending.

VIETNAM. While the Vietnam War ended six years before Ronald Reagan became president, it continued to have an impact on both **domestic policy** and **foreign policy** well into the early 1990s. A central component of President Reagan's foreign policy and his overall appeal to the American public was his promise to overcome the "Vietnam syndrome," defined as a reluctance to intervene militarily abroad because of a fear that America would become trapped in a quagmire as it did during the Vietnam War. Reagan called for a massive defense buildup and a restoration of the old-fashioned spirit of patriotism. He argued that the Vietnam War had been a just cause. Moreover, he did not seek to normalize relations with Vietnam, and he sought to identify himself with the neglected Vietnam veteran.

Vietnam figured prominently in U.S. foreign affairs in two other key ways. Even before American involvement in Vietnam had ended, Cambodia had begun to unravel, producing one of the worst massacres or cases of genocide in world history. Ultimately, Vietnamese forces intervened, bringing stability to the region. The United States sought to prod Vietnam to withdraw from Cambodia while at the same time ensuring that the Khmer Rouge, the perpetrators of the genocide, did not regain power. In 1992 Vietnam withdrew and stability of sorts was reestablished in Cambodia.

Nonetheless, tensions continued to exist between the United States and Vietnam, particularly over the issue of the prisoners of war (POWs) and those missing in action (MIA). In 1989 the U.S. Senate conducted extensive investigations into reports that the Vietnamese were holding back information on Americans still in Indochina. While the investigators concluded that there was no credible evidence of remaining American soldiers, groups of veterans continued to reject this claim. As long as this group carried political clout, which it still did as of the early 1990s, it was impossible for the United States to normalize relations with Vietnam.

Even so, increasing numbers of Americans traveled to Vietnam. Growing out of these journeys and business interests in the region, President George Bush declared, "We can begin writing the last chapter of the Vietnam War." Of course, Bush still wanted to play both sides of the street. In 1992, his campaign team hammered at **William (Bill) Jefferson Clinton**'s Vietnam War record, emphasizing that Clinton had finagled his way out of the draft. Clinton overcame this criticism, yet the very fact that Bush chose to use it suggested that the United States was still years away from overcoming the Vietnam syndrome.

Suggested Readings: H. Bruce Franklin, *M.I.A. or Mythmaking in America* (1993); Alf Louvre and Jefrey Walsh, eds., *Tell Me Lies about Vietnam: Cultural Battles for the Meaning of the War* (1988); Marilyn Young, *The Vietnam Wars, 1945–1990* (1991).

Related Entry: Vietnam Veterans Memorial.

VIETNAM VETERANS MEMORIAL. On November 11, 1982, seven years after the last American died in Vietnam, a memorial was dedicated in a wooded section of the mall in Washington, D.C., not far from the Lincoln Memorial. Its design was quite unlike any other memorial in Washington. It was constructed of 140 black granite panels, placed in a V shape, with one wall extending toward the Washington Monument and the other toward the Lincoln Memorial. Inscribed on the panels, which resemble large gravestone tablets, were the names of the approximately 58,000 American servicemen and -women who were killed in Vietnam. The construction and dedication of the memorial was made possible entirely by private contributions. The memorial's design was chosen in May 1981 from over 1,400 entries. The winner was a Yale architecture student, Maya Ying Lin.

Some harshly criticized the winning design. One Vietnam War veteran called it a "black gash of shame," and **H. Ross Perot,** one of the financiers of the memorial, publicly expressed his disapproval. Nevertheless, the memorial's developers went ahead with construction of the winner's design, offering only a few modifications such as adding a flag and a brief inscription that honored the sacrifice and devotion of the Vietnam soldier. Within a short period, despite the criticism, the designer and selection committee had been vindicated, as the monument became one of the most visited in the nation and proved the most moving in the capital.

Nancy and Ronald Reagan at Vietnam Veterans Memorial, November 11, 1988. Reagan Library.

The memorial's dedication ceremony consisted of a three-hour-long parade, with elaborate floats and fighter planes soaring overhead. The names of all the men and women listed on the tablets were read. President Ronald Reagan lit a candle and declared, "Everyone is now beginning to appreciate that they were fighting for a just cause." This statement and the ceremony itself reflected Reagan's efforts to restore American patriotism and dovetailed with the administration's defense buildup and hawkish posture around the globe.

Since its dedication, hundreds of thousands of people have visited the granite walls, leaving mementos to the fallen soldiers, touching individual names, and taking rubbings. In 1992, the Smithsonian Museum opened an exhibit entitled "Personal Legacy: The Healing of the Nation," which was made up primarily of 500 items left at the memorial, representing a tiny fraction of the 25,000 that have been collected. At a tenth anniversary dedication ceremony, President George Bush proclaimed, "We remember the names of the veterans because we cherished them as individuals, as

Paul Volcker meets with President Reagan, December 14, 1981. Reagan Library.

sons and daughters, brothers and sisters, spouses, neighbors and friends." Bush added that the memorial "has fostered unity and healing among millions of Americans."

Suggested Readings: Robin and Barry Schwartz, "The Vietnam Veterans Memorial: Commemorating a Difficult Past," *The American Journal of Sociology* 97, no. 2 (1991) p. 376; "War and Remembrance," *History Today* 43 (1993).

Related Entry: Vietnam.

VOLCKER, PAUL. (September 5, 1927, Cape May, N.J.– .) Chairman, Federal Reserve Board, 1979–1987.

While the post of chairman of the **Federal Reserve Board** was created in the early decades of the twentieth century, it was not until the early 1980s that the holder of the position became a household name. This was largely due to the significant role that Paul Volcker played while chairman of "the Fed" from 1979 through 1987.

Volcker received his B.A. from Princeton (1949) and a M.A. in political economy from Harvard (1951). He worked as a research assistant for the Federal Reserve Bank during the summers of 1950 and 1951 and spent nearly two years at the London School of Economics. Afterward, he held a series of government positions, including undersecretary of monetary affairs (1969–1975). In July 1979, President **James (Jimmy) Earl Carter** nominated Volcker to head the Federal Reserve Board, and Volcker was shortly thereafter confirmed for the post.

Even though he was originally a Carter nominee, Volcker came to play an increasingly important role after Ronald Reagan took power. He single-mindedly pursued a tight money policy in order to fight **inflation,** which had risen to double digits during Carter's last year in office. Volcker believed that high inflation not only hurt consumers but also discouraged investment and savings, both of which were crucial to the long-term expansion of the **U.S. economy.** Knowing that his monetary policy would produce a recession, he pursued the policy, nonetheless.

In 1983 President Reagan reappointed Volcker to a second term as chairman of the Federal Reserve Board, confirming, as many had said all along, that Volcker's monetary policy dovetailed with Reagan's domestic and economic agenda. Volcker supported Reagan's goal of deregulating numerous industries. He retired in 1987 as head of the Federal Reserve Board and was replaced by **Alan Greenspan,** another fiscal conservative.

Suggested Readings: William Greider, *Secrets of the Temple* (1987); Paul Volcker and Toyoo Gyahlen, *Changing Fortunes: The World's Money and the Threat to American Leadership* (1992).

Related Entries: Deregulation; Domestic Policy; Recessions.

VON DAMM, HELEN A. (May 4, 1938, Ulmerfeld, Austria– .) Personal Secretary to President Ronald Reagan and Director, White House Personnel, 1981–1983; Ambassador to Austria, 1983–1987.

Helen A. Von Damm, an Austrian native who fled the war-ravaged Austrian countryside as a youth, returned almost a half-century later as the U.S. ambassador. Her appointment represented a personal triumph yet, at the same time, was seen by many as an affront to the professionalism of the State Department. Von Damm, who had been Ronald Reagan's secretary when he was governor of California and as president (from 1981 to 1983), may have received the post because of her personal differences with **Nancy Davis Reagan** and some of the president's closest aides, such as **Michael Keith Deaver.** Unwilling to fire her, the president found Von Damm a comfortable diplomatic post. However, anonymity did not follow Von Damm when she relocated overseas. While ambassador she created a major scandal when she divorced Byron Leads, her third husband, to marry Peter Gurtler (age thirty-nine), the owner of Sacher Hotel and a man seven years her junior. Also while ambassador, Von Damm caused a scandal through her attire. Shortly after remarrying, she attended a ball wearing a low-cut gown, which First Lady Nancy Reagan found inappropriate.

Von Damm was a very visible ambassador. She brought Henry Kissinger, Frank Sinatra, and other American luminaries to Vienna and arranged a personal visit between the president of Austria, Rudolph Kirchschlager, and President Reagan. Even though most people agreed that American-Austrian relations improved during Von Damm's tenure, she was eventually forced to resign in 1987, in large part because of Nancy Reagan's furor over what she saw as her scandalous behavior. Shortly after resigning, Von Damm wrote her autobiography, *At Reagan's Side* (1989). In it she portrayed Nancy Reagan as petty, while at the same time painting herself as one of the president's steadiest supporters. Nancy Reagan was not the only woman in the Reagan administration with whom Von Damm had differences. She was known to mock **Elizabeth Hanford Dole** as "schoolmarmish" and dismissed what she considered **Jeane Jordan Kirkpatrick**'s coarse behavior as simply her "wrong time of the month."

Suggested Readings: Helen Von Damm, *At Reagan's Side* (1989); *New York Times,* February 27, 1985, p. 1.

"VOODOO ECONOMICS". During the 1980 campaign for the Republican presidential nomination, George Bush called Ronald Reagan's economic proposal to cut taxes, raise defense spending and balance the federal budget at the same time "voodoo economics." By this statement, Bush meant that Reagan's policies would not work. Once he became Reagan's running-mate, however, Bush stopped criticizing Reagan's proposals. As Vice President and later as a presidential candidate, moreover, Bush championed Reagan's economic programs and record, even denying that he had uttered the phrase. Only after NBC news showed a video clip of Bush calling Reagan's plan "voodoo economics" did he retreat from his specific denial.

Suggested Readings: Robert J. Genetski, *Taking the Voodoo Out of Economics* (1986); Robert Ortner, *Voodoo Deficits* (1990).

Related Entry: Reaganomics.

W

WALSH, E. LAWRENCE. (January 8, 1912, Port Maitland, Nova Scotia, Canada– .) Independent Counsel, Iran-contra investigation, 1986–1994.

In December 1986, Lawrence Walsh was named the independent counsel (special prosecutor) in the investigation of the **Iran-contra affair.** At the time he had a reputation for honesty and hard work. However, nearly eight years later, when he issued his final report, he had lost a good deal of support from Republicans and Democrats alike. The former proclaimed that he had developed a personal vendetta against the Ronald Reagan and George Bush administrations, while the latter lamented the fact that Walsh's investigation had taken so long and produced so few concrete results.

As special prosecutor of the Iran-contra affair, Walsh assembled a sizable team to unravel it and to pursue prosecutions where appropriate. Throughout he faced opposition, including a suit filed by **Oliver North** that challenged the law under which Walsh had been appointed—and that North lost. Walsh's task was further complicated by the fact that congressional investigators had granted immunity, in exchange for testimony, to most of the individuals involved in the affair. To make matters even worse, Walsh's pursuit of convictions was hindered by government classification rules that limited what evidence he could introduce in court. As a result, Walsh had to drop several key charges and watch helplessly as appeals courts overturned or set aside the convictions of various defendants on technical grounds. In his final report, Walsh argued that the Reagan administration had intentionally deceived Congress and the public about the scandal. At the same time, he found no credible evidence of criminal activity by the president or vice president. Many former members of the Reagan and Bush administrations termed the report biased. President Reagan issued a 125-page rebuttal which termed the report "innuendo and opinion instead of proof." Even many of Walsh's supporters questioned the length and cost of his investigation.

Walsh grew up in Queens, New York. He received his B.A. (1932) and law degree (1936) from Columbia University, working part of the time as a merchant seaman to pay for his college expenses. His first job was with Hiram C. Todd, a special prosecutor appointed to investigate corruption in the District Attorney's Office in Brooklyn, New York. Shortly afterward, Manhattan district attorney and future presidential candidate Thomas Dewey appointed him to help in the famous investigation of the Mafia in New York. In 1941 Walsh went to work for Davis, Polk and Wardwell, one of the best-known law firms in the nation. Two years later, on Thomas Dewey's election as governor of New York, Walsh returned to the public sector as Dewey's assistant legal counsel. For much of the rest of his career, Walsh alternately took posts with the public and private sector, including stints as a federal district court judge and deputy attorney general. At each step he added to his reputation for integrity, as reflected by his election as president of the American Bar Association in 1975.

Walsh is married to Mary Alma Porter. They have one daughter, Elizabeth, and he has two children by a previous marriage.

Suggested Readings: *Facts on File* (1994); E. Lawrence Walsh, *Iran-Contra: The Final Report* (1994).

WAR ON DRUGS. A major theme of both the Ronald Reagan and George Bush presidencies was a "war on drugs," which was launched in response to the dramatic increase in drug usage and associated crime in American society. Despite much fanfare, money spent, high-profile arrests and convictions, and the doubling of the prison population, the Reagan-Bush years concluded without a victory in the war.

On September 14, 1986, President Reagan and First Lady **Nancy Davis Reagan** delivered their first joint television address to announce a "national crusade" against drug abuse. The goal of this effort, the Reagans declared, was to create a "drug-free" America. The following day, President Reagan called for a $900 million drug program, which included increased efforts to stop the international trafficking of drugs, tougher federal penalties for drug-related crimes, and funding for drug education and treatment. Along with this proposal, President Reagan signed an executive order which mandated widespread drug testing of federal employees. In October, Congress passed a $1.7 billion antidrug program (nearly double the appropriations called for by the president), and Reagan signed the bill into law.

Two years later, in its last act, the 100th Congress passed another omnibus antidrug bill. The new law called for spending $2.8 billion to help fight the spread of drugs in American society. The bill provided for the death penalty in drug-related murders, increased penalties for even minor users of drugs, and allocated more money for drug education and treatment. Because of the **Gramm-Rudman-Hollings Act (Balanced Budget and Emergency Deficit Control Act of 1985),** however, only $500 million of the $2.8 billion could actually be spent during 1989.

On September 5, 1989, in the first televised address of his presidency, President George Bush unveiled his own war on drugs. His plan called for spending $7.9 billion, nearly half of which would go to law enforcement. Arguing that Bush's plan did not provide enough for drug treatment and education, Democrats in Congress added an additional $900,000 to the president's request, passing an $8.8 billion antidrug measure. Bush signed this measure into law in 1990.

Bush's war on drugs also included several high-profile arrests and trials of international drug figures. In September 1989, Eduardo Martinez Romero, the reputed financier of the Colombian drug cartel, was extradited to the United States and indicted on charges of money laundering. Later in the year U.S. armed forces invaded Panama, captured Panamanian leader Manuel Noriega, whom the federal government had previously indicted on drug-trafficking charges, extradited him to the United States, and ultimately convicted him and sent him to jail.

Despite billions of dollars of new expenditures and a rapid increase in the number of arrests and prisoners (many on drug charges), the impact of this war on drugs was largely unsuccessful. For instance, in 1985 the Drug Enforcement Administration (DEA) seized 18,129 kilograms of cocaine, while seven years later, the DEA seized nearly 80,000 kilograms of cocaine. In the same time period, the number of federal convictions for drug-related crimes nearly doubled, as did the number of convictions for violations of state drug-related laws. However, no sooner had one drug peddler been arrested than another took his or her place. While some surveys suggested that drug use among high school students declined during the early 1990s, the decline was relatively small and may have been a temporary phenomenon. To make matters worse, it appeared that violent drug-related crimes were on the increase. Murder rates rose, especially among men and women in the most drug-infested areas. Meanwhile, those individuals like Baltimore Mayor Kurt Schmoke, who compared the war on drugs to Prohibition in the 1920s and suggested that the nation adopt a different approach—namely, decriminalize drugs and spend the money collected from their legal yet controlled distribution on drug education and treatment—found their voices largely drowned out by still louder calls for even tougher laws and more police.

Suggested Readings: Dan Baum, "Tunnel Vision: The War on Drugs, 12 Years Later," *ABA [American Bar Association] Journal,* March 1993, p. 70; Steven B. Duke, *America's Longest War: Rethinking Our Tragic Crusade Against Drugs* (1993); Christina Johns, *Power, Ideology and the War on Drugs* (1992).

Related Entries: Bennett, William John; Crime Bill; "Just Say No."

WATT, JAMES GAIUS. (January 31, 1938, Lusk, Wyo.– .) Secretary of the Interior, 1981–1983.

Ronald Reagan's first secretary of interior, James Watt, spent his youth on a farm in rural Wyoming. When he was in the eighth grade he moved with his family to Wheatland, Wyoming, the county seat of the Platte County, where his father practiced law. Watt excelled in school and at athletics. He left Wheatland to attend the University of Wyoming in Cheyenne, where he earned his B.A. (1960) and law degree (1962). Upon graduation from law school, Watt went to work in Washington, D.C., for Senator Milward L. Simpson. For the next twenty-eight years he alternated between working for the private and public sectors. This included serving as legal counsel for the United States Chamber of Commerce and as vice chairman of the Federal Power Commission. He earned a reputation as an advocate of industrial and business development and an opponent of environmentalism. Before he accepted the post of secretary of the interior, he had become one of the leaders of the so-called "sagebrush rebellion," a loose collection of individuals and businesses that opposed mounting government regulations of western lands.

Watt's nomination to head the Interior Department was not well received by environmental groups. As one conservationist suggested, appointing Watt to this sensitive post was like "hiring a fox to guard the chickens." More so than probably any of his other appointees, Watt remained a controversial figure and a constant target of liberal criticism. He attracted controversy because of his background and because he was responsible for implementing the Ronald Reagan administration's environmental policies, which favored big business and marked a dramatic swing away from the more proenvironmental policies of the previous

Secretary of Interior James Watt, with President Reagan and Secretary of the Treasury Donald Regan, February 27, 1981. Reagan Library.

decade. Watt's decision to allow for new oil drilling along the Pacific coast, his **deregulation** of the mining industry, and his opening of wilderness areas to commercial use and development garnered him sharp criticism. His simultaneous decision to hike the cost of entrance fees to the national parks provoked further complaints. Controversy also followed Watt because he did little to quiet his critics. On the contrary, he fed them ammunition through his blunt and sometimes off-color remarks. On one occasion he simultaneously offended Jews, blacks, women, and American Indians. To make matters worse, Watt defended the Reagan administration's policies by suggesting that he personally enjoyed God's support. Watt even offended mainstream rock music fans by banning the musical group the Beach Boys from performing on the mall during July 4th festivities in Washington, D.C., an action that troubled even the president and the first lady, who were fans.

While Watt had his staunch supporters, who saw him as an agent for real change in Washington, in time they could not stave off calls for his resignation. By fall 1983 administration insiders were calling for Watt's departure on politically pragmatic grounds alone. In his letter of resignation, Watt acknowledged that "a different type of leadership" would best serve the president. National Security Adviser **William Patrick Clark,** an old friend of Reagan, took Watt's place.

Watt is married to Leilani Bomgardner. They have two children.

Suggested Readings: Deanne Kloepfer, *The Watt/Clark Record* (1984); Jonathan Lasch, *A Season of Spoils: The Story of the Reagan Administration's Attack on the Environment* (1984); James Watt, *The Courage of a Conservative* (1985).

Related Entry: Environment.

WEBSTER, WILLIAM H. (March 6, 1924, St. Louis, Mo.– .) Director, Federal Bureau of Investigation, 1978–1987; Director, Central Intelligence Agency, 1987–1991.

William Webster became the first person to head both the Federal Bureau of Investigation (FBI) and the Central Intelligence Agency (CIA). Webster received his B.A. from Amherst (1947) and law degree from Washington University in St. Louis (1949). He served as both the U.S. attorney general and as a district court judge for the Eastern District of Missouri. In 1973, he was promoted to the U.S. Court of Appeals, a post he left in 1978 to take over as the director of the FBI. At the time, it was a troubled agency due to allegations of misconduct under its only previous director, J. Edgar Hoover. After a decade with the FBI, during which he helped reestablish morale at the agency and restore its esteem with the public, President Ronald Reagan nominated him to become director of the CIA. As was the FBI, the CIA was in a state of turmoil, growing from several recent spy scandals and the **Iran-contra affair,** in which former CIA director **William Joseph Casey** had been implicated. Even though Webster lacked foreign policy experience, he easily won confirmation. Webster retired from the CIA in 1991. He left an agency that was on the verge of having to redefine its mission, from one that focused on the **Soviet Union** to one that did not, due to the end of the cold war.

Suggested Readings: Brian Duffy, "A New Spy Order at the CIA," *U.S. News & World Report,* May 20, 1991; Stephen Engleberg, "William Webster," *New York Times Biographical Service,* December 1988, p. 1281; William Webster, *The Search for Justice* (1983).

WEDTECH SCANDAL. In the mid-1980s, several of President Reagan's top advisers and former aides, including Attorney General **Edwin Meese**

III, **Michael Keith Deaver,** and **Lyn Nofziger,** along with a number of prominent Democratic politicians, became embroiled in the Wedtech scandal. In 1981 and 1982, Welbilt Wedtech (Wedtech for short), a defense firm, had sought Department of the Army contracts to manufacture standard engines. As a minority-owned business, it qualified for contracts awarded under a special no-bid basis. Wedtech enlisted the help of E. Robert Wallach, a long-time friend of Meese, to help win the contract. Wallach solicited Meese's help. When an independent prosecutor was appointed to determine if Meese's actions on the behalf of Wallach constituted a violation of the law, further complications arose. Meese was represented by Wallach in this investigation, leading some to charge that this impeded Meese's own investigation of possible improper activities by Wallach. Nofziger, New York congressman Mario Biaggi, and several other prominent New York politicians were similarly implicated in a variety of questionable actions.

In 1987, Nofziger was indicted and convicted for breaching the 1978 Government Ethics Act in connection with Wedtech's attempt to gain a government contract. His conviction was overturned in 1988. Biaggi was convicted on corruption charges and expelled from the U.S. House of Representatives. Meese was never indicted for violating the law, but the scandal induced his resignation as attorney general.

Suggested Readings: *Facts on File* (1987); *Facts on File,* (1988); *Historic Documents* (1988) p. 496.

Related Entry: House of Representatives, United States.

WEIDENBAUM, MURRAY LEW. (February 10, 1927, Bronx, N.Y.– .) Chairman, Council of Economic Advisers, 1981–1982.

In January 1981, President Ronald Reagan nominated Murray Weidenbaum, an economics professor at the University of Washington and a member of the conservative think tank, the American Enterprise Institute, to chair the Council of Economic Advisers. One of Weidenbaum's advantages was that he already had governmental experience, having served as the assistant secretary of the treasury during the first two years of the Richard Nixon administration. While the basic structure of the president's economic policy had already been established by other Reagan aides, such as **David Alan Stockman,** Weidenbaum was expected to help gain passage of Reagan's programs. He pushed Congress to foster **deregulation,** accept the president's proposed budget and a tax cut, and, perhaps most important, to accept the administration's argument that these policies would produce a balanced budget and a growing economy. When the **U.S. economy** went into a recession, Weidenbaum argued that it would be short-lived and that the pain was part of the necessary medicine to curing the ill of high **inflation.**

As the **budget deficit** began to grow, Weidenbaum backed away from one of the fundamentals of **Reaganomics,** that a balanced budget would accompany the tax cuts. Rather he suggested that a balanced budget was not "one of the fundamentals of the program for economic recovery." Shortly after Weidenbaum made this statement, he abruptly resigned. This led some to argue that Weidenbaum disagreed with Reagan's unwillingness to modify his program so as to decrease the growth of the budget deficit. Others, however, linked Weidenbaum's departure to the severity of the recession, casting him as the fall guy for the Reagan administration.

Weidenbaum was raised in Brooklyn, the son of a Jewish taxicab driver. He attended public high school and earned his B.A. from the City College of New York (1948), an M.A. from Columbia University (1949), and a second master's degree and a Ph.D. from Princeton University (1958). During the 1950s and 1960s he worked in both the private and public sectors as an economist, writing noteworthy articles on the defense industry. Weidenbaum became an expert on revenue sharing, a goal he promoted while a member of the Richard Nixon administration. During the latter half of the 1970s, Weidenbaum headed the Center for the Study of American Business at Washington University, which explored the history of free enterprise in the United States. This included a major study that calculated the cost of regulation, which served as ammunition for the deregulatory policies of the Reagan administration. Weidenbaum is married to the former Phyllis Green. They have three children.

Suggested Readings: *Current Biography* (1982) p. 434; Murray Weidenbaum, *The Future of Business Regulation* (1979); Murray Weidenbaum, *Rendezvous with Reality: The American Economy after Reagan* (1988).

Related Entries: Deregulation; Recessions.

WEINBERGER, CASPAR WILLARD. (August 18, 1917, San Francisco, Calif.– .) Secretary of Defense, 1981–1987.

Caspar Weinberger was one of President Ronald Reagan's most influential cabinet members. As secretary of defense from 1981 until 1987, when he resigned in the midst of the **Iran-contra affair,** he directed the

Defense Secretary Caspar Weinberger in Situation Room, May 18, 1987. Reagan Library.

biggest peacetime military buildup in U.S. history. Throughout his tenure he was considered a hawk and a staunch advocate of increasing the size of the nation's arsenal. Weinberger lobbied Congress hard to appropriate funds for a vast array of weapons, from the **MX (missile, experimental) missile** to the **Strategic Defense Initiative (Star Wars).** He supported selling arms, such as the **Airborne Warning and Control System (AWACS),** to even lukewarm allies of the United States. He backed the president's decision to invade of **Grenada,** attack **Libya,** and backed the contras in **Nicaragua.**

Weinberger received his B.A. (1938) and law degree (1941) from Harvard University. He served in the army for four years during World War II and clerked for two federal judges. After completing his clerkships, he went to work for the San Francisco law firm of Heller, Ehrman, White & McAuliffe. In 1952 he was elected to the California State Legislature and in the 1960s, after leaving this body, he became one of the leaders of the state's Republican Party. He was one of Ronald Reagan's earliest and closest advisers.

From 1972 to 1973 Weinberger headed the Office of Management and Budget under President Richard Nixon, earning the nickname "Cap the Knife" for his ability to cut spending. From 1973 until 1975 he served as Secretary of Health, Education and Welfare. Between 1975, when he left Washington, and 1981, when he returned as secretary of defense, Weinberger worked as an executive with the Bechtel Group, the large construction firm where **George Pratt Shultz** worked.

In June 1992 a federal grand jury indicted Weinberger on five felony counts of lying to Congress and obstructing justice during the Iran-contra investigation. Ironically, along with George Shultz, Weinberger had not been an advocate of the scheme to divert funds obtained from arm sales to the Iranians to the contras. Weinberger pleaded not guilty to all the charges, adamantly insisting that he was the target of a vendetta launched by the special prosecutor, **E. Lawrence Walsh.** In late September 1992 a federal judge dismissed the charge of obstructing justice. On Christmas Eve 1992, President George Bush pardoned Weinberger on all the remaining charges. Walsh reacted with astonishment, stating, "It's hard to find an adjective strong enough to characterize a president who has such contempt for honesty—and such a lack of sensitivity to the picture of a president protecting a cabinet officer who lies to Congress."

Weinberger is married to the former Jane Dalton, and they have two children. In 1990 he wrote *Fighting for Peace,* which credited the arms buildup during the Reagan years with winning the cold war.

Suggested Readings: H. Haflendorn and J. Schissler, eds., *The Reagan Administration: A Recontruction of American Strength* (1988); Caspar Weinberger, *Fighting for Peace: Seven Critical Years in the Pentagon* (1990).

Related Entry: Defense Spending.

WELFARE. Ronald Reagan's condemnation of welfare stood at the center of his program and his appeal to the American public. During his campaign for governor of California, in 1966, Reagan linked "welfare cheats" with wasteful government spending, high taxes, and urban riots. As a candidate for president and while in the White House, he repeated this claim, lashing out at big government and liberal social programs left over from the 1960s. However, neither as governor of California nor as president did he achieve the dismantling of the modern welfare system. Certain programs were cut and spending for others was reduced, but the welfare system itself remained intact.

Early on in his presidency, Reagan called for a reduction in spending for a number of domestic programs, including urban aid, medicare, food stamps, and subsidies for school meals. Early in his administration, he managed to get Congress to terminate the Comprehensive Employment Training Administration (CETA), which provided job training for the chronically unemployed. Reagan also convinced Congress to slash funding for public housing. As a result, by the time he left office, the ratio between federal dollars spent on defense compared to that spent on human resources, which encompassed various welfare programs, had flip-flopped. In 1980 approximately 28 percent of the federal budget went for human resources and about 22 percent to defense, but by 1987, 28 percent of the federal budget went to pay for defense and only about 22 percent for human resources. However, overall spending on social programs continued to rise, especially for the two biggest entitlements, Social Security and medicare. While Congress cut funding for other welfare programs, it never reduced spending as much as he proposed. Moreover, Reagan himself refused to push for cuts in social security and proposed only minor reforms in medicare. As **David Alan Stockman,** Reagan's director of the Office of Management and Budget, argued, the president chose for political reasons not to take aim at the most popular entitlements, thus ensuring an increase in the deficit and undercutting his own philosophical criticisms of the dangers of a strong central government.

In his final two years in office, Reagan turned away from abolishing welfare to working with Congress on reforming the welfare system. On October 13, 1988, following long and arduous negotiations, he signed into law the Family Support Act of 1988, perhaps the biggest change in the welfare system since the creation of the New Deal. It directed states to move capable Aid for Families with Dependent Children (AFDC) recipients off the welfare rolls. In return, the bill promised child care and additional support for women who participated in the program. (States were given leeway to tailor their own programs to fit the broad goal of helping single parents with children move into the workforce.) Reagan also signed into law a bill that reformed medicare, expanding coverage to include catostrophic illnesses while at the same time increasing premiums.

During the 1988 campaign, both presidential candidates, George Bush and **Michael Stanley Dukakis,** spoke in favor welfare reform. However, as president, Bush did little on this front. In August 1990 a White House Domestic Policy Council issued an options paper on welfare. Lacking a clear emphasis, it went nowhere. Welfare reform was further stalled by the **Persian Gulf War** and by Democratic opposition to reducing welfare payments. As some noted, recipients of AFDC had already suffered from a reduction in benefits in real terms, in spite of the fact that overall spending on AFDC had gone up. Not surprisingly, during the 1992 campaign, welfare cropped up as a major political issue. **William (Bill) Jefferson Clinton** promised to end welfare as the nation knew it, and then Bush chimed in, promising further reforms.

Suggested Readings: Dilys M. Hill, "Domestic Policy in an Era of Negative Government," in *The Reagan Presidency: An Incomplete Revolution?*, ed. Dilys M. Hill, Raymond A. Moore and Phil Williams, (1990); Michael B. Katz, *The Undeserving Poor: From the War on Poverty to the War on Welfare* (1989); Frances Fox Piven and Richard Cloward, *The New Class War: Reagan's Attack on the Welfare State and Its Consequences* (1982).

Related Entries: Domestic Policy; Election of 1992; Poverty.

WIRTHLIN, RICHARD BITNER. (March 15, 1931, Salt Lake City, Ut.–) Political Strategist for Ronald Reagan, 1980–1981.

Richard Wirthlin served as a political strategist for Ronald Reagan during both of his campaigns and during the early years of his presidency. Wirthlin earned his B.S. from the University of Utah in 1956 and his M.A. (1957) and Ph.D. (1964) in economics from the University of California at Berkeley. A specialist in statistics and polling, he chaired the Department of Economics at Brigham Young University from 1964 to 1969. Simultaneously he developed a private consulting firm. In 1969 he left academia to concentrate on his own business, first as president and chairman of the board of directors of Decision/Making Information and then as the chief operating officer of the Wirthlin Group (both located in MacLean, Va.).

Based on his political expertise, he joined the Ronald Reagan–George Bush presidential campaign in 1980, working as their chief pollster. As the election approached, he worked as the director of planning and evaluation. Many credited Wirthlin and his polling for the directions that Reagan took during the campaign and in his first year in office. In part due to Wirthlin's data, Reagan focused on cutting taxes and increasing **defense spending**, rather than on more divisive, social issues. In addition, Wirthlin helped the president identify certain wedge issues that strengthened Reagan's support among traditional Democratic voters both in the South and in many blue-collar suburbs.

Wirthlin is married to Jeralie Chandler. They have three children.

Suggested Reading: Lou Cannon, *Reagan* (1982).

Related Entry: Election of 1980.

WOMEN'S RIGHTS. The Ronald Reagan–George Bush years were often described as the worst of times for women in America. In a widely read book published in 1991, Susan Faludi contended that they were years of "backlash" (*Backlash*). Evidence of this could be seen in politics, culture, and economics, she contended. The Equal Rights Amendment (one of the core goals of the women's movement, which had neared ratification by the states during the mid-1970s) lay dead, a victim of the **New Right** campaign against it. The right to an **abortion** stood on the verge of being overturned by Reagan appointees to the **Supreme Court.** Right-to-life groups had helped defeat numerous prochoice candidates on the local, state, and federal level. The call for traditional values, Faludi and other feminists contended, displayed the backlash against the women's movement. **Poverty** among women was on the increase. Even the entertainment world, according to Faludi and others, illustrated this backlash. All of a sudden, female actresses were finding it difficult to obtain parts in which they could play strong women. As one critic observed, perhaps the strongest female part during the 1980s was *Tootsie,* which was played by a man dressed as a woman.

However, Faludi captured only part of the picture. In spite of Presidents Reagan's and Bush's championing of traditional values, by 1990 only 26 percent of all households consisted of a traditional family (defined as a husband, a wife, and children under age eighteen living at home), down from 40 percent in 1970. By 1983 the percentage of women in the workforce reached 50 percent, and this number continued to grow. While many women encountered a glass ceiling, which limited their ability to advance in the workplace, overall the earnings gap between men and women narrowed. The number of professional women, such as doctors, lawyers, and professors, skyrocketed. Even though feminists did not gain comparable worth legislation, the federal government provided tax credits for child care and momentum for federal parental leave legislation built. Furthermore, the Clarence Thomas–Anita Hill hearings brought the issue of sexual harassment to the fore and helped a number of women candidates win election in 1992.

Lastly, Faludi and most other feminists down played the fact that in spite of the traditional values rhetoric, both Reagan and Bush appointed several prominent women to top posts. **Jeane Jordan Kirkpatrick** served as Reagan's ambassador to the United Nations and achieved more prominence in the field of foreign policy than had any woman in U.S.

history. **Elizabeth Hanford Dole** served in the cabinets of both Reagan and Bush. **Sandra Day O'Connor** became the first female **Supreme Court** justice, and **Margaret Debardeleben Tutwiler** worked as a presidential spokesperson. Even during the 1970s, the era in which the women's movement seemed flush with success, women had not held so many high government posts.

Suggested Readings: Sylvia Bashevkin, "Confronting Neo-Conservatism: The Anglo-American Women's Movement under Thatcher, Reagan and Mulroney," *International Political Science Review* (July 1994) vol. 15, p. 275; Flora Davis, *Moving Mountains* (1991); Susan Faludi, *Backlash* (1991).

Related Entry: Thomas-Hill Hearings.

WRIGHT, JAMES (JIM) CLAUDE. (December 22, 1922, Fort Worth, Tex.– .) Speaker, U.S. House of Representatives, 1987–1989.

During the 1980s, Jim Wright, a Democratic congressman from Texas, was one of the most powerful people in Washington. He dutifully served as the House majority leader throughout most of Ronald Reagan's tenure, rallying Democrats against the president's policies on many occasions. When House Speaker **Thomas (Tip) Philip O'Neill, Jr.,** announced that he would not seek reelection, Wright achieved his long-term goal to become speaker of the House. However, not long after he assumed the top spot in Congress, scandals regarding his behavior began to emerge. The nonprofit watchdog group Common Cause called for the House Ethics Committee to investigate royalties that he had received from his book, *Reflections of a Public Man* (1984), which some cast as a payoff for political favors. Others questioned Wright's dealings with federal bank officials, which were charged with regulating troubled savings and loan banks with which Wright had ties. For over a year charges and countercharges flew back and forth between Wright's accusers, such as Republican **Newton (Newt) Leroy Gingrich,** and Wright himself. Finally, on May 31, 1989, Wright declared he would give up his post as speaker and resign from the House of Representatives, thus bringing to an end one of the more remarkable political careers in modern political history. He was never convicted of any wrongdoing.

Wright studied at the University of Texas and then enlisted in the army when World War II broke out. At war's end, Wright quickly involved himself in politics, successfully running for the state legislature in 1946. He quickly earned a reputation as a staunch liberal due to his support for various **civil rights** measures. These positions eventually cost Wright his seat (in 1949), but they did not end his political career, as he became mayor of Weatherford, Tex., and president of the League of Texas Municipalities. In 1954 he defeated Democratic incumbent Wingate Lucas in the congressional primary and went on to defeat his Republican opponent. For the following thirty-five years, his Fort Worth district dutifully reelected him every two years. While Wright was initially considered very liberal, in the 1970s and 1980s he moderated his views and stances. For example, in 1978 the liberal group Americans for Democratic Action rated Wright as having voted favorably only 45 percent of the time.

In 1972 he married a former staff member, Betty Hay. They have four children. Wright also has a daughter from a previous marriage, which ended in divorce.

Suggested Readings: John M. Barry, *The Ambition and the Power* (1989); *Current Biography* (1979) p. 45.

Related Entry: House of Representatives, United States.

Y

YELTSIN, BORIS NIKOLAYEVICH. (February 1, 1931, Sverdlovsk, Soviet Union– .) President of Russia, 1991– .

Boris Yeltsin was trained as an engineer and became a member of the Communist Party in 1961. When **Mikhail Sergeyevich Gorbachev** assumed power in 1985, Yeltsin assumed the post of first secretary of the Moscow City Party Committee. He quickly established himself as an adversary of hard-liners within the Communist Party and as a critic of Gorbachev, arguing that reform was proceeding too slowly. A charismatic and sometimes temperamental leader, he quickly gained a strong following. While Gorbachev was still in power, many Americans distrusted Yeltsin, seeing him as power hungry and unstable. However, after Yeltsin stood up to the military coup that sought to depose of Gorbachev, he gained a good deal of admiration in the United States.

Following the coup it quickly became clear to the George Bush administration that Yeltsin, and not Gorbachev, was the most important Russian leader. Accepting this shift in power as a fait accompli, the Bush administration determined that it needed to develop good relations with him. In January 1992, U.S. Secretary of State **James (Jim) Addison Baker III** announced that United States would initiate an emergency airlift of food to the former Soviet Republics. Shortly afterward, Yeltsin traveled to the United States to attend a special summit of fifteen leaders at the United Nations. During the trip he met with President Bush at Camp David and addressed a joint session of Congress. Later in the year, Yeltsin attended the annual G-7 (Group of Seven) economic summit, where he gained a $24 billion aid package for Russia. At the end of the year, President Bush and Yeltsin signed the **Strategic Arms Reduction Treaty (START)**, dramatically reducing the number of nuclear weapons held by the two nations.

Suggested Readings: Michael R. Beschlos and Strobe Talbot, *At the Highest Level* (1994); Neil Felshman, *Gorbachev, Yeltsin and the Last Days of the Soviet Empire* (1992); Vladimir Solovev, *Boris Yeltsin* (1992); Boris Yeltsin, *Against the Grain* (1990).

Related Entries: Communism, Collapse of; Summits, Economic (G-7).

YUPPIES. During the mid-1980s, *yuppies* became the moniker for the baby boomer generation. *Newsweek* called 1984 the "Year of the Yuppie." Other magazines, newspapers, and television spokespersons, from newscasters to late-night television hosts, paid much attention to this group of Americans. Standing for Young, Upwardly mobile, Urban Professionals, the term *yuppies* was never very precise. It meant different things to different people at different times. Some considered yuppies to be the hippies or radicals of the 1960s—or their younger brothers and sisters—who had grown up and gone to work on Wall Street, Madison Avenue, or at some other corporate address. Others used the term *yuppies* to describe the generation that had come of age since the 1960s. Enjoying the benefits of the economic boom of the mid-1980s, yuppies supposedly rejected the rebellious ideas of the 1960s in favor of Ronald Reagan's domestic agenda. For example, Jerry Rubin, a famous antiwar protester of the 1960s, turned to helping young professionals network so as to further their careers. In addition, whether *yuppies* stood as a term of admiration or denigration depended in part on who used it and on what occasion. Even the exact number of people who actually fit the media's loose definition of the term was a matter of dispute. While those who used the term as a means to argue that the 1980s had given rise to a widespread phenomenon, economists noted that only about 5 percent of the baby-boom generation earned enough to qualify as yuppies. Many men and women who were technically yuppies disagreed sharply with President Reagan's conservative social and cultural views and his **foreign policy**.

Suggested Readings: Bill Barol, "The Eighties Are Over," *Newsweek*, January 4, 1988, p. 40; Joseph Barry, ed., *Yuppies Invade My House at Dinnertime* (1987); Douglas Foster, "Post-Yuppie America," *Mother Jones*, February–March 1992, p. 16.

TIMELINE

1980	
Nov. 4	Ronald Wilson Reagan elected president.
1981	
Jan. 20	Ronald Reagan inaugurated as fortieth president; 52 American hostages held in Iran since November 1979 released.
Jan. 23	Labor Department reports that the inflation rate was 12.4 percent in 1980, second double-digit increase in two years.
Feb. 18	President Reagan proposes increased defense spending, decreased taxes, and domestic spending in speech to Congress.
Feb. 23	State Department releases "White Paper" which claims that rebels in El Salvador are receiving aid from Cuba, Soviet Union, and other communist regimes.
March 6	Reagan administration announces plan to sell AWACS and other advanced weapons to Saudi Arabia.
March 10	President Reagan sends budget proposal for fiscal year 1982 to Congress. Calls for spending $695.3 billion, with a projected deficit of $45 billion. Budget includes making budget cuts for 200 programs, in addition to those previously proposed by Jimmy Carter.
March 18	Secretary of State Alexander Haig claims that the Soviet Union is promoting terrorism and seeks to establish a beachhead in Central America.
March 20	In Poland, Solidarity declares nationwide strike.

March 30	John W. Hinckley, Jr., attempts to assassinate Reagan outside Washington Hilton. James Brady (Reagan's press secretary), a Secret Service agent, and a Washington, D.C., policeman are also shot.
April 1	Aid to Nicaragua ($15 million) suspended by the United States due to Nicaraguan support of leftist rebels in El Salvador.
April 11	President Reagan returns to the White House from the hospital.
April 24	Grain embargo on the Soviet Union lifted by Reagan.
May 2	Reagan's policy toward Central America and proposed cuts in social spending are the focus of the largest antiwar demonstration in the capitol since Vietnam War ended.
May 4	Federal Reserve Board increases discount rate again, to 14 percent, as part of its effort to curb inflation.
May 6	United States expels Libyan diplomats and closes Libya's Washington, D.C., mission.
May 7	House of Representatives approves Reagan's budget, 270–154.
May 13	Pope John Paul II shot in Vatican.
June 3	Supreme Court Justice Potter Stewart announces his retirement, as of July 3, 1981.
July 7	President Reagan nominates Sandra Day O'Connor to fill Stewart's seat on the Court.
July 16	Reagan administration declares that it favors a political, not a military, solution in El Salvador.
July 21	President Reagan attends first G-7 economic summit in Canada.
July 29	Prince Charles of England marries Lady Diana Spencer. Modified tax cut passed by U.S. House of Representatives, 238–195.
August 3–5	Air traffic controllers union goes on strike. President Reagan fires striking workers.
August 13	President Reagan signs tax cut, which will reduce top bracket by 25 percent over three years, into law.
Sept. 19	Over 250,000 labor union members join anti-Reagan demonstration in Washington, D.C.
Sept. 25	Sandra Day O'Connor sworn in as first female Supreme Court justice in U.S. history.
Oct. 2	As part of the military buildup, President Reagan declares that the United States will build B-1 bomber and MX missiles. The latter will be temporarily based in existing silos.

Oct. 6	Egyptian President Anwar Sadat assassinated in Cairo.
Nov. 6	Unemployment up to 8 percent in October, suggesting that the economy has entered a recession.
Nov. 18	In a televised address, President Reagan declares he will not deploy Pershing and other intermediate-range nuclear missiles in Europe if the Soviet Union agrees to dismantle similar weapons.
Nov. 30	United States and Soviet Union commence arms control talks in Geneva.
Dec. 10	Reagan calls for Americans to leave Libya as relations worsen between that two countries.
Dec. 13	Solidarity leaders are arrested and martial law declared in Poland.
Dec. 14	Israel officially annexes the Golan Heights, which it has held since the 1967 "Seven Days' War."
Dec. 18	United States supports United Nation's resolution condemning Israel's annexation of the Golan Heights.
Dec. 23	Limited sanctions against Poland announced by U.S. government.
Dec. 28	Declaring that the Soviet Union is responsible for the crackdown in Poland, President Reagan places economic sanctions on it.

1982

Jan. 4	National Security Adviser Richard Allen resigns. William P. Clark is to take his place.
Jan. 8	AT&T broken up into twenty-two "baby bells"; Justice Department drops antitrust suit against IBM.
Jan. 26	Reagan calls for "New Federalism" in state of the union address.
Jan. 28	A massacre in El Salvador by government forces is reported by press.
Feb. 24	Reagan proposes an economic and military plan for the Caribbean.
March 4	General John Vessey, Jr., named head of Joint Chiefs of Staff.
March 10	Embargo of Libya announced by Reagan administration.
March 31	President Reagan denounces nuclear freeze movement.
April 2–3	Falkland Islands War begins.
April 15	Reagan administration presents a school voucher plan.
April 22	Right-wing leader Robert d'Aubuisson elected president of El Salvador.
April 23	Inflation declines 0.3 percent, the first drop in a year.

April 30	United States declares its support for Great Britain in the Falkland Islands War.
May 7	Unemployment for the month of April is up to 9.4 percent, the worst since World War II, as the recession deepens.
June 12	A massive nuclear freeze demonstration takes place in New York City.
June 21	John W. Hinckley, Jr., found not guilty by reason of insanity.
June 25	Alexander Haig resigns as secretary of state. George Shultz is nominated to succeed him.
June 30	Equal Rights Amendment to the Constitution dies.
July 19	Poverty rate rises to 14 percent, the highest since 1967.
July 22	Murray L. Weidenbaum, chairman of the Council of Economic Advisers, resigns.
July 27	Reagan administration certifies that El Salvador is making progress in human rights.
August 1	Martin S. Feldstein named as new chairman of the Council of Economic Advisers.
August 9	John W. Hinckley, Jr., committed indefinitely to mental institution.
August 25	U.S. Marines join peacekeeping force in Beirut, Lebanon.
August 28	Human rights violations on the rise according to U.S. embassy and Catholic Church in El Salvador.
Sept. 13	Special prosecutor reports that Labor Secretary Raymond Donovan has committed no crimes.
Oct. 1	Balanced Budget Amendment to the Constitution fails in the House of Representatives.
Oct. 15	Agreement to sell grain to the Soviet Union is announced.
Nov. 2	Democrats gain twenty-six seats in the House of Representatives midterm election. The number of Democrats and Republicans in the Senate remains the same.
Nov. 5	Unemployment up to 10.4 percent as recession peaks.
	Don Hodel nominated to replace James Watt, who had resigned as secretary of interior.
Nov. 10	Soviet leader Leonid Brezhnev dies and is replaced by Yuri Andropov.
Dec. 7	Congress refuses to fund the MX missile.
Dec. 16	Environmental Protection Agency (EPA) head Anne Burford (Gorsuch) cited for contempt by the House of Representatives.

1983

Jan. 3	Presidential commission forms to study alternative ways to base the MX missile.
Jan. 5	Five cents per gallon gasoline tax increase signed into law by President Reagan.
Jan. 12	Margaret Heckler to replace Richard Schweiker as head of the Department of Health and Human Services.
	Kenneth Adelman to succeed Eugene Rostow as head of the Arms Control and Disarmament Agency.
Jan. 21	Inflation way down to 3.9 percent, from 8.9 percent in 1982.
Jan. 25	In state of the union address, President Reagan calls for a freeze of domestic spending and continued increases in military spending.
Feb. 4	Unemployment declines to 10.4 percent, down from 10.8 percent in January, as signs of an end to the recession emerge.
Feb. 7	Environmental Protection Agency (EPA) official Rita Lavelle dismissed by Reagan.
March 9	Anne Burford (Gorsuch) resigns as head of EPA, to be replaced by William Ruckelshaus.
March 23	In a nationally televised address, President Reagan calls for development of space-based antiballistic missile system, or Strategic Defense Initiative (Star Wars).
April 11	A presidential commission calls for production of 100 MX missiles to be based in existing silos.
April 18	A bomb explodes at the U.S. embassy in Beirut, Lebanon, killing sixty, including seventeen Americans.
April 20	Social security reform bill signed into law by President Reagan.
	Government reports that GNP rose dramatically in first quarter of 1983, signaling the end of the recession.
May 25	Funds for the MX missile released by Congress.
June 7	Relations between the United States and Nicaragua deteriorate, as the United States orders twenty-one Nicaraguan officials to leave the country immediately in response to the expulsion of U.S. diplomats from Nicaragua.
June 18	Reagan to nominate Paul Volcker to second term as head of the Federal Reserve Board.
July 1	Final phase of the tax cut goes into effect.

August 21	Benigno Aquino, leader of the opposition in the Philippines, is assassinated.
August 27	Massive civil rights march takes place in Washington, D.C., on the anniversary of the Great March of 1963.
Sept. 1	Korean Airline flight 007 shot down by Soviet airplane.
Sept. 21	Gross national product (GNP) grew at 9.7 percent in the second quarter according to the government, providing evidence of the recovery of the economy.
Oct. 5	AFL-CIO endorses Walter Mondale for Democratic nomination for president.
Oct. 13	William Clark to become new secretary of interior.
Oct. 17	Robert McFarlane to replace Clark as national security adviser.
Oct. 23	Truck-bomb explodes at U.S. Marines headquarters in Beirut, Lebanon, killing over 225 Americans.
Oct. 25	U.S. military forces invade Grenada.
Nov. 18	Aid to Nicaraguan contras approved by Congress.
Dec. 8	U.S.-Soviet arms control talks in Geneva end without date for new ones set by United States or Soviet Union.
Dec. 12	Terrorists bomb U.S., French, and other embassies in Kuwait.

1984

Jan. 11	Kissinger Commission issues report recommending an $8 billion economic aid package and increased military aid to El Salvador.
Jan. 23	President Reagan nominates Edwin Meese to replace William French Smith as attorney general.
Jan. 25	Claiming in his state of the union address that there is "renewed energy and optimism," Reagan calls on Congress to cooperate in an effort to reduce the deficit.
Feb. 7	U.S. Marines to be withdrawn from Lebanon by end of the month.
March 20	School prayer amendment to the Constitution fails to gain necessary two-thirds majority in the Senate.
April 9	Nicaragua files suit in World Court against United States for placing mines in its harbor and supporting guerrilla raids.
April 10	Senate approves nonbinding resolution condemning mining of the Nicaraguan harbor.
April 30	Reagan signs scientific and cultural exchange accords with China while on a six-day journey there.

May 6	Napoleon Duarte, a moderate, elected president of El Salvador.
May 24	Five former El Salvadoran national guardsmen found guilty of the 1980 murder of U.S. churchwomen.
May 29	Saudi Arabia receives 400 Stinger missiles from the United States to help it defend itself as the Iran-Iraq war escalates.
June 22	Eleven Latin American nations meet in Columbia to discuss international debt crisis. They seek easing of terms of their loans.
June 25	U.S. Senate goes along with House of Representatives decision to cut off all aid to Nicaraguan contras.
July 18–19	Walter Mondale and Geraldine Ferraro nominated by Democratic Party for president and vice president, respectively.
August 22	Reagan and Bush renominated by Republican Party.
Sept. 20	Another suicide bombing in Lebanon, this one at the U.S. embassy annex, kills fourteen Americans.
Sept. 21	Congress and Reagan administration work out compromise on MX missile.
Oct. 7	Walter Mondale scores a victory against President Reagan in their first debate.
Oct. 21	Reagan performs much better in his second debate with Mondale.
Nov. 6	Reagan and Bush reelected in a landslide. Republicans maintain majority in the Senate; Democrats maintain comfortable margin in the House of Representatives.
Nov. 22	Secretary of State George Shultz and Soviet Foreign Minister Andrei Gromyko announce they will meet and restart arms talks in Geneva, Switzerland, in January 1985.
Dec. 3	Poisonous gas leaks from a Union Carbide plant in Bhopal, India, killing over 2,000 people.
Dec. 22	Bernie Goetz shoots four youths on a subway train in New York City.

1985

Jan. 8	Chief of Staff James Baker and Secretary of the Treasury Don Regan announce that they will swap jobs.
Jan. 20	Reagan inaugurated for a second term.
Jan. 30	Jeanne Kirkpatrick announces her resignation as ambassador to the United Nations.
Feb. 6	In state of the union address, Reagan urges Congress to adopt major tax reform.

March 11	Mikhail Gorbachev becomes new Soviet leader.
March 12	Soviet Union and United States resume arms control negotiations in Geneva, Switzerland.
March 15	Raymond Donovan resigns to fight charges that he committed fraud and larceny before becoming secretary of labor.
April 7	Gorbachev announces a moratorium on the deployment of medium-range nuclear missiles.
May 1	Reagan administration announces trade embargo against Nicaragua.
May 5	Reagan goes to Bitburg Cemetery in Germany during a longer trip to Europe.
June 14–30	Terrorists hijack a Trans World Airlines (TWA) flight from Athens, killing an American and holding others hostage. United States refuses to make concessions. All remaining passengers are finally released.
July 9	David Stockman announces that he will resign as head of Office of Management and Budget.
July 20	Martial law declared by government of South Africa.
August 8	Two Americans killed by terrorist car-bomb at U.S. air base in West Germany.
Sept. 9	Reagan administration announces limited economic sanctions against South Africa.
Oct. 7–11	Palestinian terrorists hijack cruise ship *Achille Lauro,* killing an American passenger. U.S. Air Force planes divert civilian airplane with the hijackers aboard and arrest the terrorists.
Oct. 18	The Defense Department announces that it will test all military personnel for acquired immunodeficiency syndrome (AIDS).
Nov. 19–20	Reagan and Gorbachev meet for first summit in Geneva.
Dec. 12	Reagan signs Gramm-Rudman deficit reduction bill.
1986	
Jan 28	Space shuttle *Challenger* explodes after takeoff, killing all seven crew members.
Feb. 4	In state of the union address, President Reagan focuses on the need to strengthen family values and cut the budget deficit.
Feb. 7	Haiti's President François (Papa Doc) Duvalier ousted, seeks asylum in France.

Feb. 22–25	Rebellion in Philippines leads to overthrow of Ferdinand Marcos.
March 18–19	Reagan and Canadian Prime Minister Brian Mulroney meet to discuss ways to reduce acid rain.
March 24–25	U.S. military planes shot at by Libyan missiles. United States retaliates by bombing Libyan military sites.
April 2	Terrorists bomb TWA flight enroute to Athens from Rome, killing four Americans.
April 5	Terrorists bomb disco in West Berlin, killing three U.S. soldiers.
April 13	U.S. planes bomb Libya in retaliation for alleged sponsorship of terrorism.
April 26	Nuclear power plant in Chernobyl, Ukraine, explodes, killing many and contaminating areas reaching as far west as France.
May 25	Major fund-raiser for the homeless held by the group Hands Across America.
May 29	Special prosecutor to investigate former Reagan aide Michael Deaver.
June 17	Supreme Court Chief Justice Warren Burger announces resignation. Reagan nominates William Rehnquist to be chief justice and names Anthony Scalia to the Court.
July 3–6	Statue of Liberty ceremonies held in New York City.
July 7	Supreme Court strikes down major provisions of Gramm-Rudman.
July 26	After sixteen months in captivity, American hostage freed in Lebanon.
August 16	U.S. Senate and House approve tax reform (Reagan signs on Oct. 22).
Sept. 14	President and Nancy Reagan, in joint news conference, announce "national crusade" against drugs.
Sept. 18	Philippines President Corazon Aquino addresses Congress.
Oct. 11–12	Reagan and Gorbachev meet at summit in Iceland.
Oct. 17	Congress passes antidrug bill and Simpson-Mazzoli immigration bill.
Nov. 4	In midterm elections the Democratic Party scores big, winning back control of Senate and increasing its majority in the House of Representatives.
Nov. 6	First reports of Iran-contra affair appear, describing the exchange of arms for hostages.

Nov. 14	Financier Ivan Boesky penalized $100 million for insider trading.
Nov. 25	Reagan administration acknowledges that Nicaraguan contras received funds from arms-for-hostages deal with Iran. National Security Adviser John Poindexter and Oliver North both resign.
Nov. 26	Tower Commission appointed to investigate Iran-contra affair.
Dec. 2	Frank Carlucci appointed new national security adviser.
Dec. 6	President Reagan admits that he made a "mistake" in decision to trade arms to Iran for hostages.
Dec. 11	South Africa declares near-total news blackout on black unrest.
Dec. 19	Lawrence Walsh named special prosecutor to investigate Iran-contra affair.
1987	
Jan 27	Gorbachev criticizes Communist Party and calls for major reform.
Feb. 2	Central Intelligence Agency (CIA) director William Casey resigns.
Feb. 3–4	President Reagan's veto of Water Quality Control Act overridden by House and Senate. Seen as victory for environmentalists.
Feb. 9	Robert McFarlane, former national security adviser and a major player in the Iran-contra affair, attempts suicide.
Feb. 26	Tower Commission releases report critical of Reagan administration, yet finds no criminal wrongdoing in Iran-contra affair.
Feb. 27	Reagan's chief of staff, Donald Regan, replaced by Howard Baker.
March 4	In televised address, Reagan accepts "responsibility" for the mistaken actions in the Iran-contra affair, although he admits no criminal wrongdoing.
March 23	The United States offers military protection to tankers in the Persian Gulf from fighting in the Iran-Iraq war.
March 25	Supreme Court upholds affirmative action.
April 2	U.S. Senate overrides Reagan's veto of public works program. (The House of Representatives had overridden his veto on March 31.)
April 22	Supreme Court upholds death penalty in a case that had ruled it was racially biased.

May 5	Iran-contra hearings begin.
May 8	Democratic presidential hopeful Gary Hart withdraws from race following reports that he had rendezvoused with model Donna Rice.
May 17	U.S. warship *Stark* hit by Iraqi missile in Persian Gulf; thirty-seven U.S. sailors killed.
May 19	William Webster becomes new director of CIA.
May 25	Raymond Donovan, former secretary of labor, acquitted of all criminal charges.
May 31	Reagan calls for widespread testing in his first speech on AIDS.
June 2	Alan Greenspan nominated to replace Paul Volcker as chairman of Federal Reserve Board.
June 16	Bernie Goetz acquitted of all charges stemming from subway shooting except for illegal gun possession charge.
July 1	Robert Bork nominated by President Reagan to replace retiring Supreme Court Justice Lewis Powell.
July 23	AIDS commission appointed by Reagan.
July 25	Secretary of Commerce Malcolm Baldrige killed during rodeo practice.
August 7	Costa Rica, El Salvador, Guatemala, Honduras, and Nicaragua sign tentative peace accord.
August 25	Stock market reaches record high. Dow Jones Industrial Average hits 2,722.42.
August 28	Coup fails in Philippines. United States displays support for Aquino.
Sept. 21	U.S. helicopters fire on Iranian ships laying mines in the Persian Gulf.
Oct. 1	Secretary of Transportation Elizabeth Dole resigns to devote her time to her husband's presidential campaign.
Oct. 3	Trade pact agreed to by United States and Canada.
Oct. 8	Jerry Falwell resigns as head of PTL.
Oct. 16	Tanker carrying U.S. flag in the Persian Gulf hit by Iranian missiles.
Oct. 19	Stock Market crashes. Dow Jones falls 508 points, in worst single-day decline in exchange's history.
Oct. 23	Robert Bork's nomination to Supreme Court rejected by U.S. Senate.
Oct. 29	Reagan nominates Douglas Ginsburg to Supreme Court.
Nov. 5	Defense Secretary Caspar Weinberger resigns. Reagan nominates Frank Carlucci to post.

Nov. 11	Reagan nominates Anthony Kennedy for vacant post on Supreme Court.
Nov. 18	Congress issues Iran-contra report, declaring that President Reagan must assume "ultimate responsibility" for the affair.
Dec. 8	At summit in Washington, D.C., President Reagan and Soviet President Gorbachev sign Intermediate-range Nuclear Forces (INF) Treaty.
Dec. 10	Trade deficit reaches record of $17.3 billion for one month. Michael Deaver found guilty of perjury.
Dec. 18	Ivan Boesky receives three-year prison sentence.
Dec. 21	Guilty verdict returned by jury for three of four white teenagers in Howard Beach (New York) racial incident.

1988

Feb. 3	Congress rejects aid to the contras. Anthony M. Kennedy confirmed to seat on Supreme Court.
Feb. 4	U.S. grand jury indicts Panamanian leader Manuel Noriega on drug charges.
Feb. 8	Robert Dole upsets Vice President George Bush in Iowa caucus.
Feb. 16	Bush and Michael Dukakis are big winners in New Hampshire primary.
March 16	United States sends troops to Honduras to guard against alleged incursions by Nicaraguan Sandinista forces.
March 23	Nicaraguan Sandinistas and contras sign cease-fire.
April 8	Former Reagan aide Lyn Nofziger sentenced to jail for breaking ethics law.
April 14	Agreement for Soviet troop withdrawal from Afghanistan is signed.
April 24	Secretary of Education William Bennett reports that education system in the United States is still "at risk."
May 16	Surgeon General C. Everett Koop issues report that terms cigarettes addictive drugs.
May 24	Reagan vetoes plant closing bill.
May 27	INF treaty ratified by U.S. Senate.
May 29–June 1	Reagan and Gorbachev hold summit in Moscow.
July 3	U.S. cruiser *Vincennes* mistakenly shoots down Iranian civilian airliner, killing all 290 passengers.
July 5	Attorney General Edwin Meese resigns.

July 7	Savings and loan crisis begins to become apparent. Cost of collapse of Texas institutions alone is estimated at $152 billion.
July 18–21	Democratic Party nominates Michael Dukakis and Lloyd Bentsen for president and vice president.
August 10	Bill to pay reparations to Japanese-Americans interned by U.S. government during World War II is signed by Reagan.
August 11	Dick Thornburgh confirmed as new Attorney General.
August 15–18	Republican Party nominates George Bush and Dan Quayle for president and vice president.
Sept. 25	Bush and Dukakis hold first presidential debate.
Oct. 13	Bush and Dukakis hold second presidential debate.
Oct. 22	Congress passes massive war on drugs legislation.
Nov. 8	Bush easily wins presidential election over Michael Dukakis, yet Democrats maintain majority in the House and Senate.
Nov. 30	Kohlberg, Kravis, and Roberts purchases RJR Nabisco for $25 billion in biggest corporate takeover ever.

1989

Jan. 4	U.S. and Libyan fighter jets clash over the Mediterranean Sea.
Jan. 11	President Reagan delivers farewell address.
Jan. 20	Bush inaugurated as forty-first president.
Jan. 23	Affirmative action programs narrowed by Supreme Court ruling regarding set-aside program for Richmond, Virginia.
Feb. 6	Savings and loan bailout plan unveiled by President Bush.
Feb. 15	Withdrawal of Soviet troops from Afghanistan completed.
March 3	Robert McFarlane sentenced in case stemming from Iran-contra affair.
March 17	Richard Cheney's nomination to be secretary of defense confirmed by U.S. Senate. Former Senator John Tower's nomination had been previously rejected.
March 24	Exxon *Valdez* runs aground in Alaskan waters, spilling massive amounts of oil into a key wilderness area.
April 5	Solidarity Party legalized in Poland.
April 18	Bill granting nearly $50 million in humanitarian aid to contras is signed by President Bush.
May 4	Colonel Oliver North convicted on charges stemming from Iran-contra affair.

May 31	Speaker of the House Jim Wright announces his resignation due to ethical misconduct.
June 4	Chinese troops crush demonstration in Tiananmen Square, Beijing.
June 5	U.S. sales of military weapons to China suspended by President Bush in response to China's crackdown on the prodemocracy movement.
June 6	Thomas Foley becomes new speaker of the House of Representatives.
June 14	Congress unable to override Bush's veto of bill to raise minimum wage.
June 21	Supreme Court overturns law prohibiting flag burning.
June 27	Lyn Nofziger's conviction overturned.
July 5	Colonel Oliver North fined $150,000 and sentenced to 1,200 hours of community service.
August 9	$166 billion bailout of savings and loans signed into law by President Bush.
August 24	Solidarity leader Tadeusz Mazowiecki becomes premier of Poland, one of the first signs of the collapse of communism in Eastern Europe.
Sept. 5	Bush unveils $7.9 billion war on drugs plan.
Sept. 20	F. W. de Klerk becomes Prime Minister in South Africa.
Sept. 27	Bush asserts that education is in need of widespread reform at a meeting of the nation's governors at the University of Virginia.
Oct. 23	Hungarians commemorate anniversary of 1956 uprising against Soviet domination.
Nov. 1	Compromise minimum wage bill approved by Congress.
Nov. 7	Blacks elected to key governmental posts. Douglas Wilder becomes first black governor in U.S. history, and David Dinkins becomes New York City's first black mayor.
Nov. 9	Berlin Wall falls, as East Germany opens its borders with West Germany.
Dec. 1	Communist Party relinquishes sole leadership in Eastern Germany.
Dec. 2–3	Bush and Gorbachev hold summit in Malta.
Dec. 7	Soviet Republic of Lithuania ends Communist Party's monopoly of power.
Dec. 12–17	Wave of democracy sweeps through Latin America. Central American nations sign peace plan. Chile's military dictator,

	Agusto Pinochet, loses election. Brazil holds first presidential election in nearly thirty years.
Dec. 20	U.S. forces invade Panama.
Dec. 22	Romania's communist leader, Nicolae Ceauşescu, flees the country.
Dec. 29	Vaclav Havel, foe of the Communist Party, elected leader of Czechoslovakia.
1990	
Jan. 3	Manuel Noriega surrenders to U.S. forces in Panama.
Jan. 28	Poland's Communist Party disbands.
Feb. 3	Reformer, Dimitur Popov, becomes Prime Minister in Bulgaria.
Feb. 11	Nelson Mandela, leader of the African National Congress, is released from prison in South Africa.
Feb. 13	An engine of corporate takeovers, Drexel Burnham Lambert brokerage firm, files for bankruptcy. The firm rose and fell with Michael Milken its star trader.
Feb. 25	Sandinista leader Daniel Ortega defeated by Violeta de Chamorro in presidential election in Nicaragua.
March 13	Communist Party's political monopoly comes to an end in the Soviet Union.
April 7	John Poindexter convicted on charges stemming from the Iran-contra affair.
	Controversial art exhibit by Robert Mapplethorpe charged with being obscene by grand jury.
April 24	Michael Milken, multimillionaire junk bond trader, pleads guilty to criminal charges.
June 1	Bush and Gorbachev sign trade and weapon agreements at a summit in Washington, D.C.
June 26	Bush reneges on famous "no new taxes" pledge.
July 6	North Atlantic Treaty Organization (NATO) to devise a new strategy in the wake of the end of the cold war.
July 16	Ukraine declares sovereignty.
August 2	Iraq invades Kuwait.
August 7	U.S. troops sent to Saudi Arabia by President Bush.
August 25	UN Security Council approves of resolution allowing for embargo and use of force against Iraq.
Oct. 2	David Souter confirmed as new Supreme Court justice.
Oct. 5	Robert Mapplethorpe and a Cincinnati contemporary arts center are aquitted on all obscenity charges.
Oct. 22	Civil Rights Act of 1990 vetoed by President Bush.

Oct. 27	Congress passes budget bill, which includes new taxes agreed to by President Bush. Amendments strengthening Clean Air Act passed by Congress.
Nov. 6	In midterm elections, Democrats increase their control of both houses of Congress.
Nov. 8	Bush increases number of U.S. troops in Saudi Arabia to 400,000.
Nov. 29	United Nations authorizes the use of force in the Persian Gulf against Iraq if its troops are not withdrawn from Kuwait by January 15, 1991.
1991	
Jan. 12	Congress passes a resolution approving the use of force in the Persian Gulf.
Jan. 17	U.S.-led forces commence air attacks on Iraq in Persian Gulf War.
Jan. 18	Iraq initiates scud missile attacks on Israel in an attempt to widen the Persian Gulf War.
Feb. 1	Apartheid laws to be repealed according to plan announced by South Africa's president, F. W. de Klerk.
Feb. 24	U.S. led forces commence ground offensive in Persian Gulf War.
Feb. 25	Scud missile fired by Iraq kills twenty-eight U.S. soldiers in Dahran, Saudi Arabia.
Feb. 27	Bush declares Kuwait liberated and orders ground assault halted, as Persian Gulf War comes to a rapid end with very few U.S. casualties.
March 3	Iraq accepts peace terms.
	Videotape shows Los Angeles policemen beating Rodney King.
April 4	EPA announces that the planet's ozone layer is being depleted by pollution.
April 21	The government reports that the United States has been in an economic recession since October 1990.
June 11	A $1.5 billion loan package to the Soviet Union approved by President Bush.
June 17	Legal foundation of apartheid repealed by South Africa's parliament.
June 27	Thurgood Marshall to resign from Supreme Court.
July 1	Warsaw Pact formally comes to an end.
July 5	Bank of Credit and Commerce International (BCCI) assets are seized.

July 10	Economic sanctions against South Africa are lifted by the United States.
July 22	A peace agreement between the Croatians and Serbs in the former Yugoslavian republic is rejected by Serbian nationalists.
July 31	Strategic Arms Reduction Talks I (START-I) Treaty signed by the United States and Soviet Union.
August 19–29	Coup against Gorbachev fails. Boris Yeltsin comes to power, and the Communist Party disbanded.
Sept. 25	Peace agreement signed by government and rebel forces in El Salvador.
Sept. 30	Jean-Bertrand Aristide, Haiti's democratically elected leader, is thrown out of power by a military junta.
Oct. 6–15	Confirmation hearings for Supreme Court nominee Clarence Thomas grab the nation's attention, as former Thomas aide Anita Hill accuses him of sexual harassment. Thomas nonetheless narrowly wins confirmation by full Senate.
Nov. 20	California Senator Alan Cranston reprimanded by U.S. Senate committee for his actions in association with the Keating Five scandal.
Dec. 4	Terry Anderson, the last American hostage in Lebanon, is released.
Dec. 8	A new nation, the Commonwealth of Independent States, takes the place of the former Soviet Union.

1992

Jan. 10	The government announces that unemployment rose to 7.1 percent in December as recession worsens.
Feb. 1	Bush and Yeltsin hold a summit at Camp David. Haitian refugees forcibly repatriated by U.S. Coast Guard.
Feb. 18	Bush and former Massachusetts Senator Paul Tsongas win the New Hampshire primaries (Republican and Democratic, respectively), although Republican challenger Pat Buchanan does surprisingly well.
Feb. 24	General Motors reports that it lost a record $4.45 billion in 1991, one further sign of the severity of the recession.
March 18	The Senate fails to override Bush's veto of a law that would have stripped China of its most-favored nation status.
April 9	Former Panamanian leader Manuel Noriega found guilty on drug charges.

April 29	Riots erupt in Los Angeles following not-guilty verdict in the trial of four white policemen who had been videotaped beating Rodney King.
May 7	Michigan ratifies the so-called Madison Amendment (which limits congressional ability to raise its own pay), making it the twenty-seventh Amendment to the U.S. Constitution.
May 13	Campaign finance reform bill vetoed by President Bush.
May 30	UN Security Council imposes sanctions against Yugoslavia for its support of Serbian forces in Bosnia and Herzegovina.
June 16	Bush and Yeltsin meet in Washington, D.C. Caspar Weinberger indicted on perjury and obstructing justice charges stemming out of the Iran-contra affair.
June 26	Lawrence Garrett, secretary of the navy, resigns due to Tailhook scandal.
June 29	Right to abortion upheld, five to four, by the Supreme Court. At the same time, the Court rules in *Casey* v. *Planned Parenthood* that Pennsylvania could restrict abortions.
July 1	Motor voter bill vetoed by President Bush.
July 16	Democratic Party nominates Bill Clinton and Albert Gore as its presidential and vice presidential candidates. Independent Ross Perot declares that he is withdrawing from the presidential race.
July 29	BCCI scandal leads to the indictment of Democratic Party leader Clark Clifford.
August 5	Four white police officers involved in Rodney King beating indicted of violating the federal Civil Rights Act of 1964.
August 12	United States, Canada, and Mexico agree to the North American Free Trade Agreement (NAFTA).
August 13	James Baker announces that he will resign as secretary of state to focus on Bush's presidential campaign.
August 20	Republican Party renominates Bush and Quayle.
Oct. 1	Ross Perot announces that he is back in the race for the presidency.
Oct. 5	Bush's veto of bill regulating Cable Television overridden by both houses of Congress.
Oct. 19	Perot, Clinton, and Bush hold the last of three presidential debates.
Nov. 3	Bill Clinton elected president. Both houses of Congress remain in the hands of the Democratic Party.

Dec. 9	U.S. troops lead an invasion of Somalia as part of the UN-sponsored Operation Restore Hope.
Dec. 24	Bush pardons Caspar Weinberger and several other former Reagan administration figures in connection with Iran-contra affair.
Dec. 31	President Bush tours Somalia.

1993

Jan. 20	Clinton inaugurated as forty-second president of the United States.

APPENDIX: A STATISTICAL PROFILE OF THE REAGAN-BUSH YEARS

The following figures provide a statistical profile of the Reagan-Bush years. Figure A.1 traces the approval ratings, measured by the Gallup Poll, of President Reagan and President Bush. It provides a visual representation of the ups and downs of these administrations from January 1981 to December 1992. Many of the graphs show the performance of the economy; others deal with government spending and debt.

Figure A.1
Approval Rating for Reagan and Bush: Do you approve or disapprove of the way the president is handling his job?

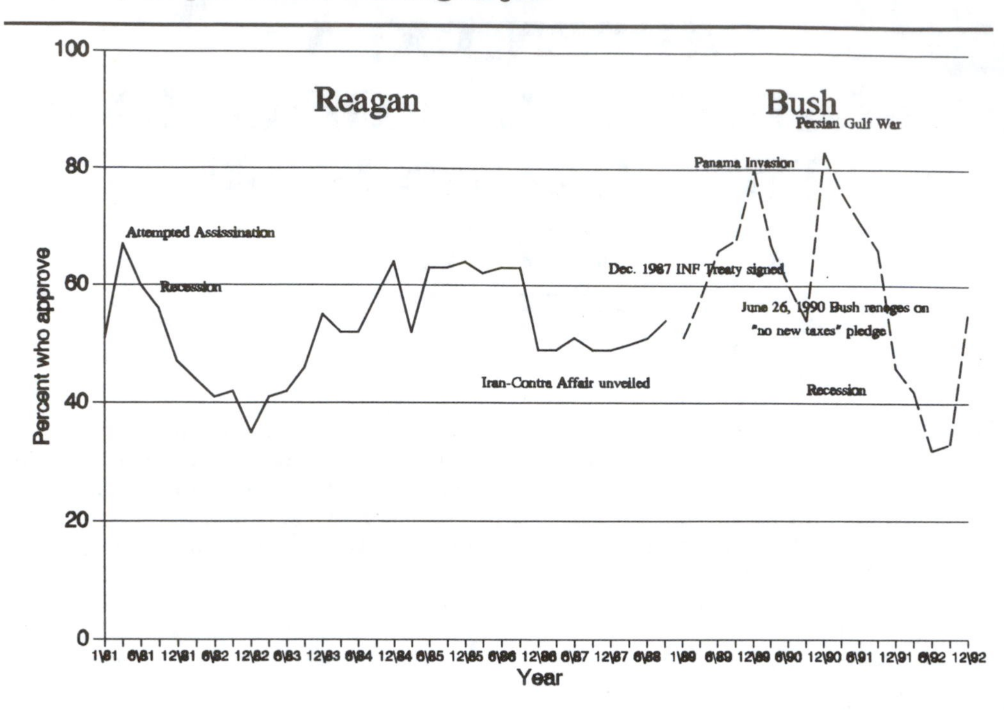

Figure A.2
Gross Domestic Product (1987 dollars)

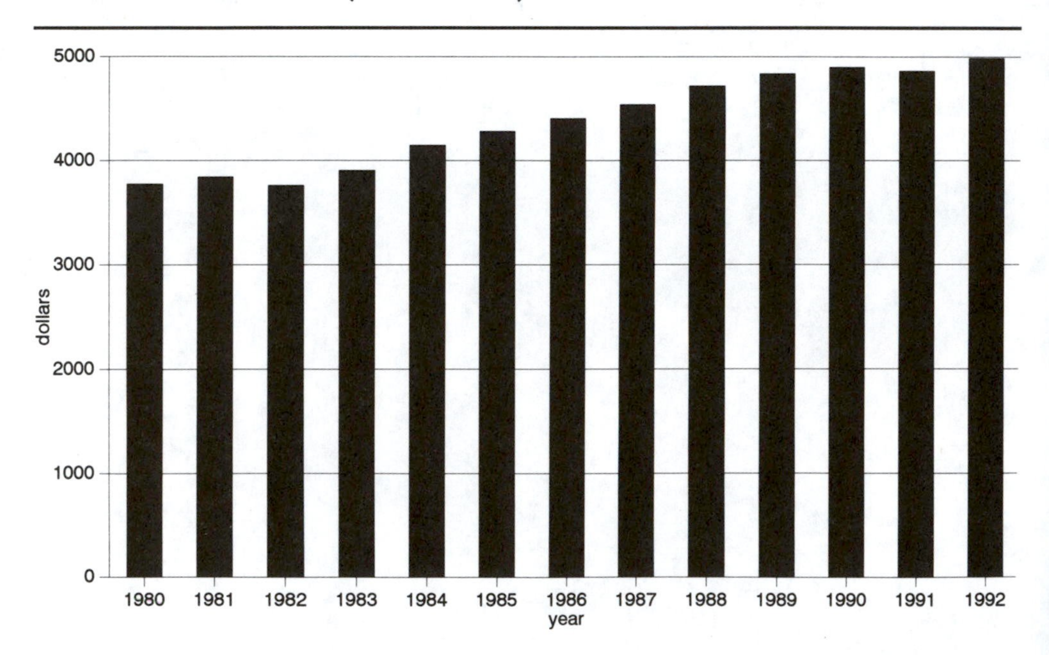

Figure A.3
Growth Rate (Adjusted for Inflation)

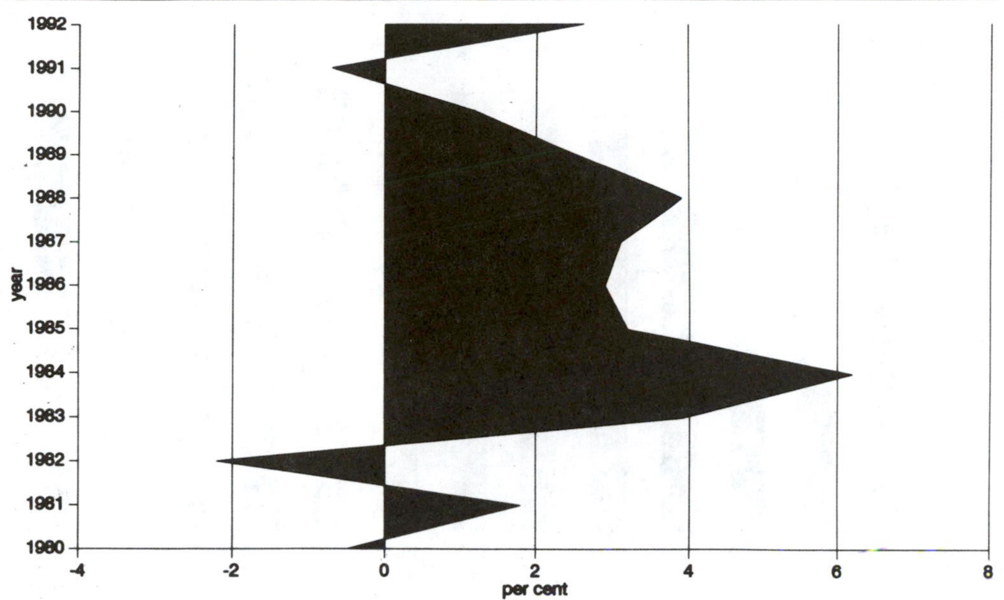

Figure A.4
Job Growth (Number of Employed Workers)

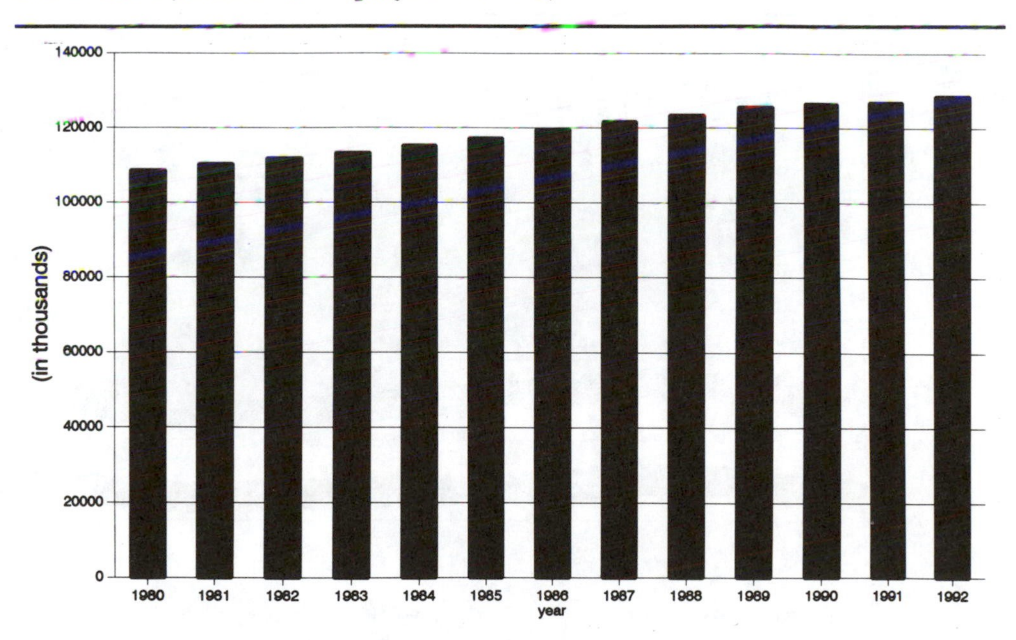

Figure A.5
Disposable Income, per capita (1987 dollars)

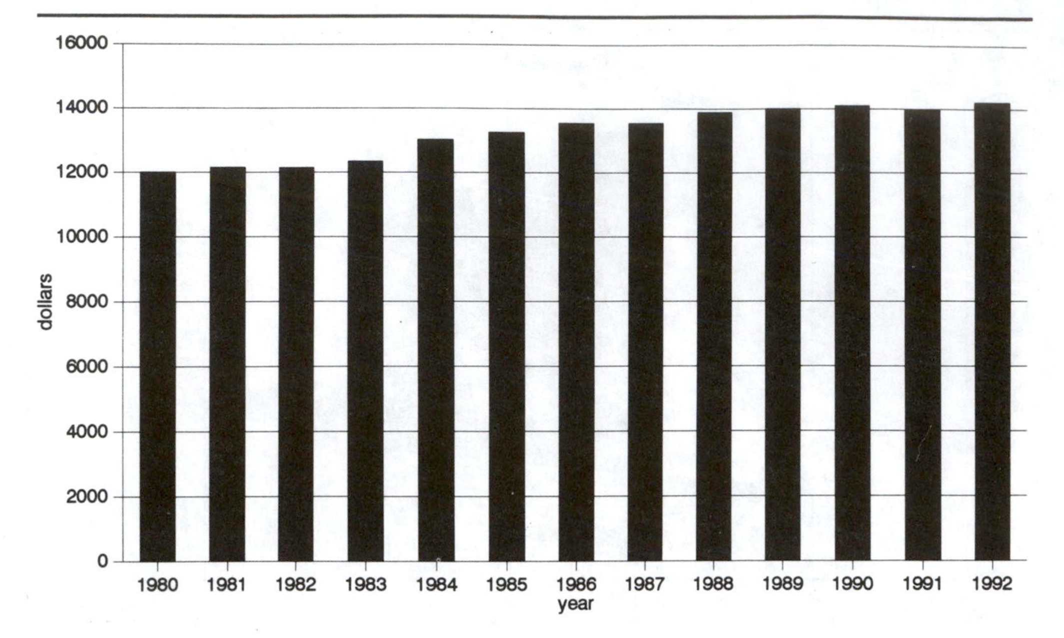

Figure A.6
Poverty Rates by Race

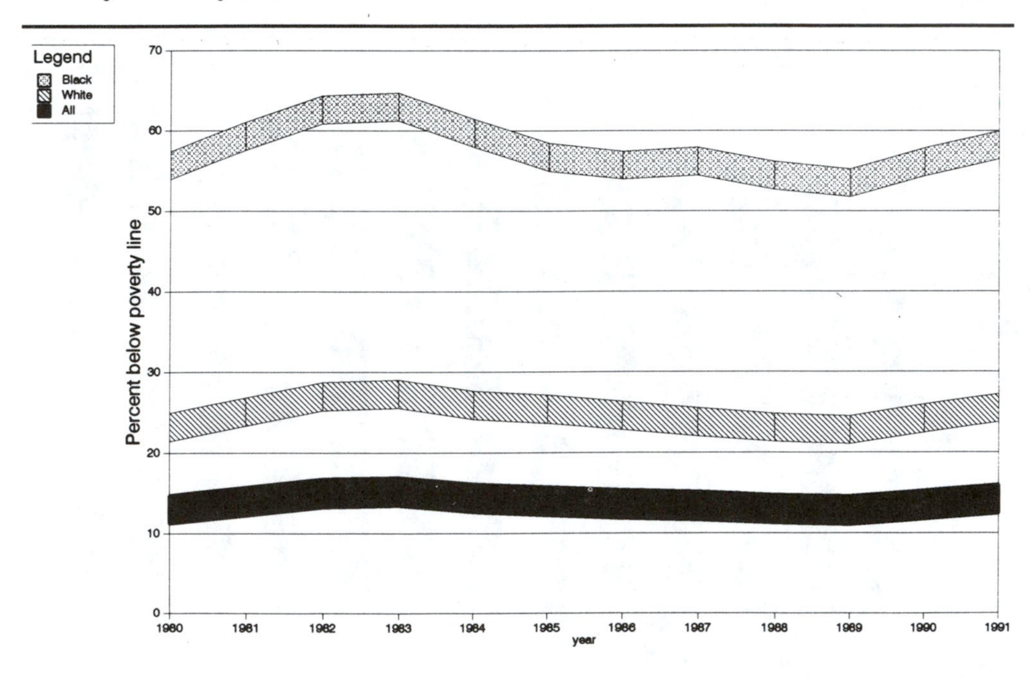

Figure A.7
Income Distribution (Household, by Income, Percent Distribution)

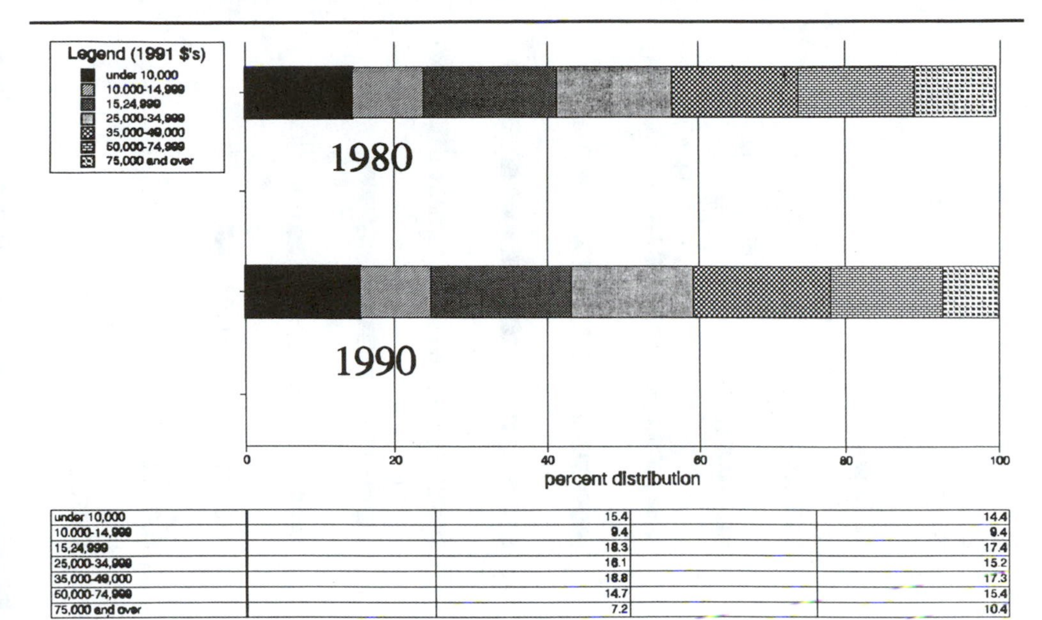

under 10,000		15.4		14.4
10.000-14,999		9.4		9.4
15,24,999		18.3		17.4
25,000-34,999		16.1		15.2
35,000-49,000		18.8		17.3
50,000-74,999		14.7		15.4
75,000 and over		7.2		10.4

Figure A.8
Interest Rates

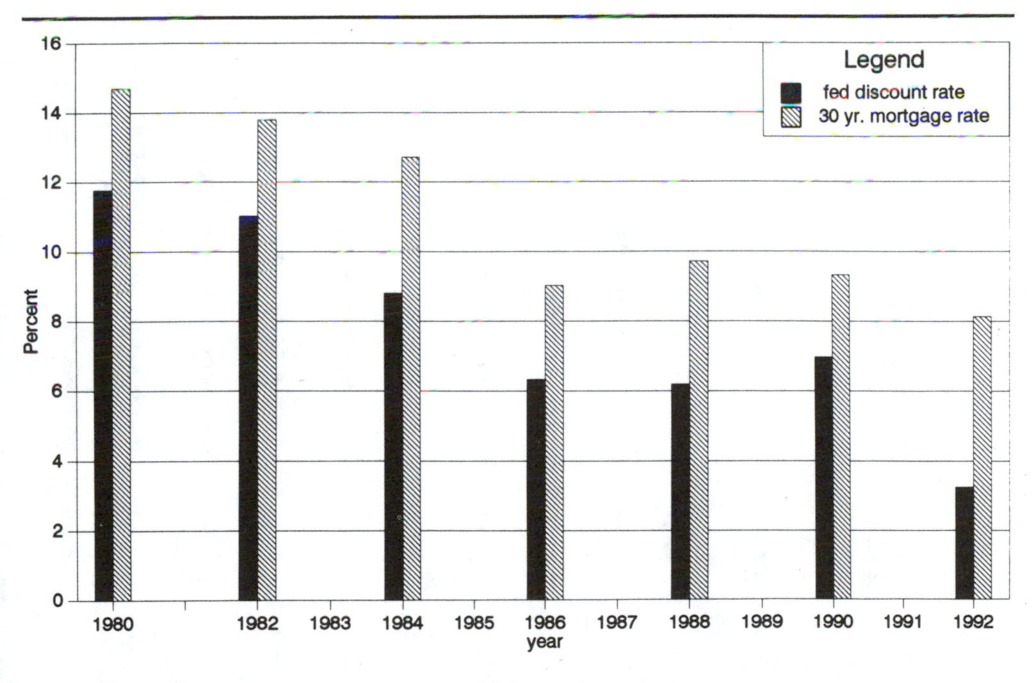

Figure A.9
Trade Deficit

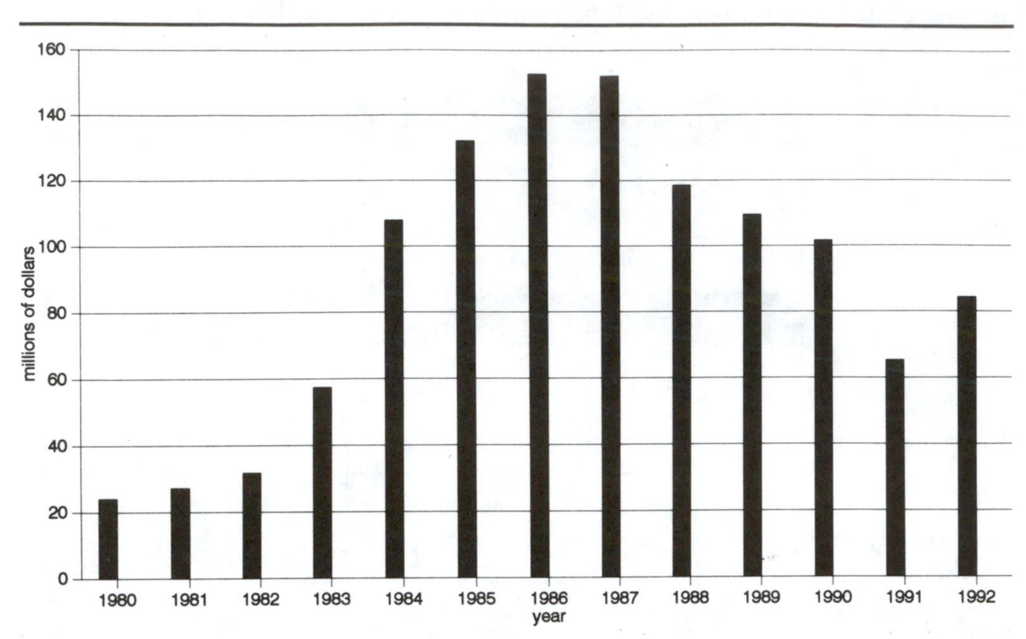

Figure A.10
Government Spending (Federal Outlays)

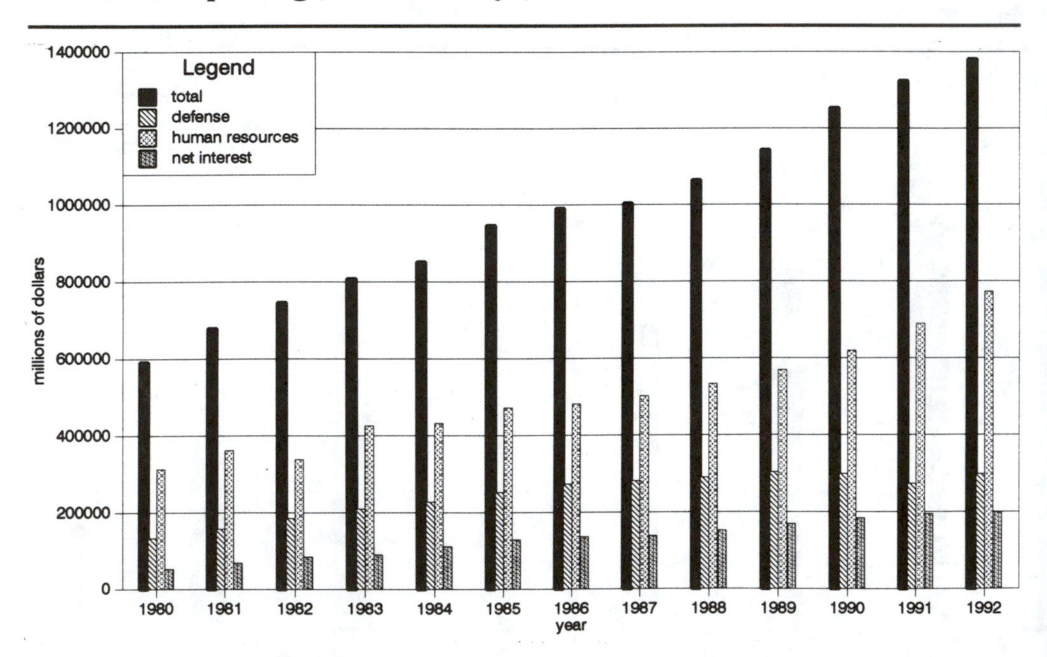

Figure A.11
Defense Spending

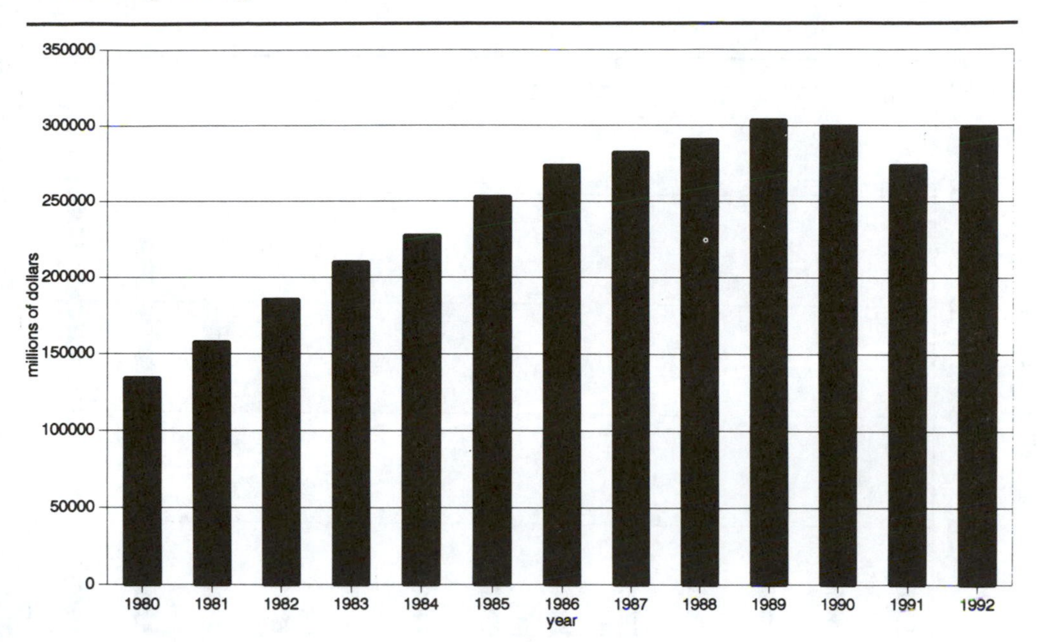

Figure A.12
Federal Deficit

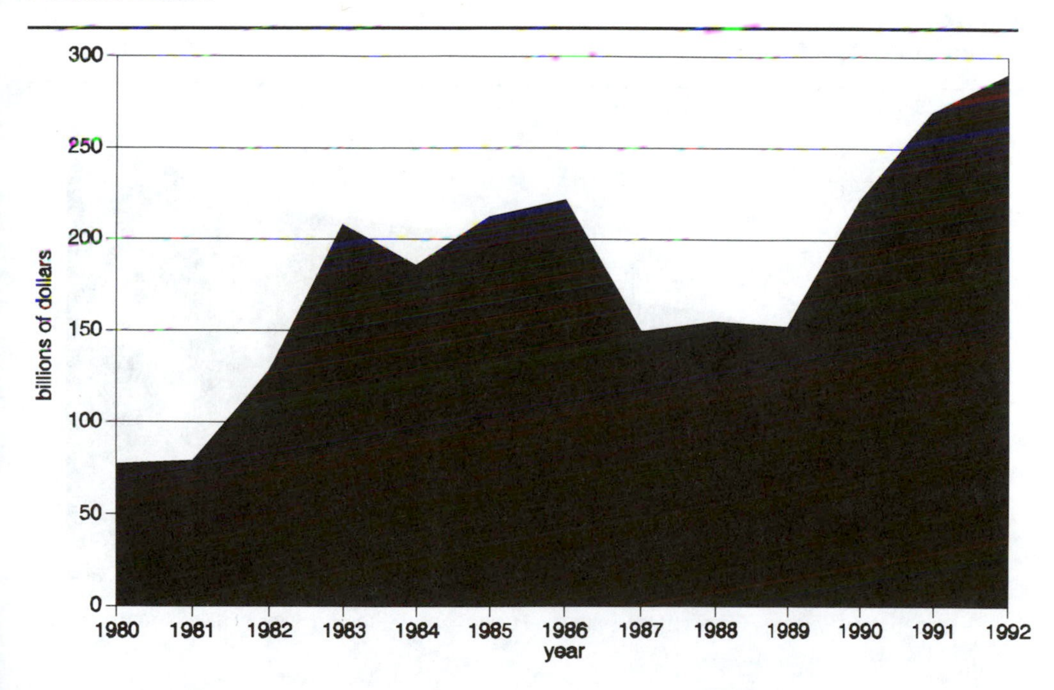

Figure A.13
National Debt

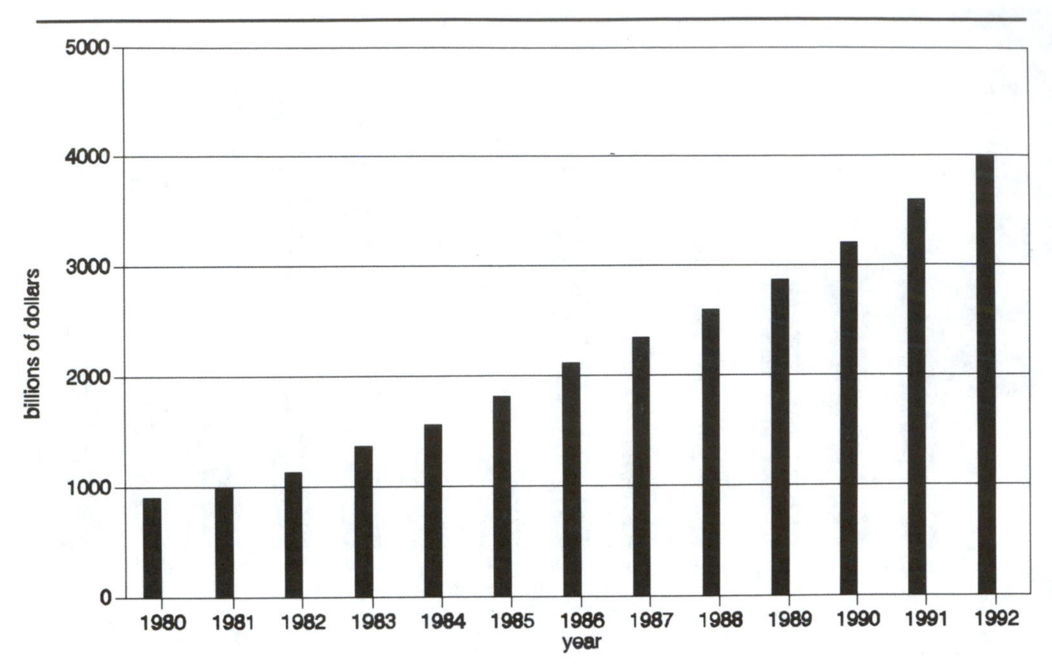

Figure A.14
National Debt as Percentage of GNP

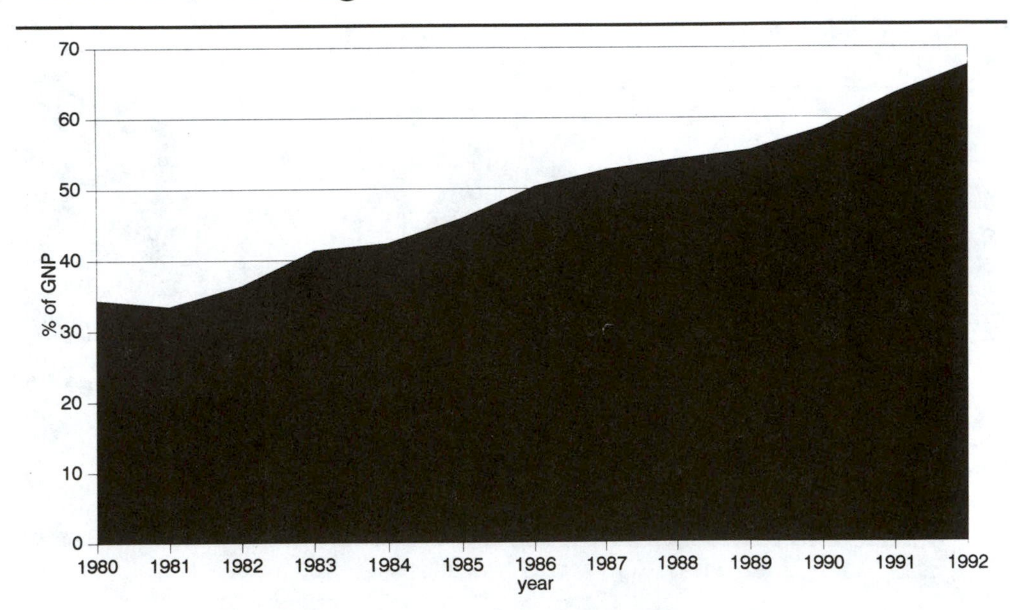

INDEX

Page numbers that appear in **bold** indicate main entries.

About the Author

PETER B. LEVY is Associate Professor of History at York College, York, Pennsylvania. He is the author of *100 Key Documents in American Democracy* (Greenwood Press, 1993), *Let Freedom Ring: A Documentary History of the Modern Civil Rights Movement* (Greenwood Press/Praeger, 1992), and *The New Left and Labor in the 1960s*. He is currently working on a case study of the race relations in Cambridge, Maryland, an analytical overview of the civil rights movement, and a reader on the 1960s.